TWENTIETH-CENT  TRY

A Critica ⌣ ⌣

(1900 to the Neo-Avantgarde)

TWENTIETH-CENTURY ITALIAN POETRY

A Critical Anthology
(1900 to the Neo-Avantgarde)

edited by
Éanna Ó Ceallacháin

t

Published by
Troubador Publishing Ltd
9 De Montfort Mews
Leicester LE1 7FW, UK
Tel: (+44) 116 255 9311
Email: books@troubador.co.uk
Web: www.troubador.co.uk

Series Editor
Professor George Ferzoco
University of Bristol, UK

ISBN: 978-1906221-003

Typesetting: Troubador Publishing Ltd, Leicester, UK

For Anna and Gemma

The younger looks to the older
And the older looks to the world;
I look to the pair of them.

(Paul Durcan, *Man With Two Daughters*)

Contents

Acknowledgements

I am grateful to the British Academy for a research grant that facilitated the research undertaken in the preparation of this anthology. Further support was provided by the Faculty of Arts at the University of Glasgow, in the form of additional funding and the granting of research leave.

I would like to thank my colleagues in the Italian Section of the School of Modern Languages and Cultures at Glasgow for the support and encouragement they have provided throughout the years in which this project has occupied so much of my time and energy.

Above all, I am grateful to my wife Arabella and my daughters Anna and Gemma: they have sustained and encouraged me with their patience and understanding, and they have provided the inspiration, perseverance and optimism that have allowed me to complete this volume.

Bibliographical Note

In the course of this volume, frequent references are made to a number of important anthologies and other general critical texts.

In the endnotes to the various chapter introductions and in the body of the notes on the texts themselves, the works listed below are often cited by author and title, or by using recognizable shortened forms of their titles.

In addition, the introduction to each chapter contains an alphabetical list of further titles, some of which are also referred to by author (and title, where necessary) in the notes to the texts.

General critical texts and anthologies

Anceschi, Luciano, *Le poetiche del Novecento in Italia: studio di fenomenologia e storia delle poetiche*, nuova ed. accresciuta e aggiornata, a cura di Lucio Vetri (Venice: Marsilio, 1990)

Barberi Squarotti, Giorgio, *La poesia del Novecento: morte e trasfigurazione del soggetto* (Caltanisetta-Roma: Sciascia, 1985)

Cucchi, Maurizio, and Stefano Giovanardi, eds, *Poeti italiani del secondo Novecento: 1945-1995*, I Meridiani (Milan: Mondadori, 1996)

Curi, Fausto, *La poesia italiana nel Noveecento* (Roma-Bari: Laterza, 1999)

Debenedetti, Giacomo, *Poesia italiana del Novecento: quaderni inediti* (Milan: Garzanti, 1974)

Fortini, Franco, *I poeti del Novecento* (Roma-Bari: Laterza, 1977)

Fortini, Franco, *Saggi italiani* (Milan: Garzanti, 1987)

Jones, Frederic J., *The Modern Italian Lyric* (Cardiff: University of Wales Press, 1986)

Lorenzini, Niva, ed., *Poesia del Novecento italiano: Dal secondo dopoguerra a oggi* (Roma: Carocci, 2002)

Lorenzini, Niva, ed., *Poesia del Novecento italiano: Dalle avanguardie storiche alla seconda guerra mondiale* (Roma: Carocci, 2002)

Lorenzini, Niva, *Il presente della poesia: 1960-1990* (Bologna: Il Mulino, 1991)

Lorenzini, Niva, *La poesia italiana del Novecento* (Bologna, Il Mulino, 1999)

Luperini, Romano, P. Cataldi and F. d'Amely, *Poeti italiani: il Novecento* (Palermo:

Palumbo; Università per Stranieri di Siena, 1994)

Manacorda, Giuliano, *Storia della letteratura italiana contemporanea 1940-1996* (Roma: Editori riuniti, 1996)

Mengaldo, Pier Vincenzo, ed., *Poeti italiani del Novecento* (Milan: Mondadori, 1978)

Picchione, John, and Lawrence Smith, eds., *Twentieth-Century Italian Poetry: An Anthology* (Toronto: University of Toronto Press, 1993)

Pozzi, Gianni, *La poesia italiana del Novecento: da Gozzano agli ermetici* (Turin: Einaudi, 1965)

Ramat, Silvio, *La poesia italiana 1903-1943: quarantuno titoli esemplari* (Venice: Marsilio, 1997)

Ramat, Silvio, *Storia della poesia italiana del Novecento* (Milan: Mursia, 1976)

Sanguineti, Edoardo, ed., *Poesia italiana del Novecento* (Turin: Einaudi, 1969)

Segre, Cesare, and Carlo Ossola, *Antologia della poesia italiana: Novecento*, 2nd edn (Turin: Einaudi, 2003)

Introduction

Lyric poetry may be characterized as a poetic genre based on an individual viewpoint and expressing a range of essentially subjective moods, emotions or opinions.[i] And indeed, much of the ferment of Italian lyric poetry in what we may call its modern period, from the end of the nineteenth century to the second half of the twentieth, has revolved precisely around the question of subjectivity. Writers grapple with varying degrees and forms of subjectivity of the individual poetic voice, and/or the need for some objectivity in relation to surrounding realities: in short they struggle to define the role, the potential and the expressive limitations of what we may call the *io lirico*. The issue has been placed, repeatedly, at the heart of attempts by critics and poets to construct a literary or historiographical overview of the modern Italian lyric. Giorgio Barberi Squarotti, for example, sums up the central problem of 'modern' (i.e. post-Romantic) Italian poetry as an ongoing quest for 'liberation' from the tyranny of the 'subject', the self, a search for a 'punto di vista diverso dall'"io" come fonte del discorso poetico'.[ii] He outlines a number of different ways in which twentieth-century poets have responded to the 'impasse' represented by the power of the *io lirico*: from the ironic undermining of the lyrical persona on the part of the *crepuscolari*, to the hermetics' retreat from communication into form, to the Montalean choice of allegorical modes; from the Futurists' desire to 'annihilate' the *io* in the image of the machine, to the various attempts to construct a 'collective subject' through forms of poetic realism. Notwithstanding these approaches, however, there are also, as the critic notes, constant recurrences of the idea of the poet as *vate* (i.e. poet with an inspired or quasi-prophetic voice), and of poetry as 'interpretazione autorizzata e autentica del mondo', from Ungaretti to Pasolini, in their own different ways. Nevertheless, for Barberi Squarotti, it is the broad phenomenon of a 'rifiuto dell'io' that dominates this period, as manifested in the search for other expressive codes and in competing ideas of poetry as 'azione, invenzione, finzione'.[iii]

Guido Mazzoni takes a slightly different approach to the question, but one which also focuses on the problematic nature of the *io lirico*. For Mazzoni, there is an underlying idea of poetry, persisting well into the twentieth century, whose origins reach back to a broadly romantic model of lyricism that emerged in the eighteenth century. It is the idea of an art form that, unlike narrative or theatrical writing, only 'makes sense' if one is willing or able to invest fragments of individual experience with a 'universal' significance.[iv] It is this aspect, the legitimacy of the *io* and its ability to speak for a 'coro sociale invisibile', that becomes increasingly untenable from the late nineteenth century onwards, and is directly challenged by a succession of avant-garde movements from the turn of the twentieth century to the 1950s and '60s. Paradoxically, however, while challenging the legitimacy of the *io*, twentieth century poetry can be seen in some respects to take 'egocentricity' to its extreme limits, as one is often left with a poetic voice that is still subjective, but bereft of the 'significato universale' that originally characterized the lyric genre. Instead other models emerge: the ironic persona, ostentatiously self-marginalizing; the 'theatrical' persona drawing attention to its own performances; the narcissistic persona, untroubled by any broader meanings beyond the self; and the regressive persona, exploring preconscious or subconscious levels of language.[v] All, in their own ways and through various modes of formal expression, are responses to a reality in which the meaning and integrity of individual experience have become deeply problematic.

Taking a longer perspective, the question of the *io lirico* and its function, its status and ability to dominate poetic discourse, has roots that reach deep into Italian literary history, leading back to the two great poetic models, Dante and Petrarch. Indeed the development of Italian poetry in the twentieth century may be seen in some ways as a story of the re-emergence and reassertion of a Dantesque inheritance in the face of a centuries-long domination by a Petrarchan paradigm. This latter model of lyricism, with the emphasis on timeless introspection, viewpoints of subjective interiority and a preoccupation with linguistic purity and formal perfection, is frequently challenged in the modern period by a widening of the linguistic spectrum to embrace a plurality of registers, the use of allegorical forms, an engagement with historical reality, and a readiness to problematize the figure of the poet's own persona as a character, albeit in the first person, within the work. Certainly there are exceptions to this, indeed very significant ones such as Ungaretti, who, as Niva Lorenzini notes, for all the undoubted modernity of his subject matter and vision, perpetuates the Petrarchan line through his 'lettura simbolica, atemporale dei dati della realtà'.[vi] Indeed, for much of the mid-twentieth century, this model of lyricism was seen as the dominant one, not least due to the excessive prestige and critical attention accorded to the Hermetic poets over several decades. Lorenzini, however, like other critics in recent decades, questions the supposed hegemony of a 'linea petrarcheggiante', and underlines the importance of other voices, from those of the *crepuscolari* to Montale and Sereni, that reach out to a broader European dimension, voices that grapple with the technical or material aspects of writing, discovering 'il pensiero sensoriale, lo spessore del corpo' while eschewing any 'assolutezza'; voices, in short, that move in alternative directions, '*contro quella lirica, dopo quella lirica*'.[vii] And, recalling again the model of Dante, it should not be forgotten that one expressive feature that frequently underpins the shift away from forms of pure lyricism is the widespread adoption of narrative or quasi-narrative modes (one need only think of Saba, Caproni or Sereni, or even, at some points, the 'hermetic' Luzi).[viii]

Questions of lyrical subjectivity and the viewpoint of the poetic persona are closely related to the broad issue of what we may call poetic realism: to what extent can or should poetry engage directly with the objective reality of the world in its socio-economic, material or historical dimensions? This issue is foregrounded by the poet and critic Edoardo Sanguineti in the important introduction to his 1969 anthology, *Poesia italiana del Novecento*. In an overview of the period that is avowedly ideological in its framework and motivations, Sanguineti highlights the emergence of 'un fronte di realismo' during the period of avant-garde experimentation in the early years of the century, a 'front' broad enough to include the prosaic but genteel objects and figures of the crepuscular Gozzano and the proto-futurist provocations of the radical Lucini. This alternative model of poetry, as carried on in different ways in the work of the work of Futurists, *vociani*, and 'realist' writers as diverse as Pavese and Pasolini, constitutes, from the left-wing critic's viewpoint (writing in the wake of the neo-avantgarde experimentalism of the 1960s), an important counterbalance to the block formed by the acknowledged *maestri* such as Ungaretti, Saba and Montale, the poets of the 'bella biografia', whose approach to poetry Sanguineti sees as a form of 'cerimonia protettiva' in the face of historical reality.[ix]

While the picture drawn by Sanguineti is clearly based on a specific perspective of ideological opposition to the political and literary establishment of the time, it can nonetheless, in the bold lines of its opinionated positions, provide one useful framework in which to view the complex and shifting movements and tendencies of some seven decades of poetry. And while one may question, for example, the inclusion of Saba or Montale along with Ungaretti in a grouping of supposedly 'anti-historical' lyricists at the heart of the century, it is undoubtedly true that tensions between forms of lyricism, more or less detached from the objective realities and pressing needs of the here-and-now, and other forms of poetic discourse that seek to respond to those needs and to explore and even shape those realities, are a recurring feature of critical and literary debate. In some cases, it is relatively easy to assign poets and their works to one or other of these poles: much of Ungaretti's work, along with that of the hermetic generation, falls easily into the first category, while, for example, works by the Futurists, Pavese, Pasolini or (in parts) the 1960s *neoavanguardia* can be seen to come under the latter heading. In other cases, however, it is a dichotomy whose usefulness is less certain, whether we consider the subtly articulated co-presence of the subjective and the objective, private and public, in Montale's work, the peculiar personal realism of Saba, or the gradual evolutions in the poetry of Zanzotto or Sereni.

Indeed any attempt at the schematic reduction of such a multi-faceted and inherently complex body of work runs the risk of gross over-simplification. One may also, of course, apply entirely different frameworks, distinguishing for example between writers who seek broadly to embrace and develop elements of the poetic tradition and those determined to break with the tradition or overturn it.[x] Similarly, one might trace a fault-line between poets for whom the communication of a message (whether ideological, spiritual or otherwise) is paramount, and those concerned primarily with exploring the possibilities of form and language itself (for example Rosselli). The literary mappings that emerge from any such analyses will always be, to some degree, tentative or provisional, subject to the overlapping of groupings or tendencies ('stratifications' that can be found, on occasion, even within the works of an individual writer), not to mention the complex interplay of generational and geographical relationships.[xi]

The issue of generational relationships brings us to the thorny question of chronological periods. It is implicit in what we have discussed already that a straightforward division into more-or-less arbitrary blocks of time would, in itself, shed little light on the complex development of the genre through Italy's turbulent history from 1900 to the end of the 1960s (on this latter time limit, see further discussion below). However, in terms of basic orientation, it may be useful to sketch out a number of what we might call 'time zones' rather than periods (the term would reflect the artificial or merely conventional nature of divisions that have no visible boundaries and are regularly ignored by those who, willingly or not, travel between them). A possible (and resolutely undogmatic) set of dates is as follows: (1) *1900-1920: The years of avant-garde experimentation*; (2) *1915-1945: The decades of lyrical introspection*; (3) *1945 onwards: Realism and existential lyricism*; (4)

1960 onwards: Neo-avantgarde experimentalism. Clearly, such time zones are broadly sketched and do not form entirely discrete units, but overlap at various points.[xii] The starting date of 1900 is, of course, somewhat arbitrary, and the avant-garde period then continues beyond the end of the First World War, even as voices of modern lyrical introspection, such as Ungaretti and Saba, are already emerging. The next watershed date, 1945, is again a conventional one, a kind of shorthand for the deep and far-reaching cultural changes arising from the fall of Fascism and the formation of the new Italian political structures over a number of years in the 1940s. It should also be noted that a strong current of lyrical modernism continues well into the post-war period. The third zone indicates the emergence and co-existence of various forms of realism and a shift away from ideas of lyrical purity towards forms of expression more open to historical contamination, even on the part of lyrical voices such as Montale or Sereni. It is a phase that continues, in the work of many poets, well into the 1960s and 1970s (and beyond). The final phase is that of the *neoavanguardia*, whose official birth is marked by the publication in 1961 of the volume *I Novissimi* and the subsequent formation of the Gruppo 63. The work of the neo-avantgarde poets, meanwhile, begins during this same period to influence numerous others who do not belong, formally or informally, to their ranks. Thus even a brief overview such as this throws up immediate areas of over-simplification and potential contradiction (and it must be stressed that it does not take account of some other specific phenomena, such as the tendency towards an anti-avantgarde 'return to order' in the years following the First World War). Furthermore, there are many other ways of mapping periods and temporal developments, depending on the perspectives and purposes of the critics concerned.[xiii] Nevertheless, a broad overview of chronological phases such as that suggested above may, provided that one is aware of its limitations, serve as a useful general tool, a set of provisional coordinates to be superimposed, judiciously, on a map whose actual boundaries and contours are often unstable and multi-dimensional.

Mengaldo offers a further useful framework for orientation within the 'quadro pluralistico, policentrico' that is Novecento poetry.[xiv] In a masterly essay on the development and characteristics of the 'lirica moderna', he outlines the forms and modes in which a 'grande stile', or some form of high lyric style, may credibly survive in an age that has seen the unravelling of some of the very ideas of individual integrity and identity on which such a style may be based. The critic convincingly sketches a 'dichotomy' between two major tendencies in the mid- to late-twentieth century: 'C'è da un lato la tendenza di chi si richiama a un filone *orfico-sapienziale* e attraverso la poesia intende affermare niente di meno che una *verità* in qualche modo trascendentale: [...] Dall'altro c'è quella di coloro che praticano invece una poesia *esistenziale*, e s'accontentano di partecipare a un'*esperienza*'.[xv] With reference to the post-Montale generation, in the first tendency he includes Luzi and Zanzotto, with their 'parola [...] impositiva e quasi intimidatoria', whereas the second tendency would include Bertolucci, Caproni and Sereni, whose poetic language is 'comunicativa e interrogativa'. Projecting backwards in time, it is not too difficult (although neither is it unequivocally simple) to add the name of Ungaretti to the first tendency and Montale to the second. Of course, this is, in itself, another schematic reduction, which cannot hope to do justice to the full complexity of many decades of poetic production. It is a dichotomy which refers, avowedly, to the area of 'grande stile', an idea of mainstream lyricism that tends to exclude more extreme varieties of formal or other experimentalism.[xvi] However, while acknowledging the risk of being seen to impose a 'Manichean' dichotomy, Mengaldo does not conceal his preference for the second of the two tendencies: if the Luzian approach is to defend heroically the besieged fortress of lyric poetry, the others 'escono per le strade, si mescolano ai nemici e sparano rasoterra'.[xvii] The sympathies of this anthology, as may be evident at times from the selection of authors and texts (as well as through the textual commentaries), lie predominantly with the voices of this latter, 'existential' and 'interrogative' line.

The question of the selection of texts raises a number of further issues. Perhaps most obvious is that of the overall temporal parameters applied. This anthology does not purport to cover the entire span of twentieth-century poetry, but broadly the period from the emergence of the *avanguardia storica* in the years following 1900 to that of the *neoavanguardia* in the 1960s. This does not mean the complete exclusion of texts published after 1969: within the selections from the works of Montale, Sereni, Zanzotto, Rosselli, Luzi, Sanguineti, there are indeed works from well into the 1970s. However, in broad terms, these are presented here as developments of expressive forms and thematic or symbolic paradigms that were already established by the late 1960s. In discussing the difficulty of constructing a poetic canon for the contemporary era, the era of the postmodern, Pietro Cataldi makes some interesting observations on what distinguishes this more recent period from the preceding one. Suggesting that an idea of 'non-integrazione' or marginality has characterized 'modern' poetry since at least the time of Baudelaire and Leopardi, Cataldi remarks that it is the paradigmatic application of this idea (or indeed, of any such underlying stance), 'il paradigma della modernità', that has in recent decades become exhausted. Taking his cue from the decision by Segre and Ossola in their 1999 *Antologia della poesia italiana* to exclude any author born after 1930, the critic observes: 'Dall'opera dei nati fino al fatidico 1930 si esprime, anche se in forme di volta in volta diverse e contrarie, quello che in filosofia si sarebbe detto un sistema, un principio via via distruttivo e ricostruttivo [...]. Nell'opera dei poeti successivi si registra la necessaria rinuncia a ogni prospettiva totalizzante, la dimissione perfino della maschera di classici'.[xviii] The texts included in the present anthology belong, essentially to that earlier 'modern' period: for all the opposing movements and polemics, revolutions and reactions, these are, on the whole, texts that can speak to one another within the paradigm of modernity. The landscape of the post-1968 world will be confronted from a fresh perspective by new voices from younger generations, who will shape its poetic imagination in their own ways.

The more invidious task of the anthologist, however, having marked out the terrain to be explored, lies in the selection of particular texts by particular authors and, necessarily, the exclusion of others. There is little about this process that can claim to be truly objective. As one eminent anthologist, Giancarlo Majorino, wryly observes: 'L'antologia appartiene a un genere fraudolento; finge obiettività dove non può che esistere soggettività, l'autore fa quello che vuole'.[xix] Notwithstanding this disclaimer, the selection and structuring of the present anthology have, as far as possible, been carried out with some broad guiding principles in mind. Firstly, in terms of structure, I have avoided, in general, the division of texts and authors into groupings by period. The notable exception is the first chapter, presented explicitly as a survey of the first two decades of the century. The varied make-up of this miscellaneous chapter arises directly from its function as a contextualizing overview, in which the roots of various currents and tendencies discussed in subsequent chapters can be traced. Two later chapters, those on the hermetic generation and on the *neoavanguardia*, can be seen, in part, as groupings of texts by period. In each case, however, the selection of poems by one particular author (respectively, Luzi and Sanguineti) takes us beyond the historical period represented by the remaining texts, a period from which the development of the major figure emerges with a clearer sense of meaning and purpose. One further chapter, 'Engaging with reality', has an entirely composite or miscellaneous structure, following the development of a broad literary approach and thus also facilitating the inclusion of a wider range of voices (albeit each represented only through a single text). The decision, however, to base the bulk of the volume on a structure of 'monographic' chapters was made in the firm conviction that in order to gain any depth of insight into the work of a given poet, the most useful initial tool is the reading of as wide a sample as reasonably possible of the writer's work. The reading of one text often informs the reading of another, whether through direct intertextual allusions, or by allowing an awareness of broader elements of continuity or diversity of themes, imagery, language and tone deployed by the same author over time. For example, any single poem from Montale's later years is difficult to decode satisfactorily without having reference to the work of his earlier 'major' period. Similarly, an awareness of the later development of Sereni's work allows the reader to trace elements in his earlier poems that may not emerge at first sight. Clearly, in some cases, considerations such as these will also have a bearing on the selection of individual texts, chosen to construct a guided pathway for the reader through the broader landscape of a given author's work. Ultimately, however, decisions on the inclusion of particular poems are often, as Majorino suggests, a matter of personal taste.

One aspect of the selection which cannot fail to be noted is the shortage of female voices. This is not, I hope, a result of any anti-feminist prejudice on my part, but rather reflects, like other inclusions and exclusions, a combination of factors: on the one hand, personal critical preferences for particular authors and texts, and, on the other hand the unavoidable fact that, as a literary genre existing in the real world of male-dominated publishing and criticism in Italy, poetry was for much of the twentieth century a form dominated by male authors. Certainly, one might have included in an anthology such as this work by writers like Antonia Pozzi, Alda Merini or Maria Luisa Spaziani. Similarly, there are various other male writers who could very well have figured if a slightly wider selection had been possible (Camillo Sbarbaro, Vincenzo Cardarelli, Attilio Bertolucci, Sandro Penna, or Giorgio Orelli). What is undoubtedly true, however, is that in any putative anthology covering more recent decades (from the 1970s onwards), the presence of female voices would be wide-ranging and of fundamental importance in characterizing the poetry of the period.

The process of selecting of texts for the present volume has also, necessarily, been influenced by an awareness of the particular purpose and potential readership of an anthology spanning two languages and cultures. This anthology is aimed primarily at advanced undergraduate readers, and as such, it presumes a good working knowledge of contemporary Italian. It is, patently, not a volume of translations, but it does seek to fulfil a role analogous in part to that of translation, a role of mediation on both a linguistic and also on an intercultural level, as it aims to make these Italian texts available to an Anglophone, Italian-reading audience. The word 'available' is crucial here, as understood in the richest sense possible: not merely presenting the texts but providing tools for the reader to access them, whether in terms of elucidation of individual words and phrases or in terms of contextual information, conceptual maps and interpretative keys. While I have not sought to avoid certain authors or styles simply because they may be seen as particularly challenging in their literal meanings or figurative ramifications, I have, almost inevitably, gravitated towards individual texts that allow for a reasonable possibility of being decoded, and hopefully enjoyed, by a non-native speaker: see for example the poems chosen from the work of the hermetic poets, or those of Amelia Rosselli, where undoubtedly other, less decipherable texts could have been selected. A wider range of poems and of interpretative materials is, in most cases, fairly easily available, as indicated in the bibliographies of texts and further reading. But any amount of guidance on further reading is of limited use if the reader does not find something that can engage her/his interest and facilitate the reading of the texts initially presented.

In this respect, one might argue that it would have been more useful to prepare a bilingual edition, or a volume solely of annotated translations without the Italian source texts (it would certainly have been a more straightforward task). However, neither approach would have necessarily addressed a key aim of this book, which is not only to open up unknown texts to the reader on a level of literal comprehension, but also to invite, or indeed demand, a critical reading of the poems themselves, a reading that takes full account of the linguistic, formal and, in short, aesthetic specifities of the original texts in the source language. In this regard, I would broadly subscribe to the viewpoint of Pietro Cataldi, in his observations on the methodology and functions of textual commentaries (observations made in the context of Italian monolingual student editions and anthologies). Cataldi stresses the fundamental importance of comprehension on a literal (or denotative) level before one can approach problems of interpretation (on a connotative level): 'il dato connotativo acquista rilevanza e significato solamente alla luce di quello denotativo'.[xx] Thus, in Cataldi's model, there is an explicit separation between an initial stage of 'parafrasi' and the subsequent interpretative stage of 'commento'. Clearly, in the present anthology, the explanatory notes do not follow a rigorous division along these lines: rather they provide elements of paraphrasing, translation and literal explanation intermingled with interpretative comment. Nevertheless, even if the notes do contain an interweaving of paraphrase and comment, they also seek to avoid confusing the two functions. The primary aim of the notes is the clarification of literal meaning, without which any aspiration to an interpretative reading is futile. Certainly the notes also provide numerous and frequent interpretative suggestions and references to secondary sources, but these are intended to constitute additional support and impetus for the task of reading the texts themselves. As Cataldi observes, the paraphrasing or commentary 'non deve dare appagamento ma curiosità verso il testo'. Along with the basic function of opening up the comprehension of difficult texts, the notes or commentary must try to stimulate a critical reading, to strive for 'l'educazione a una fruizione critica', exploiting a particularly rich niche-space of 'criticità'.[xxi] Thus this anthology hopes to maximize the potential for critical thinking provided by texts that have been written with such an intensity of formal and conceptual awareness, texts that frequently demand of the reader a high degree of intellectual and emotional commitment, and can provide in return a deeply rewarding intellectual and aesthetic experience.

Endnotes

i   De Mauro *Dizionario della lingua italiana* (Paravia: 2000) gives the definition: 'genere di poesia incentrato sulla soggettività'; whereas the Zingarelli, *Vocabolario della lingua italiana* (Bologna: Zanichelli, 1996) gives: 'forma di poesia ove prevale l'espressione di temi soggettivi, come stati d'animo ed esperienze interiori'. According to *the Concise Oxford Dictionary of Literary Terms*, ed. Christopher Baldick (Oxford: Oxford University Press, 1996), the word 'lyric' indicates 'any fairly short poem expressing the personal mood, feeling, or meditation of a single speaker (who may sometimes be an invented character, not the poet)'. The definition goes on to note the additional connotation of a 'song-like quality' often associated with the term.

ii   Giorgio Barberi Squarotti, *La poesia del Novecento: morte e trasfigurazione del soggetto* (Caltanisetta-Roma: Sciascia, 1985), pp. 9 and 11.

iii   *ibid.*, pp. 10-11.

iv   Guido Mazzoni, *Forma e solitudine: un'idea della poesia contemporanea* (Milan: Marcos y Marcos, 2002), pp. 12-13.

v   *ibid.*, pp. 16-17.

vi   Niva Lorenzini, *La poesia italiana del Novecento* (Bologna: Il mulino, 1999), p. 9.

vii   Lorenzini, *La poesia italiana del Novecento*, pp. 10 and 13.

viii   See Pier Vincenzo Mengaldo, *Poeti italiani del Novecento* (Milan: Mondadori, 1978), pp. xxiv-xxvi.

ix   Edoardo Sanguineti, *Poesia italiana del Novecento* (Torino: Einaudi, 1969), pp. xliii and lvii.

x   This distinction is crucial for Fausto Curi: see his *Poesia italiana nel Novecento* (Roma-Bari: Laterza, 1999), p. vii.

xi   On geographical factors and the interplay of groupings and individuals in the formation of various 'currents' or 'koinè stilistiche', see Mengaldo, *Poeti italiani del Novecento*, pp. xliv-xlvii.

xii   Guido Guglielmi discusses the overlapping of various poetic currents around the mid-century point: 'L'ieri convive con l'oggi, il continuo con il discontinuo'. Guido Guglielmi, 'La poesia italiana alla metà del Novecento', in *Genealogie della poesia nel secondo Novecento. Giornate di studio, Siena 23-24-25 marzo 2001*, a cura di Maria Antonietta Grignani (Pisa-Roma: Istituti editoriali e poligrafici internazionali, 2002), pp. 15-33 (p. 15) [special edition of *Moderna*, 3 (2001)].

xiii   For Cucchi and Giovanardi, for example, the years 1945-50 represent a crucial boundary, the beginning not only of a new period but a veritable new 'canon', replacing the previous dominance of 'monostilismo' with various expressions of 'objective' reality. See Introduction in *Poeti italiani del secondo Novecento, 1945-1995*, a cura di Maurizio Cucchi and Stefano Giovanardi, I Meridiani (Milan: Mondadori, 1996), pp. xi-lx (pp. xi-xviii). Ermanno Krumm outlines four periods in the structure of his anthology: the first two coinciding broadly with phases (1) and (2) as I have outlined above, the third, 'Il cuore del secolo', taking in aspects of my phases (3) and (4), and the fourth covering the years from the 1970s onwards. See *Poesia italiana del Novecento*, a cura di Ermanno Krumm (Milan: Skira, 1995). Mengaldo's periodization is broader (and, he notes, deliberately 'elastic'), with an initial avant-garde phase, then the block formed by the inter-war years, followed by a single post-war period seen as containing a range of reactions to the previous lyrical/post-symbolist hegemony (see *Poeti italiani del Novecento*, pp. l-lxiii). Many other examples could be cited. Lorenzini warns, however, of the futility of describing developments in blocks or decades, even when referring to a relatively clear and uncontroversial demarcation point such as that of 1945. See Lorenzini, *La poesia italiana del Novecento*, pp. 121-22.

xiv   Lorenzini, *La poesia italiana del Novecento*, p. 11.

xv   Pier Vincenzo Mengaldo, 'Grande stile e lirica moderna', in *La tradizione del Novecento. Nuova serie* (Florence: Vallecchi, 1987), pp. 7-24 (p. 19). Italics are the author's own. The term 'orfico' here means something like mystical or esoteric, referring to an idea of poetry as an almost sacred pursuit of truth.

xvi   Even in the area of more experimental writings, one might be tempted on occasion, *mutatis mutandis*, to apply similar distinctions, as for example between the somewhat peremptory tones of Sanguineti's early experimental work and the more uncertain stance of Porta. Of course the parallel is at best partial and approximate: I do not wish in any sense to suggest that Sanguineti represents an 'orphic' tendency, but simply that, at that particular stage of his work, there is a quality that might be classified as 'parola impositiva'. However, even such a tentative analogy highlights the need to guard against trying to make all textual phenomena fit within an arbitrary interpretative framework.

xvii   Mengaldo, 'Grande stile e lirica moderna', p. 20.

xviii   Pietro Cataldi, 'La fine del canone. I poeti e il postmoderno', in *Genealogie della poesia nel secondo Novecento. Giornate di studio, Siena 23-24-25 marzo 2001*, a cura di Maria Antonietta Grignani (Pisa-Roma: Istituti editoriali e poligrafici internazionali, 2002), pp. 149-56 (p. 151-2) [special edition of *Moderna*, 3 (2001)].

xix   Giancarlo Majorino, *Poesia e realtà: 1945-2000* (Milan: Tropea, 2000), p. 24. Mario Lunetta gives an even more jaundiced view of the process as 'quella presuntuosa operazione da piccolo padreterno letterario che è l'allestimento di un'antologia'; Mario Lunetta, *Poesia italiana oggi* (Roma: Newton Compton, 1981), p.18.

xx   Pietro Cataldi, *Parafrasi e commento: nove letture di poesia da Francesco d'Assisi a Montale* (Palermo: Palumbo, 2002), p. 22. Cataldi also notes in passing (p. 20) the analogy between the exercise of explanatory paraphrasing and translation. In some ways, indeed, it might be argued that to opt for explanatory notes without translating the texts is to offer a kind of extreme case of 'foreignizing' translation.

xxi   Cataldi, *Parafrasi e commento*, pp. 28 and 17. The methodology advocated by Cataldi is applied to notable effect in the anthology *Poeti italiani: il Novecento*, ed. by Romano Luperini, P. Cataldi and F. d'Amely (Palermo: Palumbo; Università per Stranieri di Siena, 1994).

1

The avant-garde years

In Italian poetry, as in the arts and literature of most European countries, the work produced by a new generation active from around 1900 through to the end of the First World War was characterized by a remarkable range and intensity of innovation and experimentation. This phenomenon is reflected in the widespread use of the historiographical label *avanguardia storica* to refer to the more innovative writers of this period in Italy (a label that serves also to distinguish them from the 'neo-avantgarde' of the 1960s). However, the term *avant-garde* (originally a military term, meaning 'advance guard'), as used in the title of this chapter, must not be understood in too limited a sense. The work most immediately associated with this term in the Italian context, that of the Futurists, in fact represents only one aspect of a diverse and richly-complex period. Thus the selection of poems presented here ranges from the desolation of Corazzini's 'povero poeta sentimentale' to Marinetti's bombastic propagandism, to the more anguished expressionism of Rebora and Campana. Nevertheless, as we shall see, these poets may have more in common than immediately meets the eye.

Before discussing the poets of this early period, however, brief mention must be made of two names which are otherwise notably absent from this anthology: Giovanni Pascoli and Gabriele D'Annunzio. These very important figures, whose writing straddles the nineteenth and early twentieth centuries, are inescapably *present* to the writers represented here and, of course, to their contemporary readers. It is very much in their shadow that our 'avant-garde' poets begin to write. Pascoli (1855-1912) evokes a disappearing world of rural Italy, and yet, balanced between tradition and innovation, gives no straightforwardly idyllic vision. While generally maintaining traditional metrical forms in his verse, Pascoli subtly introduces 'lower' linguistic registers, the language and imagery of the everyday and the ordinary, as seen through 'childlike' eyes in his 'poetica del fanciullino'

(1897).[i] Some lines from *Myricae* (1894) can give a taste of Pascoli's characteristic tone of quiet wonder, here in a limpid, impressionistic evocation of the sights and sounds of Nature (the description of an approaching thunderstorm), in which we find a passing allusion to a recurring Pascolian motif, that of the home as a place of refuge in a threatening world: 'Un bubbolío lontano...//Rosseggia l'orizzonte,/ come affocato, a mare;/ nero di pece, a monte,/ stracci di nubi chiare:/ tra il nero un casolare:/ un'ala di gabbiano' ('Temporale').[ii] For all his simplicity, however, the poet/*fanciullino* is seen to have access to special insights, can find and reveal hidden truths about the world, and thus achieves a kind of privileged or visionary status.

D'Annunzio (1863-1938), on the other hand, is the decadent aesthete par excellence. A man of enormous energy and talent, he achieved fame, notoriety and a peculiarly modern kind of celebrity as a poet, novelist, playwright, seducer of women and, in 1919, even as a militaristic adventurer leading his own private army in the occupation of the Adriatic port of Fiume, denied to Italy in the aftermath of the First World War (an episode which served as an example and inspiration to that other great self-publicist, Mussolini). His work glorifies art, beauty and sensual experiences and, it might be added, often tends to glorify the author himself. With his own personal reading of the philosopher Nietzsche, he puts himself forward as a kind of poetic 'superman', bestowing upon himself the role of *Vate* or visionary bard, whose aesthetic sensibilities place him beyond conventional morality. His poetry is extraordinarily rich, full of flamboyant linguistic invention and technical accomplishment, leading often to an almost hypnotic, musical memorability. In his greatest poetic work, *Alcyone* (1903), he describes a mystical and heroic communion with Nature, exemplified here in the closing lines of 'Meriggio', where the poetic *io* becomes one with the overpowering sensual experience of summer noon-time: 'Non ho più nome né sorte/ tra gli uomini; ma il mio nome/ è Meriggio. In tutto io vivo/ tacito come la Morte// E la mia vita è divina'.[iii]

While these two writers display highly contrasting human and artistic temperaments, both derive much of their poetic vision, though in different ways, from the hugely influential lesson of the French nineteenth-century Symbolists.[iv] Poets such as Baudelaire, Mallarmé and Rimbaud in the second half of the nineteenth century had led the way in exploring the world through poetic analogies, in search of hidden 'correspondences' between things, as well as between outward, sensory experiences and secret underlying truths, accessed through the instruments of verbal 'alchemies' and musicality. In their own ways, both Pascoli and D'Annunzio perpetuate the symbolist legacy. Each of them seeks to encapsulate an experience of the 'sublime', something beyond the contingencies of mere everyday reality, accessed through the special power of poetic language to create musical effects and analogies, to invest objects and situations with mysterious, universal signficance. Thus their work has been categorized by Sanguineti as converging in an experience of 'antirealismo poetico' (a label which also reflects Sanguineti's artistic and ideological preference for a more 'realistic' vein of poetry).[v] Both writers have a conception of the poetic *io* as fundamentally privileged, the bearer of special truths, which involves a degree of 'evasione dal presente' and 'fuga nell'irrazionale'.[vi] In this sense, they are destined to be widely rejected by poets of the new century, for many of whom such an idea of poetry becomes untenable. But their influence, especially in terms of form and language, and as a reservoir of poetic imagery, continues to be felt for many decades. They are inescapable whether as 'modelli' or 'antimodelli' for their successors, who so often reject ideologically the overall notions of the poet's role upheld by Pascoli and D'Annunzio, but cannot simply turn their backs on such a vast formal and linguistic inheritance.[vii]

The first broad group of poets (and it is very much an informal grouping) to whom the label of avant-garde may be applied, are the *poeti crepuscolari* (represented here by Corrado Govoni, Sergio Corazzini and Guido Gozzano).[viii] At first sight, this poetry of melancholy scenes, abandoned dusty objects and moribund young men may seem anything but *avant-garde* (in the obvious sense of 'up-to-date') in the age of machines, speed and mass-production. But, in fact the work of the *crepuscolari* represents the first significant challenge to the received image of the poet and of poetry itself in the new century. Here (with the inevitable benefit of hindsight), we can perceive the early signs of a real crisis affecting the ideological and artistic certainties which underpin the work of Pascoli and D'Annunzio. The two great *fin-de-siècle* poets, for all their technical brilliance and indeed their thematic and formal innovations, still inhabited a world in which the status of the poet was not in doubt: he was the purveyor of special insights into the mysteries of the world and the individual consciousness. In this respect, perhaps the most important unifying element in the work of the *crepuscolari* is their profound questioning of the poet's role. But if they seek to cast aside various masks such as that of the D'Annunzian superman or that of Pascoli's innocent *fanciullino*, they do so only to subsitute them with ironic, understated masks of their own making. Thus when Guido Gozzano, the most engaging and most interesting of the Crepuscular voices, declares 'Io mi vergogno, / sì, mi vergogno d'essere un poeta', his 'shame' is declared in a passage full of anti-D'Annunzian irony.

This, and similar declarations by, for example, Corazzini and Palazzeschi, are a reflection of a broader crisis and uncertainty concerning the role of the intellectual in a society undergoing rapid change. In an era of industrialization and amidst the early development of consumerism, but in an era also of great political uncertainties (both in internal Italian politics and in the fragile balance of international power), the poet starts to become part of the urban mass, albeit marked by the dubious privilege of ironic self-awareness. Even as Gozzano distances himself from the heroic image of the D'Annunzian *vate*, he is aware of his own absurdity, as embodied in the anti-heroic figure of Totò Merumeni (see text below). This kind of de-sacralization of the poetic *io* will lead eventually to the image of the poet as clown or absurd performer and brings with it, implicitly or explicitly, the degradation of the artistic process and product (as proclaimed by Palazzeschi, a poet with a foot in both the crepuscular and futurist camps: see 'Lasciatemi divertire').

A recurring motif in Crepuscular poetry is that of sickness and decay: indeed the stark reality of physical illness in the form of the tuberculosis which cut short the lives of both Gozzano and Corazzini seems almost absurdly appropriate to the poetics of the entire grouping. Their world is dominated by images of twilight (both literal and figurative), hospitals, convents, beggars, old ladies, combining to create melancholy atmospheres, more often than not within interior settings. The objects catalogued in these faded villas or neglected gardens are not invested with any portentous symbolic meanings, do not lead to any revelation of absolute truth, but serve to bring the vocabulary of the ordinary, the 'unpoetic' to centre stage (see 'Ne la corte' by Govoni). Indeed, formally, the poetry is characterized by a mixture of the elevated and the everyday, the injection of the prosaic into the world of the lyric, often achieving notable effects of ironic contrast on the level of language and tone, as well as on the thematic level (a celebrated example is in Gozzano's 'La Signorina Felicita' where 'Tagli le camicie' forms an arresting rhyme with 'E non mediti Nietzsche').[ix] The work of the *crepuscolari* opens up the world of the understated, the unremarkable events and paraphernalia of middle-class life as a new dimension for poetic exploration. One poem by Marino Moretti memorably begins: 'Piove. È Mercoledí, sono a Cesena' ('A Cesena', in *Il giardino dei frutti*, 1915). Words such as these, in their humdrum ordinariness, and in the fragmented rhythm of the poetic line, quietly characterize the early stages of a wider poetic revolution.

On the face of it, the *crepuscolari* have little in common with the next significant avant-garde group, that of the Futurists. Futurism was a clearly defined movement, a conscious coming together of like-minded writers and artists with highly public and noisily-declared revolutionary intent. Filippo Tommaso Marinetti launched the movement in Paris in 1909 with his first *Manifesto del futurismo*, a generic glorification of speed, machines and war (the latter notoriously hailed as 'sola igiene del mondo'), all trumpeted as worthy subjects for literature, accompanied by a corresponding repudiation of the past and of conventional morality.[x] From an initial emphasis on *verso libero* (verse not conforming to the rigid patterns of traditional poetic metre), Marinetti's manifestos soon moved on to the theory of 'parole in libertà' (1912-13), advocating the complete breakdown of conventional syntax and the radical renewal of the very concept of poetry, giving rise to 'tavole parolibere', innovative typographic arrangements of words and non-verbal elements, with striking, if at times somewhat facile, visual effects. These are artefacts, indeed, which arguably do not even belong to the genre of poetry as such (but one of the great Futurist preoccupations was the idea of innovative syntheses between the literary and other arts).[xi] From the beginning, Futurists espoused nationalistic and politically reactionary views, supporting Italian colonial expansionism, expressing often violently misogynistic attitudes, exulting in industrialization and the world of mass production and campaigning enthusiastically for Italian intervention in the First World War.[xii] Subsequently, indeed, the movement became closely identified with Fascist ideology and, despite attempts to rehabilitate futurism culturally in later decades, this ideological baggage has not easily been discarded. Critics have also observed a gap between Futurist theory and practice, sometimes admitting the cultural importance of the movement while taking a more jaundiced view of the actual literary results. Thus Fortini writes 'È il "testo" futurista che non "funziona" quasi mai [...]', adding that the most successful 'futurist' poets are those least intimately linked to the movement itself (including two of those represented here, Palazzeschi and Soffici).[xiii]

The typical futurist themes of war, the urban landscape (seen in a surreal perspective) and modern technology (particularly the exhilirating new technology of aviation) are all found in the texts by Marinetti, Folgore and Soffici reproduced below. Meanwhile, Palazzeschi's 'Lasciatemi divertire' epitomizes the more playfully iconoclastic side of the movement's assault on literary institutions and traditional poetic values. Palazzeschi's gleeful devaluation of the poetic word goes hand-in-hand with the further degradation of the lyrical *io* (as seen also in his clownish self-portrait as 'saltimbanco dell'anima mia' in the poem 'Chi sono?'). Thus Palazzeschi's work points to hidden areas of convergence between Futurism and crepuscular poetry. Palazzeschi himself began by writing verse broadly in the crepuscular mould (though always marked out by a note of playful vitality), and then went on to embrace the new movement from its outset, attracted not least by its delight in scandalizing the bourgeois reader. But there is a basic continuity of approach in his desire to challenge the idea of the sublime in poetry, to deny the poetic word any special aura or privilege. (The interaction between Crepuscular and Futurist poetry is also embodied in Corrado Govoni, who, after his distinctly 'twilight' beginnings, went on take part in the Futurist experiment in the second decade of the century).[xiv]

Italian Futurism was undoubtedly a movement of great cultural significance on a European scale, prefiguring and influencing similar avant-garde experiments elsewhere, such as Dadaism or Russian Futurism, as well as creating an aesthetic which would be appropriated notably by Fascist propagandism. And in the more specifically literary context, it served spectacularly to introduce new, urban-technological realities into poetic discourse, to break definitively all taboos concerning what was or was not permissible in poetry, whether in content or in terms of formal expression. On the other hand, however, it contained from the outset a fatal tendency to believe rather too much in its own rhetoric. At its worst, Marinettian futurism became a kind of gross parody of D'Annunzian vainglory, exploding notions of the sublime only to instigate its own 'neo-sublime industriale'.[xv]

An altogether more problematic, interiorized path of ethical speculation and tormented self-questioning was taken by the poets associated with the Florentine literary journal *La Voce* (published in two phases: 1908-14 and 1914-16). The final two poets in this first chapter, Clemente Rebora and Dino Campana (along with contemporaries such as Piero Jahier, Camillo Sbarbaro and Giovanni Boine), can be brought together under the admittedly approximate label of *poeti vociani*. These diverse, highly individual writers have been described as Italy's 'expressionists': poets in whose work profound ethical and intellectual anguish, tensions between individualism and moral order, are reflected in unresolved formal tensions, violently energetic language and a tendency towards fragmentation of the poetic line (though often still within the general constraints of traditional metre). Unlike in futurist poetry, here the *io lirico* survives, but is stretched to the limits of its coherence and identity. These are writers who give poetic expression to one of the great themes of European Modernism: that of the divided self, alienated against a background of an often grotesque urban environment (we may think of Pirandello and Svevo in Italy, or, further afield, T.S. Eliot). Thus for example in Sbarbaro's *Pianissimo* (1914), we find the figure of the sleep-walker, surrounded by a sterile, meaningless cityscape: 'Invece camminiamo./ Camminiamo io e te come sonnambuli./ E gli alberi son alberi, le case/ sono case, le donne/ che passano son donne, e tutto è quello/ che è, soltanto quello che è' ('Taci, anima stanca di godere'). Both Rebora and Campana are in many ways difficult to place easily within any overall movement or grouping (as reflected in the texts below), but their broad association with *La Voce* and its expressionistic tendencies is a useful key to approaching their highly-charged, intensely personal poetry.

One may ask, in conclusion, how appropriate is the term *avant-garde* to encompass all the experiences represented in this first chapter. Clearly it cannot be applied across the board in the narrow sense of a single, self-conscious, pioneering movement. These poets have very different intellectual backgrounds and formations, hold the most varied ideological views and subscribe to literary values and systems of belief that are both diverse and also subject to change over time. Nevertheless, I believe it is both possible and helpful to view them in a common perspective of change and innovation, to speak of a period of the *avant-gardes*. From the tearful impotence of Corazzini's 'povero poeta', to the impertinence of Palazzeschi's 'saltimbanco', from Marinetti's assault on the idea of the poetic, to Rebora's forced conjunction of *poesia/sterco*, we witness the breakdown of notions of poetry as an art form with a special, privileged status and the comprehensive undermining of the very idea of the lyric poet, the priest-like figure who can access rarefied truths and insights. This is not to say that such an image of the poet will not return in various forms (we need only look to Ungaretti and to the subsequent mystifications of *ermetismo*): but when it does, it cannot fail to be conditioned by the break with tradition which has occurred. Meanwhile, there has been a huge upheaval in terms of formal expression, poetic language has been variously 'contaminated' by injections of technological realism, prosaic tones and rhythms of everyday speech, as well as extravagant, provocative experimentalism. In short, these poets, whether in groups or as individuals, have sought new dimensions and turned their backs on received notions of the poetic Sublime.[xvi]

Corrado Govoni

Govoni (1884-1965) came from a prosperous farming background near Ferrara. He published his first book of poems, *Le fiale*, in Florence in 1903. After several more volumes in a broadly similar vein, along with contributions to journals such as *La Voce* and *Lacerba*, his attraction to Futurism was manifested in works such as *Poesie elettriche* (1911) and *Rarefazioni e parole in libertà* (1915). He remained something of an outsider to Futurism proper, however, always maintaining a voice in which quite diverse poetic currents came together in a highly individual manner. While there may be some superficial echoes of Pascoli's domestic intimacy, Govoni posits no vision of the sublime or the transcendent, but rather, as in the text reproduced here, paints a picture of an unremarkable reality transfigured through surprising visual and aural effects (and suggestive of personal, human affections). In later years, he published many further works of poetry and prose, though never equalling the originality of his early work.

Sergio Corazzini

Sergio Corazzini (1886-1907) spent most of his life in his native Rome, where he died of tuberculosis at the age of just twenty one. He published several collections of verse between 1904 and his death, including *Piccolo libro inutile* (in 1906, in collaboration with his friend Alberto Tarchiani), in which the text reproduced here appears. Corazzini's 'fanciullo triste' undoubtedly echoes Pascoli's 'fanciullino', but with a darker tonality of existential anguish and with no hint of the other's privileged status. 'Desolazione del povero poeta sentimentale' presents the stereotypical image of the crepuscular poet: a weeping, self-pitying, consumptive youth, an image which lends itself all too easily to ridicule and parody, but which also encapsulates a genuine search for a sort of authenticity in self-humiliation: an anguished awareness of poetry's 'uselessness'. There is certainly less irony in Corazzini's poetry than in some other *crepuscolari* (especially Gozzano): indeed, an element of introspective, confessional sincerity is underlined by the presence of religious motifs. Meanwhile, the physical world of objects is not strongly present, other than as a symbolic reflection of the poet's interior drama.

Guido Gozzano

Guido Gozzano (1883-1916) lived most of his life between his family's country home in Agliè, near Ivrea, and the city of Turin, capital of the former kingdom of Piedmont, with its now declining aristocratic glories (the new industrial Turin is absent from Gozzano's verse). Like Corazzini, Gozzano suffered from tuberculosis, which severely conditioned his life from 1907 onwards and killed him at the age of 32. Generally regarded as the most important of the crepuscular poets, his influence on subsequent generations is far-reaching. Like other *crepuscolari*, he was much exercised by the sway held over contemporary poetry by D'Annunzio, who is often the target of his polemical or ironic antagonism, but also an inescapable model, the implicit *alter ego* of Gozzano's lyrical voice. Gozzano gives definitive expression to the repertoire of crepuscular themes and imagery: dusty nineteenth-century interiors viewed through a lens of ironic nostalgia, indecisive or inept protagonists (often framed in narrative or quasi-dramatic sequences with unremarkable female figures), an ambience of faded bourgeois prosperity and fading cultural and moral certainties. His work is full of apparent contradictions: he adopts the 'closed', codified metrical forms of the lyric tradition (typically rhyming stanzas of hendecasyllables), but within these constraints he deploys the registers and tonalities of colloquial speech, causing, as Montale notes, 'sparks to fly' in the collisions between 'l'aulico [the elevated] e il prosaico'.[xvii] Though apparently frozen in a nineteenth-century world of sepia prints, he points towards key concerns of twentieth-century literature: the alienation of the divided self (despite its ironic masks of self-satisfaction); the problematic relationship with a world devoid of meaning and value. Despite his declarations of 'shame' at the title of poet, and of the futility of poetry itself, he still expresses himself in a virtuosic poetic vein, rich in literary allusiveness. In short, irony, at multiple levels, is the key to Gozzano's poetry. He published two books of verse in his lifetime, *La via del rifugio* (1907) and *I colloqui* (1911), from which the poem below is taken. He also wrote many prose works (including children's stories).

Aldo Palazzeschi

Aldo Palazzeschi (1885-1974) was a multi-faceted writer. A native of Florence, he began writing poetry in a crepuscular vein, publishing several collections between 1905 and 1909. *L'incendiario* (1910) marks a shift towards a more futuristic manner (though he maintained his distance from the more militaristic and right-wing Futurist ideologies). In fact, Palazzeschi's poetry, in its avant-garde individuality, belongs fully neither to Crepuscularism nor to Futurism. His early work contained many typical crepuscular motifs and images, but these are treated with a playful sense of irony and the grotesque, and it is this delight in the game, in playing with the signifier as much as the signified, that comes to the fore in his more Futuristic work. By the time of *L'incendiario* (the fire-raiser), published by Edizioni Futuriste di "Poesia" in 1910, Palazzeschi's work has moved beyond the discreet parody of the sublime practised by other *crepuscolari* and speaks with an impertinent iconoclastic voice of its own, as he gleefully desecrates the altars of poetry. Still, a common thread links him to the more understated *crepuscolari*: this is, as Sanguineti observes, 'la linea dei poeti che si negano come tali'.[xviii] He became a successful novelist in subsequent decades (as well as publishing further collections of verse in the last years of his life).

Filippo Tommaso Marinetti

The founder of Futurism, Filippo Tommaso Marinetti (1876-1944) was born in Egypt of Italian parents and studied in Paris before settling in Italy (his early works of prose and poetry were in French). In Milan in 1905, he founded the journal *Poesia*, which was later to become a key forum for futurist work. Following the first *Futurist Manifesto* (1909), he remained the guiding spirit of the movement, publishing many further manifestos and polemical tracts, as well as creative works. He was an enthusiastic participant in the First World War and his subsequent support of Fascism was rewarded in 1929 with membership of the Accademia d'Italia (a paradoxical outcome given his long-standing anti-academic rhetoric).

Marinetti's poetry itself is perhaps less important than his broad cultural influence. He and his followers were among the first to grasp the importance of the changes taking place in the nature and role of art in industrial, consumeristic society. Indeed they were quick to appropriate the language and techniques of commercial promotion as they celebrated the products of industrial and technological growth. The boundaries between creative and theoretical/promotional writing are sometimes rather blurred: the two often appear together and, indeed, the manifesto itself becomes one of Marinetti's most memorable genres. As regards poetic technique, a key document is his 1912 *Manifesto tecnico della letteratura futurista*, declaring the abolition of syntax, grammar and punctuation and trumpeting the advent of 'parole in libertà', words in a kind of free-associative continuum. In this manifesto, the 'whirling propellor' of an aeroplane passing over industrial Milan announces the new imperatives: 'Bisogna distruggere la sintassi, disponendo i sostantivi a caso, come nascono [...] Si deve usare il verbo all'infinito [...] abolire l'aggettivo [...] Abolire anche la punteggiatura [...] distruggere nella letteratura "l'io" [...]'.[xix] *Zang Tumb Tumb* was published two years later: subtitled 'Parole in libertà', it treats the archetypal Futurist themes of war and destruction in a 'multilinear' discourse, without an identifiable poetic *io*, while notable effects are achieved by the use of innovative typographical devices and the widespread adoption of onomatopoeic or imitative language. The text as a whole does run the risk of indulging in technical novelty for its own sake, a novelty which can quickly lose its appeal and descend into somewhat banal repetition. Nevertheless, a technically iconoclastic work such as this must be seen as an important precursor for a vast range of experimental modernism in European literature.

Luciano Folgore

Omero Vecchi (1888-1966) followed the widespread practice among Futurists of adopting a more dashing pseudonym (his real name could scarcely have been less 'futuristic'). Though something of a minor figure, he is described by Mengaldo as the most poetically 'gifted' of the Futurist vanguard, perhaps precisely because he is less bound by some of the movement's more extreme technical and ideological tenets.[xx] He published several volumes of verse and *parole in libertà*, including *Il canto dei motori* (1912) and *Ponti sull'oceano* (1914), from which the text included here is taken. He later went on to write somewhat more conventional poetry, as well as humorous verse (including some delightful parodies of other modern poets) and narrative and theatrical work.[xxi]

Ardengo Soffici

The Florentine writer and painter Ardengo Soffici (1879-1964) spent several formative years studying as an artist in Paris and was closely associated with the Futurist mainstream in the period immediately before and during the First World War. His most interesting poetic work is contained in the volume *Bïf§zf+18. Simultaneità. Chimismi lirici*, published by Edizioni della "Voce" in 1915. However, he subsequently went along with the 'return to order' of the post-war years, adopting elements of neoclassical style and rhetoric.

Bïf§zf+18 includes Marinettian *parole in libertà* in the *Chimismi* section, as well as the *versi liberi* of the section *Simultaneità* (including the poem reproduced here), where Soffici's openness to other avant-garde experiences (such as that of the French poet Apollinaire) can also be perceived. The notion of 'simultaneity' also points to a non-linear juxtaposition of images and sensations which shares features with cubist painting. Like other Futurists, Soffici tends on the one hand to cast aside the lyrical *io*, along with any notions of the sublime or the sacred, centring his discourse instead on the multiple, fragmentary, objective phenomena of contemporary life, bombarding the reader with tactile, auditory and above all visual sensations and perceptions. And yet, the poetic *io* is still very much in evidence, as in the moments of more 'heroic' subjectivism in 'Aeroplano', though this is leavened by salutary doses of irony, recalling Palazzeschi's lightness of touch (one may recall Palazzeschi's 'saltimbanco', for example, on encountering a figure in Soffici's poem 'Noia': 'Vestito da clown allora,/ Infarinato, dipinto,/ [...]/ Poter ballare,/ Cantare,/ Ridere:/ Ultimo dio in maschera sur un filo[...]').

Clemente Rebora

A native of Milan and a graduate of the University there, Rebora (1885-1957) went on to teach in technical schools. His first collection, *Frammenti lirici*, was published by *La Voce* in 1913, reflecting his sympathies with that journal's ideals. He was severely traumatized by his experiences in the First World War. In the 1920s, he underwent a profound spiritual crisis, leading to his embracing of Catholicism in 1929 and his ordination as a Rosminian priest in 1936. He continued to write poetry (largely of a religious character) in his later years.

    Frammenti lirici is usually regarded as his most significant work, and a key text within the expressionistic climate of *La Voce*. Rebora's verse is full of violent formal and ethical tensions and inner divisions. The choice of a 'fragmentary' genre is part of this overall tension, giving a sense of concentrated, but discontinuous intellectual energy as the poetic voice struggles to find meaning in a chaotic reality. Rebora's use of language is higly individual, with a marked presence of harsh consonantal combinations and frequent effects of assonance and alliteration. The verb is invested with a particular intensity (see the extremely expressive verb-sequences in the texts reproduced here). Lexical choice veers between the rarefied and the bluntly concrete, syntax is often contorted, while enjambements and changing metre (between tradional metrical forms and *verso libero*) create effects of disharmony and discontinuity. Underlying his work is the quest for some kind of order or absolute, frustrated by the anarchy of the surrounding world.

Dino Campana

Campana (1885-1932) is often seen as a sort of 'poète maudit' in the mould of the nineteenth-century French poet Rimbaud, an image supported in various ways by the themes and style of his work, and the circumstances of his life.

Born in Marradi (Tuscany), he suffered from a young age from episodes of mental illness, which would lead to various periods of confinement in psychiatric institutions, and even, on occasions, imprisonment. He never completed his university studies, but embarked on a number of solitary journeys, even venturing as far as South America. After a brief but stormy relationship with the writer Sibilla Aleramo in 1916-17, he was committed in 1918 to a mental institution near Florence, where he remained until his death in 1932.

Campana was in contact with the Florentine avant-garde circles associated with the journals *Lacerba* and *La voce* (he published work in both of these), but he remained on the margins of these groupings. After Soffici lost the only manuscript of his poems in 1913, Campana re-wrote them apparently from memory and went on to publish them in his home-town of Marradi in 1914 with the title *Canti Orfici*: a collection of verse interspersed with lyrical prose pieces which was destined to be his only major published work.[xxii] The term 'orphic' in the title reflects an idea of poetry as a vehicle for exploring the mysterious or the esoteric in search of some absolute truth, broadly within the symbolist tradition. However, there is a wide expressive range in the poems, including repeated images of the journey or voyage, hallucinatory or expressionistic depictions of the city and its inhabitants (particularly in nocturnal scenes, including marginal figures such as prostitutes), as well as the anguished exploration of an alienated, rootless lyrical self. In Sanguineti's words, Campana brings the whole 'patologia della coscienza poetica collettiva' into the 'vortex' of his images, 'delle sue parole di ossessione, dei suoi incubi di musica, dei suoi ritmi impossibili'.[xxiii]

Endnotes

[i] See 'Il fanciullino', in Giovanni Pascoli, *Prose*, vol. 1, a cura di Augusto Vicinelli (Milan: Mondadori, 1956), pp. 5-56.

[ii] In Pascoli, *Poesie*, a cura di Antonio Baldini (Milan: Mondadori, 1948), p. 86.

[iii] In D'Annunzio, *Versi d'Amore e di Gloria*, vol. 2 (Milan: Mondadori, 1950), p. 644.

[iv] On the importance of French symbolism more generally, see Shirley Vinall, 'French Symbolism and Italian Poetry 1880-1920', in *Symbolism, Decadence and the Fin de Siècle: French and European Perspectives*, edited by Patrick McGuinness (Exeter: Exeter University Press, 2000).

[v] Edoardo Sanguineti, introduction to *Poesia italiana del Novecento*, p. xxxiii.

[vi] Niva Lorenzini, *La poesia italiana del Novecento*, p. 19.

[vii] See P. V. Mengaldo, *Poeti italiani del Novecento*, pp. xxxviii-xxxix. For 'modelli'/'antimodelli', see Lorenzini, *La poesia italiana del Novecento*, p.17. See also Fausto Curi, *La poesia italiana nel Novecento*, pp. 15-20.

viii   The term 'poesia crepuscolare' (twilight poetry) was coined as a derogatory label by the critic Giuseppe Antonio Borgese in 1910, although, as Lorenzini points out (p. 38), he was crticizing a whole swathe of contemporary verse, including work which we would regard as closer to Futurism. On the idea of 'crepuscolarismo', see also Giuseppe Savoca and Mario Tropea, *Pascoli, Gozzano e i crepuscolari* (Roma-Bari: Laterza, 1976), pp. 89-93.

ix   See 'La Signorina Felicita ovvero la felicità' (ll. 308-311), in Gozzano, *Tutte le poesie*, a cura di Andrea Rocca, I Meridiani (Milan: Mondadori, 1980), p. 178.

x   'Fondazione e Manifesto del Futurismo', in Filippo Tommaso Marinetti, *Teoria e invenzione futurista*, a cura di Luciano De Maria, I Meridiani (Milano: Mondadori, 1983), pp. 7-14.

xi   An interesting example of a 'paroliberista' text by Cangiullo, seen in different versions, with one including musical elements, can be found in Matteo D'Ambrosio, *Futurismo e altre avanguardie* (Naples: Liguori, 1999), pp. 25-32.

xii   On the Futurist eroticization of war, see Lucia Re, 'Futurism, Seduction, and the Strange Sublimity of War', *Italian Studies*, 59 (2004), 83-111.

xiii   Franco Fortini, *I poeti del Novecento* (Roma-Bari: Laterza, 1977), p. 11.

xiv   A key critical text on the complex interrelationships between these tendencies is Francois Livi, *Tra crepuscolarismo e futurismo: Govoni e Palazzeschi* (Milan: Istituto Propaganda Libraria, 1980).

xv   Sanguineti, *Poesia italiana del Novecento*, p. xlviii. See also Lorenzini, *La poesia italiana del Novecento*, pp. 52-56.

xvi   See Lorenzini, *La poesia italiana del Novecento*, p. 32.

xvii   Eugenio Montale, 'Gozzano dopo trent'anni', now in *Il secondo mestiere*, I Meridiani (Milan: Mondadori, 1996), pp. 1270-80.

xviii   Sanguineti, *Poesia italiana del Novecento*, p. xlvi.

xix   Marinetti, *Teoria e invenzione del futurismo*, pp. 46-50.

xx   Mengaldo, *Poeti italiani del Novecento*, p. 236.

xxi   An example of his humorous verse is 'L'importo sepolto', an incisive parody of Ungaretti: '...Ora/ me ne vado/ a letto/ volentieri/ perchè/ sono stanco/ di questi/ grandi pensieri'. See Luciano Folgore, *Il libro delle parodie* (Milan: Ceschina,1965), p. 109.

xxii   On the relationship of the published work to the 'original' manuscript, discovered among Soffici's papers in 1971, see the introduction to *Canti Orfici*, edizione critica a cura di Giorgio Grillo (Florence: Vallecchi, 1990), pp. vii-xxxviii.

xxiii   Sanguineti, *Poesia italiana del Novecento*, p. lv.

Poetic texts

Govoni
Poesie (1903-1958) (Milan: Mondadori, 2000)
A selection of texts is also available in:
Poesie (1903-1959), a cura di Giuseppe Ravegnani (Milan: Mondadori, 1961)

Corazzini
Poesie edite e inedite, a cura di Stefano Jacomuzzi (Torino: Einaudi, 1982)

Gozzano
Tutte le poesie, a cura di Andrea Rocca, I Meridiani (Milan: Mondadori, 1980)
See also annotated editions:
Poesie, a cura di E. Sanguineti (Torino: Einaudi, 1990)
Poesie, a cura di Giorgio Barberi Squarotti (Milan: Rizzoli, 1977)

Palazzeschi
Opere giovanili (Milan: Mondadori, 1958).
(This volume of the complete works contains the main poetic collections.)
Poesie, a cura di Sergio Antonielli (Milano: Mondadori, 1971).

Marinetti
Poetic texts and manifestos are in:
Filippo Tommaso Marinetti, *Teoria e invenzione futurista*, a cura di Luciano De Maria, I
     Meridiani (Milano: Mondadori, 1983).
See also the preface by Aldo Palazzeschi for a colourful memoir of Marinetti in 1910.

Folgore
Ponti sull'oceano: versi liberi e parole in libertà (Milan: Edizioni Futuriste di Poesia, 1914)
There is no recent edition of Folgore's poetry, but selections can be found in the major
anthologies such as those by Sanguineti, Mengaldo, Segre and Ossola.

Soffici
Opere, vol. IV (Firenze: Vallecchi, 1961)

Rebora
Le poesie, a cura di Gianni Mussini e Vanni Scheiwiller (Milano: Garzanti, 1994)

Campana
Canti Orfici, a cura di Fiorenza Ceragioli (Milan: Rizzoli, 1989)
Canti Orfici, edizione critica a cura di Giorgio Grillo (Florence: Vallecchi, 1990)
See also facsimile reproduction of the first edition: *Canti Orfici* (Florence, Libreria Chiari,
1994); and Dino Campana, *Opere e contributi*, a cura di E. Falqui (Florence: Vallecchi, 1973).

Further reading

Asor Rosa, Alberto, 'Canti Orfici di Dino Campana', in *Letteratura Italiana: Le opere*, vol. IV, i: *L'età della crisi*, (Torino: Einaudi, 1995), pp. 333-404

Baldissone, Giusi, *Filippo Tommaso Marinetti* (Milan: Mursia, 1986)

Bellini, Eraldo, *Studi su Ardengo Soffici* (Milan: Vita e Pensiero, 1987)

Curi, Fausto, *Corrado Govoni*, (Milan: Mursia 1964)

D'Ambrosio, Matteo, *Futurismo e altre avanguardie* (Naples: Liguori, 1999)

De Maria, Luciano, ed., *Per conoscere Marinetti e il futurismo* (Milan: Mondadori, 1981)

Del Serra, Maura, *Dino Campana* (Florence: La Nuova Italia, 1974)

Fortini, Franco, 'Frammenti lirici di Clemente Rebora', in *Letteratura Italiana: Le opere*, vol. IV, i: *L'età della crisi*, (Torino: Einaudi, 1995), pp. 237-63

Galimberti, Cesare, *Dino Campana* (Milan: Mursia, 1967)

Gentilini, Anna Rosa, ed., *Dino Campana alla fine del secolo* (Bologna: Il Mulino, 1999)

Guglielmi, Guido, *L'udienza del poeta: Saggi su Palazzeschi e il futurismo* (Turin: Einaudi, 1979)

Guglielminetti, Marziano, *Clemente Rebora* (Milan: Mursia, 1982)

Jacobbi, Ruggero, *Invito alla lettura di Dino Campana* (Milan: Mursia, 1976)

Jacomuzzi, Stefano, *Sergio Corazzini* (Milan: Mursia, 1963)

Lenzini, Luca, *Gozzano* (Palermo: Palumbo, 1992)

Livi, Francois, and M. Zingone, eds, *"Io non sono un poeta": Sergi Corazzini (1886-1907): Atti del Convegno internazionale di studi, Roma, 11-13 marzo 1987* (Roma: Bulzoni, 1989)

Livi, Francois, *La parola crepuscolare: Corazzini, Gozzano, Moretti* (Milan: Istituto Propaganda Libraria, 1986)

Livi, Francois, *Tra crepuscolarismo e futurismo: Govoni e Palazzeschi* (Milan: Istituto Propaganda Libraria, 1980)

Lorenzini, Niva, 'I colloqui di Guido Gozzano', in *Letteratura Italiana: Le opere*, vol. IV, i: *L'età della crisi*, (Torino: Einaudi, 1995), pp. 149-175.

Marchetti, Giuseppe, *Ardengo Soffici* (Firenze: La Nuova Italia, 1979)

Marinari, Dora, ed., *Gozzano e i poeti 'crepuscolari'* (Roma: Bonacci, 1985)

Memmo, Francesco P., *Invito alla lettura di Aldo Palazzeschi* (Milano: Mursia, 1976)

Montale, Eugenio, 'Gozzano dopo trent'anni', in *Il secondo mestiere* (Milano: Mondadori, 1996), pp. 1270-80.

Pullini, Giorgio, *Aldo Palazzeschi* (Milano: Mursia, 1972).

Ramat, Silvio, *La poesia italiana 1903-1943* (Venezia: Marsilio, 1997)

Re, Lucia, 'Futurism, Seduction, and the Strange Sublimity of War', *Italian Studies*, 59 (2004), 83-111

Salaris, Claudia, 'Manifesto tecnico della letteratura futurista di F. T. Marinetti' in *Letteratura Italiana: Le opere*, vol. IV, i: *L'età della crisi*, (Torino: Einaudi, 1995), pp. 177-209.

Salaris, Claudia, *Filippo Tommaso Marinetti* (Florence: La Nuova Italia, 1988)

Salaris, Claudia, *Luciano Folgore e le avanguardie* (Florence: La Nuova Italia, 1997).

Sanguineti, Edoardo, *Guido Gozzano: indagini e letture* (Turin: Einaudi, 1975)

Sanguineti, Edoardo, *Tra liberty e crepuscolarismo* (Milano: Mursia, 1977)

Savoca, Giuseppe, and M. Tropea, *Pascoli, Gozzano e i crepuscolari* (Roma-Bari: Laterza, 1976)

Vinall, Shirley, 'French Symbolism and Italian Poetry 1880-1920', in *Symbolism, Decadence and the Fin de Siècle: French and European Perspectives*, edited by Patrick McGuinness (Exeter: Exeter University Press, 2000)

Contents

CORRADO GOVONI

From *Armonia in grigio et in silenzio* (1903)

Ne la corte — Tre stracci ad asciugare
sul muricciolo accanto il rosmarino
Una scala seduta. Un alveare
vedovo, su cui giuoca il mio micino.

Un orciuolo che à sete sul pozzale   5
di marmo scanalato da le funi.
Dei cocci gialli. Un vaso vuoto. Un fiale
che à vomitato. Dei fogliami bruni.

— Su le finestre — Un pettine sdentato
con due capelli come dei pistilli.   10
Un astuccio per cipria. Uno sventrato
guancialino di seta per gli spilli.

Una scatola di belletto. Un guanto
mencio. Un grande garofano appassito.
Una cicca. Una pagina in un canto   15
piegata, da chissà mai quale dito!

— Per l'aria — La docile campana
d'un convento di suore di clausura.
Una lunga monotonia di zana.
Un gallo. Una leggera incrinatura   20

di vento. Due rosse ventarole
cifrate. Delle nubi bianche. Un treno.
Un odore acutissimo di viole.
Un odore acutissimo di fieno.

'Ne la corte...'

This untitled poem is taken from Govoni's second collection, *Armonia in grigio et in silenzio* (Florence, 1903), where already from the title a 'crepuscular' atmosphere is established. Yet, notwithstanding certain melancholy elements typical of crepuscularism, there is a peculiar freshness and directness in Govoni's observation of the world, unlike the greyer tones of some *crepuscolari*. Here we are presented with a typical catalogue of ordinary objects, all observed within one of the enclosed spaces so characteristic of crepuscular poetry. The poem proceeds by accumulation of substantives, juxtaposed in a paratactic structure (without conjunctions or formal indications of logical connection). It is written in conventional hendecasyllabic metre, but note also the strong punctuation marks which fragment the poetic line, creating strikingly jerky rhythmic effects, undermining any sense of a musical flow (e.g. ll. 1, 7). We may also observe the emphatic use of terms from the 'lower', more everyday linguistic register in rhyming positions ('**rosmarino-micino**', '**sdentatato-sventrato**'). In this inventory of objects, the lyrical *io* has been reduced to an almost invisible presence (the very antithesis of D'Annunzio).

1-4:   '**stracci**': rags, immediately puts the focus on concrete, mundane objects; '**muricciolo**': the first of several diminutive forms used in the poem, giving a reductive sense of intimacy, of insignificant, minimal details. (also underlined phonically by other occurrences of the grouping '[c]ci'); '**accanto il**' : accanto al; '**scala seduta**' probably a folded ladder (or lying down); '**alveare vedovo**': lit. 'widowed beehive', here, abandoned by bees.

5-8:   '**orciuolo**': dim. of 'orcio': terracotta jar; '**à sete**': 'ha sete'; '**pozzale**': pozzo; '**scanalato**': furrowed by rope marks; '**vomitato**': spilled out its contents. Here, as in the first and third stanzas, images evoke melancholy abandonment and squalor, broken, and predominantly useless objects, leading to a cumulative sense of meaninglessness.

9-16:   Objects of an an interior, but viewed from outside; '**pistilli**': female parts of the flower; '**astuccio per cipria**': powder (make-up) case; '**sventrato/ guancialino...**': the expressive force of the brutal adjective ('ripped open') is underlined by the contrast with the delicacy of the silk pin-cushion; '**belletto**': make-up; '**mencio**': limp; '**cicca**': cigarette-end; '**un canto**': a corner.

17-20:   These lines broaden the scope of the word-picture, introducing more variety of colour and light impressions. '**convento**': an image, much used by the *crepuscolari*, of enclosure, of lives lived at second hand; '**zana**': cradle (suggests monotonous rocking). Images become more unconnected, in a freely impressionistic sequence.

20-21:   '**incrinatura // di vento**': the sense is that the air itself is broken or cracked by the wind. The marked enjambement (see also others elsewhere in poem), along with the full stops in both these lines, greatly disrupts the otherwise regular hendecasyllabic metre.

23-24:   The close structural similarity between the final lines underlines the uneasy juxtaposition between '**viole**' (a distinctly decorative image) and '**fieno**' (decidedly 'unpoetic').

SERGIO CORAZZINI

From *Piccolo libro inutile* (1906)

Desolazione del povero poeta sentimentale
[extracts]

I
Perché tu mi dici: poeta?
Io non sono un poeta.
Io non sono che un piccolo fanciullo che piange.
Vedi: non ho che le lagrime da offrire al Silenzio.
Perché tu mi dici: poeta?   5

II
Le mie tristezze sono povere tristezze comuni.
Le mie gioie furono semplici,
semplici così, che se io dovessi confessarle a te arrossirei.
Oggi io penso a morire.

III
Io voglio morire, solamente, perché sono stanco;   10
solamente perché i grandi angioli
su le vetrate delle catedrali
mi fanno tremare d'amore e di angoscia;
solamente perché, io sono, oramai,
rassegnato come uno specchio,   15
come un povero specchio melanconico.

Vedi che non sono un poeta:
sono un fanciullo triste che ha voglia di morire.

[...]

VI
Questa notte ho dormito con le mani in croce.
Mi sembrò di essere un piccolo e dolce fanciullo   20
dimenticato da tutti gli umani,
povera tenera preda del primo venuto;
e desiderai di essere venduto,
di essere battuto
di essere costretto a digiunare   25
per potermi mettere a piangere tutto solo,
disperatamente triste,
in un angolo oscuro.

VII
Io amo la vita semplice delle cose.
Quante passioni vidi sfogliarsi, a poco a poco,   30
per ogni cosa che se ne andava!
Ma tu non mi comprendi e sorridi.
E pensi che io sia malato.

VIII
Oh, io sono, veramente malato!
E muoio, un poco, ogni giorno.   35
Vedi: come le cose.
Non sono, dunque, un poeta:
io so che per esser detto: poeta, conviene
viver ben altra vita!
Io non so, Dio mio, che morire.   40
Amen.

Desolazione del povero poeta sentimentale

In this text (unlike the poem by Govoni above), the *io* is very definitely present, but only to be debased and humiliated: the lyrical voice gives us neither an exaltation of life nor of poetry itself. Rather, both are brought down to the level of suffering and illness, overshadowed by the presence of death. But any suggestion of solemnity or lyrical elevation is circumvented by the comprehensive lowering of the tone, and the focus on 'simplicity' and ordinariness. Potentially pretentious elements of self-pity and self-deprecation are expressed in a disarmingly direct, communicative manner and offset by hidden threads of irony. The metre is innovative in its unpredictability with a prevalence of long, hypermetric lines tending towards the tonalities and rhythms of the spoken, unpoetic word.

1-5:   The generic '**tu**' (perhaps on one level a poetic alter ego) draws the reader in to an intimate dialogue, though not without a note of potential conflict or antagonism (see part VII). **l.2**: the poem's central assertion, reinforced by the question in ll. 1 and 5, denies the identity and role of 'poet'; (one may, however, also allow for an ironic slant to this affirmation, in so far as Corazzini is rejecting the existing idea of the poet, but subtly asserting a new 'negative' model); '**Silenzio**': capitalization introduces the poem's religious thread.

6-9:   The poet's resigned melancholy is flaunted, exaggerated, along with a preference for the 'ordinary' and for self-abasement, as he refuses to engage in vitalistic optimisim; '**arrossirei**': I would blush (the lyrical posture is presented as an embarassment).

10-18   More decorative, decadent elements here, as in other *crepuscolari*, reflect the influence of French and Belgian symbolists such as Jules Lagorgue, Paul Verlaine, Francis Jammes and others ('**vetrate**': here, stained glass). **ll. 15-16**: the mirror is an important image, encapsulating the breakdown of the poetic *io*, the dissolution of its independent identity which is devalued as a mere appearance (mirrors recur in other crepuscular poems).
         (Parts IV and V, omitted here, contain further statements of the 'vanity' of poetry and additional religious elements.)

19-28:   The motif of regression to childhood is given a morbid development here. The distinctly masochistic features of the poet's fantasy underline his diametric opposition to the D'Annunzian vision of the poet as 'superman'; '**preda**': prey; '**digiunare**': to go hungry.

29-33:   The focus shifts (ll. 30-31) on to the ebbing of physical vitality, the approach of death; '**sfogliarsi**': to lose their leaves (or drop like leaves); '**Ma tu non mi comprendi…**': suggests a more ambivalent approach to the reader (who is perhaps unwilling to engage seriously with his inner drama), part of a broader ambivalence regarding the institution of poetry, (a precursor perhaps is in Baudelaire's famous line: 'hypocrite lecteur, mon semblable, mon frère').

34-41:   The bald truth of Corazzini's physical condition, as opposed to any literary game for the reader's benefit, and in stark contrast to any false optimism; **ll.**

37-39: lines heavy with irony – the refusal or inability to embrace life is again clearly antithetical to D'Annunzio's aesthetic whereby art is identified with life itself. **'Amen'**: sets the seal on the tone of religious pathos implicit throughout the poem.

GUIDO GOZZANO

From *I colloqui* (1911)

Totò Merùmeni

I

Col suo giardino incolto, le sale vaste, i bei
balconi secentisti guarniti di verzura,
la villa sembra tolta da certi versi miei,
sembra la villa-tipo, del Libro di Lettura...

[...]

II

Totò ha venticinque anni, tempra sdegnosa,
molta cultura e gusto in opere d'inchiostro,
scarso cervello, scarsa morale, spaventosa
chiaroveggenza: è il vero figlio del tempo nostro.   20

Non ricco, giunta l'ora di «vender parolette»
(il suo Petrarca!...) e farsi baratto o gazzettiere,
Totò scelse l'esilio. E in libertà riflette
ai suoi trascorsi che sarà bello tacere.

Non è cattivo. Manda soccorso di danaro   25
al povero, all'amico un cesto di primizie;
non è cattivo. A lui ricorre lo scolaro
pel tema, l'emigrante per le commendatizie.

Gelido, consapevole di sé e dei suoi torti,
non è cattivo. È il buono che derideva il Nietzsche: 30
«... in verità derido l'inetto che si dice
buono perché non ha l'ugne abbastanza forti...»

Dopo lo studio grave, scende in giardino, gioca
coi suoi dolci compagni sull'erba che l'invita;
i suoi compagni sono: una ghiandaia rôca,   35
un micio, una bertuccia che ha nome Makakita...

III
La Vita si ritolse tutte le sue promesse.
Egli sognò per anni l'Amore che non venne,
sognò pel suo martirio attrici e principesse
ed oggi ha per amante la cuoca diciottenne.   40

Quando la casa dorme, la giovinetta scalza,
fresca come una prugna al gelo mattutino,
giunge nella sua stanza, lo bacia in bocca, balza
su lui che la possiede, beato e resupino...

IV
Totò non può sentire. Un lento male indomo   45
inaridì le fonti prime del sentimento;
l'analisi e il sofisma fecero di quest'uomo
ciò che le fiamme fanno d'un edificio al vento.

Ma come le ruine che già seppero il fuoco
esprimono i giaggioli dai bei vividi fiori,   50
quell'anima riarsa esprime a poco a poco
una fiorita d'esili versi consolatori...

V
Così Totò Merùmeni, dopo tristi vicende,
quasi è felice. Alterna l'indagine e la rima.
Chiuso in sé stesso, medita, s'accresce, esplora, intende   55
la vita dello Spirito che non intese prima.

Perché la voce è poca e l'arte prediletta
immensa, perché il Tempo — mentre ch'io parlo! — va,
Totò opra in disparte, sorride, e meglio aspetta.
E vive. Un giorno è nato. Un giorno morirà.   60

Totò Merùmeni

The title **'Totò Merùmeni'** is an ironic distortion of one used by Baudelaire (and originally by the Latin poet Terence): 'Heautontimoroumenos', a Greek word meaning 'one who punishes himself'.

1-4:   The villa is an archetypal crepuscular setting. However, **ll.3-4** introduce an ironic self-awareness into the text, and signal clearly that Totò is a lightly-masked portrait of Gozzano himself; yet even in this identification, he distances himself from his creation (**'secentisti'**: in the style of the 1600s; **'guarniti...'**: decorated with plants; **'villa-tipo'**: stereotypical villa).
(The rest of section I, ll. 5-16, omitted here, elaborates on the villa and its other inhabitants: the young man's mother, great-aunt and deranged uncle.)

17-20:   Totò's cultural pretensions contrast with his inherent weaknesses, making him a 'man of our time'; **'tempra sdegnosa'**: haughty temperament; **'opere d'inchiostro'**: works in ink (literature); **'chiaroveggenza'**: clear-sightedness.

21-24:   Totò assumes a (spurious) stance of noble renunciation rather than 'sell' his intellect as a lawyer or a journalist; **'vender parolette'** is from Petrarch (CCCLX), where it refers to the law (studied by Gozzano). Gozzano's work is full of literary allusions, usually not so explicit: thus **'baratto'** is a form of 'barattiere' (fraudster) found in Dante (*Inferno* XI, 60); **'gazzettiere'**: journalist. Such allusions produce layers of tonal irony. **'l'esilio'**: exile, retreat into isolation; **'trascorsi...'**: youthful errors (best left untold), suggesting a less than virtuous character. A further allusion to Dante can be seen in **'sarà bello tacere'** (cf. *Inferno IV*, 104).

25-28:   A portrait of the worthy bourgeois gentleman, generous with his patronage of the poor and weak. (The repetition of **'non è cattivo'** begins to have a hollow ring however.) **'primizie'**: early fruit crop; **'scolaro'**: schoolboy; **'commendatizie'**: letters of reference.

29-32:   **'Gelido...'**: suggests an unfeeling self-awareness; **'torti'**: faults. Gozzano quotes Nietzsche's *Thus spoke Zarathustra*, where the philosopher derided weakness disguised as goodness (Nietzsche is the subject of **'derideva'**). Thus Totò's characterization as weak, inept, an anti-heroic figure, sets him in opposition to the 'superman'. Note the striking collision of registers in the rhyme *Nietzsche-dice*; **'l'ugne'**: fingernails.

33-36:   His companions are: a hoarse bluejay (**'ghiandaia'**), a cat (**'micio'** is an affectionate, domestic term) and a monkey (cf. Govoni, 'Ne la corte', l.4).

37-44:   Here the image of the aggressive D'Annunzian erotic hero is comprehensively overturned. Totò has not succeeded in grasping Life's prizes . The capitalized **'Vita'** and **'Amore'**, reminiscent of the great Poet, are here the active agents, in contrast with Totò's passive stance (**'ritolse'**: took back). Similarly, imagined conquests of **'attrici e principesse'**, give way to the reality of the 18-year-old servant girl. Note Totò's marked passivity in the erotic encounter: she is the active partner, he lies 'supine' (his 'active' verb, **'la possiede'** must be read ironically); **'martirio'**: suffering (of love); **'scalza'**: barefoot; **'beato'**: contented.

45-48:   **'sentire'**: here, 'to have feelings'; **'indomo'**: invincible; the **'male'** which 'dried him up' is given in **l.47**: his habit of analytical sophistry (**'sofisma'**). Here there is a distinctly darker note in the portrayal of his bleak inner life.

49-52:   The darker tone is immediately attenuated by the image of irises (**'giaggiole'**) blooming in a burnt out building, just as Totò's 'burned' (**'riarsa'**) soul is 'consoled' by his own verse. But here Gozzano's irony is double-edged. Even as he mocks Totò's angst and 'slender' (**'esili'**) consolatory verse, he also mocks those who see his own work in such terms.

53-60:   The poem closes on a picture of renunciation and withdrawal from life; **'l'indagine e la rima'**: philosophical thought and poetry; **'s'accresce'**: grows (intellectually); **'la vita dello Spirito'**: refers to Benedetto Croce's Idealistic philosophy, increasingly influential in these years. **'Perché la voce è poca...'**: A further ironic self-portrayal, deprecating the 'smallness' of his 'voice' in the face of poetry itself (**'l'arte prediletta'**) and of Time; **'opra'**: works ['opera']. **l.60**: A bleakly disillusioned picture of a life consisting solely of birth and death.

ALDO PALAZZESCHI

From *L'incendiario* (1910)

Lasciatemi divertire
(Canzonetta)

Tri tri tri,
fru fru fru,
uhi uhi uhi,
ihu ihu ihu.

Il poeta si diverte,   5
pazzamente,
smisuratamente.
Non lo state a insolentire,
lasciatelo divertire
poveretto,   10
queste piccole corbellerie
sono il suo diletto.

Cucù rurù,
rurù cucù,
cuccuccurucù!   15

Cosa sono queste indecenze?
Queste strofe bisbetiche?
Licenze, licenze,
licenze poetiche.
Sono la mia passione.   20

Farafarafarafa,
Taratararatarata,
Paraparaparapa,
Laralaralarala!

Sapete cosa sono?   25
Sono robe avanzate,
non sono grullerie,
sono la ... spazzatura
delle altre poesie.

Bubububu,   30
fufufufu,
Friù!
Friù!

Se d'un qualunque nesso
son prive,   35
perché le scrive
quel fesso?

Bilobilobilobilobilo
blum!
Filofilofilofilofilo   40
flum!
Bilolù. Filolù.
U.

Non è vero che non voglion dire,
vogliono dire qualcosa.   45
Voglion dire...
come quando uno si mette a cantare
senza sapere le parole.
Una cosa molto volgare.
Ebbene, così mi piace di fare.   50

Aaaaa!
Eeeee!
Iiiii!
Ooooo!
Uuuuu!   55
A! E! I! O! U!

Ma giovinotto,
diteci un poco una cosa,
non è la vostra una posa,
di voler con così poco   60
tenere alimentato
un sì gran foco?

Huisc... Huisc...
Huisciu... sciu sciu,
Sciukoku... Koku koku,   65
Sciu
ko
ku.

Come si deve fare a capire?
Avete delle belle pretese,   70
sembra ormai che scriviate in giapponese,

Abì, alì, alarì.
Ririri!
Ri.

Lasciate pure che si sbizzarrisca,   75
anzi, è bene che non lo finisca,
il divertimento gli costerà caro:
gli daranno del somaro.

Labala
falala   80
falala...
eppoi lala...
e lalala, lalalalala lalala.

Certo è un azzardo un po' forte
scrivere delle cose così,   85
che ci son professori, oggidì,
a tutte le porte.

Ahahahahahahah!
Ahahahahahahah!
Ahahahahahahah!   90

Infine,
io ho pienamente ragione,
i tempi sono cambiati,
gli uomini non domandano più nulla
dai poeti: 95
e lasciatemi divertire!

Lasciatemi divertire

In this text, the *io* is cynical, subversive, anarchic. With an overt, almost theatrical presence, distinctly non-lyrical, the poetic persona puts himself forward also for potential public ridicule (and the mocking crowd is given its own voices, emphasizing that the *io* is no longer at the centre of a unitary discourse). Subtitle: '**Canzonetta**': a form of light or sentimental verse, echoed ironically here in the overall shape of the text, though the poem is written in *versi liberi*.

1-4:   These lines, along with every second subsequent stanza, are composed entirely of meaningless or infantile sounds, constituting the protagonist's 'poetic text' which causes such outrage to the 'audience'.

5-12:   '**smisuratamente**': beyond measure (typifying Palazzeschi's exuberant language); '**insolentire**': insult; '**corbellerie**': nonsense; '**poveretto**' suggests a tone of smug condescension, reflecting the conventional outlook of the listeners. A feature of this text is co-presence of different (and competing) voices. In these lines, we have the voice of an indeterminate 'narrator' of sorts, separate from the protagonist (identifiable with the poet's own perspective).

16-20:   The outraged voice of the public, followed by the poet's playful response. '**bisbetiche**': absurd, nonsensical; '**licenze poetiche**': poetic licence usually refers to a permissible infraction of convention, but here the 'licence' is clearly all-encompassing. The poet's only criteria are his own 'delight' (l. 12) and 'passion'.

25-29:   The use of terms from a low or banal register speaks of a radical devaluation and demystification of the idea of poetry; '**robe avanzate**': left-over 'stuff' (emphasising the mundane nature of the poetic product); '**grullerie**': stupidities; '**spazzatura**': rubbish. The voice presents his poetry as material rejected by polite literature and society.

34-37:   The impatient voice of the public, expressing a conventional view that poetry should make sense, have some value; '**nesso**': logical connection; '**prive**': lacking; '**fesso**': fool. The rhyme emphasizes a comic contrast.

44-50:   The 'poet' justifies his 'nonsense'. But the 'sense' he defends is in fact a lack of meaning: it is the pure pleasure of enunciation. l.49: an ironic mimicry of the 'crowd's' viewpoint.

57-62:   Again, a patronizing tone is evident in '**giovinotto**' ('voi' is used here as the polite singular). The audience suspects the poet of insincerity ('**posa**': pose) and dismisses his work as inadequate to the needs of poetry; '**un sì gran foco**': conventional view of the poetic tradition as a sacred flame, to be served humbly; '**alimentato**': fed, nourished.

63-71:   If anything, the protagonist's 'text' becomes even more bizarre, more of a regression to infantile babbling, more alien to the sounds of Italian. One may speculate that these 'alien' sounds allude to the contemporary fashion for the Japanese 'haiku' form (as reflected in the irritated response of the listeners).

75-78:   The crowd no longer even attempts to address the 'poet': their contempt highlights the communicative gulf opening between contemporary poetry and its audience. Meanwhile this discussion among the listeners underlines the presence of multiple voices and viewpoints. **'Si sbizzarrisca'**: indulge himself; **'somaro'**: ass (fool).

84-87: 'azzardo': risk; **'a tutte le porte'**: 'around every corner'. The audience's invocation of 'professors' is a wry critique of the stifling conservatism of academic culture.

88-90: **'Ah ah'** is the conventional representation of laughter ('ha ha'). The poet's 'text' reaches its climax in pure non-semantic pleasure.

91-96: A slightly more sobre note here, as the poet acknowledges his complete loss of status (but this is immediately overturned in the playful defiance of the closing line).

FILIPPO TOMMASO MARINETTI

From *Zang Tumb Tumb* (1914)

BILANCIO DELLE ANALOGIE

(1ª SOMMA)
  Marcia del cannoneggiamento futurista colosso-leitmotif-maglio-genio-novatore-ottimismo fame-ambizione *(TERRIFICO ASSOLUTO SOLENNE EROICO PESANTE IMPLACABILE FECONDANTE)*
zang tuumb tumb tumb
(2ª SOMMA)
  difesa Adrianopoli passatismo minareti dello scetticismo cupole-ventri dell'indolenza vigliaccheria ci-penseremo-domani non-c'è-pericolo non-è-possibile a-che-serve dopo-tutto-me-ne-infischio consegna di tutto lo stock in stazione-unica = cimitero
(3ª SOMMA)
  intorno ad ogni obice-passo del colosso-accordo cadere del maglio-creazione del genio-comando correre ballo tondo galoppante di fucilate mitragliatrici violini monelli odori-di-bionda-trentenne cagnolini ironie dei critici ruote ingranaggi grida gesti rimpianti *(ALLEGRO AEREO SCETTICO FOLLEGGIANTE AEREO CORROSIVO VOLUTTUOSO)*
(4ª SOMMA)
  intorno a Adrianopoli + bombardamento + orchestra + passeggiata-del-colosso + officina allargarsi cerchi concentrici di riflessi plagi echi risate bambine fiori fisch-di-vapore attese piume profumi fetori angosce *(INFINITO MONOTONO PERSUASIVO NOSTALGICO)* Questi pesi spessori rumori odori turbini molecolari catene reti corridoi di analogie concorrenze e sincronismi offrirsi offrirsi offrirsi offrirsi in dono ai miei amici poeti pittori musicisti e rumoristi futuristi
zang-tumb-tumb-zang-zang-tuuumb tatatatatatata picpacpam
pacpacpicpampampac *uuuuuuuuuuuuuuu*

ZANG-TUMB
TUMB-TUMB
TUUUUUM

From *Zang Tumb Tumb*

Zang Tumb Tumb is a lengthy text (well over 100 pages), perhaps more akin to a prose poem than a lyric poem. Applying the tenets of the *Manifesto tecnico* (re-published in the same volume) it evokes vividly the sights, sounds and sensations experienced by Marinetti as a war correspondent during the siege of Adrianopoli (Edirne) in the Balkan war of 1912.

'Bilancio delle analogie': in this final section of the work we find a summing-up of key groups of images or analogies. For all Marinetti's innovative fury, the interest in intuitive 'analogies' owes much to the established Symbolist canon (see Ramat, *La poesia italiana 1903-1943*, pp. 115-123, on his hidden 'lyricism').

'1ª somma':
Depicts the bombardment of the town. Marinetti is clearly on the side of the besieging Balkan League forces against the defending Turks. **'maglio'**: hammer; **'novatore'**: innovator; **'zang tuumb tumb tumb'**: onomatopoeic rendition of the sound of artillery shells. Note the sequence of adjectives in parenthesis: though he preached the abolition of adjectives in his *Manifesto tecnico*, he soon modified this view and in *Distruzione della sintassi* (1913) advocated a new type of 'aggettivo semaforico', to be used in long sequences, isolated in parenthesis and thus 'illuminating' entire zones of the text.

'2ª somma':
The defenders are characterized as *passatisti* and thus deplorably weak and inert, procrastinating (**'ci-penseremo-domani'**) and indifferent (**'dopo-tutto-me-ne-infischio'**), in a sequence culminating in **'= cimitero'**: the past and its advocates are 'dead'.

'3ª somma':
Further impressions of the besieging forces, now in an even more surreal, non-rational associative sequence. **'obice'**: artillery piece (howitzer); **'passo del colosso'**: the 'colosso' is the besieging force (cf. 1st and 4th parts), seen here as taking giant steps by means of its artillery; **'accordo'**: musical chord; **'violini...'**: highly incongruous images, difficult to interpret rationally (**'odori-di-bionda trentenne'** suggests an eroticization of war); **'monelli'**: naughty boys; **'ingranaggi'**: cogs; **'folleggiante'**: tending towards madness.

'4ª somma':
Typical sequence of nouns linked by **'+'**: Marinetti theorized this use of mathematical signs in lieu of conventional syntax in his *Manifesto tecnico*; **'Questi pesi spessori etc.'**: Marinetti offers the convergence (**'concorrenze e sincronismi'**) of tactile sensations, sounds, smells, sights as a 'gift' to the futurist movement before the text culminates in further onomatopoeic battlefield effects. (Compare this with the use of 'nonsense' sounds by Palazzeschi above: Marinetti's stance is rather serious and intense, whereas Palazzeschi is always smiling, playful.)

LUCIANO FOLGORE

From *Ponti sull'oceano* (1914)

Fiamma a gas

Lampione scultore,
scultore di cose mai vedute,
forse ridicolo,
ma pieno di buon umore.
Lampione scultore,   5
questa notte barili, barili
di vento.
Ubbriacatura completa:
sbattute sul casamento
della tenebra   10
alto diecimila piani senza lumi,
capitomboli sul selciato,
piruette nel fango,
esercizi di traballamento
sull'elastico sensibile della pioggia.   15

Lampione scultore,
pel vicolo questa notte
pochissime cose;
un pisciatoio a tettoia
che tu inghiotti e ridai   20
con mutevole forma di donna,
un carretto abbandonato,
enorme uccello
con ali di ruote,
e un'ombra di cane   25
o meglio, un lungo cane d'ombra.

Benone scultore,
abbozzatore
e deformatore;
eccoti un uomo filosofo,   30
mantello nero nero.
L'abbranchi? No.
Soltanto la testa.
Decapitazione superba,
e schiaffi e colpi di luce   35
sul torso che cammina lo stesso.

Poi gonnelle, gambuccie
e mani fugaci;
famiglie toccate,
mangiate,   40
digerite nell'enorme budello
del buio,
inseguite sull'angolo;
teste a triangolo,
ricopiate,   45
rimpastate,
segate sui muri;
padri seri, mamme gravi
trasformati in ridicoli fantocci,
e mezzi visi che se ne vanno,   50
e occhi chiusi e riaperti
da lancette fulminee di luce.

Infine un ubbriaco:
nera linea spezzata di canti a sghimbescio
Sosta della tua luce;   55
acutissima voglia rattenuta.
Quasi, quasi...
No, no che passi
unica serietà della notte,
vagabonda pensosità della vita.   60
Le tue schiere di luce
presentano le armi
sino in fondo al vicolo.

Domani all'alba
l'ultima pisciata di giallo   65
sul lampionaio impettito,
l'ultima smorfia sotto
gli scappellotti del sole
vilissimo illuminatore
di cose,   70
contro te, lampione scultore,
creatore di mondi originali
di forme.

Fiamma a gas

This poem presents an urban streetscape (typical scenario of the Futurist), under the distorting effects of artificial illumination, a spectacle which Folgore enthusiastically celebrates as a form of spontaneous 'sculptural' creativity. Written in *versi liberi*, the poem is structured around a sequence of nouns and nominal phrases, giving the world of objects and appearances absolute centrality, with verbs reduced to a minimum. Folgore's highly visual impressionism leads to surrealistic effects, in a vision reminiscent at times of Pirandello's grotesque *umorismo*.

1-15:   'Lampione scultore': a typical Futurist coupling of nouns creates an instantaneous analogy between the street-light and a sculptor. There follows a series of surrealistic images of a rainy, windy night; 'barili': barrels; 'casamento...': block of flats (the darkness is portrayed as an enormous dark building); 'capitomboli sul selciato': head-over-heels on the pavement; ll. 14-15: 'balancing exercises on the sensitive elastic of the rain'.

16-26: The objects in the 'vicolo' (alleyway), a public urinal ('pisciatoio') and a cart, are transformed by the lamplight; The light 'swallows' ('inghiotti') the public toilet and 'gives it back' as the form of a woman; the cart becomes a huge bird, its shadow a dog.

27-36: The figure of a man is grotesquely decapitated by the light falling on a walking torso. 'Benone': 'Well done'; 'abbozzatore': sketcher; 'filosofo': man as a rational creature is debunked by the Futurist. 'L'abbranchi?': 'do you grasp him?'.

37-52: Now entire families are caught, 'eaten' by the light; 'gambuccie': little legs; 'budello': bowel; 'teste a triangolo': heads distorted by light and shadow; ll. 45-47: [heads] 'copied, re-shaped, cut off', cast as shadows on the walls; 'fantocci': puppets (a kind of humorous de-humanization, with echoes of Pirandello); 'lancette...': arrows of light.

52-63: The appearance of a drunk in the light threatens momentarily to change the tone. 'nera linea...': a highly effective, almost abstract visual/auditory impression: 'black broken line of crooked songs'; ll. 56-60: following an unspecified 'voglia rattenuta' (restrained wish), there is a moment of hesitation, followed by a hasty dismissal of any 'serietà' or 'pensosità' (suggesting a potentially darker tone, below the surface of the poem). 'schiere', 'ranks' of lights lined up (like soldiers on parade) along the street.

64-73: Dawn will end the surreal spectacle, bringing mere reality. 'l'ultima pisciata...': 'the last pissing of yellow'; 'lampionaio impettito': upright, erect, lamplighter; 'smorfia': grimace; 'scappellotti': blows; The sun is a 'vilissimo' (mean, worthless) illuminator of reality, as against the creative energy of artificial, technological light.

ARDENGO SOFFICI

From *Bïf§zf+18. Simultaneità. Chimismi lirici* (1915)

Aeroplano

Mulinello di luce nella sterminata freschezza, zona elastica della morte;
Crivello d'oro, girandola di vetri, venti e colori:
Si respira il peso grasso del sole
Con l'ala aperta, W. Spezia, 37, sulla libertà.

La terra, ah! case, parole, città,   5
Agricoltura e commercio, amori, lacrime, suoni,
Fiori, bevande di fuoco e zucchero;
Vita sparsa in giro come un bucato;
Non c'è più che una sfera di cristallo carica di silenzio esplosivo, enfin!

Oggi si vola!   10

C'è un'allegria più forte del vino della Rufina con l'etichetta del 1811:
È il ricordo del nostro indirizzo scritto sul tappeto del mondo.
La cronaca dei giornali del mattino e della sera,
Gli amici, le amanti a perpetuità, il pensiero trascinato nei libri,

E le mille promesse: 15
Cambiali in giro, laggiù, nella polvere e gli sputi,
Fino alla bancarotta fraudolenta, fatale per tutti.

Stringo il volante con mano d'aria,
Premo la valvola con la scarpa di cielo;
Frrrrrr frrrrrr frrrrrr, affogo nel turchino ghimè,   20
Mangio triangoli di turchino di mammola,
Fette d'azzurro;
Ingollo bocks di turchino cobalto,
Celeste di lapislazzuli,
Celeste blu, celeste chiaro, celestino,   25
Blu di Prussia, celeste cupo, celeste lumiera;
Mi sprofondo in un imbuto di paradiso.
Cristo aviatore, ero fatto per questa ascensione di gloria poetico-militare-
[sportiva

[handwritten: macho glorification of the self, of the 'io' lirico]

Sugli angioli rettangolari di tela e d'acciaio.
Il cubo nero è il pensiero del ritorno, che cancello con la mia lingua   30
                    [accesa e lo sguardo di gioia
Dal bianco quadrante dell'altimetro rotativo.

Impennamento erotico fra i pavoni reali delle nuvole;
Capofitto nelle stelle più grandi, color di rosa;   *[handwritten: fetishization of the machine]*
Vol plané nello spazio-nulla:
Il mio cuore meteora si spande come uno sperma nell'abisso fecondo   35
                    [di sangue.
A me questa solitudine; non ho più che la materia etere del mio cervello
Per una creazione sola autentica e definitiva.
A 6207 metri incipit vita nova. *[handwritten: → Dante's words, irony]*
L'infinito ha un profumo di frutta matura,
Di benzina, *[handwritten: → echoes Leopardi]*   40
Di cosce, di poppe, di capelli pettinati dopo la doccia,
Delle mie ascelle che adoro;
Il gelo infiammato del cocomero tuttato a lungo nel pozzo.
Bacio la vulva del firmamento, senza rumore.
Le scintille di musica che punteggiano il rombo entusiastico dei cilindri   45
                    [e dell'elica
Son l'eco del fischio dei più alti uccelli.
Navigo nell'assoluto, mia patria, e vorrei dimenticare il corpo che
                    [sempre è con noi
La forma della libellula matematica che è il mio destino,
La mia storia, e i vostri ultimi radiotelegrammi umani.

Se si potesse disfarsi di questa malinconia degli apparecchi simpatici!   50
La saggezza è cosa di tutti e si mangia col pane ogni giorno;
Basta non vomitare, amico Sancho; e ripetiamo al barbero omicida
                    [mascherato di specchi:
«Dulcinea del Toboso es la mas hermosa mujer del mundo».

Dormire, cantare in questa ricca fiamma di purità
Difficile.   55
Ho compiuto tutti i corsi dell'arte e del vizio e posseggo il documento
                                    [ufficiale.
Ho inventato tre sensi, la chimica della fantasia, la resurrezione di tutte
                                    [le cose,
La transustanziazione dell'arcobaleno,
E la volatilizzazione esilarante dell'etica;
Ho finito i miei nervi sulla quadruplice tastiera degli amori: 60
Ho goduto le gialle viscere di una zucca, una vergine capra;
En rêve j'ai baisé ma soeur morte,
E visto naufragare la divinità con un gran peto di gelsomino
Nel verde di una mominette preparata con tutta sapienza
Al caffé dei due Magot, in piazza Saint-Germain des Prés a Parigi.   65

La nostra vita è un grappolo d'agresto che ho troppo ardentemente
                                    [succhiato;
Mi asciugo la bocca col tovagliolo indaco del cielo.
La mia gamba è lunga e secca,
E calzo il n. 41 come Arthur Rimbaud.
Dovrò forse morire e 37 anni fra colonne d'ametista?   70
Mais je ne marche plus.

Città, vedo ancora la geometria di fosforo sulla coltre nera di notte:
Piazze, strade,
Cerchi di treni lungo i paesaggi réclame,
Vermi smarriti sur una mappa di cartapesta.   75
Vedo ancora le lumiere titoli dei drammi ai teatri:
Giulietta e Romeo, King Lear,
La vida es sueño, Amleto,
Le Monde où l'on s'ennuie.
Tutti i fiumi finiscono troppo presto nel mare   80
Troppo stretto e duro;
I più bei fiori hanno una forma che si trova divulgata in tutti
                                    [i trattati di botanica
E non barattano mai fra loro le tinte e gli odori.
Le donne, oh! hanno la mente troppo vicina alle chiappe, o troppo lontana;
Gli uomini, il loro pensiero puzza di Dei e di piedi;   85
E per un'anima che ha una bella cravatta o un asprì di moda gloriosa,
Quanti soffritti d'aglio sotto il vermiglione dei tetti, in quel golfo
                                    [di verde persiana.

Ah! non ritornerò che fuliggine d'ossa bruciate.

Senza addio né rimpianti, alzo la quota;
Lancio sempre più in alto le stelle filanti dei miei desideri;   90
Stabilisco la mira degli occhi ubriachi:
Su, su, su, ancora una trincea d'oltremare!
Bisogna prender d'assalto le mitragliatrici furibonde del solleone.

Aeroplano

The iconoclastic irreverence of Futurism is strongly in evidence in this poem, as is the delight in the language and imagery of technology, aggressive eroticism and war.

1-4:   The accumulation of nouns sets a strongly Futuristic opening tone with a heady mix of sensory impressions. '**Mulinello**': whirlwind; '**crivello**': sieve; '**girandola**': (toy) windmill; '**Si respira il peso...**': note non-logical simultaneity of different senses; '**W. Spezia, 37**': probably a registration number written on the aircraft's wing (La Spezia: Ligurian port).

5-10:   The multiple phenomena of ordinary life (note again, accumulation of nouns) are reduced to a uniform level of unimportance, as compared with the elation of flight. '**bucato**': laundry; '**enfin**': ('in the end') first of several snatches of French, reflecting Soffici's period of immersion in Parisian cultural chic.

11-17:   '**Rufina**': well-known Tuscan wine. The poet's inebriating '**allegria**' lies in remembering the world left down below, seen in various images of 'writing' on the earth's surface, everyday human commitments characterized as questionable transactions, like unreliable cheques circulating ('**cambiali**'), leading to a squalid universal 'bankruptcy'.

18-31:   The poetic *io* makes a decisive entrance in a series of vigorous 1st-person verbs in these lines. '**volante**': control stick; '**valvola**': throttle; '**turchino ghimé**': deep turquoise (the start of an exuberant catalogue of shades of blue); '**turchino di mammola**': violet blue; '**Ingollo bocks...**': 'I swallow tankards of cobalt blue'; '**imbuto**': funnel; '**Cristo aviatore**': the Futuristic exaltation of flight is given an almost blasphemous pseudo-religious twist here; '**angioli rettangolari...**': rectangular angels (aeroplanes); '**tela**': canvas. l. 30: a hint of a darker inner reality, the 'black cube' of returning to earth, which is quickly banished by further elation as the altimeter turns.

32-49:   The poet's flight takes on explicit sexual overtones (a frequent motif in Futurist poetry): he is likened to sperm in the womb, he assigns erotic bodily analogies to the smells of 'infinity' (l. 41), and characterizes his flight as a daring sexual conquest of the heavens (l. 44). '**Impennamento**': upward flight; '**Capofitto**': headlong; '**Vol plané**': glide; '**l'abisso fecondo di sangue**': 'fertile abyss of blood' (the womb). There follows an implicit analogy between physical fertility and the creative imagination in the 'matter/ether' of the brain. '**incipit vita nova**': an allusion to the opening of Dante's *Vita Nuova*, transferred from a framework of spiritual love to a more carnal futuristic concept of the sublime; '**cosce... poppe**': thighs... breasts; '**ascelle**': armpits; l. 43: 'the ice-cold of watermelon kept in a well'. The incongruous sexualization of the ascent reaches its apogee with '**Bacio la vulva del firmamento**'. ll. 45-46: Note the fusion of auditory sensations (music, engine's roar, bird calls); ll. 47-49: Tensions persist between the desire for a kind of mystical experience and the overwhelming presence of concrete reality in the text; '**libellula matematica**': mathematical dragonfly (the aircraft); '**vostri ultimi radiotelegrammi...**': probably the 'messages' of human communication which tie him to the world.

50-53: l. 50: again, the paradoxical wish to get rid of machines (no matter how 'simpatici'); **'Sancho'**: Sancho Panza (in Cervantes' Don Quixote); **'barbero'**: Spanish, barber; l. 53: 'Dulcinea of Toboso is the most beautiful woman in the world'

54-65: A dazzling résumé of the poet's life experiences and achievements, from 'art' to 'vice', with a fantastic appraisal of his own aesthetic inventiveness, his creation of new 'senses', new modes of perception; **'transustanziazione...'**: 'transubstantiation of the rainbow'; transubstantiation, the Catholic doctrine of the actual transformation of bread and wine into the body and blood of Christ, is used here to indicate a kind of profane aesthetic mysticism (remember that Soffici was also a painter); **'volatilizzazione dell'etica'**: evaporation of ethics. ll. 60-65: from a catalogue of fantastically morbid sexual experiences, he proceeds to a surreal depiction of the death of the divine, 'drowned' in alcohol; **'tastiera'**: keyboard; **'goduto'**: here, enjoyed in a sexual sense. **'En rêve j'ai baisé...'**: 'In a dream I screwed my dead sister' (the first edition was even stronger : 'En rêve j'ai baisé ma vieille mère/ J'ai enculé mon père mort'); **'peto di gelsomino'**: 'jasmine fart'; **'mominette'**: a drink made from absinthe or pastis; **'due Magot'**: the Deux Magots, a famous Parisian café.

66-71: A sense of jaded satiety, leading to an ironic comparison with the French poet and adventurer Rimbaud (much loved by Soffici) and considerations of mortality. **'agresto'**: type of bitter grape; **'calzo il n. 41'**: I take shoe size 41; l. 70: Rimbaud died at 37 (Soffici was 36 in 1915); **'Mais je ne marche plus'**: French idiom: 'but I won't be taken in/ won't go along with this anymore'.

72-79: The nocturnal view of the city from the air leads on to further deprecation of human existence. ll. 74-75: surreal image of trains as worms on a papier maché map; **'coltre'**: quilt; **'paesaggi réclame'**: advertisement landscapes. ll. 76-79: illuminated theatre signs.

80-87: Images of disillusionment and distaste for social relationships: l. 84: a contemptuous view of women, typical of Futurist misogyny (**'chiappe'**: buttocks); l. 85: scornfully dismisses both 'thought' and religion; **'asprì'**: fashionable plume made of bird feathers; **'soffritto d'aglio'**: frying garlic, an evocation of the banal reality under decorative rooftops.

88-93: A final flourish of almost D'Annunzian overtones, as the poet declares he will overcome all natural, physical barriers and will return to earth only as burnt remains; **'fuliggine'**: soot; **'alzo la quota'**: I increase altitude; **'stelle filanti'**: shooting stars; **'mira'**: aim l. 92: a note of Marinettian militarism (**'trincea d'oltremare'**: trench overseas, i.e. in colonial wars); **'mitragliatrici furibonde del solleone'**: 'furious machine-guns of the summer heat'.

sensations of death, recklessness, daring + risk all related to myth of Icarus in flight.

CLEMENTE REBORA

From *Frammenti lirici* (1913)

Frammenti lirici, III

Dall'intensa nuvolaglia
Giù — brunita la corazza,
Con guizzi di lucido giallo,
Con suono che scoppia e si scaglia —
Piomba il turbine e scorrazza   5
Sul vento proteso a cavallo
Campi e ville, e dà battaglia;
Ma quand'urta una città
Si scàrdina in ogni maglia,
S'inombra come un'occhiaia,   10
E guizzi e suono e vento
Tramuta in ansietà
D'affollate faccende in tormento:
E senza combattere ammazza.

Frammenti lirici, III

In the original edition the 'fragments' were untitled, but this poem was given the title 'Turbine' (whirlwind) in a subsequent edition.

1-7:   The first half of the poem is an evocative description of a storm or whirlwind ('**turbine**'), which descends ('**piomba**') from the clouds and rushes ('**scorrazza**') across the countryside, assaulting it violently ('**dà battaglia**'). '**nuvolaglia**': widespread clouds (initiates one of the 'harsh' rhyme sequences in the poem); '**brunita la corazza**': with shining armour (the image is of the storm as an attacking warrior - continued in l. 6, where the storm is 'riding forward on the wind'); '**guizzi**': flashes; '**si scaglia**': shatters (one of several verbs beginning with an intensifying 's'); '**ville**': villages ('campi e ville' is the object of verb 'scorrazza').

8-14:   Considers the encounter between the storm and urban, civilized humanity (the contrast with the natural scene is marked clearly by '**Ma**'). The theme of the city is introduced here not in its superficial technological manifestations (beloved of the Futurists), but as a human, existential dimension. '**si scardina**': breaks up; '**maglia**': link in chain-mail (armour); '**s'inombra…**': 'darkens like an eye-socket' ('**occhiaia**': 'bags' under eyes, or, eye-socket). The direct, physical violence now becomes transformed into something apparently less potent (**si scardina, senza combattere**), but also much more disquieting, interiorized in the perspective of the city-dweller, who lives in an uneasy relationship with the world, marked by dark anxiety. '**Tramuta**': transforms (subject of verb is still '**turbine**', objects are the nouns in previous line); '**affollate faccende**': the 'crowded business' of the urban mass - the storm becomes part of their 'ansietà/tormento'; '**e senza combattere…**': regardless of its physical violence, the storm becomes part of the deadly alienation of urban life. The sense of profound disharmony between man and nature precludes any symbolist identification with the natural world.

Frammenti lirici, **XLIX**

O poesia, nel lucido verso
Che l'ansietà di primavera esalta
Che la vittoria dell'estate assalta
Che speranze nell'occhio del cielo divampa,
Che tripudi sul cuor della terra conflagra,   5
O poesia, nel livido verso
Che sguazza fanghiglia d'autunno
Che spezza ghiaccioli d'inverno
Che schizza veleno nell'occhio del cielo
Che strizza ferite sul cuor della terra,   10
O poesia nel verso inviolabile
Tu stringi le forme che dentro
Malvive svanivano nel labile
Gesto vigliacco, nell'aria
Senza respiro, nel varco   15
Indefinito e deserto
Del sogno disperso,
Nell'orgia senza piacere
Dell'ebbra fantasia;
E mentre ti levi a tacere   20
Sulla cagnara di chi legge e scrive
Sulla malizia di chi lucra e svaria
Sulla tristezza di chi soffre e accieca,
Tu sei cagnara e malizia e tristezza,
Ma sei la fanfara   25
Che ritma il cammino,
Ma sei la letizia
Che incuora il vicino,
Ma sei la certezza
Del grande destino,   30
O poesia di sterco e di fiori,
Terror della vita, presenza di Dio,
O morta e rinata
Cittadina del mondo catenata!

Frammenti lirici, XLIX

This 'fragment', also untitled, is a declaration of Rebora's poetics. Thus it gives us a clear insight into an idea of poetry as a genre full of contradictions and ambivalence. It engages with all of reality, from the sublime to the degraded, while remaining a 'humble' art-form, not given to mystical elevation but seen rather as a means of attempting to comprehend the world from within.

1-5:   In these lines, full of tensions, the subject of the various verbs is **'poesia'** (as also in ll. 7-10). **'Divampa'**: burns; **'tripudi'**: joys; **'conflagra'**: burns (ll. 4-5: note bringing together of elevated and lowly: **'cielo'/'terra'**).

6-10:   **'livido'**: dark, leaden colour; **'sguazza fanghiglia'**: wallows/splashes mud; **'schizza'**: squirts. Note stiking sequence of verbs with initial intensifying 's-'; l. 10: 'which squeezes out wounds over the heart of the world'.

11-19:   **'stringi'**: gather together; **'dentro'**: within [us]; **Malvive svanivano'**: 'barely alive, were fading away'. Note alliteration and assonance underlining the 'labile' nature of human thought and action (**'gesto'**); **'varco'**: opening; **'disperso'**: lost; **'orgia'**: frenzy; **'ebbra'**: drunk;

20-24:   **'cagnara'**: confused noise (of *letterati*; as opposed to superior silence of poetry, which rises up **'a tacere'**); **'chi lucra e svaria'**: those who profit and deceive; **'accieca'**: intransitive: those who 'are blinded'; l. 24: Note the direct contradiction with preceding lines, highlighting poetry's shifting, ambiguous nature.

25-34:   Following a series of higly positive images, the poem closes with its most striking, almost oxymoronic, contradictions: **'sterco'**: excrement; **'rinata'**: reborn. l. 34: 'enchained citizen of the world'; poetry is ultimately chained to reality, it is inescapably of this world.

From *Poesie sparse* (1913-1927)

Voce di vedetta morta

C'è un corpo in poltiglia
Con crespe di faccia, affiorante
Sul lezzo dell'aria sbranata.
Frode la terra.
Forsennato non piango: 5
Affar di chi può e del fango.
Però se ritorni
Tu uomo, di guerra
A chi ignora non dire;
Non dire la cosa, ove l'uomo   10
E la vita s'intendono ancora.
Ma afferra la donna
Una notte, dopo un gorgo di baci,
Se tornare potrai;
Sóffiale che nulla del mondo   15
Redimerà ciò ch'è perso
Di noi, i putrefatti di qui;
Stringile il cuore a strozzarla:
E se t'ama, lo capirai nella vita
Più tardi, o giammai.   20

Voce di vedetta morta

This poem, first published in 1917, is included in *Poesie sparse* (1913-1927) in the collected poems. It is a disturbing poem in many respects, presenting the nightmarish vision of a dead soldier along with his haunting words (**'vedetta'**: look-out, sentry). The poem may usefully be compared to Ungaretti's 'Veglia': both evoke similar experiences, centred on the terrible image of a dead comrade. However, Ungaretti turns the traumatic event into lyrical discourse, sublimating the horror in poetry: 'ho scritto/ lettere piene d'amore'. He tries to essentialize, to purify (as reflected in the sparing form). Rebora, on the other hand, displaces the lyrical *io* to give 'voice' to the dead man's disenchantment. He refuses to sublimate the grim reality, so that his poetry remains deeply 'impure', dedicated to expressing uncomfortable, unreconciled tensions, with an open, challenging conclusion.

1-6:   The poem begins with the horror of the decomposing corpse: **'in poltiglia'**: rotting; **'crespe di faccia'**: wrinkled face; **'affiorante'**: emerging; **'lezzo'**: stench; **'sbranata'**: torn to pieces; **'frode la terra'**: the earth is fraud (almost certainly an echo of Leopardi's 'A se stesso': 'fango/ è il mondo'); **'Forsennato'**: out of my mind; **'affar di chi può'**: 'a matter for those who can'.

7-11:   Here the voice of the dead look-out takes over (although the transition is not clearly marked - it is also in part the voice of the poet). **'di guerra... non dire'**: 'do not tell [this] to those who do not know about war'; **'ove l'uomo... ancora'**: slightly ambiguous, probably: 'where man and life can still be understood'.

12-20: Only in the intensity of personal experiences may something of all this be revealed and, possibly, understood. **'afferra'**: grasp (expressing a need to violently embrace life); similarly, **'gorgo'**: whirlpool, an intense, overwhelming experience; **'Sóffiale'** [soffia a lei]: whisper to her; **'nulla...'**: there is no apparent redemption of the horror, the loss suffered, even in love; **'putrefatti'**: decomposed; **'Stringele il cuore'**: squeeze her heart; again, the violence of the language and the image reflect the desperation, the anguish of the 'voice' (the violence of war seems to contaminate even the imagined love scene, which is overwhelmed by the horror); **'a strozzarla'**: to the point of strangling her; **ll. 19-20**: again, ambiguous lines: *either*, 'you will know whether she loves you later, or never', *or*, 'if she loves you, you will understand [all this], later, or never'. Probably the latter interpretation is more satisfactory, in line with the poem's overall yearning for some sense, some understanding of the incomprehensible. This *may* come through the difficult intensity of life, of love, but equally, may never be possible.

DINO CAMPANA

From *Canti Orfici* (1914)

L'invetriata

La sera fumosa d'estate
Dall'alta invetriata mesce chiarori nell'ombra
E mi lascia nel cuore un suggello ardente.
Ma chi ha (sul terrazzo sul fiume si accende una lampada) chi ha
A la Madonnina del Ponte chi è chi è che ha acceso la lampada – c'è   5
Nella stanza un odor di putredine: c'è
Nella stanza una piaga rossa languente.
Le stelle sono bottoni di madreperla e la sera si veste di velluto:
E tremola la sera fatua: è fatua la sera e tremola ma c'è
Nel cuore della sera c'è,   10
Sempre una piaga rossa languente.

L'invetriata

This poem reflects Campana's difficult relationship with the symbolist tradition: an initial lyrical evocation of evening is interrupted, leaving the poet's persona with only an inner 'wound'. The anguished intensity of the text is reflected formally in its metrical irregularity (several lines are beyond any recognized verse measure), frequent enjambements and notable elements of syntactic fragmentation.

1-3: The opening atmosphere is one of lyrical contemplation, with **'fumosa'** giving a sense of indefinite outlines, blurred further by the window pane (**'invetriata'**) through which the evening 'pours' or 'mixes' (**'mesce'**) its light, creating an intense, seemingly painful (**'ardente'**) impression on the poet (**'suggello'**: seal).

4-5: The opening **'Ma'** abruptly breaks any spell, and the sense of disruption is underlined formally by the fragmented, problematic syntax of these lines, where the first question (**'chi ha ... [acceso]'**) is interrupted structurally by the parenthesis and then by the second formulation of the question (**'chi è ...'**). The source of the interruption is the lighting of a lamp to the statue of the Madonna, an apparently inconsequential act, which, with its introduction of a human presence, opens the way for a more problematic perception of reality.

6-7: The smell of decay (**'putredine'**) may be a realistic detail (perhaps from the river), but acquires strong figurative overtones through its juxtaposition with the open wound (**'piaga'**) of l. 7, which, in occupying the poem's interior setting, seems to characterise the poet's inner reality, bringing a cruder level of suffering than the 'suggello ardente' of l. 3. The enjambement around 'c'è' creates a sense of dislocation and discontinuity in the fabric of reality.

8-11: The description of the evening sky, through personification and the rather precious imagery of **'madreperla'** (mother of pearl) and 'velvet', now seems almost a parody of symbolist modes, as the images appear 'fatuous' in comparison with the poet's inner 'wound'. In l. 9, there is a clear progression from the first part, where the delicate personification of evening is continued with the emphasis on the verb **'tremola'** (trembles), to the second part, where the emphasis is more bluntly on the 'fatuous' nature of the spectacle: **'è fatua la sera'**. The second **'tremola'** is the adjective 'tremulous'. The 'wound' within the *io* is now transferred to the whole scene (with an opposite direction of movement to that of the opening lines). The repetition of **'piaga rossa languente'** is the most visible instance of a pattern of repetition that creates an almost obsessive effect throughout the text.

2

Giuseppe Ungaretti (1888-1970)

Out of the tumult of the avant-garde years, Giuseppe Ungaretti's early work emerges with an unmistakable lyrical voice whose influence will be strongly felt across large areas of Italian poetry throughout the first half of the century and beyond. Ungaretti was born and brought up in Alexandria in Egypt, where his parents (originally from Lucca) had settled.[i] He was given a European education (attending first the Istituto Don Bosco, and then from 1904, the École Suisse Jacot), but the landscape of the Egyptian desert left a deep impression in his memory and his imagination: against a background of nature's harshness and life's precariousness, he gained a sense of the intensity of the mirage, the illusion, the mystical insight. In 1912 he moved to Paris to study at the Sorbonne, an experience which was of fundamental importance for his cultural formation, opening up the world of avant-garde art and writing and bringing him into direct contact with figures such as the poet Apollinaire, as well as a number of writers associated with the Italian Futurist movement (including Soffici, Palazzeschi and Papini). He began writing poetry at this time, some of which as published in 1915 in Italy in the futurist journal *Lacerba*.

He moved to Milan in 1914, espoused the interventionist cause (calling for Italy's entry into the First World War against Austria) and, upon war breaking out in 1915, he volunteered for active service. His time spent on the North-Eastern Italian front (in the mountainous Carso region, the scene of fierce fighting and atrocious conditions) constituted a defining moment for Ungaretti's poetic production.[ii] He developed a highly-individual style, in which elements of the avant-garde experimentalism characteristic of these years (both in France and in Italy) are combined with an intensely lyrical vision.[iii] Perhaps the most striking innovation is on the level of metre, where

55

Ungaretti radically fragments the traditional poetic line, highlighting the isolated, single word, which is given a new intensity by the surrounding silence of the blank page. There is, in some texts, a graphic, heightened realism, grounding these poems in the collective horror of the historical moment, and yet Ungaretti's work remains clearly within the symbolist line of descent (leading back to Mallarmé, among others), with a central emphasis on formal refinement, unexpected verbal combinations and intuitive analogies and an almost mystical faith in the value of the poetic word itself as a potential instrument of transcendence: '[…] io credevo in una poesia dove il segreto dell'uomo (fin da allora) trovasse in qualche modo un'eco, credevo nella poesia dell'inesprimibile'.[iv] A first group of poems was published in 1916 as *Il porto sepolto*, which then formed the core of an expanded collection, *Allegria di naufragi*, in 1919, which was in turn subsumed into *L'allegria* (1931). These, more than any others, are the poems which guarantee Ungaretti his place in the modern Italian canon. In them, even as he crystallizes certain elements of the avant-garde experimentalism of the preceding years, Ungaretti also places the lyrical 'io' once again at the centre of Italian poetic discourse.

There is a marked change in Ungaretti's work in the 1920s. In his second collection, *Sentimento del tempo* (1933), he seeks to align his poetry with 'il canto della lingua italiana […] nella sua costanza attraverso i secoli', most notably through reclaiming the hendecasyllable.[v] This is part of a more general return to traditional models (as advocated notably by the journal *La Ronda* in the early 1920s), a widespread reaction against the experimental excesses of the previous two decades, a 'return to order' whose effects can be found across many artistic fields and in different European cultures, and which also carries ideological overtones, particularly with the rise of Fascism in Italy.[vi] A further element of return to tradition comes at Easter 1928 with Ungaretti's re-embracing of Christian faith following a spiritual crisis, as reflected subsequently in several texts in *Sentimento*.[vii] An explicitly Christian mysticism can also be found in a number of poems in *Il Dolore*, published in 1947, perhaps his most intensely personal body of work, with a stylistic extravagance reflecting the poet's anguish at the loss of his young son during his years teaching at the University of Sao Paulo in Brazil (1936-42).

After his return to Italy in 1942 he settled again in Rome where he became Professor of Italian Literature. In the post-war years he went on to publish several further collections, including *La terra promessa* (1950), *Un grido e paesaggi* (1952), *Il taccuino del vecchio* (1960), and he became a prominent public figure. His later work remains alive to experimentation and innovation (although there are also moments when formal bravura threatens to overwhelm his more authentic voice). But there is no doubting the importance of Ungaretti's legacy in establishing, with his earlier poetry, the stylistic and thematic paradigms of a modern lyricism which would dominate Italian poetry for decades. It was a model of poetry primarily as introspection and transcendence, a quest for perfection and essentiality of form, at times almost a mysticism of the word, with the poetic *io* as purveyor of privileged insights.

Notes

[i] For biographical details, see: Ungaretti, *Vita d'un uomo. Tutte le poesie*, a cura di Leone Piccioni, I Meridiani (Milan: Mondadori, 1969), pp. lvii-lxiii; Leone Piccioni, *Vita di Ungaretti* (Milan: Rizzoli, 1979); Walter Mauro, *Vita di Giuseppe Ungaretti* (Milan: Camunia, 1990).

[ii] On the Carso battlefield and its meaning for Ungaretti, see Sergio Campailla, '"Il Carso non è più un inferno": Significato di un'esperienza', in *Atti del Convegno Internazionale su Giuseppe Ungaretti, Urbino 3-6 ottobre 1979* (Urbino: 4Venti, 1981), pp. 838-45.

[iii] There is also a partly-submerged vein of fervid nationalism in some texts, notably 'Italia', with its cry of 'Sono un poeta / un grido unanime /...', expressing the poet's atavistic sense of unity with the the land of his ancestors. On tensions between more 'peaceful' and 'belligerent' aspects in *L'allegria*, see Vivienne Hand, 'Ambiguous Joy: Contradictions and Tensions in Giuseppe Ungaretti's *L'allegria*', *The Italianist*, 16 (1996). However, Hand is perhaps too ready to ascribe an unequivocally 'pro-war' intent to 'Italia', whose meaning may lie rather in Ungaretti's response to the *crepuscolari* and their declarations of 'non-poethood'. See Stefano Jacomuzzi, '"Sono un poeta": 'L'affermazione ungarettiana di fronte al rifiuto della recente tradizione', in *Atti del Convegno Internazionale*, pp. 1079-85.

[iv] Ungaretti, *Vita d'un uomo. Saggi e interventi*, a cura di Mario Diacono e Lucian Rebay, I Meridiani (Milan: Mondadori, 1974), p. 818.

[v] See *Vita d'un uomo. Saggi e interventi*, pp. 274-5. See also *Vita d'un uomo. Tutte le poesie*, pp. lxxi-lxxii for a slightly different version.

[vi] Franco Fortini, writing from a left-wing perspective, links Ungaretti's stylistic reaction directly with his early support for Fascism: 'L'adesione di Ungaretti al fascismo fu, in questo senso, adesione a una immagine letteraria della tradizione patria'; Fortini, *I poeti del Novecento*, p. 76 . In this respect, see Ungaretti's 1927 essay 'Originalità del fascismo' (*Saggi e interventi*, pp. 149-53); see also notes, including letters from Mussolini to Ungaretti (*ibid.*, pp. 909-11). Carlo Ossola gives a concise and balanced account of Ungaretti's relationship with Fascism in *Giuseppe Ungaretti* (Milan: Mursia, 1975), pp. 441-45. Various others have at times tried to minimize his pro-Fascist leanings (e.g. Mauro, *Vita di Giuseppe Ungaretti*, pp. 64-65; Giampaolo Papi, *Il primo Ungaretti* (Bari-Roma: Lacaita, pp. 154-55).

[vii] On his 'conversion', see Piccioni, *Vita di Ungaretti*, pp. 159-62.

Poetic texts

Collected poems
Vita d'un uomo. Tutte le poesie, a cura di Leone Piccioni, I Meridiani (Milan: Mondadori, 1969)
This brings together the main individual collections:
L'Allegria (1931); *Il sentimento del tempo* (1933); *Il Dolore* (1947); *La terra promessa* (1950); *Il taccuino del vecchio* (1960).

Prose texts

Vita d'un uomo. Saggi e interventi, a cura di Mario Diacono e Luciano Rebay, I Meridiani (Milan: Mondadori, 1974).

Further reading

Bo, Carlo, and others, *Atti del Convegno Internazionale su Giuseppe Ungaretti, Urbino 3-6 ottobre 1979* (Urbino: 4Venti, 1981)

Boroni, Carla, *Giuseppe Ungaretti. Dall'"innocenza" alla "memoria"* (Venezia: Corbo e Fiore, 1992)

Cambon, Glauco, *La poesia di Ungaretti* (Turin: Einaudi, 1976)

Ferola di Sabato, Dora, *Letture di Giuseppe Ungaretti* (Napoli: ESI, 1995)

Giachery, Emerico, *Luoghi di Ungaretti* (Napoli: Edizioni scientifiche italiane, 1998)

Guglielmi, Guido, *Interpretazione di Ungaretti* (Bologna: Il Mulino, 1989)

Hand, Vivienne, 'Ambiguous Joy: Contradictions and Tensions in Giuseppe Ungaretti's L'allegria', *The Italianist*, 16 (1996), 76-116.

Jones, Frederic J., *Giuseppe Ungaretti: poet and critic* (Edinburgh University Press, 1977)

Luti, Giorgio, *Invito alla lettura di Giuseppe Ungaretti* (Milano: Mursia, 1974)

Mauro, Walter, *Vita di Giuseppe Ungaretti* (Milan: Camunia, 1990).

Ossola, Carlo, *Giuseppe Ungaretti* (Milan: Mursia, 1975)

Ossola Carlo, ed., *Il porto sepolto*, (Milan: Il Saggiatore, 1981) [annotated edition]

Papi, Giampaolo, *Il primo Ungaretti* (Bari-Roma: Lacaita, 1988)

Piccioni, Leone, *Per conoscere Ungaretti* (Milan: Mondadori, 1971)

Piccioni, Leone, *Ungarettiana* (Firenze: Vallecchi, 1980)

Piccioni, Leone, *Vita di Ungaretti* (Milan: Rizzoli, 1979)

Siciliano, Vincenzo, *Giuseppe Ungaretti* (Teramo: Giunti Lisciani, 1994)

Suvini-Hand, Vivienne, *Mirage and Camouflage: Hiding behind Hermeticism in Giuseppe Ungaretti's L'Allegria* (Leicester, Troubador, 2000).

Contents

From *L'allegria* (1914-1919)

General note on editions: Ungaretti's texts, especially those of *L'allegria*, were subject to a great deal of revision. The texts given here are taken from *Vita d'un uomo. Tutte le poesie* (1969). The poems of *L'allegria*, written between 1914-1919, first saw the light as *Il porto sepolto* (1916), then as *Allegria di naufragi* (1919) and subsequently in the 1931 edition titled *L'allegria*, with a further, definitive edition in 1942.

Ricordo d'Affrica

Il sole rapisce la città

Non si vede piú

Neanche le tombe resistono molto

Ricordo d'Affrica

From the book's opening section, 'Ultime' (subtitled 'Milano 1914-1915'), which contains the 'last' poems of an early, pre-war vein, this poem gives us a dream-like vision of Alexandria in the desert sunlight. The form is pithy, laconic, although the poetic line is not yet subject to the extreme fragmentation of the following years (here we have the classic metres of *novenario, quinario, endecasillabo*). The memory of Egypt is of a physical world – the world of life (**'città'**) and death (**'tombe'**) – lacking in any permanence or solidity, tenuous to the point of disappearing, suggesting perhaps the proximity of a mystical experience or truth, a motif which would return in many forms throughout Ungaretti's verse; **'rapisce'**: lit. 'kidnaps' (carries off).

In memoria

Locvizza il 30 settembre 1916

Si chiamava
Moammed Sceab

Discendente
di emiri di nomadi
suicida
perché non aveva piú
Patria   5

Amò la Francia
e mutò nome

Fu Marcel
ma non era Francese   10
e non sapeva piú
vivere
nella tenda dei suoi
dove si ascolta la cantilena
del Corano   15
gustando un caffé

E non sapeva
sciogliere
il canto
del suo abbandono   20

L'ho accompagnato
insieme alla padrona dell'albergo
dove abitavamo
a Parigi   25
dal numero 5 della rue des Carmes
appassito vicolo in discesa

Riposa
nel camposanto d'Ivry
sobborgo che pare   30
sempre

[Handwritten annotations:]
tension between title + subheading
timeless vision, place outside of time colliding with dark reality
patriotism of the ex-pat
embodiment of alienation of the individual in urban environment
insight/truth/prayer even?
crepuscolari voice?

in una giornata
di una
decomposta fiera

sense of abandonement + neglect
MELANCHOLY

E forse io solo   *sense of loss,*   35
so ancora
che visse

Question of lost identity

In memoria

The opening poem in the group that was first published as *Il porto sepolto* in 1916. Like the other texts in this series, it bears a precise indication of a time and place in the war zone, marking it as part of a poetic 'war diary'. However the personal/memorial theme here sets the poet's account of his war experiences within the context of a larger sense of crisis of the self, the modernist crisis of the dislocated individual, of uncertain identity and alienation. Sceab, a close boyhood friend of Ungaretti's in Alexandria, joined him in Paris but committed suicide there in 1913. Ungaretti, in a 1963 interview, called the poem 'il simbolo di una crisi delle società e degli individui che ancora perdura [...]' (*Saggi e interventi*, 818-19; see also Piccioni, *Vita di Ungaretti*, 36-38). Sceab's death was given very different expression in an earlier text in French, 'Roman cinéma', a more discursive combination of realistic detail and dark irony (see *Tutte le poesie*, pp. 361-62). Comparison of the two shows the extent to which Ungaretti strives in 'In memoria' for a stark essentiality of both content and form. Although the poem contains a strong sense of narrative in the sequence of past tense verbs, it is a narrative largely unadorned by detail and centred instead on abstractions contained in isolated key words like '**suicida**', '**Patria**', '**vivere**', focusing the reader's attention on concepts such as lost identity and, notably, Sceab's failure to sublimate this through '**il canto**' (ll. 18-21), clearly a reference to Ungaretti's sense of his own poetry as having a redemptive or elevating function. Lines are frequently reduced to 1, 2 or 3 words (although forming fragments of longer, recognizable metres).

1-21: '**Patria**': The upper case here points to the presence of an idea of nationalism that comes to the surface occasionally in *L'allegria*. It is part of a broader atavistic quest for belonging on the part of Ungaretti the displaced Italian. While in this text the concept of 'Homeland' remains generic, almost spiritual, elsewhere, at its most extreme, it overlaps with elements of the bellicose nationalism that characterized futurism and later the Fascist regime. See 'Italia' with its 'grido unanime' (*Tutte le poesie*, p. 57). On tensions between pro- and anti-war sentiments, see Hand, 'Ambiguous Joy...'. '**cantilena**: singsong melody; '**sciogliere**': to release; '**abbandono**': solitude, isolation.

22-37: Notwithstanding Ungaretti's flirtation with futurist modes and motifs, he draws also on other areas of the contemporary verse tradition: these lines bring in a quasi-crepuscular tonality in the evocation of a faded Parisian alleyway ('**appassito vicolo**'), the imagery of the '**camposanto**' (cemetery) in the desolate '**sobborgo**' with its air of a '**decomposta fiera**' (crumbling fair) and the somewhat emphatic pathos of the closing lines highlighting the isolation of the poetic voice ('**io solo**'). However, the poem could, arguably, be said to close on a positive tone with '**visse**' (see also the close of 'Veglia').

Il porto sepolto

Mariano il 29 giugno 1916

Vi arriva il poeta
e poi torna alla luce con i suoi canti
e li disperde

Di questa poesia
mi resta quel nulla   5
d'inesauribile segreto

Il porto sepolto

Written, like most of these texts, in the war zone, this poem gave its title to the first
published collection of Ungaretti's work in 1916. The title refers to the ancient port
of Pharos near Alexandria, subject of archaeological investigations during Ungaretti's
youth (see *Tutte le poesie*, pp. 519-20, 523; *Saggi e interventi* p. 817, Mauro, *Vita di
Giuseppe Ungaretti*, pp. 40-41, Piccioni, *Vita di Ungaretti*, pp. 49-52). A particularly
rich reading of this poem is in Ossola's annotated edition of the original 1916
collection, *Il porto sepolto* (Milan: Il Saggiatore, 1981), pp. 19-31.

1-3:   'Vi': 'there' (= 'ci' in more common usage); '**disperde**': disperses.
4-6:   These lines typify his sense of the poet's task as a privileged, sacred, almost
        mystical one. While he can access mysterious depths and convey hidden
        things to the world, there remains for him (and for him alone – '*mi* resta')
        some unfathomable secret, identified both with poetry and 'il nulla' (see also
        the disappearing physical world of 'Ricordo d'Affrica'). In 1963, recalling the
        role of the desert and the mirage in his early work, he states: '[…] l'origine
        della poesia è il contatto con Dio, è il contatto dell'uomo che non sa, che non
        potrà mai sapere. Quel contatto così che l'illumina, e in un modo impreciso
        perché non è dato di conoscere che vagamente il mistero che non sarebbe
        altrimenti mistero' (*Saggi e interventi*, p. 817).

Veglia
Cima Quattro il 23 dicembre 1915

Un'intera nottata
buttato vicino
a un compagno
massacrato
con la sua bocca   5
digrignata
volta al plenilunio
con la congestione
delle sue mani
penetrata   10
nel mio silenzio
ho scritto
lettere piene d'amore

Non sono mai stato
tanto   15
attaccato alla vita

Veglia

'**Veglia**': vigil; '**Cima Quattro**': 'Peak no. 4'; as for many other poems, the location is given using a military designation, increasing the sense of diaristic immediacy.
'**digrignata**': with bared, grinding teeth; '**plenilunio**': full moon; '**congestione**': swelling. Here Ungaretti's lyrical voice confronts directly the brutal reality of war and death. He does so with graphic realism in the depiction of his comrade's corpse: indeed the choice of vocabulary and imagery tends towards a kind of heightened expressionism with the shock of terms such as '**massacrato**', the '**bocca digrignata**' grinning fiercely at the full moon, the '**congestione**' of swollen hands. The stark power of the imagery is underlined by the phonic sequence in '-ata/o' (perhaps the most unremarkable of rhymes in Italian, but here it lends a simple, uncompromising force to the text): *nottata-buttato-massacrato-digrignata-penetrata*. The poem is a prime example of Ungaretti's extreme fragmentation of the poetic line, with key-words repeatedly appearing in isolation, the surrounding blank page underlining their evocative power: '[...] di solito, a quei tempi, ero breve, spesso brevissimo, laconico: alcuni vocaboli deposti nel silenzio come un lampo nella notte, un gruppo fulmineo d'immagini [...]' (*Tutte le poesie*, p. 517). As elsewhere, there are clear debts to Futurism (absence of punctuation, relative lack of verbs in favour of participle

forms, desire to shock), but Ungaretti's achievement is to integrate such features within the concentrated lyricism of a formally balanced text, with a coherent lyrical and ethical voice, what Ungaretti called a 'pienezza di contenuto morale' (*Saggi e interventi*, p. 298). (On Ungaretti and the avant-gardes, see Ossola, pp. 178-92). Out of the horror of the scene emerges paradoxically a message of love and life. His 'letters of love' (a transparent metaphor for poetry itself) gain poignancy and intensity from the surrounding slaughter, just as the isolated word gains from the silence of the blank page, and the text ends on an affirmation of **'vita'** (comparable to the often-quoted close of another poem, 'Sono una creatura': 'la morte / si sconta / vivendo' – *Tutte le poesie*, p. 41). This reflects Ungaretti's overwhelming tendency towards some form of transcendence or lyrical sublimation of reality, a paradoxical quest for 'allegria' in the midst of horror and violence.

In dormiveglia
Valloncello di Cima Quattro il 6 agosto 1916

Assisto la notte violentata

L'aria è crivellata
come una trina
dalle schioppettate
degli uomini   5
ritratti
nelle trincee
come le lumache nel loro guscio

Mi pare
che un affannato   10
nugolo di scalpellini
batta il lastricato
di pietra di lava
delle mie strade
ed io l'ascolti   15
non vedendo
in dormiveglia

In dormiveglia

Here the poet combines the violent reality of battle with more fantastical elements, as sensory impressions blend into dream-like images in his **'dormiveglia'** (half-sleep).

1-8:   The image of night as **'violentata'** (raped) may recall the Futurist battle-cry of 'let us kill the moonlight!', but here the image carries a greater seriousness of intent. **'crivellata...schioppettate'**: 'riddled, like lace, with gunshots'; **'ritratti'**: withdrawn (past part. of *ritrarre*); **l.8**: any suggestion of war-like dynamism is overturned ironically here.

9-14:   The sound of gunfire changes into that of a 'crowd of stone-workers' (l.11), chiselling paving stones (**'lastricato'**) in the poet's home (the reference is to Alexandria – see note in *Tutte le poesie*, p. 524). It is one of several forms of fantastical escape from reality found in these poems.

I fiumi

Cotici il 16 agosto 1916

Mi tengo a quest'albero mutilato
abbandonato in questa dolina
che ha il languore
di un circo
prima o dopo lo spettacolo   5
e guardo
il passaggio quieto
delle nuvole sulla luna

competing elements

spiritual overtones

Stamani mi sono disteso
in un'urna d'acqua   10
e come una reliquia   *cleansing water*
ho riposato

L'Isonzo scorrendo
mi levigava – *polished*
come un suo sasso   15

Ho tirato su
le mie quattr'ossa
e me ne sono andato
come un acrobata
sull'acqua   20

Mi sono accoccolato
vicino ai miei panni
sudici di guerra
e come un beduino – *spiritual*
mi sono chinato a ricevere   25
il sole

Questo è l'Isonzo
e qui meglio
mi sono riconosciuto
una docile fibra   *achieves harmony*   30
dell'universo   *with universe*
in backdrop of horror,
almost as a result
of horror

Il mio supplizio
è quando
non mi credo
in armonia   35

Ma quelle occulte
mani
hidden hands = flow of river
che m'intridono
mi regalano
la rara felicità   40

Ho ripassato
le epoche
della mia vita

Questi sono
i miei fiumi   45

Questo è il Serchio
al quale hanno attinto
sense of self through childhood memory
duemil'anni forse
di gente mia campagnola
e mio padre e mia madre   50

Questo è il Nilo
che mi ha visto
nascere e crescere
e ardere d'inconsapevolezza
nelle estese pianure   55

Questa è la Senna
e in quel suo torbido
mi sono rimescolato
e mi sono conosciuto

Questi sono i miei fiumi   60
contati nell'Isonzo

all flow into eachother = construct his sense of self.

Questa è la mia nostalgia
che in ognuno
mi traspare
ora ch'è notte   65
che la mia vita mi pare
una corolla
di tenebre

like a flower of darkness
- lyrical image of
beauty mixed with
image of death

realism of war
sublimated into lyrical
response = tends to dominate
his poetry.

I fiumi   *looking for mystical sense of being one with the universe*

This is the longest poem in this collection, and in it the poet is seen taking stock of his life on both a personal and a creative level. While it is, above all, a contemplative piece, a lyrical and spiritual meditation, the references to the chaos and destruction of war provide an essential counterbalance and reminder of the context (see ll. 1 and 22-23, along with the references to the Isonzo, the river of the battle zone, and the recurrence of words like 'questo', 'qui', 'ora').

1-15:   'dolina': doline, a type of circular depression typical of rocky limestone regions like the Carso. 'languore / di un circo': there is a hint of crepuscular melancholy in the image of the deserted circus ring. 'come una reliquia': the image of the poet as a relic in an urn and the idea of a quasi-ritualistic bathing open up a strand of religious imagery running through the poem; 'levigava': polished.

16-26:   'le mie quattr'ossa': a self-deprecating colloquialism (my scant/few bones) describing his swimming; Jones suggests the image of the 'acrobat' may recall Christ's walking on water, and goes on to note the echo of Islamic ritual in the image of the bedouin (Jones, p. 80); 'accoccolato': crouched; 'sudici': filthy.

27-35:   The central moment of mystical communion with the cosmos, paradoxically occurring 'qui meglio', i.e. here, in the midst of war, more effectively than elsewhere. Such moments represent 'harmony', whose absence is 'supplizio' (torment).

36-40:   'occulte mani...m'intridono': the secret 'hands' of the waters (or, more profoundly, the forces of cosmic harmony – see *Tutte le poesie*, p. 524) that 'knead' him; 'felicità': the momentary, ineffable 'allegria' of the book's title (which, in its earliest version, was the 'happiness of shipwrecks', a momentary ecstasy emerging out of chaos and tribulation).

41-61:   In cataloguing 'his' rivers, evoked here in the Isonzo, the poet recapitulates his personal and cultural formation and values. 'Il Serchio': the river of Lucca in Tuscany, representing Ungaretti's atavistic sense of belonging and race-memory; 'attinto': past participle of 'attingere' (draw water); 'il Nilo': the Nile embodies the unselfconscious ('inconsapevole') intensity of his youthful 'burning' in the landscape of desert plains; 'la Senna': the Seine marks his passage into intellectual maturity and self-knowledge.

62-68:   The closing stanza seems to retreat somewhat, with nightfall, from the search for an intense, mystical moment of harmony into a more individual, melancholy vision of personal 'nostalgia' which now runs through all the remembered rivers, as the poet leaves us with the slightly precious (or self-indulgent?) image of his life as a 'corolla' (the part of the flower formed by the petals) made up of 'darkness'. While it may recall the note of melancholy or pathos in the opening 'circus' scene, it is on another level a typically strong Ungarettian paradox juxtaposing positivity and negativity in mutual interdependence.

Pellegrinaggio

Valloncello dell'Albero Isolato il 16 agosto 1916

In agguato
in queste budella
di macerie
ore e ore
ho strascicato   5
la mia carcassa
usata dal fango
come una suola
o come un seme
di spinalba   10

Ungaretti
uomo di pena
ti basta un'illusione
per farti coraggio

Un riflettore   15
di là
mette un mare
nella nebbia

'**Pellegrinaggio**': the title, 'pilgrimage' suggests a spiritual quest.

1-8:   '**In agguato**': lying in ambush; There follows a gritty portrayal of the poet
         amidst the brutalizing, filthy reality of the battlefield, evoked in a series of
         strongly marked lexical choices, underlining the dehumanizing effects of war:
         '**budella**' (bowels); '**macerie**' (ruins/rubble); '**strascicato**' (dragged);
         '**carcassa**' (normally used for a dead animal); '**fango**'; '**suola**' (sole of a shoe);
         ll.9-10: like a hawthorn seed.
11-14:   Characteristically, a dichotomy is posited between negative and positive
         ('**pena**' and '**coraggio**') hinging around the possibility of an '**illusione**'.
15-18:   The moment of illusion or escape is described in a highly concentrated
         image, in which a realistic detail ('**riflettore**': searchlight) is transfigured in a
         leap of impressionistic fantasy, as the beam of light through the fog
         transports the poet to a seascape, or rather 'puts' the sea, an image with strong
         associations of his youth in Alexandria, into the fog of the battlefield, thus
         transforming the earlier '**ore e ore**' of horror into an instant of spiritual, inner
         calm.

La notte bella

Devetachi il 24 agosto 1916

Quale canto si è levato stanotte
che intesse
di cristallina eco del cuore
le stelle

Quale festa sorgiva   5
di cuore a nozze

Sono stato
uno stagno di buio

Ora mordo
come un bambino la mammella   10
lo spazio

Ora sono ubriaco
d'universo

La notte bella

This poem depicts one of the elusive moments of 'armonia' (see 'I fiumi'), in a series of rarefied lyrical images.

1-4:   He asks what 'song' arose in the night that 'weaves' (**'intesse'**) the stars with a 'crystalline echo of the heart'.

5-6:   **'sorgiva'**: (adj.) fresh, like spring-water. The sense of these concentrated lines is problematic due to the highly-telescoped syntactical structure. Perhaps: 'What freshly-sprung festivity of the heart [arose] for/at nuptials'. The surprising juxtaposition of different semantic areas with **'festa'/'sorgiva'/'cuore'** recalls the synaesthetic combinations beloved of the French symbolist poets and points to Ungaretti's belonging within a tradition of introspective lyrical speculation;

7-13:   **'stagno'**: pool; **'Ora…'**: In opposition to the past darkness of l.7, this is the moment of harmony or 'allegria', partly an image of inward-looking regression, like a suckling child (**'mammella'**: breast), partly one of ecstatic expansion of the consciousness.

Mattina
Santa Maria La Longa il 26 gennaio 1917

M'illumino
d'immenso

Mattina

Famously the shortest poem in *L'allegria*, this text has come to epitomize the stark minimalism of Ungaretti's early work. The poem essentially renders an experience of epiphany, or transcendence, such as that of 'I fiumi' or 'La notte bella', in extremely concentrated form, reduced to its fundamental elements: morning, light, immensity (each of which can be read both literally and metaphorically). As occurs elsewhere, the two single-word lines can be used to reconstruct a longer line of classical italian poetic metre, in this case, a perfect *settenario*. The historical or autobiographical context is apparently discarded (but note that the indication of place and date contains more words than the text itself); only the moment of spiritual illumination, of cosmic harmony, is expressed. Ungaretti's own note on the meaning of 'allegria' gives a useful insight into this idea of a momentary, spiritual illumination in the midst of death: 'Esultanza che l'attimo, avvenendo, dà perché fuggitivo, attimo che soltanto amore può strappare al tempo, l'amore più forte che non possa essere la morte' (*Tutte le poesie*, p.517).

From *Sentimento del Tempo* (1919-1935)

L'isola
1925

A una proda ove sera ere perenne
Di anziane selve assorte, scese,
E s'inoltrò
E lo richiamò rumore di penne
Ch'erasi sciolto dallo stridulo   5
Batticuore dell'acqua torrida,
E una larva (languiva
E rifioriva) vide;
Ritornato a salire vide
Ch'era una ninfa e dormiva   10
Ritta abbracciata a un olmo.

In sé da simulacro a fiamma vera
Errando, giunse a un prato ove
L'ombra negli occhi s'addensava
Delle vergini come   15
Sera appiè degli ulivi;
Distillavano i rami
Una pioggia pigra di dardi,
Qua pecore s'erano appisolate
Sotto il liscio tepore,   20
Altre brucavano
La coltre luminosa;
Le mani del pastore erano un vetro
Levigato da fioca febbre.

L'isola

One striking difference between the poems of *L'allegria* and those of the second collection becomes apparent even on a cursory glance at this text: from the isolated word, Ungaretti has moved to the continuous length of the full poetic line. Thus, on the metrical level, we find in this poem a combination of *settenari*, *novenari* and some *endecasillabi*. Along with the return of punctuation and major shifts in language and theme, this reflects the poet's realignment with tradition (see introduction above). Instead of the immediacy of sensory impressions and graphic realism, there is here a slower, more articulated meditation. History (in the immediate sense) is absent, time is now that of myth and tradition, duration rather than instant. The landscape too has changed, reflecting in part Ungaretti's move to Marino in the hills outside Rome. This is a highly-literary text, where the classical imagery and stylized language express what is primarily a culturally-mediated vision of beauty and formal perfection.

1-3:   '**una proda**': a shore, presumably that of the 'island', but it is clear that this is a place of the imagination, outside of time, rather than a physical location. (See Ungaretti's note: 'Il paesaggio è quello di Tivoli. [...] è un punto separato dal resto del mondo, non perché lo sia in realtà, ma perché nel mio stato d'animo posso separarmene'. *Tutte le poesie*, p. 537). In this sense the island here is a literary topos, a place of refuge or escape (see *Atti del Convegno...*, p. 869); '**di anziane selve assorte**': relates back to '**sera**' ('evening ... of ancient, contemplative woods'); '**scese**': *passato remoto* of *scendere*; the subject of the verb is not specified but can be taken to be the 3rd person poetic persona, 'he'. Note the greater detachment inherent in this, compared to the frequent 1st person singular in *L'allegria*; '**s'inoltrò**': proceeded inwards/onwards.

4-6:   The sense is: 'a sound of feathers, which had been released from the strident [sound, provoking his] heartbeat, of the water, called his attention'; '**ch'erasi sciolto...**': 'che si era sciolto', the inversion of syntax is part a deliberate use of an archaic, highly literary style (see also for example vocabulary such as: '**ove**', '**selve**','**larva**', '**ninfa**', '**appiè**', '**dardi**'). This type of language, along with an intensely assonant texture, has led critics to speak of a D'Annunzian influence.

7-8:   'he saw a spirit (waning and waxing)'; notice here the rich musicality of the texture with the repetition of *l-a-r-v-i* sounds continuing in the following lines.

9-11:   '**Ritornato a salire**': 'going back up again' (completes a movement of descent and re-ascent recalling that of 'Il porto sepolto'); '**una ninfa**': the vision becomes clarified as that of a nymph embracing an elm tree. Jones (p.99) suggests it is 'the vision of a classical form of beauty'

12-13: This is a wholly interior journey for 'him'('**In sé**'), wandering from artificial image ('**simulacro**') to true one.

14-16: Read: 'L'ombra s'addensava [thickened] negli occhi delle vergini come sera appiè [at the foot] degli ulivi': the eyes of these mysterious virgins recalls the shade of olive trees in a fantastical, classical landscape.

17-18: The branches 'distill a slow rain of darts', perhaps the shafts of sunlight between the trees.

19-24: Sheep and shepherd complete the arcadian scene, while the imagery borders on the surreal, as the meadow becomes a 'luminous quilt' (**'coltre'**) that the sheep graze (**'brucavano'**), the shepherd's hands become 'glass polished by slight fever', another enigmatic image suggesting that any potentially realistic textures are turned into a highly-polished, artificial ones under the fantastical light (which may have a feverish quality). Here we can see how, despite the return to elements of the poetic tradition, the poem remains uncompromisingly modern, with quasi-surreal analogies (in a symbolist vein) straining any logical thread and forcing the reader into an intuitive interpretation. It is a style which, with its inward-looking concern with formal perfection, its ready embracing of obscure imagery (notably nature imagery) and its unexpected analogies and juxtapositions, would become an important reference point for the *ermetici* in the following years (see chapter on *ermetismo*, below).

Di luglio
1931

Quando su ci si butta lei,
Si fa d'un triste colore di rosa
Il bel fogliame.

Strugge forre, beve fiumi,
Macina scogli, splende,   5
È furia che s'ostina, è l'implacabile,
Sparge spazio, acceca mete,
È l'estate e nei secoli
Con i suoi occhi calcinanti
Va della terra spogliando lo scheletro.   10

Di luglio

A searing vision of the summer landscape. In a 1965 interview, the poet declares: '[...] l'estate è la mia stagione, la stagione che mi brucia fino a farmi arido – l'estate della mia infanzia – la stagione del sole che continua a rodere anche quando già tutto è stato roso' (*Saggi e interventi*, p. 838).

1-7:   **'lei'**: the summer (as clarified in l.8), that 'throws itself' upon the landscape; **'fogliame'**: foliage; **'strugge forre'**: it melts/consumes gorges; **'Macina scogli'**: it grinds up rocks; **'acceca mete'**: it 'blinds' (i.e., obscures) destinations, the points at which one aims.

8-10:   **'occhi calcinanti'**: 'burning eyes' ('calcinare' means to 'calcine', or heat to the point of oxidization); **'Va ... spogliando'**: progressive verb form, meaning it continually strips bare the earth's skeleton. We are left with a rather darker version of the almost mystical evocations of desert landscapes found elsewhere (see 'Ricordo d'Affrica'), as the sun becomes a sinister destructive force (a foretaste of the terrible vision of nature in 'Tu ti spezzasti').

From *Il Dolore* (1937-1946)

directed at son

Tu ti spezzasti 'You broke'

nightmareish brutual + unbearable cruelty of world = unforgiving

1

I molti, immani, sparsi, grigi sassi
Frementi ancora alle segrete fionde
Di originarie fiamme soffocate
Od ai terrori di fiumane vergini
Ruinanti in implacabili carezze,   5
 – Sopra l'abbaglio della sabbia rigidi
In un vuoto orizzonte, non rammenti?

E la recline, che s'apriva all'unico
used to climb tree Raccogliersi dell'ombra nella valle,
7Araucaria, anelando ingigantita,   10
Volta nell'ardua selce d'erme fibre
Piú delle altre dannate refrattaria,
Fresca la bocca di farfalle e d'erbe
Dove dalle radici si tagliava,
 – non la rammenti delirante muta   15
Sopra tre palmi d'un rotondo ciottolo
In un perfetto bilico
Magicamente apparsa?

small bird *delicate, fragility of boy*
Di ramo in ramo fiorrancino lieve,   *against harsh*
Ebbri di meraviglia gli avidi occhi *landscape* 20
WONDER
Ne conquistavi la screziata cima,
Temerario, musico bimbo,
Solo per rivedere all'imo lucido *sea abyss*
D'un fondo e quieto baratro di mare
Favolose testuggini   *exuberant youth + curiosity*25
Ridestarsi fra le alghe.

Della natura estrema la tensione
E le subacquee pompe,
Funebri moniti. *omens*

disembodied

2

Alzavi le braccia come ali   *transform boy*   30
E ridavi nascita al vento   *into angelic*
Correndo nel peso dell'aria immota.   *figure*

Nessuno mai vide posare
Il tuo lieve piede di danza.   *fragile*
                                      vision of happiness

3
Grazia, felice,   35
Non avresti potuto non spezzarti
In una cecità tanto indurita
Tu semplice soffio e cristallo,
                         like a flash of light:
Troppo umano lampo per l'empio, *intensity +*
Selvoso, accanito, ronzante   *brevity*   40
Ruggito d'un sole ignudo.

Direct human trauma
that typifies his work.

Tu ti spezzasti

In *Il Dolore* Ungaretti's poetry is convulsed by the acute experience of 'dolore' (grief/suffering) on several levels: the death of his brother in 1937 is followed by that of his 9-year-old son Antonietto in 1939, after which comes the collective trauma of the Second World War (especially the German occupation of Rome in 1943-44). The relatively detached quest for formal perfection found in *Sentimento del tempo* is overtaken by raw emotion, as seen in this poem, where there is an immediacy reminiscent of certain texts in *L'allegria*. However, where once the poet's emotions were distilled into concentrated flashes, here they flood onto the page in an accumulation of lexical excess and syntactical contortions.

This poem evokes a landscape in Brazil, where Ungaretti lived from 1936 to 1942 and where his son died of appendicitis in 1939 ('**Tu ti spezzasti**': 'You broke'). The fragile figure of the boy is overwhelmed by this alien, hostile landscape, depicted in a rapid succession of images of almost hallucinatory intensity, with a 'baroque' extravagance of descriptive detail, seen particularly in the hyperbolic profusion of adjectival forms. (Ungaretti himself described the importance of the baroque, as experienced by him in the fabric of Rome, for the genesis of *Sentimento del tempo*, writing of the baroque as an expression of 'orrore del vuoto', in passages that resonate strongly with our text – see *Tutte le poesie* pp. 529-36.) Though far removed from the bare intensity of his early work, 'Tu ti spezzasti' is one of Ungaretti's finest poems, so rich in artifice and yet saved from any empty mannerism by its formal tensions and by its intense emotional power

1-7:   The opening stanza gives a vision of a primeval landscape in Brazil, frightening in its excesses but also in its emptiness ('**vuoto orizzonte**'). Leopardi clearly provides a 'rhetorical model' for Ungaretti here, with the anguished '**non rammenti?**' (don't you remember?) recalling the opening question of 'A Silvia', similarly addressed to an embodiment of youth and grace who was crushed by a hostile Nature. But the parallel ends there, as Ungaretti mirrors the terrors of Nature in a 'sublime paroxysm' of language (see Cambon, *La poesia di Ungaretti*, pp.159-61). Syntax is contorted, with the basic elements of the question ('I molti ... sassi ... non rammenti?') separated by a furious accumulation of subordinate clauses dominated by adjectival and participle forms. '**immani**': enormous; '**Frementi...**': a vision of nature still vibrating with the energy of catastrophic primeval events ('still trembling from the secret slings of primeval smothered fires or from the terrors of virgin torrents rushing down in implacable caresses'); '**l'abbaglio della sabbia**': 'the dazzle of [sunlight on] the sand'.

8-18:   As in stanza 1, tortuous syntax with inversions of the expected sequence of clauses breaks up the basic sentence, which is: '**E la recline** [leaning] ... **araucaria** ['monkey-puzzle tree']... **non la rammenti...?**'. '**che s'apriva ... valle**': a clause qualifying 'Araucaria'; '**anelando ingigantita**': panting, made gigantic; **ll. 11-12**: 'turned [directed] to the arduous flint with/by its solitary fibres, more resistant than the other damned ones [other trees]'. A sense of extreme conditions and the fragility of life is encapsulated again in adjectival expressions in this stanza: **'ardua'**, **'dannate'**, **'refrattaria'**, **'delirante muta'** (an almost oxymoronic pairing, suggesting an overall tension between anguished expressionism and overwhelmed silence); **l.16:** 'on top of a round stone three spans across'; **'magicamente apparsa'**: the 'magic' nature of its balancing suggests also extreme precariousness. The dense sequence of hendecasyllables finally begins to give way to a variety of shorter lines in ll.17-18, opening the way for a more varied rhythm and tempo in the succeeding sections.

19-29: The tone initially changes with the depiction of the boy climbing the tree, all lightness and grace, but his view from the top is of a fantastical yet unsettling natural world. **'fiorrancino lieve'**: delicate firecrest (a small bird); **'Ebbri'**: drunk; **'ne'**: of the tree; **'screziata cima'**: dappled summit. His sense of avid wonder and fearlessness (**'temerario'**) momentarily transform the scene with lightness and musicality (consigned again to the abundance of adjectives), but what he sees ('fabulous turtles awakening') is located in the disquieting 'shining depth' (**'imo lucido'**) of a sea-abyss (**'baratro di mare'**). This is now seen by the poetic voice as part of a series of omens (**'moniti'**), deriving from the 'extreme tension of nature', itself expressed in a line of syntactic tension: **'Della natura estrema la tensione'**.

30-34: The boy's vitality and grace prevail again momentarily, in a pause of almost Leopardian idyllic recollection, as the stylistic and tonal extravagance of the poem is briefly suspended. **'come ali'**: prefigures perhaps the transformation of the boy into a spiritual, angelic figure; **'ridavi nascita...'**: 'you gave birth to the wind again'.

35-41: The fragile vision of happiness, encapsulated in the delicately punctuated *quinario* of l.35 is now overwhelmed by the merciless flood of negativity and destructiveness in the longer lines of the close, echoing the inhuman atmosphere of the opening stanzas and again expressed through a baroque accumulation of adjectival forms. **l. 36:** 'you could not have not broken'. **'Troppo umano lampo'**: the boy is a 'flash' of light (suggesting both intensity and brevity) but too human in the face of the 'roar' (**'ruggito'**) of the naked sun, which is **'empio'** (impious, cruel), **'selvoso'** (wild), **'accanito'** (dogged), **'ronzante'** (buzzing or droning).

Non gridate più

Cessate d'uccidere i morti,
Non gridate più, non gridate
Se li volete ancora udire,
Se sperate di non perire.

Hanno l'impercettibile sussurro, 5
Non fanno più rumore
Del crescere dell'erba,
Lieta dove non passa l'uomo.

Non gridate più

In *Il Dolore*, the echoes of contemporary events come to the forefront in the section 'Roma occupata', where a kind of baroque expressionism is again present in a number of longer poems, such as 'Mio fiume anche tu' (where it is combined with an explicitly Christian mysticism). Perhaps more effective in addressing the contemporary tragedy, however, are the simplicity and economy of this text in which the poetic voice calls for a quiet humility, rather than any angry rhetoric, in remembering the dead and listening to their voices.

1-4:   The poem revolves around the opening paradox, suggesting that the dead may ultimately be more alive than the living (see also 1.4). As ever in Ungaretti, there is a tendentially spiritual or mystical element here.

5-8:   **'sussurro'**: murmur; **'crescere dell'erba'**: the image of the quietly growing grass suggests a natural cycle of regeneration and renewal, to which man must give due attention and careful respect.
Unusually, this poem contains a direct address to a public *voi* rather than the personal lyrical discourse of the *io* (periodically addressing a series of *tu* figures), as found in most of Ungaretti's verse. And yet, the poet remains true to the intimate, reflective vein of his most authentic work, never embracing realism solely in the name of political engagement. In this respect, it is interesting to compare a poem by Quasimodo, 'Milano, agosto 1943' (note the historical specificity of the title), where an apparently similar theme is treated, but to very different effect. Quasimodo deliberately gives us a chronicle of horror and despair, without any sublimating element, but with rhetorical fervour in the service of his broadly left-wing, humanitarian message: 'Non toccate i morti, così rossi, così gonfi: / lasciateli nella terra delle loro case: / la città è morta, è morta.'

From *Il Taccuino del Vecchio* (1960)

Ultimi cori per la terra promessa

no. 24

Mi afferri nelle grinfie azzurre il nibbio
E, all'apice del sole,
Mi lasci sulla sabbia
Cadere in pasto ai corvi.

Non porterò più sulle spalle il fango,   5
Mondo mi avranno il fuoco,
I rostri crocidanti
L'azzannare afroroso di sciacalli.

Poi mostrerà il beduino,
Dalla sabbia scoprendolo   10
Frugando col bastone,
Un ossame bianchissimo.

*****

no. 27

L'amore più non è quella tempesta
Che nel notturno abbaglio
Ancora mi avvinceva poco fa
Tra l'insonnia e le smanie,

Balugina da un faro   5
Verso cui va tranquillo
Il vecchio capitano.

Ultimi cori per la terra promessa

Following on from the title of his 1950 collection (*La terra promessa*, in which Ungaretti gives voice to mythic figures such as Dido and Palinurus), this series of 27 short poems, dated 'Roma 1952-1960', has the unmistakable feel of a potentially valedictory text. Here we find pithy meditations on time, life, love and death. The tone is quietly contemplative, with a simplicity of diction in some respects reminiscent of his early work.

no. 24:
The poet invokes a death which, in removing temporal/physical concerns (the 'mud' of the world) would return him to purity in harmony with the desert.

1-4:   'Mi afferri ... Mi lasci...': Both verbs are in the present subjunctive (3rd pers. sing.), meaning: 'Let the kite (i.e., bird of prey) grasp me .... and let him drop me...'; 'grinfie': claws; 'apice': apex, zenith; 'in pasto ai corvi': to be eaten by the crows.

5-8:   'Mondo': 'cleansed': he will have been cleansed by fire, by the 'crowing beaks', and the 'stinking biting' of the jackals.

9-12:   The figure of the bedouin brings us back to the atmosphere of some of the earliest poems; 'frugando': digging, delving; 'ossame': set of bones. The mystical aspiration to unity with nature is given a stark formulation here.

no. 27:
The imagery here recalls the 'shipwreck' and the old 'sea-dog' of the short 1917 poem 'Allegria di naufragi', but now the urgency and drama of the journey, the 'tempests' of younger years, are replaced by the quiet certainty of impending arrival; 'abbaglio': dazzlement. 'avvinceva': bound or entranced; 'Balugina': It [love] flickers, glimmers. As in all of Ungaretti's work, these texts are underpinned by an essentially spiritual or religious outlook and a sense that physical existence is a journey towards some other state.

3

Umberto Saba (1883-1957)

Saba seems to swim against the tide of contemporary poetry in the first half of the twentieth century: and yet although he followed, with his apparent literary conservatism, a direction 'diametrically opposed' to the mainstreams of 'poesia pura' and hermeticism, his poetry is, arguably, more firmly immersed in the life and culture of his times than that of some of his more up-to-date contemporaries.[i] It is easy to draw connections between the individuality of his style and the particular geographical, cultural and family circumstances of his birth and upbringing: Saba himself linked his Triestine origin with the fact that he was, at least initially, 'un arretrato' in cultural terms.[ii] And the frankly autobiographical focus of so many of his poems means that it is difficult to ignore some key facts of the writer's existence: from his childhood experiences (an absent father and the early trauma of separation from his *balia*, or wet-nurse) to the vagaries of personal relationships (the sometimes tempestuous marriage to Lina, as well as other erotic involvements) to the painful process of self-exploration through psychoanalysis, to the experience of racial persecution (Saba was Jewish and went into hiding during the war years).[iii]

However, the peculiarity of Saba's poetic style amounts to more than a mere accident of geography and life events. The poet himself maintains that his 'conservatism' is an innate characteristic, rather than deriving from his specific cultural ambience, while Fortini characterizes his 'anachronism' as a 'stylistic choice'.[iv] In fact, Saba's poetry is more complex than any broad label such as 'conservative' or 'traditional' might suggest, just as its apparent communicative innocence is often 'ingannevole'.[v] On the one hand, he adopts metrical and formal structures that signal a clear continuity with the classic Italian tradition, from Petrarch to Leopardi. On the other hand, he combines these structures with a range of vocabulary and imagery drawn from the everyday, the prosaic, which are in turn, as it were, re-energized by the syntactical and metrical richness of canonical verse forms.[vi] The effect, at times, is one of a 'complex falsetto', a mis-match between content and form.[vii] There are some parallels between such an approach and the irony of the *crepuscolari*, with their rejection of the sublime in favour of the banal, but Saba's sensibility is quite different, solidly rooted in the sincerity of personal emotions and insistent on the authenticity of personal experience, with an overwhelming impulse towards immersion in 'la calda vita' (see 'Il Borgo'), with all its attendant problems.[viii]

The themes of Saba's poetry revolve, predominantly, around the lyric persona's direct if problematic experiences of life, presented within a quasi-narrative framework: themes such as the sights and sounds of the city (specifically of Trieste), the multifarious human lives encountered therein, the vitality and sensuality of animals, plants and other elements of nature (often filtered through the urban context), and the joy and pain of personal relationships, whether involving the intense emotional and psychological complexity surrounding the figures of the poet's mother and father, or the tender intimacy of a father's love for his child. Such themes form the subject matter of Saba's 'poesia onesta' – a phrase found in his essay 'Quello che resta da fare ai poeti', submitted in 1911 to the leading Florentine literary review *La Voce*, only to be rejected and remain unpublished until after the poet's death. The episode underlines the singular and isolated nature of Saba's poetic enterprise, as does the substance of the essay itself, in which he decries the 'insincerity' of much contemporary verse (particularly that of D'Annunzio) and pleads instead for 'onestà letteraria' advocating a process of 'selezione e [...] rifacimento' with regard to the tradition rather than a pursuit of novelty at all costs.[ix]

The singularity of Saba's poetry is manifested also in the peculiar evolution and structure of his *Canzoniere*. The title, with its Petrarchan associations, was first used by Saba in 1921 for a volume which gathered together the bulk of his poetry up to that point, arranged in chronologically and thematically articulated sections, corresponding only in part to the early volumes in which they originally appeared. This 1921 collection later became (though with various revisions) the 'Volume primo' of subsequent editions of his *Canzoniere* in 1945, 1948, 1957 (and posthumously in 1961). In the later editions, the second and third 'volumes' respectively bring together works written and published in the periods 1921-32 and from 1932 onwards. The result is a text of some complexity despite its apparent structural and chronological clarity, a carefully constructed poetic autobiography incorporating below the surface a history of reworkings and a network of thematic and formal links and echoes that provide an over-arching 'macro-textual cohesion'.[x] Meanwhile, Saba provides the reader with an invaluable companion to his own verse in the form of his *Storia e cronistoria del Canzoniere*, written between 1944 and 1947 and published under the pseudonym Giuseppe Carimandrei, a playful device allowing Saba a degree of ironic distance both in criticizing and eulogizing his own poetry, as seen for example in the opening words: 'Saba ha commesso molti errori. Ma negare la poesia di Saba sarebbe negare l'evidenza di un fenomeno naturale.'[xi]

Saba's poetry can be seen to fall into three phases, broadly following the structural division of the *Canzoniere* into three volumes. The first phase, that of the work collected in the 1921 edition of the *Canzoniere*, includes the poems of *Casa e campagna* and *Trieste e una donna*, collections that define the poet's voice and image and undoubtedly contain, as Mengaldo puts it, some of his 'capolavori assoluti'.[xii] (And it should not be forgotten that these works pre-date the early poetry of both Ungaretti and Montale, so often seen as the originators of the modern lyrical voice.) In the second phase, from the early 1920s to the early 1930s (not represented in the selection below), Saba experiments with a number of different formal and stylistic solutions while exploring a sometimes intensely introspective thematic vein (related partly to his experience of psychoanalysis in these years). The results are mixed, the style at times somewhat laboured or contrived. The volume *Parole* (1933-34) marks the opening of the third major phase, seen by some as a second high point of his work. Here more than anywhere else, Saba approaches a degree of convergence with 'la linea dominante della lirica novecentesca' (greater brevity, use of pauses to isolate images, use of analogies, etc.).[xiii]

Yet despite this move towards 'le forme essenziali della lirica', Saba does not abandon his 'vocation' as a realist.[xiv] If anything, this comes to the fore again in a number of areas of his later work (for example the section *1944*). There is, for Mengaldo, a fundamental 'solidarietà con il reale' in Saba that sets him apart from other contemporaries for whom the relationship with the world is seen in symbolic terms.[xv] However, as Fortini warns, one should not necessarily see in this a mark of 'salute' in opposition to the 'ills' of hermeticism and *novecentismo*: rather, the reality that Saba's work reveals is that of a 'radicale infermità', a divided self for whom the poetic word and the real world evoked through it are also, in part, a defence mechanism.[xvi] This surely is the sense of a famous closing line from the short poem 'Secondo congedo': 'Quante rose per nascondere un abisso!'[xvii]

The tension inherent in this line is just one aspect of the complexities and contradictions that run throughout Saba's work. His language and tonalities are ostensibly conservative and yet also distinctly modern, he is 'attardato e anticipatore, controcorrente'.[xviii] He reaches out to a community of readership and celebrates a life of shared experiences, even as he doggedly explores the inner truth of the self, the individual. Thus, in a memorable formulation (as part of an illuminating discussion of Saba's relationship with the particular artistic genre of the opera libretto) Sanguineti describes 'il sabese' – Saba's personal poetic language – with a suitably oxymoronic flourish: 'così anticamente nuovo, così difficilmente facile, così egocentricamente e egotisticamente collettivizzabile e collettivizzato'.[xix]

Endnotes

i   See Giacomo Debenedetti, *Poesia italiana del Novecento*, p. 127.

ii   *Storia e cronistoria del Canzoniere*, in Saba, *Prose*, ed. by Linuccia Saba (Milan: Mondadori, 1964), pp. 399-657 (p. 407).

iii   For biographical information, see Saba, *Tutte le poesie*, pp. lxxiii-xcii.

iv   *Prose*, pp. 407-08; Fortini, *I poeti del Novecento*, p. 50.

v   Gian Luigi Beccaria, 'Poesia di Saba', in *Umberto Saba: Trieste e la cultura mitteleuropea*. Atti del Convegno, Roma 29 e 30 marzo 1984, ed by Rosita Tardi (Milan: Mondadori, 1986), pp. 21-47 (p. 22).

vi   Curi, *La poesia italiana nel Novecento*, pp. 115-16.

vii   Fortini, *I poeti del Novecento*, p. 55.

viii   See Elvio Guagnini, *Il punto su Saba* (Roma-Bari: Laterza, 1987). pp. 38-39, and Lorenzini, *La poesia italiana del Novecento*, p. 88.

ix   'Quello che resta da fare ai poeti', in *Prose*, pp. 751-59 (753 and 759).

x   Furio Brugnolo, '*Il Canzoniere* di Umberto Saba', in *Letteratura Italiana: Le opere*, vol. IV, i: *L'età della crisi*, (Torino: Einaudi, 1995), pp. 497-559 (pp. 514-15).

xi   *Prose*, p. 405.

xii   Mengaldo, *Poeti italiani del Novecento*, p. 195.

xiii   Segre and Ossola, *Antologia della poesia italiana*, p. 282.

xiv   Curi, *La poesia italiana nel Novecento*, p. 257.

xv   Mengaldo, *Poeti italiani del Novecento,* pp. 193-94.

xvi   Fortini, *I poeti del Novecento*, p. 58.

xvii   See Romano Luperini, *Il Novecento* (Turin: Loescher, 1981), p. 247-48.

xviii   Lorenzini, *La poesia italiana del Novecento,* p. 90.

xix   Edoardo Sanguineti, 'Saba e il melodramma', in *Umberto Saba: Trieste e la cultura mitteleuropea*. Atti del Convegno Roma 29 e 30 marzo 1984, ed by Rosita Tardi (Milan: Mondadori, 1986), pp. 93-100 (p. 96).

Poetic texts

Saba's *Canzoniere*, as structured retrospectively by the author, is divided into three 'volumes' and further subdivided into individual collections, which, however, do not always correspond to the separate collections originally published. The definitive form of the *Canzoniere* can be found, along with numerous uncollected poems and significant background material in:

Tutte le poesie, a cura di Arrigo Stara, introduzione di Mario Lavagetto, I Meridiani (Milan: Mondadori, 1988).
A good anthology of Saba's poetic and prose works can also be found in:
Per conoscere Saba, a cura di Mario Lavagetto (Milan: Mondadori, 1981)

Prose texts

Prose, a cura di Linuccia Saba (Milan: Mondadori, 1964)

Further reading

Atti del Convegno internazionale 'Il punto su Saba'. Trieste, 25-27 marzo 1984 (Trieste: Ed. Lint, 1985)

Baldoni, Luca, '"Un vecchio amava un ragazzo": Homoeroticism in Umberto Saba's Late Poetry', *Italian Studies*, 60 (Autumn 2005), 221-39

Barberi Squarotti, Giorgio, 'Appunti in margine allo stile di Saba', in *Astrazione e realtà* (Milan: Rusconi, 1960), pp. 121-143

Beccaria, Gian Luigi, 'Poesia di Saba', in *Umberto Saba: Trieste e la cultura mitteleuropea*. Atti del Convegno, Roma 29 e 30 marzo 1984, ed by Rosita Tardi (Milan: Mondadori, 1986), pp. 21-47

Brugnolo, Furio, '*Il Canzoniere* di Umberto Saba', in *Letteratura Italiana: Le opere*, vol. IV, i: *L'età della crisi*, (Torino: Einaudi, 1995), pp. 497-559

Debenedetti, Giacomo, *Poesia italiana del Novecento: quaderni inediti* (Milan: Garzanti, 1974), pp. 127-73

Guagnini, Elvio, *Il punto su Saba* (Roma-Bari: Laterza, 1987)

Lavagetto, Mario, *La gallina di Saba* (Turin: Einaudi, 1974)

Pinchera, Antonio, *Umberto Saba* (Firenze: La Nuova Italia, 1974)

Portinari, Folco, *Umberto Saba* (Milan: Mursia, 1963

Raimondi, Piero, *Invito alla lettura di Umberto Saba* (Milan: Mursia, 1974)

Renzi, Lorenzo, 'A Reading of Saba's "A mia moglie"', Modern Language Review, 68 (1973), 77-83

Sanguineti, Edoardo, 'Saba e il melodramma', in *Umberto Saba: Trieste e la cultura mitteleuropea*. Atti del Convegno, Roma 29 e 30 marzo 1984, ed by Rosita Tardi (Milan: Mondadori, 1986), pp. 93-100

Contents

From *Casa e campagna* (1909-1910)

A mia moglie [extract]

Tu sei come una giovane,
una bianca pollastra.
Le si arruffano al vento
le piume, il collo china
per bere, e in terra raspa;   5
ma, nell'andare, ha il lento
tuo passo di regina,
ed incede sull'erba
pettoruta e superba.
È migliore del maschio.   10
È come sono tutte
le femmine di tutti
i sereni animali
che avvicinano a Dio.
Così se l'occhio, se il giudizio mio   15
non m'inganna, fra queste hai le tue uguali,
e in nessun'altra donna.
Quando la sera assonna
le gallinelle,
mettono voci che ricordan quelle,   20
dolcissime, onde a volte dei tuoi mali
ti quereli, e non sai
che la tua voce ha la soave e triste
musica dei pollai.

[...]

A mia moglie

The first stanza (of six) of what is probably Saba's best-known text, an unconventional, tender love-poem addressed to his wife Lina. In *Storia e cronistoria*, Saba sums up the studied naivety of the tone as follows: 'se un bambino potesse sposare e scrivere una poesia per sua moglie, scriverebbe questa' (*Prose*, 435). He also points to the 'prayer-like' overtones, something that emerges more fully with the repetitive structure of the opening line of each stanza, giving the sense of a litany: 'Tu sei come una gravida / giovenca... // Tu sei come una lunga / cagna... // Tu sei come la pavida / coniglia...// Tu sei come la rondine... // Tu sei come la provvida / formica...'. Critics have noted intertextual echoes, for example from the Old Testament *Song of songs* (Pinchera, pp. 35-36) or from St Francis' *Cantico delle creature* (Renzi, p. 81). Far from expressing any transcendent spirituality however, the 'religious' element tends towards a celebration of the created world in its concrete reality, lovingly observed. The poem is rich in rhyme and assonance and is dominated by *settenari* and *endecasillabi*.

1-5: The comparison is direct and unadorned, with the modified noun-form **'pollastra'** (pullet) establishing firmly a tone of unpretentious domesticity. The realistic details of the hen's behaviour further emphasise its (literally) down-to-earth qualities: **'... in terra raspa'** (scratches). The subject of **'si arruffano'** (are ruffled) is **'le piume'** (**'Le'**: 'a lei').

6-9: The noble aspect of the hen's bearing springs from the comparison with the woman (**'ha il ... tuo passo'**), in a curiously convoluted form of compliment; **'incede'**: walks solemnly; **'pettoruta'**: proud-chested.

10-14: In some respects, these lines re-work a paradigm of the lyric tradition dating back to the *dolce stil novo* and beyond: the exaltation of the beloved woman as a pathway to the Divine (see Renzi, pp. 82-83). But here, this is given a distinctly earthly twist: the subject is still the 'pollastra', and the praise is extended to the entire female animal kingdom, **'femmine'** rather than 'donne' (and elsewhere in the poem, the emphasis is firmly on the procreative role of the female), so that ultimately the Divine resides in the humble vitality and animal sensuality of the real world.

15-17: The comparison of line 1 is repeated, but with an additional statement of the beloved's uniqueness among women, due to her affinity with the 'femmine' of the animal world (here **'queste'**), but also, by implication, her closeness to God (as reprised at the close of the poem's final stanza).

18-24: The direct comparison with the hens is elaborated further in terms of sensory impressions, of the 'music' of their voices at evening time. It is subtly structured as a two-way, 'open' comparison (Pinchera, p. 37): initially the hens' voices are the first term of the comparison, recalling that of the woman (ll. 20-22), only to become the second term at the close (ll. 23-24). **'assonna'**: the subject is **'sera'**, the object **'gallinelle'** ('when evening makes the hens sleepy'). The voice of the woman is evoked in a moment of **'querelarsi'** (complaining of her ills), reflecting the sometimes difficult nature of Saba's relationship with Lina (also evoked elsewhere). The word **'pollai'** (hen houses) in the final rhyming position emphasises the note of domestic realism in the vocabulary and scenario of the poem.

From *Trieste e una donna* (1910-1912)

Il torrente

Tu così avventuroso nel mio mito,
così povero sei fra le tue sponde.
Non hai, ch'io veda, margine fiorito.
Dove ristagni scopri cose immonde.

Pur, se ti guardo, il cor d'ansia mi stringi,   5
o torrentello.
Tutto il tuo corso è quello
del mio pensiero, che tu risospingi
alle origini, a tutto il forte e il bello
che in te ammiravo; e se ripenso i grossi   10
fiumi, l'incontro con l'avverso mare,
quest'acqua onde tu appena i piedi arrossi
nudi a una lavandaia,
la più pericolosa e la più gaia,
con isole e cascate, ancor m'appare;   15
e il poggio da cui scendi è una montagna.

Sulla tua sponda lastricata l'erba
cresceva, e cresce nel ricordo sempre;
sempre è d'intorno a te sabato sera;
sempre ad un bimbo la sua madre austera   20
rammenta che quest'acqua è fuggitiva,
che non ritrova più la sua sorgente,
né la sua riva; sempre l'ancor bella
donna si attrista, e cerca la sua mano
il fanciulletto, che ascoltò uno strano   25
confronto tra la vita nostra e quella
della corrente.

Il torrente

On one level, a poem with a simple 'moral' (Saba notes in *Storia e cronistoria*), as captured in the image of the stream: 'la dolce vita corre inevitabilmente alla morte' (*Prose*, p. 446). But this is also a poem about Saba's memories of childhood and the figure of his mother, around whom unresolved tensions persist throughout his work.

1-4: The *tu* of this poem is the 'torrent' itself, evoked in contradictory terms from the start, **'avventuroso'** in the world of 'myth' (the poetic imagination, or perhaps childhood memory), 'poor' in reality, and indeed, revealing foul or unclean (**'immonde'**) things just beneath the surface of its stagnant pools (an image of the troubled depths of the poet's psyche); **'ristagni'**: lie stagnant.

5-6: **'il cor d'ansia mi stringi'**: 'you grip my heart with anxiety'; a Leopardian echo perhaps (from 'La sera del dí di festa': 'fieramente mi si stringe il core').

7-10: The comparison between the stream and the poet's inner life brings him to recall his own origins, to seek the positive (**'il forte e il bello'**) that he once saw in this image; **'risospingi'**: you push back.

10-16: Even from the perspective of the present (**'se ripenso...'**), and when compared to rivers and the hostile (**'avverso'**) sea (the wider experiences of adult life) the stream (**'quest'acqua'**) still holds its fascination, just as the hill (**'poggio'**) still seems a mountain. The syntax of ll.12-15 is characteristically convoluted, in the manner of the pre-*novecento* tradition, with the verb **'m'appare'** separated from its subject (**'acqua'**) by subordinate clauses and the adjectival sequence. The connotations of the stream water are, again, contradictory, as it is both **'pericolosa'** and **'gaia'** (with the mention of the washerwoman's bare feet hinting also at the stream as an image of erotic possibilities).

17-19: On the paved (**'lastricata'**) bank, the past (**'cresceva'**) and present (**'cresce'**) merge into the **'sempre'** of a timeless memory of childhood Saturday evenings.

20- 27: The core of the poem lies here, in the remembered figure of the mother, with her austere and melancholy admonition to the child, her lesson on the transience of life, which flows on ineluctably; **'sorgente'**: source. The poet leaves us with the image of the boy's perplexity expressed in typically direct, matter-of-fact terms.

Trieste

Ho attraversata tutta la città.
Poi ho salita un'erta,
popolosa in principio, in là deserta,
chiusa da un muricciolo:
un cantuccio in cui solo   5
siedo; e mi pare che dove esso termina
termini la città.

Trieste ha una scontrosa
grazia. Se piace,
è come un ragazzaccio aspro e vorace,   10
con gli occhi azzurri e mani troppo grandi
per regalare un fiore;
come un amore
con gelosia.
Da quest'erta ogni chiesa, ogni sua via   15
scopro, se mena all'ingombrata spiaggia,
o alla collina cui, sulla sassosa
cima, una casa, l'ultima, s'aggrappa.
Intorno
circola ad ogni cosa   20
un'aria strana, un'aria tormentosa,
l'aria natia.

La mia città che in ogni parte è viva,
ha il cantuccio a me fatto, alla mia vita
pensosa e schiva.   25

Trieste

Along with the following text, this forms the quintessential portrait of Saba's Trieste. Here the emphasis is on the city's atmospheric qualities and emotional associations.

1:      The opening line conveys a sense of Saba's all-embracing vision of poetry, reaching out to the reality of society and community.

2-7:   The situation described clearly echoes Leopardi's 'L'infinito': the hill; the **'muricciolo'** (little wall), a barrier creating a place of secluded contemplation (here, a **'cantuccio'**: little corner); and the sense that the known world ends here. Unlike Leopardi however, Saba turns his attention not towards the unknown infinities beyond, but down towards the city itself. l. 7: **'termini'**: subjunctive of *terminare* (following **'mi pare'**).

8-14:   Here the city becomes a veritable character in itself, a 'creatura morale' (Portinari, p. 58). These lines, with their paradoxical contradictions, are the key to the poem, especially the phrase **'scontrosa / grazia'** (surly grace), where the enjambement emphasises the almost oxymoronic tension in the poet's ambivalent attachment to his city. This is further underlined by the rhyme *piace-vorace*, the juxtaposition of **'ragazzaccio'** with **'fiore'**, and the phrase **'un amore / con gelosia'** (on the rhyme *fiore-amore*, see 'Amai', below).

15-22: As in l.1, the emphasis is on the inclusivity of the poet's gaze, taking in and 'dis-/uncovering' (**'scopro'**) the whole city from its heights to its depths; **'mena'**: leads; **'ingombrata'**: cluttered; **'s'aggrappa'**: clings. Further tensions are evident in the various attributes of **'aria'**, both **'strana ... tormentosa'** and **'natia'** (native).

23-25   The identification of the poetic *io* with his native place is at the heart of these lines (**'mia... a me.... mia'**), although a tension persists (underlined by the contradictory closing rhyme) between the positive vitality of the city (**'viva'**) and the hesitant introspection of his own life (**'schiva'**: reticent). Nevertheless, we are left with a very strong sense of warmth and belonging (notably in the repetition of **'cantuccio'**, with its overtones of refuge and safety).

Città vecchia

Spesso, per ritornare alla mia casa
prendo un'oscura via di città vecchia.
Giallo in qualche pozzanghera si specchia
qualche fanale, e affollata è la strada.

Qui tra la gente che viene che va   5
dall'osteria alla casa o al lupanare,
dove son merci ed uomini il detrito
di un gran porto di mare,
io ritrovo, passando, l'infinito
nell'umiltà.   10
Qui prostituta e marinaio, il vecchio
che bestemmia, la femmina che bega,
il dragone che siede alla bottega
del friggitore,
la tumultuante giovane impazzita   15
d'amore,
sono tutte creature della vita
e del dolore;
s'agita in esse, come in me, il Signore.

Qui degli umili sento in compagnia   20
il mio pensiero farsi
più puro dove più turpe è la via.

Città vecchia

This further portrait of Trieste is placed amidst the concrete reality of the city and its inhabitants, reflecting Saba's wish to 'fondere la sua vita a quella delle creature più umili ed oscure' (*Prose*, p. 447). Here Saba's 'aspro realismo' comes to the forefront, but it is also balanced by an element of 'severa, e pur viva e limpida, poesia morale' (Barberi Squarotti, pp. 136-7).

1-4: The **'città vecchia'** is the oldest part of Trieste, with its narrow streets and unsalubrious air, suggested in the details of darkness and puddles reflecting street lamps, but it is also teeming with life. The image of the city is, for all Saba's traditionalism, a modern one, with echoes of the avant-garde (and also of the prototypical modernist, Baudelaire).

5-8: The anonymous 'crowd' of l. 4 is here the more human **'gente'**, 'amidst' whom the *io* locates himself. Again the imagery emphasises the grimier aspects of urban life; **'lupanare'**: brothel. l. 7: inverted syntax: 'where goods and men are the detritus of ... etc.'

9-10: The core idea of the poem is here: that truth, authenticity reside in the humdrum, the everyday.

11-19: The range of images of 'reality' is extended here, from the continuing catalogue of low-life characters to the positively-connotated young woman in love. Note the shift in register from **'prostituta'** and **'femmina che bega'** (a rather uncomplimentary term for a woman, coupled with a dialect term for 'arguing'), **'dragone'** ('dragoon' or cavalry man) and **'friggitore'** (fried-food seller), to **'giovane impazzita / d'amore'**. All are finally subsumed in a quasi-religious effusion, probably best understood as an affirmation of the overarching value of life itself (Saba was not a religious man). Note the rhyme sequence (including both incongruous and more conventional or even clichéd juxtapositions): *friggitore-amore-dolore-Signore*. **'esse'**: the 'creature' of l.17.

20-22: Inversion of normal prose syntax: 'Qui in compagnia degli umili sento...'. The paradoxical nature of his insight is underlined in these lines, the 'purity' of his thought being in direct proportion to the 'foulness' (**'turpe'**) of the streets he walks.

From *Cose leggere e vaganti* (1920)

Ritratto della mia bambina

La mia bambina con la palla in mano,
con gli occhi grandi colore del cielo
e dell'estiva vesticciola: "Babbo
– mi disse – voglio uscire oggi con te".
Ed io pensavo: Di tante parvenze   5
che s'ammirano al mondo, io ben so a quali
posso la mia bambina assomigliare.
Certo alla schiuma, alla marina schiuma
che sull'onde biancheggia, a quella scia
ch'esce azzurra dai tetti e il vento sperde;   10
anche alle nubi, insensibili nubi
che si fanno e disfanno in chiaro cielo;
e ad altre cose leggere e vaganti.

Ritratto della mia bambina

This is an example of Saba's voice at its most accessible and apparently naïve, from a group of poems written with the desire 'di divertirsi e di giocare' (*Prose*, p. 475). It is both direct and charming, highly personal and yet open to the common human experience of the joys of life and love, seen here for once without any hints of darker or problematic aspects.

1-4:   A disarmingly simple portrait of the poet's daughter Linuccia (born 1910), with elements prefiguring the comparisons of the subsequent lines.

5-7   '**parvenze**': 'appearances', in the sense of visible phenomena of the world around, to which the child can be compared.

8-13   A catalogue of images of 'light' and 'wandering' things (i.e. mobile, shifting, changing), from the '**schiuma**' (foam) on the waves, to the '**scia**' ('wake' or 'trace') coming from the rooftops (trails of smoke from chimneys), to the clouds in their evanescence.

From *L'amorosa spina* (1920)

Sovrumana dolcezza
io so, che ti farà i begli occhi chiudere
come la morte.

Se tutti i succhi della primavera
fossero entrati nel mio vecchio tronco,   5
per farlo rifiorire anche una volta,
non tutto il bene sentirei che sento
solo a guardarti, ad aver te vicina,
a seguire ogni tuo gesto, ogni modo
tuo di essere, ogni tuo piccolo atto.   10
E se vicina non t'ho, se a te in alta
solitudine penso, più infuocato
serpeggia nelle mie vene il pensiero
della carne, il presagio

dell'amara dolcezza,   15
che so che ti farà i begli occhi chiudere
come la morte.

'Sovrumana dolcezza...'

The last of a set of 12 untitled poems, in which Saba celebrates a very different aspect of human relations, erotic love, with 'la malinconia di un uomo già innanzi con gli anni preso al fascino di una creatura uscita appena dall'adolescenza' (*Prose*, p. 479); a young woman named elsewhere as 'Chiaretta'.

1-3:   While exalting the 'superhuman' intensity of erotic pleasure, the poet links it firmly with mortality (hinting also perhaps at the perennial presence of guilt in connection with sexual relationships in his own problematic psychological make-up).

4-10:   The image of the **'vecchio tronco'** with its fresh sap has clear sexual overtones, although these are balanced in the following lines by the less overtly carnal aspiration to simply observe and admire; l.6: **'anche'**: here, 'ancora'.

10-14: It is her absence that most inflames the poet's desires; **'serpeggia'**: snakes through; **'presagio'**: presage.

15-17 The reprise of the opening lines contains a small but significant modification with the oxymoron **'amara dolcezza'**: on the one hand this can be seen to allude to the Petrarchan tradition of tormented platonic love with its frequent oxymoronic tensions; on the other it is a painful acknowledgment of the contradictions and tensions inherent in Saba's own poetic embracing of reality, including erotic love.

From *Parole* (1933-34)

Parole

Parole,
dove il cuore dell'uomo si specchiava
– nudo e sorpreso – alle origini; un angolo
cerco nel mondo, l'oasi propizia
a detergere voi con il mio pianto   5
dalla menzogna che vi acceca. Insieme
delle memorie spaventose il cumulo
si scioglierebbe, come neve al sole.

Parole

The collection *Parole* marks the beginning of the third 'volume' of the *Canzoniere*, in which Saba's poetry shows signs of leaning towards a 'purer' type of lyricism, with some lessening of narrative/realist elements. The title itself (of both the collection and this poem) reflects a greater interest in refining the poetic word, as does the theme of seeking a 'cleansing' of language in the quest for truth – what Saba called: 'una grande chiarificazione interna, alla quale risponde un uguale illimpidimento della forma' (*Prose*, p. 580).

1-3: The poem is addressed to language itself, to **'parole'** (the **'voi'** of ll.5-6), seen as a means of laying bare the 'heart', a 'mirror' where some original authenticity could once be found (the 'origins' may be those of mankind, or of the individual in childhood).

3-6 The poet's persona seeks a refuge 'in' the world (a significant distinction from those who would seek refuge *from* the world, away from reality), a space where language (**'voi'**: you words) can be cleansed (**'detergere'**). The 'lies' (**'menzogna'**) that 'blind' language may be washed away by his tears: an image that neatly encapsulates Saba's aspiration to emotional sincerity, no matter how painful (with an echo perhaps of his experience of psychoanalytic therapy in the preceding years); **'propizia'**: propitious, favourable.

7-8: Inverted syntax: 'the pile of fearful memories would melt'. The event is hypothetical, dependent on finding the 'oasis' in the lines above. The poet's desire is for a return to some primordial innocence, with a language untainted by memory (experience). The final analogy (with the omission of the definite article for **'neve'**) is reminiscent of certain hermetic stylistic modes (along with the introspective stance and focus on **'parole'**, **'cuore'** and **'memoria'**).

Tredicesima partita

Sui gradini un manipolo sparuto
si riscaldava di se stesso.
                             E quando
– smisurata raggera – il sole spense
dietro una casa il suo barbaglio, il campo   5
schiarì il presentimento della notte.
Correvano su e giù le maglie rosse,
le maglie bianche, in una luce d'una
strana iridata trasparenza. Il vento
deviava il pallone, la Fortuna   10
si rimetteva agli occhi la benda.

Piaceva
essere così pochi intirizziti
uniti,
come ultimi uomini su un monte,   15
a guardare di là l'ultima gara.

Tredicesima partita

One of a group of 'Cinque poesie per il gioco del calcio', in which Saba's realistic vein is very firmly continued even within *Parole*. Saba describes in *Storia e cronistoria* how he came to appreciate football relatively late in life, finding in the game, apart from the fascination of a 'spettacolo [...] bellissimo', an unexpected sense of belonging, of being 'come tutti / gli uomini di tutti / i giorni' (in the words of the poem 'Il Borgo'). This poem recalls a poorly-attended midweek game in Padua (where the poet was visiting), with the home team seeking to avoid relegation to a lower division (*Prose*, pp. 592-93).

1-2:   The emphasis is on spectators and atmosphere rather than the game itself: their huddling together for warmth emphasising the sense of solidarity sought by the poet; '**manipolo sparuto**': sparse group.

3-6:   The onset of dusk increases the somewhat bleak atmosphere; '**raggera**': radiance, halo; '**barbaglio**': glow. However, in the half-light the pitch itself 'brightens' ('**schiarì**') the sense of encroaching darkness.

7-11:   The description of the game is limited to broadly sketched movements of the different coloured '**maglie**' (shirts), overseen by blind Fortune ('**benda**': blindfold; '**si rimetteva**': presumably having briefly favoured one side, she resumes her impartiality). The emphasis on the imagery of light, with its strange iridescence, may be seen as a further reflection of the more 'lyrical' tendency of this phase in Saba's work.

12-16: The poet's gaze turns firmly again towards the spectators ('**intirizziti**': frozen), where he finds pleasure in the feeling of community ('**uniti**'), but also a hint of a privileged status: we are left with a miniature apocalyptic fantasy as these 'few' glimpse, in this struggle in the gathering darkness, some ultimate truth beyond normal reality ('**di là**').

"Frutta erbaggi"

Erbe, frutta, colori della bella
stagione. Poche ceste ove alla sete
si rivelano dolci polpe crude.

Entra un fanciullo colle gambe nude,
imperioso, fugge via.   5
                 S'oscura
l'umile botteguccia, invecchia come
una madre.
                 Di fuori egli nel sole
si allontana, con l'ombra sua, leggero.   10

"Frutta erbaggi"

This poem's subject matter is drawn from the real world of sensory experience and human presences, but it is treated with a concision not found in some of Saba's earlier work. The title, in quote marks, is the cry or shop-sign of a greengrocer.

1-3: The greengrocer's wares are presented with simple realism, but also with a notable sensuality, as objects of desire (**'sete'**), revealing secret delights, both **'dolci'** and **'crude'** (**'ceste'**: baskets; **'polpe'**: flesh of fruit).

4-5: The appearance and departure of a young boy seems a disjointed element, but can be read as another image of natural, vital energy. (There is perhaps, in the **'gambe nude'** and the admiring **'imperioso'** a hint of the homoerotic theme that emerges elsewhere in Saba's work – see Baldoni).

6-8: The shop (**'botteguccia'**, subject of both verbs here) seems bereft at the boy's departure, and the analogy with a sad, ageing mother points to a hidden theme, that of the poet's complex relationship with his own mother, which includes feelings of guilt and inadequacy: 'riprende il tema della madre […] e del fanciullo, il bel 'fanciullo imperioso' che Saba avrebbe voluto essere stato' (*Prose*, p. 605).

9-10: The closing imagery of light and lightness suggests an uncomplicated, direct participation in life which is surely more of an aspiration than a reality for the poet (whose own **'ombra'** is more of a burden).

From *1944*

Teatro degli Artigianelli

Falce martello e la stella d'Italia
ornano nuovi la sala. Ma quanto
dolore per quel segno su quel muro!

Entra, sorretto dalle grucce, il Prologo.
Saluta al pugno; dice sue parole   5
perché le donne ridano e i fanciulli
che affollano la povera platea.
Dice, timido ancora, dell'idea
che gli animi affrattella; chiude: "E adesso
faccio come i tedeschi, mi ritiro".   10
Tra un atto e l'altro, alla Cantina, in giro
rosseggia parco ai bicchieri l'amico
dell'uomo, cui rimargina ferite,
gli chiude solchi dolorosi; alcuno
venuto qui da spaventosi esigli,   15
si scalda a lui come chi ha freddo al sole.

Questo è il Teatro degli Artigianelli,
quale lo vide il poeta nel mille
novecentoquarantaquattro, un giorno
di Settembre, che a tratti   20
rombava ancora il cannone, e Firenze
taceva, assorta nelle sue rovine.

Teatro degli Artigianelli

Saba spent the winter of 1943-44 in Florence, living in hiding for fear of deportation (as a Jew) by the Nazis (among those who supported him were Carlo Levi and Eugenio Montale). This is one of a short group of poems written immediately after the liberation of the city. Here the events of history are intertwined in a direct narrative realism with Saba's individual perspective, in a poem that is, in his own words, both 'epic' and 'lyric'.

1-3:   The star (placed beside the hammer and sickle) was interpreted by Saba at the time as that of the Italian national emblem, which, to his satisfaction, he saw aligned here with the emblems of the communist Resistance; until it was pointed out to him later that this was probably the Soviet star, used by the PCI (*Prose*, p. 618); **'sala'**: auditorium. In any case, the presence of these emblems during a theatrical performance (apparently organized by the Communist party) is the visible sign of new freedoms, but also a reminder of the terrible suffering endured (ll. 2-3).

4-7:   The **'Prologo'**, speaker of the play's prologue, appears to be a war casualty (**'sorretto dalle grucce'**: supported on crutches). **'Saluta al pugno'**: the communist clenched-fist salute. His speech is initially light-hearted, and is addressed to a working-class audience (**'povera platea'**) predominantly of women and children.

8-10:   As though still uncertain of the freedom to speak, he tells of the communist ideal, the idea that 'brings souls [people] together as brothers' (**'idea'** is the subject of **'affrattella'**), before leaving the stage with a humorous jibe at the expense of the retreating Germans.

11-13: Wine, **'l'amico dell'uomo'**, is distributed at the interval. **'parco'** (adj.): frugal, scarce (referring to 'l'amico'); thus: '… all around wine frugally reddens glasses…'. The somewhat rhetorical language and use of complex syntactic structures in these and the following lines is typical of Saba's stylistic conservatism.

13-14: **'cui'**: a cui (i.e. all'uomo), thus: '…to whom [i.e. man] it [wine] heals wounds, closes painful scars'.

14-16: **'alcuno'**: archaic form for 'qualcuno', possibly referring to the poet himself, or to the many others emerging from different forms of 'exile' (**'esigli'**) or hiding. **'lui'**: wine (as personified as a 'friend' above), which provides a humane comfort and warmth. More than the abstract political ideal mentioned earlier, it is this shared experience of simple conviviality that embodies the poet's human values.

17-22: The perspective opens up to include the broader sweep of historical events, including the visibly 'objective' or prosaic elements of date and place, but also a reminder of the individual's subjective perception: **'quale lo vide il poeta'**; **'a tratti rombava…'**: at times the cannon still roared. The final image (Florence suffered heavy damage at the hands of the retreating German forces) closes the poem on a more meditative, introspective note; **'assorta'**: pensive, self-absorbed.

From *Mediterranee* (1945-1946)

Amai

Amai trite parole che non uno
osava. M'incantò la rima fiore
amore,
la più antica difficile del mondo.

Amai la verità che giace al fondo,   5
quasi un sogno obliato, che il dolore
riscopre amica. Con paura il cuore
le si accosta, che più non l'abbandona.

Amo te che mi ascolti e la mia buona
carta lasciata al fine del mio gioco.   10

Amai

Coming towards the end of his poetic career this poem is a sort of artistic testament or retrospective statement of poetics, and presents some of Saba's most memorable interpretative declarations on his own work.

1-4: The title (*passato remoto* of *amare*, repeated in each of the stanzas) foregrounds a human, emotional response to the world as a defining characteristic of Saba's approach. The tensions between, on the one hand, **'trite'**/ **'antica'** and, on the other, **'non uno osava'**/ **'difficile'** point to a basic paradox in Saba's work: the more conventional, trite or 'easy' his linguistic and stylistic choices, the more 'daring' they are and the more 'difficult' it is to write without descending into cliché and banality. The point is exemplified in the 'enchanting' rhyme *fiore-amore* (used for example in 'Trieste'). **'non uno osava'**: highlights Saba's sense of individuality and artistic isolation.

5-8: The more 'difficult' aspect of Saba's poetry includes the desire to uncover hidden 'truths' in the 'depths' (**'fondo'**) of the psyche (the allusion to 'forgotten dreams' recalls his experience of psychoanalysis). The idea of truth is central here: though it involves **'dolore'** and **'paura'**, these are part of a process of discovering truth as **'amica'** and clinging fast to it (the relative pronoun **'che'** in l.6 and the indirect pronoun **'le'** in l.8 refer back to **'la verità'**). Note the further 'easy' rhyme *dolore-cuore*.

9-10: The poet addresses the reader directly, reflecting the strongly communicative vein throughout his work, and expresses also his faith that this communicative openness is reciprocated (**'mi ascolti'**). Finally, the object of his love is his poetry itself, seen metaphorically as the best 'card' left at the end of the 'game' (the slight ambiguity in **'carta'** – card or paper – emphasises the metaphorical reference to writing). **'fine'**: usually feminine, can also be masculine when used in the sense of outcome or result.

4

Eugenio Montale (1896-1981)

Montale's poetry occupies a central position in the Italian 20th-century canon. His work ranges over six decades, spanning from the period of high modernism, coinciding with his creative peak, to that of the neo-avantgarde experimentalism of the 1960s and '70s, when, as a seemingly aloof and disenchanted observer, he continued nevertheless to participate in contemporary poetic discourse.[i]

A native of Genoa, Montale spent the summers of his youth at Monterosso in the Cinque terre on the Ligurian coast, an area whose landscape suffuses his early work. *Ossi di seppia* (1925) is an extended dialogue with that landscape and with a number of (largely unidentified) *tu* figures, as the poet's persona struggles to construct meaning in a world of bewildering natural phenomena and other mysterious presences. Montale gives us a harsh, uncompromising vision, obstinately refusing certainties and eschewing any ornamental lyrical effusion, rejecting the exotic flora favoured by 'poeti laureati' (an ironic allusion to D'Annunzio) in favour of the humbler plants of his own dessicated landscape, leading the reader down country pathways ('le strade che riescono agli erbosi / fossi dove in pozzanghere / mezzo seccate agguantano i ragazzi / qualche sparuta anguilla') to find the pungent intensity of the lemon groves ('I limoni'). While the vast presence of the sea seems sporadically to promise some other dimension, what Montale's verse reveals is the void, the absence of meaning beneath the appearances of the physical world. The frustrations and hostility of that world (but also its crumbling disintegration) are conveyed through a richly dissonant musicality, as Montale (in his own words) seeks to 'wring the neck' of the centuries-old tradition of lyrical eloquence in the Italian poetic idiom.[ii]

In 1927 Montale moved to Florence, and his second collection, *Le occasioni* (1939), reflects this geographical change, but also his growing sense of alienation from historical and political developments in Fascist Italy (he was one of the signatories of Benedetto Croce's Manifesto degli intellettuali antifascisti in 1925).[iii] The scenario of his poems becomes increasingly one of urban landscapes and interiors, in which human figures, especially the female *tu*, appear in moments of personal crisis, of leavetakings and absences, clinging desperately to private meanings in an atmosphere of deepening gloom. In this collection, and especially in its central section *Mottetti*, the poet's persona entrusts his own salvation to the figure of the beloved, inspired (among others) by the young American scholar Irma Brandeis who first came to meet Montale in Florence in 1933.[iv] The story of their tortuous relationship is revealed through glimpses of a private drama, but she is also gradually transformed into an allegorical figure of hope for collective redemption, a transposition of the angel-woman of the medieval poetic tradition into a modern secular key. The highly-elliptical, intense and sometimes obscure character of Montale's verse during these years can be seen as having an indirect relationship with the poetic habitat he shared with the emerging Florentine hermetic generation. However, Montale's poetry does not share the hermetics' tendentially mystical pursuit of lyrical purity, but finds its centre of gravity in a difficult, conflictual relationship between the *io* and historical reality, a relationship expressed often in allegorical modes.[v]

The allegorical transformation of the beloved woman comes to a head in Montale's third collection, *La bufera e altro* (1954), where, under the name of Clizia, she eventually becomes a wholly disembodied presence visiting the poet's persona in the dark years of the war (the 'storm' of the title). However, in the changed political context of post-war Italy, after a brief period of optimistic *impegno*, when the poet harboured hopes for a new dawn, 'per tutti' (see 'La primavera hitleriana', not included here below), the myth of Clizia, the expectation of future salvation, collapses. Instead the poet's search for meaning and authenticity switches to the here-and-now, the earthly world of the senses, where images of flight and quasi-spiritual elevation find a new counterpart in those of a terrestrial and earthy sensuality, embodied by the eel's writhing in the mud of fertility (see 'L'anguilla') and, subsequently, encapsulated in a passionate cycle of poems dedicated to a new muse, 'la Volpe' (the young poet Maria Luisa Spaziani, whom Montale met in 1949).[vi]

With the publication of *La bufera*, however, there began a period of poetic silence for Montale, lasting almost a decade. Now a prominent national figure, he had moved to Milan in 1948, where he became a regular contributor to the pages of the *Corriere della sera*, writing many reviews and essays on contemporary literature, art and culture, as well as a substantial number of short narrative prose pieces (a selection of which were published in 1956 as

Farfalla di Dinard). It was only after the death in 1963 of his long-term partner Drusilla Tanzi (known affectionately as Mosca) that Montale began to write verse again in earnest, composing the poems of *Xenia* in her memory, poems which were published initially in 1966 and subsequently subsumed into *Satura* (1971).[vii] This collection marks a fundamental formal and thematic renewal in Montale's verse. After the intensely emblematic style of his first three collections, which had in many ways helped to define the parameters of the Italian lyric genre throughout the mid-century period, he now appears in the unexpected guise of ironic diarist, by turns satirical, prosaic and polemical, showing, in his own words, 'il rovescio della medaglia', the other 'face' of his work, the 'retrobottega' or back-room of the poet's workshop.[viii] In this book, and those that followed through the 1970s, Montale debunked his own poetic myths, while casting a disillusioned eye over a vast range of contemporary issues and events. This new voice, no matter how recognizably personal in its notes of detachment and aristocratic disdain for the contemporary world, owes something also to the wider renewal of poetic forms underway with the work of a younger generation in the neo-avantgarde movements of the 1960s and beyond. Thus Montale, by now the unofficial poet laureate of the post-war Italian Republic (with the international recognition given by the award of the Nobel Prize in 1975) challenged his readers' expectations and assumptions up to the end (and indeed beyond, through the practical joke of the posthumous poems released over several years and collected in *Diario postumo* in 1996).

Endnotes

i   On Montale's centrality in the canon, see Romano Luperini, 'Montale e il canone poetico del Novecento italiano', in *Montale e il canone poetico del Novecento*, ed. by Maria Antonietta Grignani and Romano Luperini (Roma-Bari: Laterza, 1998), pp. 361-68.

ii   See 'Intenzioni: intervista immaginaria', now in Montale, *Il secondo mestiere: arte, musica, società* (Milan: Mondadori, 1996), pp. 1475-84 (p. 1480).

iii   For biographical details see 'Cronologia' in *Tutte le poesie*, ed. by Giorgio Zampa (Milan: Mondadori, 1991).

iv   See 'Cronologia' in *Tutte le poesie*. See also Marco Forti's introduction to *Per conoscere Montale*, rev. edn (Milan: Mondadori, 1986): Giulio Nascimbeni, *Montale: biografia di un poeta* (Milan: Longanesi, 1986); Franco Contorbia (ed.), *Eugenio Montale: immagini di una vita* (Milan: Mondadori, 1996); and Eugenio Montale, *Lettere a Clizia*, ed. by R. Bettarini, G. Manghetti, F. Zabagli (Milan: Mondadori, 2006).

v   On the allegorical nature of Montale's work, see Angelo Jacomuzzi, *La poesia di*

Montale: dagli 'Ossi' ai 'Diari' (Turin: Einaudi, 1978), pp. 69-74; and Romano Luperini, 'Note sull'allegorismo novecentesco: il caso di Montale', *Paragone (Letteratura)* 39 (1988), 54-76. See also Luperini, *Storia di Montale* (Rome-Bari: Laterza, 1986).

vi   Silvio Guarnieri recalls seeing Montale rejuvenated and energized by the relationship with Spaziani: see Guarnieri, *L'ultimo testimone* (Milan: Mondadori, 1989), pp. 51-55.

vii   On the development, themes and style of *Xenia* see Maria Antonietta Grignani, 'Storia di *Xenia*', in *Prologhi ed epiloghi sulla poesia di Eugenio Montale* (Ravenna: Longo, 1987), pp. 85-115.

viii   See interview with Annalisa Cima, 'Le reazioni di Montale', in Annalisa Cima and Cesare Segre, eds, *Eugenio Montale: Profilo di un autore* (Milan: Rizzoli, 1977), pp. 192-201 (p. 192). On the later work in general, see Éanna Ó Ceallacháin, *Eugenio Montale: The poetry of the Later Years* (Oxford: Legenda, 2001).

Poetic texts

There are two complete editions:
L'opera in versi, a cura di Rosanna Bettarini and Gianfranco Contini (Turin: Einaudi, 1980);
Tutte le poesie, a cura di Giorgio Zampa, I Meridiani (Milan: Mondadori, 1991).

These bring together the individual collections:
Ossi di seppia (1925); *Le occasioni* (1939); *La bufera e altro* (1956); *Satura* (1971); *Diario del '71 e del '72* (1973); *Quaderno di quattro anni* (1977); *Altri versi* (1981).

See also the excellent bilingual annotated edition:
Collected poems 1920-1954, translated and annotated by Jonathan Galassi (New York: Farrar, Straus and Giroux, 1998)

Useful notes are also found in:
Selected Poems, ed. by George Talbot (Dublin: UCD Foundation for Italian Studies, 2000);
Le occasioni, a cura di Dante Isella (Turin: Einaudi, 1996).

Prose texts

Prose e racconti, a cura di Marco Forti, I Meridiani (Milan: Mondadori, 1996)
Il secondo mestiere: arte, musica, società, a cura di Giorgio Zampa, I Meridiani (Milan: Mondadori, 1996)
Il secondo mestiere: Prose 1920-1979, a cura di Giorgio Zampa, I Meridiani (Milan: Mondadori, 1996)

Further reading

The critical bibliography on Montale is vast. The following are some of the more useful critical studies (including some of the main works in English), as well as indications of sources cited in the notes.

A number of important **conference proceedings** are:
Il secolo di Montale: Genova 1896-1996 (Bologna: Il Mulino, 1998)
La poesia di Eugenio Montale: atti del Convegno Internazionale, Milano 12/13/14 settembre, Genova 15 settembre 1982 (Milan: Librex, 1983)
La poesia di Eugenio Montale: atti del Convegno Internazionale tenuto a Genova dal 25 al 28 novembre 1982 (Florence: Le Monnier, 1984)
Letture montaliane in occasione dell'80° compleanno del poeta (Genoa: Bozzi, 1977)

Other sources:
Almansi, Guido, and Bruce Merry, *Eugenio Montale: The Private Language of Poetry* (Edinburgh, Edinburgh University Press, 1977).

Avalle, D'Arco Silvio, *Tre saggi su Montale* (Turin: Einaudi, 1972)

Becker, Jared, *Eugenio Montale* (Boston: Twayne, 1986)

Brook, Clodagh, *The expression of the inexpressible in Eugenio Montale's poetry: metaphor, negation, and silence* (Oxford: Oxford University Press, 2002)

Cambon, Glauco, *Eugenio Montale's poetry: A Dream in Reason's Presence* (Princeton: Princeton University Press, 1982)

Cataldi, Pietro, *Montale* (Palermo: Palumbo, 1991)

Cima, Annalisa, and Cesare Segre, eds, *Eugenio Montale: Profilo di un autore* (Milan: Rizzoli, 1977).

Contorbia, Franco, ed., *Eugenio Montale: immagini di una vita* (Milan: Mondadori, 1996)

Croce, Franco, *Storia della poesia di Eugenio Montale* (Genoa: Costa & Nolan, 1991).

Forti, Marco, ed., *Per conoscere Montale*, rev. edn (Milan: Mondadori, 1986)

Greco, Lorenzo, *Montale commenta Montale*, 2nd edn (Parma: Pratiche, 1980)

Grignani, Maria Antonietta, *Prologhi ed epiloghi sulla poesia di Eugenio Montale* (Ravenna: Longo, 1987)

Grignani, Maria Antonietta, and Romano Luperini, eds, *Montale e il canone poetico del Novecento*, (Roma-Bari: Laterza, 1998)

Guarnieri, *L'ultimo testimone* (Milan: Mondadori, 1989)

Jacomuzzi, Angelo, *La poesia di Montale: dagli 'Ossi' ai 'Diari'* (Turin: Einaudi, 1978)

Luperini, Romano, 'Note sull'allegorismo novecentesco: il caso di Montale', *Paragone (Letteratura)* 39 (1988), 54-76

Luperini, Romano, *Storia di Montale* (Rome-Bari: Laterza, 1986)

Marchese, Angelo, *Visiting angel: intepretazione semiologica della poesia di Montale* (Turin: SEI, 1977).

Mengaldo, Pier Vincenzo, 'Da D'Annunzio a Montale', in *La tradizione del Novecento* (Milan: Feltrinelli, 1975), pp. 13-106

Montale, Eugenio, *Lettere a Clizia*, ed. by R. Bettarini, G. Manghetti, F. Zabagli (Milan: Mondadori, 2006)

Nascimbeni, Giulio, *Montale: biografia di un poeta* (Milan: Longanesi, 1986)

Ó Ceallacháin, Éanna, *Eugenio Montale: The poetry of the Later Years* (Oxford: Legenda, 2001).

Pellini, Pierluigi, 'L'ultimo Montale: donne miracoli treni telefoni sciopero generale', *Nuova corrente*, 39 (1992) 289-324.

Spaziani, Maria Luisa, 'Un carteggio inedito di Montale', in *La poesia di Eugenio Montale: atti del Convegno Internazionale tenuto a Genova dal 25 al 28 novembre 1982* (Florence: Le Monnier, 1984), pp. 321-24

Talbot, George, and Doug Thompson, eds, *Montale: Words in Time* (Market Harborough: Troubador, 1998)

West, Rebecca, *Eugenio Montale: Poet on the Edge* (Cambridge: Harvard University Press, 1981)

Zambon, Francesco, *L'iride nel fango: L'anguilla di Eugenio Montale* (Parma: Pratiche, 1994)

Contents

From *Ossi di seppia* (1925)

Non chiederci la parola che squadri da ogni lato
l'animo nostro informe, e a lettere di fuoco
lo dichiari e risplenda come un croco
perduto in mezzo a un polveroso prato.

Ah l'uomo che se ne va sicuro,   5
agli altri ed a se stesso amico,
e l'ombra sua non cura che la canicola
stampa sopra uno scalcinato muro!

Non domandarci la formula che mondi possa aprirti,
sì qualche storta sillaba e secca come un ramo.   10
Codesto solo oggi possiamo dirti,
ciò che *non* siamo, ciò che *non* vogliamo.

'Non chiederci la parola...'

This is the first in a series of twenty-two untitled poems that form the central section of *Ossi di seppia* (the series bears the same title as the collection itself). This text, with its forceful refusal of certainties, its unwillingness to offer easy formulae and its resolute negativity (all centred on the functions of language itself), can be read as a poetic and philosophical manifesto for Montale's work.

1-3:   **'squadri'** ('square off'), **'dichiari'**, **'risplenda'**: verbs in the present subjunctive, all sharing the subject **'la parola'**, indicating what such a hypothetical 'word' *might* do, if it could be offered.

4:      The desolate reality of the world, where no such resplendent truth is found (**'croco'**: crocus).

5-8:   The poet indicates what he is *not* (cf. l. 12): the self-assured individual, untroubled by doubt or by his shadow (an image of all that is undefinable and shifting) cast on a 'crumbling' wall; **'canicola'**: here, high summer sunshine.

9-10:   **'che mondi possa aprirti'**: 'that *might* open up worlds for you' (present subjunctive); **'sì'**: 'rather'. The harsh consonantal effects in line 10 typify Montale's refusal of any melodious lyricism.

11-12: Encapsulating the unwavering scepticism and negativity of Montale's early work, this is frequently read as an implicit statement of dissent from the ascendant ideology of Fascism (the poem was written in 1923). The use of the first person plural, unusual within Montale's opus, has also lent itself to interpretation as expressing the collective voice of a generation of intellectuals.

Meriggiare pallido e assorto
presso un rovente muro d'orto,
ascoltare tra i pruni e gli sterpi
schiocchi di merli, frusci di serpi.

Nelle crepe del suolo o su la veccia   5
spiar le file di rosse formiche
ch'ora si rompono ed ora s'intrecciano
a sommo di minuscole biche.

Osservare tra frondi il palpitare
lontano di scaglie di mare   10
mentre si levano tremuli scricchi
di cicale dai calvi picchi.

E andando nel sole che abbaglia
sentire con triste meraviglia
com'è tutta la vita e il suo travaglio   15
in questo seguitare una muraglia
che ha in cima cocci aguzzi di bottiglia.

'Meriggiare pallido e assorto...'

This is the definitive and best-known depiction of Montale's physical and figurative landscape in *Ossi di seppia* (and, according to the poet, the earliest, dating to 1916). The poetic persona is no more than a suggested presence through the infinitive verb forms, as the landscape itself takes centre stage, with its typical elements of burning heat, harsh and inexplicable flora and fauna, and the key image of an insurmountable barrier.

1-4: '**Meriggiare**': from 'meriggio' (noon), meaning 'to noon', to experience noontime; '**assorto**': self-absorbed; '**rovente**': burning hot; '**pruni... sterpi**': thorny bushes; '**schiocchi**': the blackbird's characteristic clucking cry of alarm, a highly-onomatopoeic element, along with the snakes' '**frusci**' (rustling)

5-8: On the cracked, arid earth, interweaving lines of ants provide evidence of an intense but unsettling and enigmatic vitality permeating the landscape; '**veccia**': vetch (plant); '**biche**': small heaps (of vegetation). Within the rich phonic texture of the poem (mostly resolved into perfect end-rhymes), the hypermetric rhyme *veccia: s'intrecciano* injects an element of dissonance and instability.

9-12: The other major element in the Montalean landscape, the sea, is a barely-glimpsed presence here, and yet it too seems a threatening, scaly, living entity ('**scaglie**': scales). Meanwhile the auditory canvas is completed with a striking depiction (through rhythmic deployment of *c* and *i* sounds) of the cicadas' screeching song ('**scricchi**') that pervades the Mediterranean midday heat; '**calvi picchi**': bare peaks.

13-17: '**com'è tutta... / in questo seguitare...**': 'how all of life and its suffering is [summed up] in this act of following a high wall'. The figurative sense of the persona's experience is brought into the foreground as his continuing walk alongside an apparently endless barrier becomes an image of a profound existential frustration, of the tragic impossibility of reaching any true understanding of the world. Meanwhile, the surrounding physical reality remains unrelentingly negative and hostile. Note the continuing discordant effects of the rhyme/assonance sequence *–aglia /-iglia /-aglio* and the grating onomatopoeia of the closing line; '**cocci aguzzi**': sharp fragments.

Forse un mattino andando in un'aria di vetro,
arida, rivolgendomi, vedrò compirsi il miracolo:
il nulla alle mie spalle, il vuoto dietro
di me, con un terrore di ubriaco.

Poi, come s'uno schermo, s'accamperanno di gitto   5
alberi case colli per l'inganno consueto.
Ma sarà troppo tardi; ed io me n'andrò zitto
tra gli uomini che non si voltano, col mio segreto.

'Forse un mattino andando...'

A recurring element in *Ossi* is the hypothesis of some 'miracle', some 'accident of nature' or 'broken mesh in the net' (see 'In limine') that might allow an escape from everyday experience of life, an insight into the true nature of existence. Here, in a kind of philosophical fantasy, as the *io* turns around to glimpse the 'miraculous' event, such a moment is posited, only to be revealed as deeply problematic, as the physical world is seen to be a mere illusion. (For a reading of this poem, see Calvino's essay in *Letture montaliane*.)

1-4:   '**Forse**': a Montalean word par excellence, encapsulating his perennial uncertainty. What follows is both inebriating and terrifying, as the poet's vision unveils the vertiginous void behind perceived reality. The longed-for truth is in fact complete emptiness, an absence of any truth; '**compirsi**': to come true, come to pass.

5-8:   Even as the poet's persona momentarily catches the vision of the void, the illusion of normal perception rushes back into place as if on a 'screen'; '**s'accamperanno di gitto**': 'will suddenly take their place'; '**l'inganno consueto**': customary illusion. Once glimpsed, however, the truth cannot be unlearned: it leaves the *io* privileged with his 'secret' insight, but also fatally isolated, '**zitto**', unable to communicate with others; '**gli uomini che non si voltano**': the unreflecting others (echoing 'l'uomo che se ne va sicuro' of 'Non chiederci...'), viewed with a sense superior detachment, an aristocratic disdain for the masses which Montale would repeatedly express through his career.

From *Mediterraneo*

Avrei voluto sentirmi scabro ed essenziale
siccome i ciottoli che tu volvi,
mangiati dalla salsedine;
scheggia fuori del tempo, testimone
di una volontà fredda che non passa.   5
Altro fui: uomo intento che riguarda
in sé, in altrui, il bollore
della vita fugace – uomo che tarda
all'atto, che nessuno, poi, distrugge.
Volli cercare il male   10
che tarla il mondo, la piccola stortura
d'una leva che arresta
l'ordegno universale; e tutti vidi
gli eventi del minuto
come pronti a disgiungersi in un crollo.   15
Seguìto il solco d'un sentiero m'ebbi
l'opposto in cuore, col suo invito; e forse
m'occorreva il coltello che recide,
la mente che decide e si determina.
Altri libri occorrevano   20
a me, non la tua pagina rombante.
Ma nulla so rimpiangere: tu sciogli
ancora i groppi interni col tuo canto.
Il tuo delirio sale agli astri ormai.

'Avrei voluto sentirmi scabro ed essenziale...'

Part of 'Mediterraneo', a sequence of nine poems in which Montale conducts an ambivalent dialogue with the sea, an image that embodies an elemental life force, an unrestrained energy, that seems to both attract and repel the poet's persona, but also admonishes him for his inadequacy. Below the surface of this exchange lurks, almost certainly, an equally ambivalent dialogue with the lyrical voice of D'Annunzio, whose musical power fascinates Montale but whose ecstatic embracing of nature goes against the grain of Montale's self-conscious restraint. (See Mengaldo, 'Da D'Annunzio a Montale', pp. 79-82).

1-5:   The *io* aspires to a different relationship with the world, a somehow purifying immersion in life, as a pebble worn by the **'salsedine'** (sea-salt; an image also reminiscent of the cuttlefish bones of the collection's title). This is no comforting vision however, as seen in terms like **'scabro'** (rough), **'mangiati'**, **'scheggia'** (shard): the result could be a kind of erosion or loss of the self, in surrendering to the cold power of nature; **'ciottoli'**: pebbles; **'volvi'**: turn over.

6-9:   Even as he seems to regret his lack of communion with the sea, the poet affirms his true characteristics of self-consciousness and reflective observation. **'uomo che tarda / all'atto'**: hesitancy is a common feature of the modernist anti-hero; **'bollore'**: boiling, agitation.

10-15: **'Volli'**: pass. remoto of *volere*. These lines echo other poems in *Ossi* where Montale imagines the moment of penetrating beyond the appearances of the physical world, where 'uno sbaglio di natura ... l'anello che non tiene' might reveal an ultimate truth ('I limoni' – but see also 'Forse un mattino'). Rather than enjoying any union with nature, he is deeply sceptical about the reality of the physical world in time, seen as a machine on the verge of disintegration; **'tarla'**: 'eats away' (denoting the action of a woodworm, suggesting a structure undermined from within); **'stortura'**: mistake, or crookedness; **'leva'**: lever; **'tutti vidi'**: inversion of 'vidi tutti'; **'disgiungersi'**: disintegrate.

16-19: **'Seguito...'**: past participle: 'having followed the track...'. Montale's characteristic stance of indecisiveness would, he seems to suggest, have benefitted from the sharp 'knife' of mental certainty (but he has rejected precisely such decisiveness in 'Non chiederci la parola').

20-21: He recognizes the difference between his words (the 'books' that he 'needed') and the 'roaring' (**'rombante'**) language of the sea, though not without ambiguity, as the tone hovers between pride and regret.

22-24: Regret is swept aside as the poem closes on a note of ecstatic abandon. The *io* surrenders his doubts (**'groppi'**: knots) to the lyrical power of the sea; **'astri'**: stars. Yet there is perhaps a note of excess or inauthenticity in the term **'delirio'**. (Indeed, this romantic effusion is soon superseded by a more measured conclusion in the final poem in the sequence.)

From *Le occasioni* (1939)

A Liuba che parte

Non il grillo ma il gatto
del focolare
or ti consiglia, splendido
lare della dispersa tua famiglia.
La casa che tu rechi   5
con te ravvolta, gabbia o cappelliera?,
sovrasta i ciechi tempi come il flutto
arca leggera – e basta al tuo riscatto.

A Liuba che parte

Liuba is one of a number of enigmatic, tormented female figures of Central European origin to appear in *Le occasioni*, figures that cling to totemic objects in which their sense of identity and hopes for survival are invested (see also 'Dora Markus' and 'Carnevale di Gerti'). In a brief note added to post-war editions, Montale specifies that Liuba (like Dora Markus) was Jewish and describes the piece as 'the ending of a poem never written' (*L'opera in versi*, p. 899). The real woman, Liuba Blumenthal, left Florence in 1938 and settled in London (see Ó Ceallacháin, pp. 179-80). The poem is a masterpiece of lightness and understatement when considered against the background of the historical 'occasion', the enactment of the 1938 race laws (for further readings, see Avalle and the Isella edition of *Occasioni*).

1-4:   **'il grillo'**: refers to a traditional Florentine festival during which caged crickets were sold (and may perhaps allude to Pinocchio's 'grillo parlante', whose role also was to give counsel). Here, however, the putative cricket is supplanted by a cat, transformed in turn into a kind of domestic deity; **'focolare'**: fireplace; **'lare'**: ancient Roman family divinity and protector of the home; **'or'**: 'ora'; **'dispersa'**: the reference to the 'scattered' family suggests an idea of vulnerability and gains great poignancy with the added knowledge of her Jewish background.

5-6:   The enigmatic opening is partly explained here with the suggestion that Liuba may be carrying a cat in cage or hat-box (which thus becomes also **'la casa'**, a kind of portable embodiment of 'home'); **'rechi'**: carry.

7-8:   This miniature travelling home is transformed into a protective 'ark', whose very 'lightness' allows it to ride over (**'sovrastare'**) the waves, which in turn are an image of the 'blind times', an indirect but effective formulation of the menacing political background. This fragile but resilient ark of personal values and identity ensures her **'riscatto'** (redemption).

From *Mottetti*

Lo sai: debbo riperderti e non posso.
Come un tiro aggiustato mi sommuove
ogni opera, ogni grido e anche lo spiro
salino che straripa
dai moli e fa l'oscura primavera   5
di Sottoripa.

Paese di ferrame e alberature
a selva nella polvere del vespro.
Un ronzìo lungo viene dall'aperto,
strazia com'unghia ai vetri. Cerco il segno   10
smarrito, il pegno solo ch'ebbi in grazia
da te.
      E l'inferno è certo.

'Lo sai: debbo riperderti e non posso...'

At the centre of *Le occasioni* is a sequence of 20 short untitled poems that form, in Montale's words, 'un romanzetto autobiografico', the story of an obsessive love (*Il secondo mestiere: arte, musica, società*, p. 1490). The term 'motet' (originally a form of thirteenth-century polyphonic sacred music) reflects the fact that Montale's use of love poetry in these years owes much to the medieval tradition, especially the *dolce stil novo*, in which the beloved woman, remote and idealized, is a source of spiritual elevation. The sequence as a whole is dedicated to the figure eventually known as 'Clizia', inspired by the American Irma Brandeis, with whom Montale had an intermittent relationship from 1933-39 and who comes to embody poetically his yearning for a salvation that is both personal and political. (The fact that the first three 'mottetti' involve a different *ispiratrice* does not affect the poetic unity of the sequence, with its overall sense of development from a human to a transcendent love; see Ó Ceallacháin, 180-81). This opening poem establishes the scenario of an intense, tortured love story, marked by repeated leavetakings, in which the *io* is 'besieged' by the 'absence/presence' of the woman (*Il secondo mestiere: arte, musica, società*, p. 1490).

1: **'debbo'**: less common form of 'devo'. The juxtaposition of this with **'non posso'** immediately sets up the sense of an unbearable tension.

2-6: Each sensory impression of the city 'shakes' the *io* (**'mi sommuove'**); **'un tiro aggiustato'**: a well-aimed shot; **'lo spiro / salino'**: the salty 'breath' of the sea air; **'straripa'**: spills over; **'l'oscura primavera'**: this almost oxymoronic phrase creates an atmosphere of gloom and foreboding; **'Sottoripa'** (in the port area of Genoa) gives the poem a precise urban setting.

7-8: The port/industrial landscape: **'ferrame'**: iron materials; **'alberature'**: ships masts; **'a selva'**: like a forest. The dense assonance of l.8 is typical of Montale's phonic patterns (see also the network of assonance around the sounds of *'rip-'* / *'st-'* etc. in stanza 1); **'la polvere del vespro'**: intensifies the sense of gloomy desolation.

9-10: The situation of the poet's persona in an interior setting, besieged by a hostile world outside, is a recurring one in Montale (see Marchese, *Visiting angel*, pp. 111-19). The exact nature of the **'ronzio'** (some 'buzzing' sound) is unclear, but it is certainly unwelcome, as seen in the grating onomatopeia of l.10 (**'straziare'**: to torture).

10-12: The figurative implications of the woman's absence begin to emerge, as he now searches for a lost token of 'grace' (**'pegno'**: pledge). The Dantesque overtones become explicit in the closing line: the poet's persona is trapped in a 'hellish' scenario. In this context, many poems in *Le occasioni* involve the search for 'signs' or epiphanies of the woman, indicators of possible salvation.

Addii, fischi nel buio, cenni, tosse
e sportelli abbassati. È l'ora. Forse
gli automi hanno ragione. Come appaiono
dai corridoi, murati!

. . . .

– Presti anche tu alla fioca   5
litania del tuo rapido quest'orrida
e fedele cadenza di carioca? –

'Addii, fischi nel buio, cenni, tosse...'

1-2:   'Motet' no. 5, another leave-taking scene, with fleeting sound and sight impressions of a railway station as a train is about to depart: **'cenni'**: waves; **'sportelli abbassati'**: train windows lowered into the closed position (Isella, p. 87; this anticipates the **'murati'** of l. 4); **'È l'ora'**: the sense of time running out is a recurring motif in this collection.

3-4:   **'gli automi'**: the robots, an image of the unthinking masses (like 'gli uomini che non si voltano'), here literally 'walled in'; a vision of a mechanized, alienating world which, perhaps, is gaining the upper hand as the beloved is carried off and the *io* left alone.

The line of dots following indicates something omitted, perhaps something too private, too intense. The omission leaves the closing lines strangely isolated:

5-7:   The *io* clutches desperately at some continuing 'sign' of the beloved, in this case the imagined sound of the **'carioca'** in the rhythm of the departing train wheels (a rhythm which she too, perhaps, 'lends' to the sound of the train); **'rapido'**: a category of fast train; **'carioca'**: a type of Brazilian dance music popular in the 1930s (here it is both **'orrida e fedele'**, in keeping with the unbearable tension suffusing the 'Mottetti').

=

Ti libero la fronte dai ghiaccioli
che raccogliesti traversando l'alte
nebulose; hai le penne lacerate
dai cicloni, ti desti a soprassalti.

Mezzodì: allunga nel riquadro il nespolo   5
l'ombra nera, s'ostina in cielo un sole
freddoloso; e l'altre ombre che scantonano
nel vicolo non sanno che sei qui.

'Ti libero la fronte dai ghiaccioli...'

'Motet' no. 12, added only in the second (1940) edition of *Le occasioni*. In this poem Montale's *stilnovismo*, the transformation of the beloved into an 'angel' figure, a messenger from another sphere, is given its first explicit formulation. The real woman is now clearly absent (Brandeis is back in America), but she appears as an embodiment of both fragile hope and powerful endurance.

1-4:   The poet's persona ministers to a storm-battered angel, removing **'ghiaccioli'** (icicles) from her forehead, in a scene of tender intimacy. She has endured the ice and storms of a hostile world to come to him: **'l'alte / nebulose'**: high nebulae (increases the sense that the *tu* now belongs to an otherwordly realm). She now sleeps fitfully (**'a soprassalti'**).

5-7:   A faint, cold echo of the intense midday scenes of *Ossi di seppia*; **'allunga...nera'**: 'the shadow of the medlar tree lengthens in the square frame [of the window]'.

7-8:   Once again, the *io-tu* couple are surrounded by incomprehending 'others'; **'scantonano'**: slip away. Here the spatial divide implicit in several texts is underlined, with the *io* in his interior space protected by the presence of the *tu* and her privileged understanding, while the 'other shadows' outside are marked above all by ignorance (**'non sanno'**). There is also probably an echo of Dante's *Inferno*, where the souls of the damned are **'ombre'**.

La casa dei doganieri

Tu non ricordi la casa dei doganieri
sul rialzo a strapiombo sulla scogliera:
desolata t'attende dalla sera
in cui v'entrò lo sciame dei tuoi pensieri
e vi sostò irrequieto.   5

Libeccio sferza da anni le vecchie mura
e il suono del tuo riso non è più lieto:
la bussola va impazzita all'avventura
e il calcolo dei dadi più non torna.
Tu non ricordi; altro tempo frastorna   10
la tua memoria; un filo s'addipana.

Ne tengo ancora un capo; ma s'allontana
la casa e in cima al tetto la banderuola
affumicata gira senza pietà.
Ne tengo un capo; ma tu resti sola   15
né qui respiri nell'oscurità.

Oh l'orizzonte in fuga, dove s'accende
rara la luce della petroliera!
Il varco è qui? (Ripullula il frangente
ancora sulla balza che scoscende...).   20
Tu non ricordi la casa di questa
mia sera. Ed io non so chi va e chi resta.

La casa dei doganieri

This poem (dated 1930) belongs to a partly-submerged cycle dedicated to a different muse, known as 'Arletta', whose presence would only emerge clearly in a number of texts of the 1970s. Montale repeatedly refers to her as having died young, probably more in the sense of her function as an absent figure in his poetry than in a literal sense. In many ways, the figure and associations of Arletta belong more to the world of *Ossi di seppia* than *Le occasioni*, as is evident from the setting on the *Cinque terre* coast. The title refers to a coastguards' building near the Montale villa in Monterosso, apparently abandoned when the poet was still a child. It is a poem of lost love and personal yearning, but also an exploration of the loss brought inevitably by the passing of time in a world of uncertainty and disorientation.

1-5:   '**Tu non ricordi**': the motif of memory is introduced, only to be negated. The opening words may echo Leopardi ('Silvia rimembri ancora…'). l. 2: 'on the height overhanging the cliff'. The desolate present is juxtaposed with a past encounter with the girl, whose memory carries its own sense of anxiety, with her thoughts in a restless 'swarm' ('**sciame**'). The setting at evening time, along with other elements, lends a 'crepuscular' air to the poem and the figure of Arletta.

6-9:   '**Libeccio**': the South-West wind (here, with '**sferza**' – whips – representing a violent nature rarely seen in *Ossi*). The images of '**bussola**' (compass –which is 'crazed') and the '**dadi**' (dice) suggest an outlook of disorientation and randomness in the absence of her once-happy laughter.

10-11:   '**altro tempo**': the 'other time' of the dead, to which she and their shared memories belong, obstructs the attempted recollection, and introduces another image of time passing as a 'thread' is wound up ('**s'addipana**').

12-16:   '**Ne tengo ancora un capo**': the poet clings in vain to one end of the thread (of time/memory). The image of the blackened, spinning weathervane ('**banderuola**') intensifies the sense of disorientation seen in the previous stanza, this time with an added note of relentless menace ('**senza pietà**'). For all his desperate clinging to the thread (as repeated in l. 15), all that remains is her solitude (wherever she may be) and his darkness ('**qui**').

17-20:   The focus widens to take in the entire landscape/seascape, whose horizon seems to 'rush away', as if the physical world were on the brink of disintegration, leading to a possible '**varco**' (opening or gateway). On one level the question posed in l.18 might be imagined as that posed by the crew of the '**petroliera**' (oil-tanker), searching for the entrance to port (picking up on the '**bussola**' image earlier). On another level, however, it is surely the poet's own quest, like the search for a gap in the wall, or 'broken link in the chain' seen in *Ossi*, a search for an insight or opening into some other dimension at a moment when the normal constraints of the world within time seem about to yield. In either case, however, there is no answer but the sound of the waves ('the breaker seethes on the steeply-sloping shore') – isolated in their parenthesis, and with the typically onomatopoeic assonance of '**frangente… scoscende…**'.

21-22:   The poem's opening words return here in a hammered repetition to seal the sense of relentless irreversibility of time and loss. The shared '**sera**' evoked in stanza 1 is now only '**mia**', leaving the *io* alone and with no clear perspective.

From *La bufera e altro* (1956)

L'anguilla

L'anguilla, la sirena
dei mari freddi che lascia il Baltico
per giungere ai nostri mari,
ai nostri estuarî, ai fiumi
che risale in profondo, sotto la piena avversa,   5
di ramo in ramo e poi
di capello in capello, assottigliati,
sempre più addentro, sempre più nel cuore
del macigno, filtrando
tra gorielli di melma finché un giorno   10
una luce scoccata dai castagni
ne accende il guizzo in pozze d'acquamorta,
nei fossi che declinano
dai balzi d'Appennino alla Romagna;
l'anguilla, torcia, frusta,   15
freccia d'Amore in terra
che solo i nostri botri o i disseccati
ruscelli pirenaici riconducono
a paradisi di fecondazione;
l'anima verde che cerca   20
vita là dove solo
morde l'arsura e la desolazione,
la scintilla che dice
tutto comincia quando tutto pare
incarbonirsi, bronco seppellito;   25
l'iride breve, gemella
di quella che incastonano i tuoi cigli
e fai brillare intatta in mezzo ai figli
dell'uomo, immersi nel tuo fango, puoi tu
non crederla sorella?   30

L'anguilla

Written in 1948, this text signals the imminent end of the cycle of poems dedicated to Clizia. The allegorical narrative in which she, in her absence, represented the hope of future salvation, becomes unsustainable in the post-war world. With liberation from Fascism comes disillusionment, as Montale sees his own ideals of secular liberalism (embodied in the short-lived Partito d'Azione) marginalized in the left-right polarization of the new Italy. Meanwhile, the relationship with the real woman who inspired Clizia is now over. In his poetry, he looks for new images of energy and redemption to replace the rarefied flights of Clizia, and here he finds one in the eel, an embodiment of animal vitality, fertility and regeneration from below that becomes momentarily fused with the redeeming angel. The poem (addressed to Clizia) consists of a single sentence, a question summed up in the opening and closing lines: 'The eel [...], is it possible for you not to believe it is your sister?' (Within months, this new strand of terrestrial/animal imagery will be subsumed in a cycle of poems written for 'la Volpe', the poetic name given to Montale's new muse and lover, whom he meets early in 1949). On this poem, see especially Zambon, *L'iride nel fango*. The notes in the Galassi edition are also particularly useful here.

1-4: Montale's version of the eel's life cycle involves apparent confusion with that of the salmon, but this need not detract from the power and resonance of this image of tenacity, survival and regeneration (see Cima and Segre, *Profilo di un autore*, pp. 71 and 195); **'sirena'**: siren; suggests metaphorical attributes beyond those of mere physical vitality, including a magical allure of a potentially erotic nature.

5-10: The eel's journey is one of both emergence from below (unlike Clizia) and of penetration into the heart of the landscape: **'piena avversa'**: opposing flood water; **'di ramo... in capello'**: through ever narrower branches of the stream; **'macigno'**: sandstone; **'gorielli di melma'**: muddy channels.

11-14: At the very point of stagnation (**'acquamorta'**), the eel offers a spark or flash of light; **'una luce scoccata...'**: light 'shooting' through chestnut trees; **'guizzo'**: flash or flickering movement; **'fossi'**: ditches; **'balzi'**: crags.

15-19: Erotic overtones combine with a quasi-mystical personification of 'Love' (recalling again the *stilnovo* tradition), but this is now firmly earth-bound (**'in terra'**) and tied to sensual imagery as the streams lead it to a 'paradise of fertility'; **'torcia'**: torch; **'frusta'**: whip; **'botri'**: ditches; **'pirenaici'**: 'of the Pyrenees'.

20-25: **'l'anima verde'**: In Italian the colour green has strong figurative connotations of youth and hope (apparent here in the contrast between the 'green' of living growth and the images of arid desolation). In these lines we may see also an image of the renewal of Montale's poetry itself, even at the point of its potential exhaustion. **'arsura'**: burning heat; **'incarbonirsi'**: to burn to ashes; **'bronco'**: bare twisted branch.

26-30: The depiction of the eel as **'iride'** (rainbow) signifies the iridescent colours reflected briefly in its skin, but links immediately also to the other meaning of 'iris', as this fleeting colour is 'twinned' with the iris of Clizia's eyes, compared in turn to a gem-stone 'set' (**'incastonare'**) amidst her eyelashes.

The tensions between transcendence and earthy physicality (tensions concerning the nature and function of poetry itself) come to the fore in these lines, with their contrasting images of, on the one hand, light and purity ('**intatta**' connoting virginal purity) and, on the other, the impure world of '**fango**' in which we are necessarily immersed, but which also belongs to the *tu*. This dense figurative knot is accompanied by an intensification of the assonance and internal rhyme that runs through the poem as a whole, notably a series based around *-illa; -ello; -elli; -ella*; running from the first to the last words of the text.

Hai dato il mio nome a un albero? Non è poco;
pure non mi rassegno a restar ombra, o tronco,
di un abbandono nel suburbio. Io il tuo
l'ho dato a un fiume, a un lungo incendio, al crudo
gioco della mia sorte, alla fiducia   5
sovrumana con cui parlasti al rospo
uscito dalla fogna, senza orrore o pietà
o tripudio, al respiro di quel forte
e morbido tuo labbro che riesce,
nominando, a creare; rospo fiore erba scoglio –   10
quercia pronta a spiegarsi su di noi
quando la pioggia spollina i carnosi
petali del trifoglio e il fuoco cresce.

'Hai dato il mio nome a un albero? Non è poco...'

Written in 1949, this is part of *Madrigali privati*, a group of poems in *La bufera e altro* for Montale's new muse 'la Volpe' (Maria Luisa Spaziani). The quasi-sacred 'motet' form of *Occasioni* is now replaced by the 'madrigal', an indicator of the profane and earthly nature of these new love songs. Montale makes this distinction clear also by drawing a parallel with Dante's *Vita Nuova*: 'Qui appare l'Antibeatrice come nella Vita Nuova; come la donna gentile che poi Dante volle gabellarci come Filosofia, mentre si suppone che fosse altro...' (Greco, *Montale commenta Montale*, p. 57). On the background to these poems, see Spaziani, 'Un carteggio inedito...', where the woman behind the figure of Volpe describes their extensive correspondence. Silvio Guarnieri describes a Montale rejuvenated in these years by this intense relationship (Guarnieri, *L'ultimo testimone*, pp. 51-55). Spaziani subsequently emerged as a poet in her own right (her creative dimension is alluded to in this poem). While one may agree in part with Galassi (p. 599) that this is 'a poem about poetics, celebrating (while also undermining) the naming function of poetry', it must also be read as a passionate and sensual love poem.

1-3:   The opening question gives the sense that this poem is part of an ongoing private conversation, and indeed the poem as a whole continues this, as he apparently tries to outdo the beloved in seeking intense or striking imagery with which to portray their respective figures; **'Non è poco'**: 'It's no small thing' (i.e. it is quite significant)

3-8:   The response of the *io* is to catalogue the objects and phenomena to which he applies her name: from the elemental forces of water and fire, to his own 'cruel' destiny (**'sorte'**), to the **'fiducia sovrumana'** (superhuman trust) that she has shown by even deigning to address him. The figure of the **'rospo uscito dalla fogna'** (toad emerged from a sewer) anticipates the widespread self-abasement of the *io* in Montale's later work (it is also, of course, an allusion to the story of the frog prince); **'tripudio'**: jubilation.

8-10: The catalogue of phenomena evoked by her name culminates in the image of her **'labbro'**. This brings together elements with connotations of sensuality (**'respiro'**, **'forte e morbido'**) with the celebration of the creative power of her 'lips', contained in the very act of 'naming' (**'labbro che riesce/ nominando, a creare'**).

10-13: The poem concludes with a further catalogue of apparently unconnected objects and phenomena from the natural world. **'quercia pronta a spiegarsi du di noi'**: oak tree ready to spread over us. Note the portrayal of 'us' as a couple united under the shelter of the tree, in a tangible sensual relationship far removed from the rarefied intensity of the Clizia poems, with their emphasis on absence and mystical elevation; **'quando la pioggia spollina i carnosi / petali del trifoglio'**: 'when the rain washes the pollen off the fleshy petals of the clover'. Even the vegetation is apparently suffused with sensuality. The closing image, **'il fuoco cresce'**, suggests, like others in the Volpe poems, an intense vitality emerging from below rather than descending from on high.

From *Satura* (1971)

Xenia I, 1

Caro piccolo insetto
che chiamavano mosca non so perché,
stasera quasi al buio
mentre leggevo il Deuteroisaia
sei ricomparsa accanto a me,   5
ma non avevi occhiali,
non potevi vedermi
né potevo io senza quel luccichìo
riconoscere te nella foschia.

Xenia I, 1

Written in 1964 after the death of his wife (known affectionately as Mosca), this poem is typical of the understated, quasi-prosaic style that would come to dominate Montale's work in his final period. The title '**Xenia**' (Greek: 'gifts offered to a departing guest') suggests, perhaps, an expiatory gesture, a belated recognition of the importance in the poet's life of this woman who now posthumously becomes his last major muse (on the figure of Mosca, see Ó Ceallacháin, p. 182). The writing is far removed from the emblematic and stylistic intensity that marked Clizia's epiphanies in *Occasioni* or *La bufera*. The syntax is direct, the use of rhyme and assonance sparing, almost surreptitious (e.g.: *io* – *luccichìo* – *foschia*): part of Montale's new 'poetry that tends towards prose while at the same time refusing it' (*Il secondo mestiere: arte, musica, società*, p. 1699). The apparition of the ghost is narrated with matter-of-fact simplicity (l.5), and sets the scene for an intimate dialogue with her through the shared memories evoked throughout the series.

1-2:   '**insetto... mosca**': images echoing ironically Clizia's transcendent flights.
4:       '**Deuteroisaia**': The second book of Isaiah. The title breaks the prosaic tone and diction while introducing a surprising partial assonance with '**buio**'.
6-7:   Rather than the steely eyes of Clizia, Mosca is characterized by her defective vision and glasses (and yet, in Montale's new world of inverted values, her myopia goes hand in hand elsewhere with a curious clairvoyance and insight).
8-9:   Even the modest '**luccichìo**' (glint) of her glasses (a faint reflection of Clizia's luminous figure) is absent here, leading to the failure of recognition and of the epiphany. The repeated attempts to evoke her presence in *Xenia* serve in fact to underline her absence, along with the absence of meaning for the *io* in the post-war world.

Xenia II, 5

Ho sceso, dandoti il braccio, almeno un milione di scale
e ora che non ci sei è il vuoto ad ogni gradino.
Anche così è stato breve il nostro lungo viaggio.
Il mio dura tuttora, né più mi occorrono
le coincidenze, le prenotazioni,   5
le trappole, gli scorni di chi crede
che la realtà sia quella che si vede.

Ho sceso milioni di scale dandoti il braccio
non già perché con quattr'occhi forse si vede di più.
Con te le ho scese perché sapevo che di noi due   10
le sole vere pupille, sebbene tanto offuscate,
erano le tue.

Xenia II, 5

1-3:   A moving, intimate evocation of their life together and of his grief at her loss.
        Note the downward motion: their shared 'journey' has none of the imagery
        of ascent associated with the Clizia cycle.

4-7:   'coincidenze': travel connections; 'scorni': humiliations; 'chi crede…': the
        latest incarnation of the unthinking 'others', those who unquestioningly
        accept a 'reality' which the poet's persona now views with the most sceptical
        detachment.

10-12: In a world where all values have been inverted, Mosca's 'clouded'
        ('offuscate') eyes are in fact capable of searing insights.

Fine del '68

Ho contemplato dalla luna, o quasi,
il modesto pianeta che contiene
filosofia, teologia, politica,
pornografia, letteratura, scienze
palesi o arcane. Dentro c'è anche l'uomo,   5
ed io tra questi. E tutto è molto strano.

Tra poche ore sarà notte e l'anno
finirà tra esplosioni di spumanti
e di petardi. Forse di bombe o peggio,
ma non qui dove sto. Se uno muore   10
non importa a nessuno purché sia
sconosciuto e lontano.

Fine del '68

This poem is from 'Satura II', the long final section of the book, where Montale casts his sceptical eye over the contemporary world (as he continues to do in his subsequent volumes). The title marks this text as part of a diary or chronicle, as the poet (writing on 31 December 1968) comments on an event of global media interest, the Apollo 8 mission in which astronauts orbited the moon for the first time, producing the iconic image of a distant earth rising over the moon's horizon. It is an image of the kind of confident technological progress about which Montale was deeply sceptical.

1-5: The meditative tone of the opening is reinforced by the predominance of hendecasyllables, but any solemnity is undermined by the poet's irony (even from the end of l.1 with the addition of '**o quasi**'). The catalogue of human activity in ll.3-4 is mocked by the facile but incongruous internal rhyme sequence, as the poet looks down with aristocratic detachment from his imaginary lunar viewpoint on the spectacle of the contemporary world ('**palesi o arcane**': clearly revealed or mysterious)

5-6: Humanity (including the *io*) seems a mere afterthought. From grand abstractions to the individual, all of life is thus subsumed to form the object of the poet's bewilderment (with perhaps an ironic nod to Leopardi).

7-12: After the evocation of New Year celebrations ('**petardi**': fireworks), the tone grows darker as Montale presents the moral indifference of a world in violent turmoil. Expressions of negativity accumulate, reinforced by assonance on the sounds *n* and *o*. Here the emphasis shifts from the collective human comedy of the first stanza to the suffering of the individual. The single end-rhyme at the close, *strano-lontano*, highlights the sense of alienation and isolation seen by Montale as a universal human condition.

Nel silenzio

Oggi è sciopero generale.
Nella strada non passa nessuno.
Solo una radiolina dall'altra parte del muro.
Da qualche giorno deve abitarci qualcuno.
Mi chiedo che ne sarà della produzione.   5
La primavera stessa tarda alquanto a prodursi.
Hanno spento in anticipo il termosifone.
Si sono accorti ch'è inutile il servizio postale.
Non è gran male il ritardo delle funzioni normali.
È d'obbligo che qualche ingranaggio non ingrani.   10
Anche i morti si sono messi in agitazione.
Anch'essi fanno parte del silenzio totale.
Tu stai sotto una lapide. Risvegliarti non vale
perché sei sempre desta. Anche oggi ch'è sonno
universale.   15

Nel silenzio

1-2:   The rather prosaic chronicle of a general strike is the starting point for Montale's exploration of a wider sense of unease and isolation. The 'silence' of the title is that of the Milan apartment from which the poetic voice now speaks, and of a world that no longer addresses the *io* in any meaningful way. The structure, with each line ending in a full stop, reflects the dull inertia of the situation. There may also be an element of parody of Franco Fortini here (see Pellini, 'L'ultimo Montale', pp. 314-21).

3-4:   The once metaphysical barrier of the wall, now domesticated, cannot quite separate him from the unwelcome intrusion of contemporary noise in the form of a neighbour's radio.

7-8:   Images reinforcing the sense of isolation of the poet's persona.

9-10:   A distant echo of the longed-for 'miracles' of *Ossi di seppia*, now reduced to the seemingly commonplace malfunctions of the 'mechanisms' of life. l. 10: 'it has to happen that some mechanism/gear does not engage properly'.

11-15:   The silence is also that of the dead, and of Mosca in particular; **'in agitazione'**: 'on strike' (but used ironically of the dead, in view of its literal meaning). Mosca, however, in keeping with her ability to overturn conventional perceptions, is apparently the only vital presence in the poet's silent world (her appearance also brings the only break in the structural monotony of the text). Her figure provides an image of a private authenticity amidst the bland torpor of contemporary life. **'lapide'**: tombstone.

From *Diario del '71 e del '72*

Verso il fondo

La rete
che strascica sul fondo
non prende
che pesci piccoli.

Con altre reti ho preso   5
pesci rondine
e anche una testuggine
ma era morta.

Ora che mi riprovo
con amo e spago   10
l'esca rimane intatta
nell'acqua torbida.

Troppo spessore è intorno
di su, di giù, nell'aria.
Non si procede: muoversi   15
è uno strappo.

Verso il fondo

This is part of a vein running through the later collections on the theme of poetry itself and the possibility or otherwise of its continuing in an environment that has changed fundamentally both in personal terms and in the general cultural outlook.

1-4:   A characteristically self-deprecatory image characterizes Montale's later verse as a **'rete che strascica'** ('trawl-net'), taking only the meanest of pickings. In conjunction with the title (**'fondo'**: sea-bed), these lines suggest an idea of self-consciously touching a low-point in poetic terms (or claiming to do so).

5-8:   Continuing the metaphor, the **'pesci rondine'** (flying fish) recall his earlier *ispiratrici*, the dead turtle evokes the flightless Mosca. (But see also Contorbia, *Immagini di una vita* p. 68, for a photo of a young Montale with a sea turtle).

9-12:   The net is replaced here by hook (**'amo'**) and line: if anything an even more rudimentary implement, and certainly no more effective, with its untouched bait (**'esca'**). The idea of impoverished or threadbare equipment is echoed elsewhere in the same thematic strand, for example in 'La mia Musa', where a scarecrow- muse conducts 'un quartetto di cannucce'. The **'acqua torbida'** recalls the torbid waters ('torba') of the Florentine flood of 1966, as depicted in *Xenia II*, 14, where they became a metaphor for a debased and menacing reality besieging the poet's persona.

13-16: The very air seems almost physically oppressive (**'spessore'**: density), with perhaps a distant echo of the 'aria di vetro' in 'Forse un mattino andando...'. But, whereas there the tangible air facilitated a breakthrough in perception, here it provokes only paralysis, immobility; **'strappo'**: wrench.

5

Mario Luzi
and the Hermetic Generation

The Hermetic Generation

When the critic Francesco Flora published his book *La poesia ermetica* in 1936, his use of the term 'hermetic' marked the beginning of a long and tortuous process of critical discussion, polemics and often confusion surrounding the word itself and the poetic and critical movement that it came to encapsulate.[i] (The word *ermetico* derives from the name of Hermes Trismegistus, ancient Egyptian divinity associated with the secrets of alchemy, and hence with connotations of the esoteric, the impenetrable.) Flora used the term as part of a broad denigration of all contemporary poetry, seen as obscure and sterile, and unhealthily indebted to the French symbolist tradition. With the broad scope of his critique (one of his main targets was Ungaretti), Flora also set the scene for a widespread and enduring lack of clarity over the boundaries of 'hermetic' poetry, in terms of chronology, groupings and literary forms.

Luciano Anceschi substantially reinforced a broad, inclusive idea of *ermetismo* in his two influential anthologies, *Lirici nuovi* (1942) and *Lirica del Novecento* (1953), both of which suggested that the term was more or less synonymous with the whole area of 'lirica nuova' (including Ungaretti and Montale) that had emerged after the ferment of the avant-garde years. Although Anceschi acknowledges the 'equivocal' nature of the term *ermetico*, he is nevertheless content to use it to indicate a general atmosphere of 'crisi della parola' and 'crisi dell'uomo' in the preceding decades.[ii] Thus, Anceschi's anthologies underlined the dominance of the 'lyrical' model in Italian poetry in the first half of the century (a dominance whose legitimacy would be challenged in the following years by, among others, Pasolini, with his notion

153

of 'antinovecentismo'), and also consolidated the idea that 'hermetic' poetry
was central to the development and renewal of that lyric tradition. In the 1942
volume he celebrates *ermetismo* for bringing 'un approfondimento della
nostra lingua letteraria... un allargare il confine del senso logico delle parole,
tese all'interno da una intensa volontà di canto e di durata [...] l'aperta e veloce
libertà nell'uso delle strutture sintattiche e aggettivali in modi insoliti e
assoluti'.[iii]

In the course of the following decades, however, the use of the term
ermetismo gradually came to be more circumscribed, as it came to be applied
to a much narrower grouping of poets (known also as the 'terza
generazione'), active especially in the 1930s, or as Fortini suggests 'all'incirca
fra il 1932 e il 1942 soprattutto a Firenze'.[iv] This grouping is the focus of the
present chapter: it included young Tuscan writers such as Mario Luzi, Piero
Bigongiari and Alessandro Parronchi (all born in 1914), slightly older poets
like Salvatore Quasimodo and Alfonso Gatto (both Southerners who lived or
spent time in Florence in the 1930s) and, alongside these, critics such as Carlo
Bo, whose 1938 essay 'Letteratura come vita' is often seen as an ethical and
poetic 'manifesto' of the hermetics.[v] Nor should it be forgotten that Florence
in these years was the centre of a wider and highly significant community of
writers and critics, from Eugenio Montale to Elio Vittorini to Gianfranco
Contini, whose presence and active participation in the many literary journals
based in the city provided fertile terrain in which the work of the hermetic
poets thrived.

For its practitioners and supporters, hermetic poetry was founded on
the highest aesthetic and ethical ideals and represented a model of intense
moral commitment, achieved through literary form itself: 'letteratura [...]
come strenuo impegno di confessione e di verità [...] come costruzione di una
umanità rinnovata e salvata nella libertà pura della poesia'.[vi] It is, clearly, a
view that contains a degree of mysticism in its conception of the 'redemptive'
power of poetry: a conception of lyrical 'purity' uncontaminated by the
inauthentic, banal realities of everyday life. For the hermetic poets, in a
historical context in which any constructive political dialogue was impossible
(these are the years of the fully consolidated Fascist dictatorship), the only
space remaining for the pursuit of truth and freedom was that of literature, as
an ambivalent 'luogo d'esilio e d'asilo'. Thus, writes Lucio Vetri, the *ermetici*
turn to an exploration of an inner world, attempting to penetrate 'nel
profondo, chiuso e segreto, della coscienza', where some 'Truth' may be
found and expressed through 'obscure symbols', in language of 'estrema
concentrazione semantica [...] di indeterminata allusività'.[vii] As can be seen in
the texts, this concentration and allusivity of language can render the poetry

opaque, indeed impenetrable at times.

Unsurprisingly, the hermetic poets and their works came under hostile critical scrutiny in the decades following the fall of Fascism, the period when contentious debates between advocates of left-wing realism and formal experimentalism would leave little room for rarefied lyrical meditations. As Salvatore Quasimodo wrote in 1946 (with the zeal of the convert): 'Per quelli che credono alla poesia come a un gioco letterario [...] diciamo che il tempo della "speculazioni" è finito. Rifare l'uomo, questo è l'impegno'.[viii] The hermetics were widely portrayed as having failed in the duty of the artist to engage with historical problems. Fortini grants them a somewhat condescending partial absolution for their ideological sins ('le cose erano state più grandi di loro'), before noting that even their more successful works offer at best 'una verità ridotta e approssimativa', while Sanguineti, in his 1969 anthology, dismisses them as 'le anime belle per definizione'.[ix] Fausto Curi notes that ideas of some 'absolute' recur frequently in the hermetic poets and that a climate of pathos dominates, whereas 'reality' as such does not exist, but rather is sublimated, 'levigata e quasi consumata dal lavoro psichico e dall'attività retorico-stilistica'.[x] And yet, it is somewhat paradoxical, as Pautasso observes, that the very stance of artistic isolation that had irritated the Fascist regime would later become the basis for accusations of culpable literary escapism.[xi]

The work of these poets is often highly challenging in terms of its language, its imagery and, above all, its meaning. A catalogue of the main linguistic features of the style, drawn up by Mengaldo, examines in detail some of the more extreme forms of 'grammatica ermetica' as used by members of the Florentine grouping. The list includes: the use of 'absolute' noun forms (without articles), or of plural in place of singular, giving a sense of the abstract or emblematic (e.g. Quasimodo, 'così t'è sorella acquamorta'; 'mi parve s'aprissero voci / che labbra cercassero acque'); a general freedom in the use of prepositions (especially *a* and *di*), expressing allusive meaning or logically ambiguous relationships (Gatto, 'a respiro e a cadenza della sera / tu mi portavi in braccio al sonno'; 'Bosco d'amore a non stormire'); expression of analogies by apposition as part of a highly concentrated syntax (De Libero, 'usciva la luna / animale di tempesta'); marked use of abstractions (Luzi, 'Scendono persuasioni calde sulla terra fiorita'); use of 'precious' or erudite vocabulary; unexpected couplings of nouns and adjectives causing extreme semantic or logical tension (Luzi, 'scoscesa tortora'; Bigongiari, 'pianto astruso', 'fiori lancinanti').[xii] For Mengaldo, the recurrence of such forms confirms the existence of a veritable hermetic 'school' of poetry (although he is careful to distinguish a core grouping from those, such as Sereni, who are on the margins or tangential to it), a movement that constitutes a 'singolare avanguardia' focused on the radical renewal of poetic language.[xiii]

For Giorgio Barberi Squarotti, on the other hand, the challenging nature of the hermetic style is not exclusively a matter of language, but arises also from a fundamental crisis in the institution of lyric poetry. For all that this poetry appears to express a highly subjective vision in refined, metaphorical terms, the critic argues that it is, in fact, the *subject* that is missing in many of these texts, where the accumulation of symbols and imagery cannot be assembled in a coherent relationship to a poetic *io*, resulting in a 'liricità senza soggetto'.[xiv] The emotional charge, so highly evident in some of the language used, remains strangely abstract. Thus this poetry, which appears in some ways so conventionally lyrical (not least in predominance of nature imagery and the frequent use of metrical forms based on *endecasillabo* or *settenario*), can be seen as profoundly subverting the lyric tradition. It is based on a 'poetica antiespressiva' which, for Barberi Squarotti, is the culmination of a long process of 'distruzione dell'io' reaching back to the beginnings of twentieth-century verse.[xv]

Mengaldo concludes his discussion with the observation: 'Oggi come oggi, diciamolo francamente, i poeti ermetici veri e propri [...] sono quasi illeggibili'.[xvi] Certainly, this is true of some of the more extreme examples of hermetic writing (what Mengaldo calls 'l'ermetismo *forte*'). But indeed, the same might be said of some of the products of other avant-garde movements, whether the *parole in libertà* of the Futurists or some of the formal experiments of the Novissimi later in the 1960s. Perhaps it is this notion of radicalism of intent, seen both in formal expression and, in some cases, in a tendentially mystical vision, that is the most useful general key for the reader in approaching the work of the *ermetici*.

Mario Luzi

Luzi (1914-2005) was at the centre of the hermetic grouping, both in generational and geographic terms, but he is also the writer from that grouping whose work and cultural profile would develop in the most interesting and enduring ways. His first collection *La barca* (1935) offers already a veritable compendium of the themes and stylistic features of *ermetismo*: landscapes laden with symbolic significance, intimations of a transcendent Catholic faith, an intense and self-consciously decorative use of language and an elegant mastery of poetic metre, especially the classic hendecasyllable line. Luzi's style reaches its early maturity with his second collection *Avvento notturno* (1940), which has been seen as the definitive hermetic text ('il testo decisivo di un'intera stagione culturale'), with its 'città spettrali, paesaggi lunari, marmi e pietre preziose [...], avventi e presenze di creature celesti e terrestri'.[xvii]

In the following decades, however, while some of his contemporaries would continue with a manneristic hermeticism and others (for example Quasimodo) would seek to embrace more facile forms of realism, Luzi's poetry continues to develop from within its original line of inspiration, while succeeding in renewing its lyrical approach in authentic and at times problematic directions. Following *Primizie del deserto* and *Quaderno gotico*, comes the emblematically titled *Onore del vero* (1957), at a time when Luzi comes under the influence of Montale and Eliot more than that of his hermetic contemporaries, or indeed, more that of Dante than of Petrarch.[xviii] There is an 'apertura comunicativa' in these years, 'un linguaggio e [...] uno stile più umile e colloquiale'.[xix] While the poetry remains intensely literary and often mystical in its suppositions, there is increasingly an attempt to open up to the world of objects and of others beyond the self. It is, however, with *Nel magma* (1963) that Luzi definitively breaks the 'incantesimo dello sguardo sospeso'.[xx] There is now a fundamental shift in tone and language, an opening to the world of prose and a proliferation of voices in dialogue with the *io* and with each other.[xxi]

In some quarters (notably those for whom the hermetic tradition is flawed *a priori* on ideological or cultural grounds), Luzi has been the object of ongoing critical ambivalence or even hostility: Fortini has written perceptively on Luzi's poetry, and yet even he can pay him a rather double-edged compliment ('segue una sua stella fissa che lo illumina e lo isola'); while Curi finds an inadequacy in Luzi's relationship with the real world, 'una difficoltà di relazione, la mancanza di un rapporto vero'.[xxii]

Nevertheless, Luzi's work continues to develop in a multiplicity of directions during the last decades of his life: alongside his poetry there is a wealth of critical essays, prose writings, and, especially from the 1980s onwards, theatrical works. His poetry too continues to develop, juxtaposing lyrical and spiritual meditations with explorations of a bewildering contemporary world, as well as experimenting with a variety of formal and stylistic approaches. Indeed, if there is a constant element in Luzi's poetry, it lies in his capacity to surprise and to change, to encapsulate the 'frantumarsi della percezione' in the very form, the 'physiology' of his verse itself.[xxiii] But alongside this mutability of form is an unswerving belief that 'la parola della poesia, come ogni parola umana [...], non può che misurarsi con un'altra parola, cioè la Rivelazione'.[xxiv]

Salvatore Quasimodo

Quasimodo (1901-1968) could in some ways be regarded as something of an outsider in the context of Florentine *ermetismo*: he was some years older than Luzi and his contemporaries and as a native of Sicily he only ever spent limited periods in the Tuscan city (he worked and lived in Liguria and Milan in the 1930s).[xxv] And yet, he is often seen as a kind of founding father of the hermetic style. His first collection, *Acque e terre* (where the influence of Ungaretti is evident), was published in 1930 in Florence under the imprint of the journal *Solaria* (his introduction to the *Solaria* group came via Elio Vittorini, who was his brother-in-law). This collection, with its dream-like landscapes and refined, allusive musicality, had a significant influence on the stylistic direction of the younger poets throughout that decade. His second volume, *Òboe sommerso* (1932), develops and crystallizes some of the key formal and linguistic features of the hermetic manner.[xxvi]

During the later 1930s, there were some signs of a shift in emphasis in Quasimodo's verse, particularly with *Nuove poesie* (1942), where the poet's voice appears to reach out to a shared human experience, but it was the traumatic experience of the Second World War that led to a fundamental change in the themes and style of Quasimodo's poetry. With *Giorno dopo giorno* (1947), he adopts a new stance as civic or public poet, treating the thematic material of conflict in a rhetorical, quasi-epic style based on classical hendecasyllabic metre (see chapter *Engaging with Reality* below). The communicative and moral accessibility of this later style (which would continue to form a substantial element of his subsequent collections) was a significant element in the award of the Nobel Prize for literature in 1959. In subsequent decades, however, the value of Quasimodo's post-war work was questioned by many critics: Fortini, for example, says his embracing of 'humanistic-social' themes is 'quasi sempre infelice'; while for some his real contribution to the poetry of his time lies in his translations of ancient Greek lyrics, *Lirici greci* (1940).[xxvii]

Alfonso Gatto

A native of Salerno, Gatto (1909-1976) settled in Florence in 1937, where, a year later, he was co-founder (with Vasco Pratolini) of *Campo di Marte*, the journal which became a focal point of the hermetic group. He subsequently joined the Communist party (which he left in 1951) and was active in the Resistance. His first collection of verse, *Isola* (1932) is, along with

Quasimodo's early poetry, one of the defining texts of Florentine *ermetismo*. (It is interesting to note the recurrence of the image of the 'island', as for example in Quasimodo, and in Ungaretti's 'L'isola'.) Although the poem given in this volume is a characteristic hermetic text in its surreal imagery, allusiveness and unexpected analogies, there is, elsewhere in Gatto, a contrasting vein of concrete expression of everyday realities.

Piero Bigongiari

An exact contemporary of Luzi and also a native of Tuscany, Bigongiari (1914-1997) was highly active both as a poet and critic in hermetic circles in Florence in the 1930s and 1940s. His first collection, *La figlia di Babilonia* (1942) is a typical product of the hermetic generation: enclosed in the polished refinement of form and averse to any communicative openness, it offers a series of elegant lyrical modulations around a thematic idea of 'absence' (often involving a mysterious female *tu* figure, probably influenced in part by Montale's *Le occasioni*), all enveloped in an aura of dream or vision. Bigongiari's first collection has been described as the 'apex' of hermetic mannerism.[xxviii]

Endotes

[i] See Francesco Flora, *La poesia ermetica* (Bari: Laterza, 1936).

[ii] *Lirica del Novecento. Antologia di poesia italiana*, ed. by Luciano Anceschi and Sergio Antonielli (Florence: Vallecchi, 1953), p. lxxviii. In a preface added to the 1964 edition of *Lirici nuovi*, Anceschi still makes the broad identification between *ermetismo* and 'lirica nuova': see *Lirici nuovi*, ed. by Luciano Anceschi, 2nd edn. (Milan: Mursia, 1964), p. xii.

[iii] See the original 1942 Introduction in Anceschi, *Lirici nuovi*, pp. 3-13 (p. 5).

[iv] Fortini, *I poeti del Novecento*, p. 99. Different poetic 'generations' were outlined by Oreste Macrì in *Caratteri e figure della poesia italiana contemporanea* (Firenze: Vallecchi, 1956), with for example Ungaretti representing the first generation, Montale and Quasimodo in the second, and poets such as Luzi in the third. Silvio Ramat gives the boundaries of *ermetismo* proper as lying between the publication dates of Ungaretti's *Sentimento del tempo* [1933] and Montale's *Finisterre* [1943]. See Ramat, *L'Ermetismo* (Firenze: La Nuova Italia, 1969), p. 1.

[v] 'Letteratura come vita' was first published in the journal *Frontespizio* in 1938. Now in Carlo Bo, *Letteratura come vita*, ed. by S. Pautasso (Milan: Rizzoli, 1984).

[vi] Donato Valli, *Storia degli ermetici* (Brescia: Editrice La Scuola, 1978), p. 90.

[vii] Lucio Vetri, Appendix to Luciano Anceschi, *Le poetiche del Novecento in Italia: studio di fenomenologia e storia delle poetiche*, nuova ed. accresciuta e aggiornata

(Venezia: Marsilio, 1990), pp. 283- 319 (p. 293).

viii   Salvatore Quasimodo, 'Poesia contemporanea' (1946), in *Poesie e discorsi sulla poesia*, I Meridiani (Milan: Mondadori, 1994), pp. 263-72 (p. 272).

ix   Fortini, *I poeti del Novecento*, p. 98; Sanguineti, *Poesia italiana del Novecento*, p. lix.

x   Curi, *La poesia italiana del Noveecento*, pp. 204-206. For all this sublimation of reality, however, Curi notes mischievously that 'una diffusa tradizione orale, forse non del tutto leggendaria, vuole che certo ermetismo sia nato nei bordelli di Firenze' (p. 205).

xi   Sergio Pautasso, *Ermetismo* (Milan: Editrice Bibliografica, 1996), pp. 7-8. Pautasso vigorously defends the hermetics against a range of cultural and ideological prejudices on pp. 41-49.

xii   Mengaldo, 'Il linguaggo della poesia ermetica', in *La tradizione del Novecento. Terza serie* (Turin: Einaudi, 1991), pp. 131-57 (pp. 137-142).

xiii   Mengaldo, 'Il linguaggo della poesia ermetica', p. 155. For the poet Piero Bigongiari, *ermetismo* represented an 'avanguardia non codificata', a radical attempt to 'cercare nel fondo dell'uomo la ragione stessa del suo essere e del suo parlare'. See Éanna Ó Ceallacháin, '"L'origine della parola": An Interview with Piero Bigongiari', *The Italianist*, 14 (1994) 305-18 (p. 316).

xiv   Giorgio Barberi-Squarotti, *La poesia del Novecento: morte e trasfigurazione del soggetto* (Caltanisetta-Roma: Sciascia, 1985), chapter 9 (p. 240).

xv   *ibid.*, p. 260. Barberi-Squarotti maintains that this stance on the part of the 'true' hermetics is quite at odds with that of Quasimodo, whose lyricism he sees as genuinely subjective, more in line with that of Ungaretti (pp. 260-62).

xvi   Mengaldo, 'Il linguaggo della poesia ermetica', p. 156.

xvii   Stefano Pavarini, 'Saba, Ungaretti, Quasimodo, l'Ermetismo', in *Storia della letteratura Italiana*, ed. by E. Malato, 9: *Il Novecento* (Rome: Salerno Editrice, 2000), pp. 451-543 (p. 531); Franco Fortini, 'Di Luzi', in *Saggi italiani* (Milan:Garzanti, 1987), pp. 41-75 (p. 46).

xviii   See Mengaldo, *Poeti italiani del Novecento*, p. 650.

xix   Lisa Rizzoli and Giorgio Morelli, *Mario Luzi: La poesia, il teatro, la prosa, la saggistica, le traduzioni* (Milan: Mursia, 1992), pp. 88-89.

xx   Carlo Bo, 'Al tempo dell'ermetismo: Gatto, Luzi, Sereni', in *Storia della letteratura italiana*, ed. by E. Cecchi and N. Sapegno, 9: *Il Novecento* (Milan: Garzanti, 1969), pp. 416-38 (p. 425).

xxi   Sergio Pautasso, *Mario Luzi: Storia di una poesia* (Milan: Rizzoli, 1981), p. 90. One may note a partial convergence in this respect with aspects of Sereni's work of the same years; see Mengaldo, *Poeti italiani del Novecento*, p. 652 and *Poesia del Novecento italiano: dalle avanguardie storiche alla seconda guerra mondiale*, ed. by Niva Lorenzini (Roma: Carocci, 2002), p. 272.

xxii   Fortini, *I poeti del Novecento*, p. 152; Curi, *La poesia italiana*, p. 293.

xxiii   Lorenzini, *Il presente della poesia*, p. 147.

xxiv   Stefano Verdino, in Luzi, *L'opera poetica* (Milan: Mondadori, 1998), p. liii.

xxv   See cronologia in Quasimodo, *Poesie e discorsi sulla poesia* (Milan: Mondadori, 1971), pp. xci-xcii.

xxvi   See Mengaldo, *Poeti italiani del Novecento*, p. 587.

xxvii   See Fortini, *I poeti del Novecento*, p. 90; Lorenzini, *La poesia italiana del Novecento*, p. 112; Sanguineti, *Poesia italiana del Novecento*, p. 947.

xxviii   Ramat, *La poesia italiana 1930-1943*, p. 456.

Poetic texts

Mario Luzi
The collected edition, with detailed critical apparatus, is:
L'opera poetica, a cura di Stefano Verdino, I Meridiani (Milan: Mondadori, 1998)
This brings together the various collections:
La barca (1935); *Avvento Notturno* (1940); *Un brindisi* (1946); *Quaderno gotico* (1947); *Primizie del deserto* (1952); (All of the above collected in *Il giusto della vita*, 1960); *Nel magma* (1963); *Dal fondo delle campagne* (1965); *Su fondamenti invisibili* (1971); *Al fuoco della controversia* (1978); *Per il battesimo dei nostri frammenti* (1985); *Frasi e incisi di un canto salutare* (1990); *Viaggio terrestre e celeste di Simone Martini* (1994).
Subsequent works (not included in the collected edition):
Sotto specie umana (Milan: Garzanti, 1999); *Poesie ritrovate* (Milan: Garzanti, 2003); *La dottrina dell'estremo principiante* (Milan: Garzanti, 2004)

Salvatore Quasimodo
The complete edition of Quasimodo's poetry is:
Poesie e discorsi sulla poesia, a cura di Gilberto Finzi, I Meridiani (Milan: Mondadori, 1971).

Alfonso Gatto
Tutte le poesie, a cura di Silvio Ramat (Milan: Mondadori, 2005).
Previous selected editions are:
Poesie, a cura di F. Napoli (Milan: Jaca Book, 1988)
Poesie (Milan: Mondadori, 1961) [with introduction by Giansiro Ferrata]

Piero Bigongiari
Tutte le poesie I, 1933-1963, a cura di Paolo Fabrizio Iacuzzi (Florence: Le lettere, 1994)
Dove finiscono le tracce, 1964-1996, (Florence: Le lettere, 1996)
A selection of his work is in
Poesie (1942-1992), a cura di G. Quiriconi (Milan: Jaca Book, 1994).

Further reading

Anceschi, Luciano and S. Antonielli, *Lirica del Novecento. Antologia di poesia italiana* (Florence: Vallecchi, 1953)
Anceschi, Luciano, ed., *Lirici nuovi*, 2nd edn. (Milan: Mursia, 1964)
Barberi-Squarotti, Giorgio *La poesia del Novecento: morte e trasfigurazione del soggetto* (Caltanisetta-Roma: Sciascia, 1985)
Bo, Carlo, 'Al tempo dell'ermetismo: Gatto, Luzi, Sereni', in *Storia della letteratura italiana*, ed. by E. Cecchi and N. Sapegno, 9: *Il Novecento* (Milan: Garzanti, 1969), pp. 416-38.
Bo, Carlo, *Letteratura come vita*, ed. by Sergio Pautasso (Milan: Rizzoli, 1984)
Borello, Rosalma Salina, ed., *Per conoscere Quasimodo* (Milan: Mondadori, 1973)
Borraro, Pietro and F. D'Episcopo, eds, *Stratigrafia di un poeta: Alfonso Gatto. Atti del*

Convegno nazionale di studi (Salerno-Maiori-Amalfi 1978) (Galatina: Congedo, 1980)

Caranica, Nicu, *Capire Luzi* (Rome: Edizioni Studium, 1995).

Finzi, Gilberto, ed., *Salvatore Quasimodo: la poesia nel mito e oltre* [conference proceedings] (Rome: Laterza, 1986)

Finzi, Gilberto, *Invito alla lettura di Salvatore Quasimodo* (Milan: Mursia, 1973)

Finzi, Gilberto, *Quasimodo e la critica* (Milan: Mondadori, 1969)

Flora, Francesco, *La poesia ermetica* (Bari: Laterza, 1936)

Fortini, Franco, 'Di Luzi', in *Saggi italiani* (Milan:Garzanti, 1987), pp. 41-75.

Frassica, Pietro, ed., *Salvatore Quasimodo nel vento del Mediterraneo. Atti del convegno internazionale (Princeton, 6-7 April 2001)* (Novara: Interlinea, 2002)

Macrì, Oreste *Caratteri e figure della poesia italiana contemporanea* (Firenze: Vallecchi, 1956)

Macrì, Oreste, *La poesia di Quasimodo* (Palermo: Sellerio, 1986)

Marchi, Marco, *Invito alla lettura di Mario Luzi* (Milan: Mursia, 1998)

Mariani, Gaetano, *Il lungo viaggio verso la luce. Itinerario poetico di Mario Luzi* (Padova: Liviana, 1982).

Mengaldo, Pier Vincenzo, 'Il linguaggio della poesia ermetica', in *La tradizione del Novecento. Terza serie* (Turin: Einaudi, 1991), pp. 131-57 (pp. 137-142)

Panicali, Anna, *Saggio su Mario Luzi* (Milan: Garzanti, 1987)

Papini, Maria Carla, *Bibliografia di Piero Bigongiari* (Florence: Opus Libri, 1986)

Pautasso, Sergio, *Ermetismo* (Milan: Editrice Bibliografica, 1996)

Pautasso, Sergio, *Mario Luzi: Storia di una poesia* (Milan: Rizzoli, 1981)

Pavarini, Stefano, 'Saba, Ungaretti, Quasimodo, l'Ermetismo', in *Storia della letteratura Italiana*, ed. by E. Malato, 9: *Il Novecento* (Rome: Salerno Editrice, 2000), pp. 451-543

Ramat, Silvio, *Invito alla lettura di Piero Bigongiari* (Milan: Mursia, 1979).

Ramat, Silvio, *L'Ermetismo* (Firenze: La Nuova Italia, 1969)

Rizzoli, Lisa, and Giorgio Morelli, *Mario Luzi: La poesia, il teatro, la prosa, la saggistica, le traduzioni* (Milan: Mursia, 1992)

Salibra, Elena, *Salvatore Quasimodo* (Rome: Edizioni dell'ateneo, 1985)

Tondo, Michele, *Salvatore Quasimodo* (Milan: Mursia, 1971)

Valli, Donato, *Storia degli ermetici* (Brescia: Editrice La Scuola, 1978)

Vetri, Lucio, Appendix to Luciano Anceschi, *Le poetiche del Novecento in Italia: studio di fenomenologia e storia delle poetiche*, nuova ed. accresciuta e aggiornata (Venezia: Marsilio, 1990), pp. 283- 319

Zagarrio, Giuseppe, *Luzi* (Firenze: La Nuova Italia, 1968)

Zagarrio, Giuseppe, *Salvatore Quasimodo* (Florence: La Nuova Italia, 1974)

Contents

MARIO LUZI

From *La barca* (1935)

L'immensità dell'attimo

Quando tra estreme ombre profonda
in aperti paesi l'estate
rapisce il canto agli armenti
e la memoria dei pastori e ovunque tace
la segreta alacrità delle specie,   5
i nascituri avvallano
nella dolce volontà delle madri
e preme i rami dei colli e le pianure
aride il progressivo esser dei frutti.
Sulla terra accadono senza luogo,   10
senza perché le indelebili
verità, in quel soffio ove affondan
leggere il peso le fronde
le navi inclinano il fianco
e l'ansia de' naviganti a strane coste,   15
il suono d'ogni voce
perde sé nel suo grembo, al mare al vento.

L'immensità dell'attimo

From Luzi's first youthful collection, this poem is an example of 1930s Florentine hermeticism at its best, expressing a quasi-mystical experience of the landscape, without descending into the exaggerated mannerism found in some hermetic texts. The title is reminiscent of some of Ungaretti's moments of cosmic insight.

1-4:   The thrust of the first clause can be reduced to: '**Quando ... l'estate rapisce il canto ... e la memoria...**' ('**profonda**' qualifies '**l'estate**'). Summer 'carries off' the 'song' (sound) of the herds ('**armenti**') and the memory of the shepherds: this introduces a sense of magic in the landscape (along with quasi-classical or idyllic motifs). '**ombre**', '**paesi**': undefined plural nouns (without articles) are one of the features of 'grammatica ermetica' identified by Mengaldo (plural nouns recur throughout this poem).

4-5:   '**alacrità**' (vivacity) is the subject of '**tace**'. As part of the magical moment the 'lively activity' of the animals ('**le specie**') falls silent. The use of an abstract noun as subject is a typical hermetic device, as is its coupling, incongruous in strictly rational terms, with the adjective '**segreta**'.

6-7:   '**nascituri**': those who are about to be born; '**avvallano**': the intransitive use of this verb is unusual and highly literary, meaning to descend, go down. Note again the incongruous use of an abstraction ('**volontà**') as the site of this action (the image is clearly an image of fertility, fruitfulness, like the following lines).

8-9:   The subject of '**preme**' is '**il progressivo** *esser* **dei frutti**', i.e. the progressive 'being' (act of being, existence) of the fruits 'presses' (weighs down) branches and plains. Another striking use of an abstraction (this time a verb), which acquires an urgent and seemingly portentous physical presence.
All of the above lines (introduced by 'Quando...') construct an atmosphere of mystery and stillness but also sensual anticipation.

10-12:   The outcome of the atmosphere described is a moment of mystical insight, of 'indelible truths' manifested on earth, in terms which are physically indeterminate ('**senza luogo**') and outside rational explanation ('**senza perché**').

12-15:   '**soffio**': breath or puff of wind (possibly with overtones of divine breath?). In this '**soffio**' leafy branches ('**fronde**') bow down (note oxymoron: '**affondan leggere il peso**') and ships lean to one side, as the '**naviganti**' (voyagers, or rather, their 'anxiety' – again an abstraction) lean towards '**strane coste**'. Thus, along with the incorporeal '**verità**' comes movement and vitality in the fabric of human experience, as we tend towards the unknown, the new.

16-17:   The individual human voice emerges momentarily, but immediately disappears, both in an inner movement ('**nel suo grembo**') and beyond in the world of '**mare**' and '**vento**', as if an attempt to find or define individual identity is overwhelmed by the 'immensity' of the moment.

From *Avvento notturno* (1940)

Avorio

Parla il cipresso equinoziale, oscuro
e montuoso esulta il capriolo,
dentro le fonti rosse le criniere
dai baci adagio lavan le cavalle.
Giù da foreste vaporose immensi   5
alle eccelse città battono i fiumi
lungamente, si muovono in un sogno
affettuose vele verso Olimpia.
Correranno le intense vie d'Oriente
ventilate fanciulle e dai mercati   10
salmastri guarderanno ilari il mondo.
Ma dove attingerò io la mia vita
ora che il tremebondo amore è morto?
Violavano le rose l'orizzonte,
esitanti città stavano in cielo   15
asperse di giardini tormentosi,
la sua voce nell'aria era una roccia
deserta e incolmabile di fiori.

Avorio

The text is composed almost entirely of hendecasyllables, elegantly constructed and rich in assonance and alliteration. The title suggests an object of polished beauty, precious and with exotic connotations, as found in the landscape/dream of the text. Curi pays an ambivalent tribute to its formal perfection: 'testo eburneo, sospeso tra fulgente visione orfica e siderale artificio' (Curi, *La poesia italiana*, p. 223).

1-4: The nature imagery here has elements of the surreal as the poet depicts an exuberant enigmatic landscape that 'speaks' to us. Logic is strained in constructions such as the opening **'Parla il cipresso equinoziale'** (**'cipresso'**: cypress; **'equinoziale'**: 'of the equinox'); the exulting 'mountainous' **'capriolo'** (roe buck); or the **'cavalle'** (subject of **'lavan'**, whose object is **'le criniere'**), washing **'baci'** from their manes.

5-6: The view of the landscape widens to include elemental scenes of forest and river. Syntax is contorted: **'immensi'** qualifies the **'fiumi'** running through **'eccelse città'** (**'eccelse'**: most high or sublime).

7-8: The poem shifts explicitly to a dream-scene, suggesting a fantastic sea voyage to Olympia (an image of some classical idyll perhaps). **'affettuose vele'**: 'affectionate sails', another example of an indeterminate plural, vague and evocative (coupled also with an incongruous adjective).

9-11: Human figures are introduced (but remain ill-defined) with the enigmatic **'ventilate fanciulle'** ('windblown maidens', note literary register), who also journey to a fantastic Orient, from where they will blissfully (**'ilari'**) observe the world: an image of escape from reality but also an aspiration to an intense experience of life; **'salmastri'**: salty, evoking the sea.

12-13: Suddenly the *io* breaks in with an anguished question (**'attingere'**: to draw [water, etc.]). The quest for **'la mia vita'** interrupts the polished literary surface and energizes the text, suggesting an urgent search for meaning, for the self, beyond the poetic word; **'amore'**: perhaps a past personal relationship, or perhaps an image of poetic perfection as evoked in the preceding lines, seen as insufficient to life itself.

14-18: In some ways, a reprise of the texture of the opening lines with images of roses, 'hesitant' celestial cities, gardens, but verbs in the imperfect now characterise this as a lost scenario; **'asperse'**: sprinkled; **'la sua voce'**: 'her' voice (or, that of 'amore'?). In either case, it too is evoked as something past: it was solid (**'roccia'**), but also desolate beyond the consolatory powers of **'fiori'** (perhaps poetry itself).

From *Onore del vero* (1957)

Nell'imminenza dei quarant'anni

Il pensiero m'insegue in questo borgo
cupo ove corre un vento d'altipiano
e il tuffo del rondone taglia il filo
sottile in lontananza dei monti.

Sono tra poco quarant'anni d'ansia,   5
d'uggia, d'ilarità improvvise, rapide
com'è rapida a marzo la ventata
che sparge luce e pioggia, son gli indugi,
lo strappo a mani tese dai miei cari,
dai miei luoghi, abitudini di anni   10
rotte a un tratto che devo ora comprendere.
L'albero di dolore scuote i rami...

Si sollevano gli anni alle mie spalle
a sciami. Non fu vano, è questa l'opera
che si compie ciascuno e tutti insieme   15
i vivi i morti, penetrare il mondo
opaco lungo vie chiare e cunicoli
fitti d'incontri effimeri e di perdite
o d'amore in amore o in uno solo
di padre in figlio fino a che sia limpido.   20

E detto questo posso incamminarmi
spedito tra l'eterna compresenza
del tutto nella vita nella morte,
sparire nella polvere o nel fuoco
se il fuoco oltre la fiamma dura ancora.   25

Nell'imminenza dei quarant'anni

Luzi was 40 in 1954, and here he takes stock on a number of levels: existential and spiritual.

1-4:   An apparently more specific landscape (**'*questo* borgo'**) than that of earlier poems, but it is evoked rather than described in realistic terms: **'cupo'** (dark, sombre) immediately suggests a metaphorical as well as literal reading for this – probably Tuscan – hill town (**'borgo'**); **'altipiano'**: upland plateau. The natural elements of **'vento'**, **'rondone'** (swift), **'filo ... dei monti'** are all somewhat generic, suggesting an inner landscape within the hermetic tradition, an 'idea of landscape' with dream-like notes (see the seminal reading of this poem in Debenedetti, pp. 107-124). From the outset, however, the text is dominated by the poet's inescapable **'pensiero'**: the crisis presented here is manifested in intellectual terms first and foremost.

5-11: The second stanza presents the life of the *io*, mostly in terms of its pains: **'ansia'**; **'uggia'** (tedium); the **'strappo'** (wrench) of separation from loved ones (by death or otherwise); **'indugi'**: hesitations; **'tese'**: outstretched. Amidst the suffering, joys (**'ilarità'**) are fleeting. This evocation by rapid allusions gives these elements an exemplary air, as of human experiences with a universal value beyond those of one man. This value is what he must now seek to understand (**'comprendere'** echoing the intellectual imperative of l. 1).

12:    The feeling of pain momentarily overcomes the process. The **'albero di dolore'** is a typically concentrated hermetic image, combining life and suffering (perhaps with an allusion to the cross of Christ).

13-14: The passing of time, so painful in stanza 2, is suddenly left to continue unheeded behind him; **'si sollevano'**: rise up; **'a sciami'**: in swarms.

14-18: The answer to the anguish of the previous stanza is unequivocal: **'non fu vano ... penetrare il mondo opaco...'**. The difficult business of 'going through' the 'opaque' world *does* have meaning and value, it is the common lot of humanity, affirmed in direct, existential terms ('l'opera / che si compie [one accomplishes] ciascuno e tutti insieme'), but it also binds us together with the other world (**'i vivi i morti'**). The language becomes more symbolic and more abstract in ll. 17-20 as the religious element gradually comes to the fore: the different types of symbolic pathway, **'vie chiare e cunicoli'** (tunnels) have distinct biblical overtones. ll. 19-20 mark a definitive shift to the language of Christian belief, as merely human love gives way to the one true Love, transmitted through generations towards ever greater perfection (**'fino a che sia limpido'**).

21-23: All anguish is set aside in the certainty of faith, allowing the *io* to move forward briskly (**'spedito'**) on the 'path' of life, seen in mystical terms as a coming together (**'compresenza'**) of contradictions (**'tutto... vita... morte'**).

24-25: He can also face death with serenity, whether death as **'polvere'** (dust, i.e. physical death) or **'fuoco'** (the fire of new life), which endures beyond the existence of the physical 'flame'. The **'se'** expresses an affirmation rather than uncertainty: 'if [as is the case]'. Notwithstanding the mystical and symbolic elements, the ending, like the rest of the poem, is largely direct and communicative in style (as compared with earlier hermetic obscurity). However, as Debenedetti observes, what it communicates is in itself 'hermetic', something that goes beyond the realm of ordinary language (Debenedetti, p. 121).

From *Nel magma* (1963)

Presso il Bisenzio [extract]

[...]
Ma uno d'essi, il più giovane, mi pare, e il più malcerto,
si fa da un lato, s'attarda sul ciglio erboso ad aspettarmi
mentre seguo lento loro inghiottiti dalla nebbia. A un passo
ormai, ma senza ch'io mi fermi, ci guardiamo,
poi abbassando gli occhi lui ha un sorriso da infermo.   5
"O Mario" dice e mi si mette al fianco
per quella strada che non è una strada
ma una traccia tortuosa che si perde nel fango
"guardati, guardati d'attorno. Mentre pensi
e accordi le sfere d'orologio della mente   10
sul moto dei pianeti per un presente eterno
che non è il nostro, che non è qui né ora,
volgiti e guarda il mondo come è divenuto,
poni mente a che cosa questo tempo ti richiede,
non la profondità, né l'ardimento,   15
ma la ripetizione di parole,
la mimesi senza perché né come
dei gesti in cui si sfrena la nostra moltitudine
morsa dalla tarantola della vita, e basta.
Tu dici di puntare alto, di là dalle apparenze,   20
e non senti che è troppo. Troppo, intendo,
per noi che siamo dopo tutto i tuoi compagni,
giovani ma logorati dalla lotta e più che dalla lotta dalla
                                        [sua mancanza umiliante".
Ascolto insieme i passi nella nebbia dei compagni che si eclissano
e questa voce venire a strappi rotta da un ansito.   25
Rispondo: "Lavoro anche per voi, per amor vostro".
Lui tace per un po' quasi a ricever questa pietra in cambio
del sacco doloroso vuotato ai miei piedi e spanto.
E come io non dico altro, lui di nuovo: "O Mario,
com'è triste essere ostili, dirti che rifiutiamo la salvezza,   30
né mangiamo del cibo che ci porgi, dirti che ci offende".
Lascio placarsi a poco a poco il suo respiro mozzato dall'affanno
mentre i passi dei compagni si spengono

e solo l'acqua della gora fruscia di quando in quando.

"È triste, ma è il nostro destino: convivere in uno stesso tempo e luogo   35
e farci guerra per amore. Intendo la tua angoscia,
ma sono io che pago tutto il debito. E ho accettato questa sorte".
E lui, ora smarrito ed indignato: "Tu? tu solamente?"
Ma poi desiste dallo sfogo, mi stringe la mano con le sue convulse
e agita il capo: "O Mario, ma è terribile, è terribile tu non sia dei nostri". 40
E piange, e anche io piangerei
se non fosse che devo mostrarmi uomo a lui che pochi ne ha veduti.
Poi corre via succhiato dalla nebbia del viottolo.

Rimango a misurare il poco detto,
il molto udito, mentre l'acqua della gora fruscia,   45
mentre ronzano fili alti nella nebbia sopra pali e antenne.
"Non potrai giudicare di questi anni vissuti a cuore duro,
mi dico, potranno altri in un tempo diverso.
Prega che la loro anima sia spoglia
e la loro pietà sia più perfetta".   50

Presso il Bisenzio [extract]

As the opening text in *Nel magma*, this poem marks a major innovation in Luzi's style. Here the poet's persona is just one of the voices in a polyphonic, almost dramatic text, with strong narrative and prosaic elements, clearly set in the world of historical reality, but a reality defamiliarized by Luzi's visionary streak. The extract is the second half of the poem, which opens on a foggy, dream-like scene beside a '**gora**' (water channel), near the Bisenzio, a tributary of the Arno, where four half-recognized figures challenge the *io* regarding his non-participation in the Resistance: 'Tu? ... Non ti sei bruciato come noi al fuoco della lotta...'. To the accusatory questions (with clear overtones concerning literary *impegno* - 'Dunque sei muto?'), he responded initially: 'È difficile spiegarti'; and that his was a 'cammino ... più lungo', taking him in other directions. The scenario of a meeting with querulous figures in the fog has strong Dantesque overtones (see *L'opera poetica*, pp. 1535-36).

1-5: The style is straightforwardly narrative, with long lines exceeding standard metrical measures. '**malcerto**': the one who stops is the least dogmatic of the group. '**ciglio**': the edge (of the path or the *gora*) '**loro inghiottiti**': the other three figures, 'swallowed' by the fog; '**A un passo**': one step away from each other.

6: '**O Mario**': the poet's name (repeated 3 times), while underlining the realistic autobiographical element, also heightens the sense that this is an intensely personal exploration. Any distance between writer and poetic *io* is reduced to a minimum.

7-8: A clear suggestion here that the '**strada**' is not simply realistic but a heightened and/or symbolic reality (but bound to the '**fango**' of the world); '**tortuosa**': twisting.

9-19: The voice admonishes Luzi for his lyrical and meditative introspection, his 'tuning' ('**accordi**') of the '**orologio della mente**' to the celestial bodies, which takes him out of the 'here and now'. Instead, he is exhorted to turn ('**volgiti**') and look at the world as it is, '**questo tempo**', which requires him to reflect reality through '**mimesi**' (mimesis: representation of reality), without questioning ('**senza perché né come**'): a clear reference to the left-wing imperative of 'realism' in literature. The reality to be portrayed is that of 'our' multitude, unleashed ('**si sfrena**') in the frenzy of life (characterized in somewhat sinister terms as a tarantula bite).

20-23: He is admonished for his transcendent vision ('**puntare alto**': aim high), seen as an excess and, in a sense, a betrayal of his 'comrades' on the left who have struggled so hard and who, perhaps with a hint of disillusionment, seem disoriented in the post-Resistance world (a disorientation reflected in the long and formless l. 23); '**logorati**': worn down.

24-28: '**si eclissano**': disappear; '**a strappi**': fitfully; '**ansito**': panting. The response by the *io*, pithy and almost condescending, seems to suggest that his 'work' has a superior status serving all men. The brevity of his answer is, as he remarks, like a 'stone' in response to his interlocutor's heartfelt appeal or '**sacco doloroso vuotato**' ('vuotare il sacco': to speak one's mind, to get it off one's chest; **'spanto'**: past participle of *spandere*, to spread or spill out).

29-31:   The young man's rejection of the 'food' of salvation offered by 'Mario' begins to take on notes of anguished hurt.

32-37:   **'placarsi'**: calm down; **'mozzato dall'affanno'**: broken by panting; **'fruscia'**: rustles. The voice of the *io* remains unmoved, firm in its conviction, and begins to introduce elements linked to a providential vision of reality: **'destino', 'sorte'** (fate). He stresses the ambivalence of his position, accepting the necessary co-existence (**'convivere'**) with others and yet affirming the almost aggressive nature of the religious mystery (an ambivalence summed up in the oxymoron **'farci guerra per amore'**: his *impegno* is both spiritual and militant). **'sono io che pago tutto il debito'**: perhaps the sense that the *disimpegnati* have been unduly persecuted in post-war culture.

38-40:   The young man's tone, despite his indignation, seems ever more confused (**'smarrito'**) and desperate for some reconciliation, or more accurately, for the poet to convert to his views; **'sfogo'**: outburst; **'convulse'**: convulsive; **'dei nostri'**: on our side.

41-43:   His weeping and disappearance into the mist carry clear echoes of Dante; **'succhiato'**: sucked in.

44-50:   The figure of the poet is left to ponder all he has heard (**'il molto udito'**) amidst elements of landscape that recall his more hermetic phase: **'acqua ... gora ... nebbia'** – but alongside the hum (**'ronzano'**) of electric or telegraph wires, indicators of an 'unpoetic' reality. His last words are addressed to the self, closing this 'historical' poem on a note of renunciation, introspection and spirituality. **'potranno altri in un tempo diverso'**: on one level a realization that the present will be 'judged' as history in some future time; on another level a reference to the 'other time' of a spiritual dimension. It remains only for him to pray for true **'pietà'** on the part of the more 'perfect' souls who may judge us. **'spoglia'**: the notion of a soul stripped of its bodily 'dress' as it moves towards perfection is a further Dantesque allusion.

From *Al fuoco della controversia* (1978)

A che pagina della storia, a che limite della sofferenza –
mi chiedo bruscamente, mi chiedo
di quel suo "ancora un poco
e di nuovo mi vedrete" detto mite, detto terribilmente

e lui forse è là, fermo nel nocciolo dei tempi,   5
là nel suo esercito di poveri
acquartierato nel protervo campo
in variabili uniformi: uno e incalcolabile
come il numero delle cellule. Delle cellule e delle rondini.

'A che pagina della storia, a che limite della sofferenza...'

This text and the one following (respectively the third and sixth short fragments in the series 'Muore ignominiosamente la repubblica') illustrate the juxtaposition of spiritual transcendence and contemporary anxieties in this phase of Luzi's work. The **'lui'** here is Christ, whose second coming is anxiously awaited.

1:      The speculation on when Christ may become manifest deftly combines the poet's historical perspective with a religious idea of inevitable suffering, 'sofferenza come superamento religiosamente dotato di senso dei limiti finora sperimentati dalla vicenda umana' (Marchi, p. 66).

2-4:   The words quoted evoke Gospel references to a promised return of the Messiah (see *L'opera poetica*, p. 1611), words which, depending on their interpretation, may be seen as 'mild' (**'mite'**) or 'terrible'.

5-7:   The voice of faith emerges, with a belief in the enduring nature of the incarnation. **'nel nocciolo dei tempi'**: in the 'kernel' of time, at the heart of history; **'acquartierato'**: billeted. The military metaphor, with Christ incarnated in the 'army' of the poor in their 'proud' camp, highlights the dimension of historical *impegno* in Luzi's faith, firmly on the side of the oppressed.

8-9:   The poem closes on a note of mystical contemplation, of the divinity's individual essence (**'uno'**) and infinite manifestations (**'incalcolabile'**), summed up in serene natural imagery (cells and swallows).

Muore ignominiosamente la repubblica.
Ignominiosamente la spiano
i suoi molti bastardi nei suoi ultimi tormenti.
Arrotano ignominiosamente il becco i corvi nella stanza accanto.
Ignominiosamente si azzuffano i suoi orfani,   5
si sbranano ignominiosamente tra di loro i suoi sciacalli.
Tutto accade ignominiosamente, tutto
meno la morte medesima – cerco di farmi intendere
dinanzi a non so che tribunale
di che sognata equità. E l'udienza è tolta.   10

'Muore ignominiosamente la repubblica...'

Dating to 1977, this is a bleak response to the crises shaking Italian society and the very institutions of the Republic (in the so-called 'years of lead', of right- and left-wing terrorism). The unwieldy **'ignominiosamente'**, repeated six times in ten lines, breaks up any natural rhythm in the piece, underlining a sense of fraught abjection.

1-6:   The various onlookers at the 'ignominious' death of the State need not necessarily be identified specifically, but the orphans' quarrelling (**'si azzuffano'**) suggests the fractious democratic parties, while **'bastardi'**, **'corvi'** (crows) and **'sciacalli'** (jackals) evoke forces of extremism, violence and self-interest; **'Arrotano ... il becco'**: they sharpen their beaks; **'si sbranano'**: rip each other apart.

7-10:   Even in a poem responding so directly to the contemporary world Luzi's tendency towards a detached position comes to the fore. The assertion that everything (including death) is ignominious, except death itself, brings us into the area of enigma and oxymoron, to which – after a half-hearted attempt by the *io* to explain to a non-existent court – there is no logical or rational response. The disenchanted irony of the close is reminiscent of Montale's work of these years.

From *Per il battesimo dei nostri frammenti* (1985)

Vola alta parola

Vola alta, parola, cresci in profondità,
tocca nadir e zenith della tua significazione,
giacché talvolta lo puoi – sogno che la cosa esclami
nel buio della mente –
però non separarti   5
da me, non arrivare,
ti prego, a quel celestiale appuntamento
da sola, senza il caldo di me
o almeno il mio ricordo, sii
luce, non disabitata trasparenza...   10

La cosa e la sua anima? o la mia e la sua sofferenza?

Vola alta parola

Notwithstanding the many (very personal) forms of engagement with historical reality in his later works, a faithful dialogue with the poetic 'word' remains a constant foundation of Luzi's writing. This collection bears an epigraph from the Gospel of John: ' In lei [la parola] era la vita; e la vita era la luce degli uomini'. In this text his address to language is full of a tension between the transcendent potential of language and his need for it to stay rooted in his reality.

1-2: He urges the word to touch both heights and depths, to encompass a seemingly impossible totality of meaning; **'nadir e zenith'**: lowest and highest points.

3-4: **'talvolta'**: this miracle of total expression can, sporadically, be a reality exclaimed like a dream in our inner darkness.

5-9: The crux of his anxiety is that there should be no separation between the word and his inner truth, that poetic expression (even when it reaches the apogee of some 'celestial' insight) should not be separated from the 'heat' of human identity. (Meanwhile, on a more purely spiritual level, there is a parallel with the idea of incarnation of the divine in human form.)

9-10: The light of true expression is distinguished from the mere **'trasparenza'** of formal perfection or abstraction (a perennial danger for the hermetic text).

11: An ambiguous line. Perhaps: '[Is the word...] the thing [i.e. objective reality] and its soul [i.e. its true meaning]? or is it mine [my soul] and its suffering?' (On **'sofferenza'**, see note to 'A che pagina della storia...' above).

SALVATORE QUASIMODO

From *Òboe sommerso* (1932)

Òboe sommerso

Avara pena, tarda il tuo dono
in questa mia ora
di sospirati abbandoni.

Un òboe gelido risillaba
gioia di foglie perenni,   5
non mie, e smemora;

in me si fa sera:
l'acqua tramonta
sulle mie mani erbose.

Ali oscillano in fioco cielo,   10
labili: il cuore trasmigra
ed io son gerbido,

e i giorni una maceria.

Òboe sommerso

From the very title, this poem unfolds as a series of enigmatic images and allusions, whose rational meaning is wrapped in obscurity. The title certainly evokes an idea of musicality, perhaps the musicality of poetry itself, which is 'submerged' or hidden and must be uncovered by the poet. For Ramat, the poem is about poetic inspiration, which gains in intensity from being 'submerged' (Ramat, *La poesia italiana 1903-1943*, p. 370).

1-3:   The *io* looks for the 'gift' of **'pena'**: he seems to be searching for some intensity of emotion which is denied to him; **'avara'**: miserly; **'tarda'**: verb *tardare*, to be slow in coming. The rich assonance of l. 1 is typical of the musical quality of Quasimodo's early work. Note the decadent languor in **'sospirati abbandoni'**.

4-6:   The musical instrument is **'gelido'**, suggesting perhaps the coldness of poetic perfection, or the sense of its distance from the *io*. **'risillaba / gioia di foglie perenni'**: 'utters again the joy of perennial leaves', a typical example of 'hermetic grammar' in its incongruous combination of undefined elements. It suggests that the poetic word contains the vitality of nature, but this joy is 'not mine'; **'smemora'**: the music 'loses its memory'.

7-9   In the absence of poetry/inspiration, darkness falls. Note the logic-challenging juxtapositions **'l'acqua tramonta'** (the water 'sets', i.e. as the sun sets), and **'mani erbose'** (grassy hands). The figure of the *io* seems to blend into an ill-defined hermetic landscape.

10-12:   Nature imagery continues (note the absence of articles with **'ali'** and **'cielo'**) as the heart 'migrates' and the *io* is transformed into an inanimate element of nature. **'gerbido'**: an adjective normally applied to land, meaning uncultivated, lying fallow, and whose coupling with 'io' stretches the limits of meaning.

13:    Generalizes the sense of the poet's anguish, which affects not just his 'heart' but also **'i giorni'** (an image of shared reality within time), which are reduced to **'maceria'** (ruin). This poem offers a good example of the centrality of the *io* in Quasimodo, seen by Barberi Squarotti as a feature which distinguishes him from the exquisitely *in*expressive work of the 'true' hermetic poets (Barberi Squarotti, pp. 260-262).

Isola

> Io non ho che te
> cuore della mia razza.

Di te amore m'attrista,
mia terra, se oscuri profumi
perde la sera d'aranci,
o d'oleandri, sereno,
cammina con rose il torrente   5
che quasi n'è tocca la foce.

Ma se torno a tue rive
e dolce voce al canto
chiama da strada timorosa
non so se infanzia o amore,   10
ansia d'altri cieli mi volge,
e mi nascondo nelle perdute cose.

Isola

One of Quasimodo's recurring themes is his sense of 'exile' from his Sicilian homeland, evoked in idyllic terms as a landscape of myth and memory. The 'tu' here is the island itself. The epigraph is from a poem in the original 1930 edition of *Acque e terre*, 'Una voce', removed from later editions (*Poesie e discorsi*, p. 822).

1-6:   The 'love' of the island saddens (**'attrista'**) the poet's persona, as the evocation of place is interwoven with a vein of introspective nostalgia. The landscape is encapsulated in typically undefined terms as **'oscuri profumi ... d'aranci o d'oleandri'** (the subject of **'perde'** is **'la sera'** and the object is **'profumi'**; **'sereno'** qualifies **'torrente'**; **'foce'**: river mouth).

7-10   The **'se'** suggests that the exile's return may be merely imagined or dreamed of, an impression reinforced by the hermetic device of omitting articles with almost all the nouns here, giving a sense of generic images rather than tangible reality; **'rive'**: shores. The objects of **'chiama'** are **'infanzia o amore'**: the disembodied voice calls to the poet's love of his place along with his memories of childhood.

11-12:   The *io* cannot escape the anguish of his exile under **'altri cieli'**, which 'turns' (**'volge'**) or distracts him, but still he seeks (and finds?) refuge in the **'perdute cose'** of his lost idyll. There is a certain ambiguity at the close, as to whether the refuge is achieved or the 'hiding' is a vain attempt to escape the reality that this landscape is 'lost'.

ALFONSO GATTO

From *Isola* (1932)

Carri d'autunno

Nello spazio lunare
pesa il silenzio dei morti.
Ai carri eternamente remoti
il cigolío dei lumi
improvvisa perduti e beati   5
villaggi di sonno.

Come un tepore troveranno l'alba
gli zingari di neve,
come un tepore sotto l'ala i nidi.

Cosí lontano a trasparire il mondo   10
ricorda che fu d'erba, una pianura.

Carri d'autunno

The main image of **'carri'** (wagons) refers to a gypsy caravan, but the word may also allude to the constellations of Ursa Major and Ursa Minor (Segre and Ossola, *Antologia*, p. 519).

1-2:   The depiction of nocturnal silence in terms of 'lunar' space and of **'i morti'** establishes a setting beyond 'normal' perceptions of space and life.

3-6:   The **'carri'** of l. 3 may be the constellations, in the face of which the **'cigolío'** (creaking) of lights on gypsy carts conjures up ('improvises') some lost but apparently magical 'sleep villages' (dream places?). The difficulty of establishing a clear meaning stems partly from the highly ambiguous use of the preposition **'a'** in l. 3.

7-9:   Here the allusion to the **'zingari'** (gypsies) is made clearer, as they look forward to the **'tepore'** (warmth) of dawn. **'zingari di neve'**: another example of elliptical hermetic syntax, associating the 'zingari' with the qualities and experience of snow, on multiple and undefined levels.

10-11:   The sense may be: 'The world, appearing so distantly [slowly emerging from darkness?] reminds them [or remembers] that it was once a plain (**'pianura'**), made of grass'. It is the emergence of reality from the mysteries of night, evoked with a tremulous impressionism.

PIERO BIGONGIARI

From *La figlia di Babilonia* (1942)

Assenza

Non ha il cielo un segreto che ti culmini,
le tue risa s'iridano al vetro
della sera dolcissima di fulmini.
Al cielo sale nel tuo gesto effimero
la riga d'un diamante, lo smeriglio   5
ricalcola all'assenza una giunchiglia
morta nel sonno e al tenero fermaglio
del tuo dolore che non si può chiudere
geleranno dagli astri luci blu,
luci sorte alla piega delle labbra   10
che rimormorano arse cielo al cielo.

Dove un rapido greto si distrugge,
dove odorano (al tuo braccio?) gaggie,
segreto faccio
mia la tua pena che non ti raggiunge.   15

Assenza

This text, like many of Bigongiari's, resists attempts to paraphrase its sense logically. Its metre consists almost entirely of hendecasyllables.

1-3: The *tu* is placed in relation to a higher realm (**'cielo'**), which seems to hold no secret superior to her; **'culmini'**: culminates (subjunctive), a highly unusual transitive use of this verb. Her laughter shines iridescently on/through glass, against evening/lightning; **'s'iridano'**: assume rainbow colours (a highly Montalean image).

4-5: With her 'ephemeral gesture' (again one thinks of Montale's *Mottetti* or indeed *Finisterre* – see Ramat, *La poesia italiana*, pp. 462-3), there rises a 'diamond track' (**'riga'**) to the sky.

5-7: The syntax and semantic aspects become highly problematic here. A possible literal reading is: 'the *smeriglio* [the mineral emery] recalculates in [your?] absence a jonquil [type of daffodil] which has died in sleep'. This presumably is a further event associated with 'il tuo gesto' (l. 4).

7-11: Again a literal paraphrasing might be: 'at the tender clasp (**'fermaglio'**) of your pain, that cannot be closed, blue lights will freeze from the stars, lights that have emerged (**'sorte'**) at/from the fold of [your?] lips, which murmur, burnt (**'arse'**), [from] sky to sky'. In the lines above there are numerous examples of typical 'hermetic grammar' (Mengaldo), from the incongruous combinations of nouns, verbs and adjectives (**'lo smeriglio ricalcola'**; **'tenero fermaglio'**; **'geleranno ... luci'**) to undefined nouns (**'astri'**; **'luci'**) to the ambiguous use of prepositional links, especially 'a' (**'al vetro'**; **'all'assenza'**; **'al fermaglio'**; **'alla piega'**).

12-13: The setting for the 'action' of the closing lines seemingly involves a river bank and floral perfume. **'greto'**: dry part of a river bed (other poems allude to the Arno); **'gaggie'**: a highly perfumed evergreen plant; **'al tuo braccio?'**: the combination of an ambiguous **'a'** with the interrogative leads again to an openness of meaning.

14-15: In this setting, the *io* is introduced in the relatively unambiguous phrase **'faccio / mia la tua pena'**: 'I make your suffering mine'; **'segreto'**: qualifies the *io*, who therefore remains hidden. The relative simplicity of the proposition is, however, clouded by the final words **'che non ti raggiunge'**: if 'your' pain 'does not reach you', it is not clear in what sense it is 'yours'. We are left with the sense of an intense, troubled, quest for some identification or contact with an absent *tu*, whose presence is hinted at in the multifarious phenomena of a surreal nature (sky, stars, plants, gems), which are thus endowed with mysterious symbolic significance. Thus what Bigongiari gives us of his 'dramma amoroso' are, in Ramat's words 'più le ossessioni che i contenuti' (Ramat, *La poesia italiana 1903-1943*, p. 465).

6

Engaging with Reality

Even in the heyday of the hermetic movement, in the culturally stifling environment of the 1930s, in which so many writers chose to turn inward, there were still voices that sought to bring the reality of the external world into poetry. Indeed, as we have seen in the case of Saba (and, in less obvious ways, that of Montale also), the apparent hegemony of 'pure' lyricism and of the broadly 'hermetic' manner was never total, although those who stood outside the mainstream risked isolation, or worse, indifference and obscurity. There were also, of course, important precedents in the early avant-garde movements for a model of poetic discourse not exclusively centred on the lyrical *io* (one may think, for example, of the emphasis placed on banal objects in crepuscular poetry). In fact, an idea of poetry as a more inclusive genre, open to narrative elements, multiple voices and the direct depiction of social or other realities (whether in concrete or more impressionistic terms), can be seen to act as a hidden counterbalance to hermetic introspection even in the inter-war years. The most notable example in the 1930s is the work of Cesare Pavese, in particular his 1936 collection *Lavorare stanca*. Pavese is known primarily as the author of post-war novels such as *La luna e i falò*, but his vocation as a novelist is also reflected in the narrative and descriptive vein which dominates much of this early collection of poetry. Among other poets writing in broadly similar veins of impressionistic realism in these years, two notable voices (not represented in this anthology) are Sandro Penna (1906-1977) and Attilio Bertolucci (1911-2000), both of whom continued to publish also in the post-war decades. Bertolucci's understated lyricism evokes both emotional and physical realities in a delicate balance, whereas Penna's deceptively simple but highly-crafted style creates striking word-pictures, whose intense physicality underpins his homo-erotic themes: 'Dal portiere non c'era nessuno./ C'era la luce sui poveri letti/ disfatti. E sopra un tavolaccio/ dormiva un ragazzaccio/ bellissimo. [...]' ('Interno', from *Poesie*, 1939).

   With the fall of Mussolini in 1943, and the trauma of war and civil war culminating in the liberation from Fascism in 1945, the hidden current of what we can call poetic 'realism' suddenly becomes a highly visible one, openly challenging the supremacy of the more established, intimist, lyrical voice. The impact of a dramatic 'realtà extraletteraria' gives rise to poetry that has at its centre, in the words of Giancarlo Majorino 'l'esserci palese di quello che c'è'.[i] The decade and a half from 1945 to the early 1960s sees the emergence of new voices, new themes and new formal and stylistic approaches. Indeed, it has been suggested that if we are to insist on counting poetic history in centuries, it is in fact at this mid-century point that the foundations of a new poetic canon are laid.[ii] These are, initially, the years of neo-realism, the post-war explosion in the representations of historical and social realities, especially in the novel and cinema. The works of novelists such as Pavese, Vittorini, Calvino, as well as directors like Rossellini, depict recent and current historical events (war and Resistance, social and political struggles) with great communicative immediacy and stylistic energy. In the field of poetry, also, there were calls for a new *impegno*, or engagement with reality, a break with the monostylistic lyricism that was seen as dominating the recent past. Such demands, in particular on the part of more ideologically-driven writers and critics of the political left, coincided often with a polemical, indeed moralistic condemnation of the poetry of the preceding decades, seen indiscriminately as a uniform mass of narcissistic self-obsession, culpably divorced from reality in its preoccupation with form.[iii] However, neo-realism never became as strong a tendency in poetry as in narrative. It has been observed that neo-realist poetry was in a sense caught between on the one hand the entrenched dominance of 'hermetic' modes and language within the lyric genre, and, on the other, the emerging supremacy of narrative as the ideal communicative vehicle of the moment.[iv] Still, the neorealist climate is unmistakably present, perhaps nowhere more visibly than in the work of Salvatore Quasimodo. Quasimodo's poetry in the immediate post-war years undergoes a remarkable transformation in its themes, tone and diction, as he re-invents his voice broadly in line with the tenets of left-wing realism, and spurns the introspective lyricism of his earlier work (see chapter on the Hermetic generation above). His is an extreme example of poetic 'conversion', but the forces of change, opening the world of the poetic *io* to a historical dimension, can also be seen operating in subtler ways, perhaps the more convincing because more gradual, in the work of other poets of the hermetic generation: see for example the organic development of Sereni's verse towards quasi-realist modes, or Luzi's lyrical opening towards the world, or indeed Montale's stylistic renewal in *La bufera e altro* and subsequent collections. In the words of Ermanno Krumm, 'tutti scoprono la realtà e, indipendemente dal neorealismo, che resta sostanzialmente estraneo alla poesia, cercano una lingua in grado di parlare di ogni suo aspetto'.[v]

The late 1950s was a time of rapid transformation for Italian society. The hopes and aspirations for profound social, political and economic change in the wake of the Resistance had now been replaced by disillusionment for many on the left. With the Christian Democrats consolidated in power, there now began the years of the so-called 'economic miracle', the extraordinarily rapid boom (lasting from the mid-1950s to the early '60s) which transformed Italy in a few years from a predominantly rural economy and society into a major industrial power, with all the attendant problems of economic, social and cultural dislocation. It is at this point, rather than in 1945, that truly new directions begin to emerge, as Italian poets increasingly ground their language in a dimension of objective reality, external to the lyrical *io*, employing multiple linguistic registers and heterogeneous stylistic solutions in contrast with the predominantly 'monostylistic' approaches of the previous era.[vi]

In 1955 Pier Paolo Pasolini, along with Francesco Leonetti and Roberto Roversi, founded the journal *Officina* (meaning 'workshop', in the industrial sense), which soon became an important forum for exponents of a new literary experimentalism. *Officina* conducted a literary polemic on two fronts. On the one hand it stood against the poetics of *novecentismo*, the idea of poetry as a refined lyrical exploration of the self, aspiring to the sublime, the expression of essential, transcendent truths through forms of linguistic and stylistic purity, a line which was still seen by many as the principal axis of modern Italian poetry, from Ungaretti to the hermetics.[vii] But while rejecting this kind of literary purity, the *Officina* group also took up a position, from an independent left-wing perspective, against the overly-prescriptive ideological tenets of neorealism. The exact nature of the alternative they proposed, however, was less clear: they were always an eclectic group (Pasolini embodied within himself many of their conflicts and contradictions) and their innovative formal solutions were soon to be superseded by the more radical experimentalism of the new avant-garde (see *neoavanguardia* chapter below).[viii] Nevertheless, their emphasis on an idea of *antinovecentismo* (with Giovanni Pascoli as a distant stylistic precursor), on a kind of ethical poetry more open to narrative, realistic and impressionistic elements, served to consolidate the broadly realist current which is the subject of this chapter, and within which Pasolini's work occupies an important place, both as theoretician and practitioner.[ix] Among the other regular contributors to the intense ideological and literary polemics generated by *Officina* were the poet and critic Franco Fortini (though he was never strictly a part of the group), and Roberto Roversi (another notable poet, though not represented here below). Also Elio Pagliarani, a figure subsequently identified with the 1960s *neoavanguardia*, was initially linked to *Officina*: a fact which higlights the complexity and permeability of groupings such as these, and should warn us against seeking neat or simplistic lines of demarcation between different tendencies.

Meanwhile, there are other, more individual voices represented in this chapter, for whom the choice of realistic or narrative modes represents not so much an ideological imperative, but a vocation deeply rooted in their nature as artists. This is certainly the case for Giorgio Caproni, who, though he starts to write and publish verse in the 1930s is ultimately more open to the influence of Saba than to the rarefied allusiveness of the lyrical mainstream of those years. As for the generation emerging after the Second World War, we find idiosyncratic voices such as those of Giovanni Giudici and Giovanni Raboni, both of whom make their very personal contributions to the poetry of the so-called *linea lombarda*, identified initially by Anceschi in 1952.[x]

The poems brought together in this chapter can be seen to engage, albeit in different ways and with different intentions on the part of their authors, with the reality of the world beyond the self, beyond the individual's inner life. In bringing the work of these poets together here, however, it is not my intention to suggest the establishment of any simplistic critical construct of 'realist' poetry, just as the main focus on the key post-war years should not be taken to indicate a rigid division into historically-determined periods. On the contrary, the fact that many of these poets start to write in the 1930s and that some go on into 1980s and '90s underlines the presence of overlapping, interweaving currents. The equally important fact that 'pure' lyricism continues to be an important element in the poetry of the second half of the century further demonstrates the necessarily schematic, not to say reductive, nature of critical or historiographical categories such as 'realism', 'hermeticism' or 'lyricism'. There are many different ways of distinguishing and defining the trends and movements that make up the complex poetic history of the period in question.[xi] In bringing together a number of 'realistic' poems here (whether realistic in form or in content, or both), the intention is to highlight the importance of this broad current over many decades, but also to show some of the many possible approaches to poetic realism and the vast diversity of the resulting texts.

Cesare Pavese

A native of the Langhe area of Piedmont, Cesare Pavese (1908-1950) studied in Turin and went on to become part of the important anti-Fascist intellectual circles there. In 1935 he was arrested for anti-Fascist activities and sent into internal exile (*confino*) in Calabria for a year. His collection of poems *Lavorare stanca* was published in 1936. Meanwhile he worked on translations (particularly of American authors) and on his own novels, which would be published throughout the 1940s. He committed suicide in 1950, the year of publication of his novel *La luna e i falò*.

Appropriately for a writer who would achieve fame primarily as a novelist, Pavese's early poetic work has a strong narrative element. In contrast to the lyrical introspection which dominated the poetry of the 1930s, Pavese's poems look outwards to the surrounding social environment. His poems often tell stories, offering glimpses of the lives of ordinary people against a background of objective realities, expressed in language full of everyday, prosaic elements, with tonalities of the spoken word in the long narrative lines: 'Mio cugino ha una faccia recisa. Comprò un pianterreno/ nel paese e ci fece riuscire un garage di cemento/ con dinanzi fiammante la pila per dar la benzina/...' ('I mari del sud'). And while the isolation of individuals, their problematic relationships and mutual incomprehension, can have timeless significance, there is also a sense of the particular historical context of such alienation in Fascist Italy. This world is given formal expression in a highly personal, original poetic idiom: in long poetic lines, Pavese uses language drawn from a variety of registers, with frequent recourse to the 'lower' or more colloquial registers and a notable presence of the concrete vocabulary of physical reality. In the text reproduced here, as in others, the lyrical *io* is entirely displaced by the narrating voice of a character (in this case, Deola, a prostitute), whose thoughts are intermingled with the direct speech of other voices.[xii]

Salvatore Quasimodo

See paragraph on Quasimodo in the chapter: *Luzi and the Hermetic Generation*.

Giorgio Caproni

Although a contemporary of the hermetic generation, Caproni (1912-1990) follows a distinctive and highly individual poetic path, one of 'melodismo e prosaicità autobiografica' that avoids the mainstream of *novecentismo* and finds parallels, especially in his earlier periods, in the work of Saba, not least in his accomplished capacity to 'cantare e narrare insieme'.[xiii] A native of Livorno, Caproni lived in Genoa from the age of ten, and would later move to Rome, where he worked as a teacher. Recurring themes in his work are those of the city, the figure of his mother, and the journey, all of which contribute to a common thematic strand of 'exile'.[xiv] While the world of objects, places and human presences looms large in his work, these are often felt to be 'outside' of historical reality, placed in a realm of private 'innocence' and authenticity.[xv] The echoes of Saba are most apparent in Caproni's (partial) adoption of fixed verse forms of the pre-*Novecento* tradition and in the exquisite charm with which the poet's personal urban landscapes are evoked. Caproni's port-cities of Livorno and Genova, evoked in all their sensory detail, recall Saba's Trieste in several respects, and indeed the cycle of 'love-poems' in *Il seme del piangere*, dedicated to the imagined figure of the poet's mother as a young woman, must surely remind us of some of Saba's idiosyncratic love poems, with their tormented psychological background beneath an apparently simple surface. In Caproni's later work there is an increasing centrality of existential or quasi-religious questioning, although the latter is always more concerned with doubt and absence than with any positive faith.

Pier Paolo Pasolini

Pasolini (1922-1975) made his mark on Italian culture across a wide range of creative and critical activities: from the Friulian dialect poetry of the early years (in *La meglio gioventù*), to the poetry of ideological and civic *impegno* of the later 1950s; from the novels set amidst the Roman underclass (*Ragazzi di vita* in 1955, and *Una vita violenta* in 1959) to his emergence as an internationally recognized cinema director in the 1960s and 1970s; a prodigious creative output which was underpinned by a constant presence as critic and commentator, and through which Pasolini became an embodiment of cultural dissent.[xvi] A left-wing radical outside of party orthodoxy, he is a figure whose image came ultimately to be dominated by the tragic and violent circumstances of his death in 1975, apparently at the hands of a casual lover (a murder which has continued to give rise to conspiracy theories over the years).

Through the pages of *Officina* from 1955 onwards, Pasolini gave trenchant expression to his belief in the need for a formal and ethical renewal in Italian poetry, in the face of the dominant lyrical line. Pasolini espoused a new vision of narrative poetry which would bring together individual lyrical sensibilities and broader ethical and political perspectives, expressed in a language which, while realistic and concrete, should also be marked by formal and stylistic experimentation and innovation, including the use of multiple registers of tone and vocabulary, from the abstract and ideological to the concrete and realistic and indeed the lyrical. One of his preferred genres is the *poemetto* (extended narrative poem), typically, as in the example reproduced here, written in *terzine*, lengthy sequences of tercets linked together, albeit loosely, by rhyme: it is a form whose model can be found in Pascoli, but also, ultimately, in Dante, both writers whose work resonates, in different ways, with that of Pasolini.

Franco Fortini

Fortini (1917-1994) was not only a poet but also a critic, academic and essayist, as well as a cultural and ideological commentator whose influence was widely felt throughout the post-war decades in Italy. Although his roots are generationally and geographically close to the Florentine hermetics, his poetry follows different pathways. His participation in the Resistance is reflected in his 1946 collection *Foglio di via*, where along with hermetic elements, echoes of the broader neo-realist trend can clearly be discerned. His subsequent work continues to be politically engaged, but he keeps a critical distance, both as poet and thinker, from left-wing party orthodoxies. Though associated with *Officina*, Fortini also eschews linguistic experimentalism. His *impegno* is concerned with a dogged pursuit of intellectual rigour and poetic authenticity rather than any facile representational realism. The result is often poetry of considerable density and complexity, not to mention ambiguity and contradictions, between 'esigenze rivoluzionarie' and, in formal terms, 'valori della tradizione'.[xvii]

Elio Pagliarani

Pagliarani (1927–) was one of the five poets included in Giuliani's 1961 anthology *I Novissimi*, marking him unequivocally as part of the *neoavanguardia* (see relevant chapter below). Despite this, and notwithstanding the innovative character of his work and his extensive involvement in the *Gruppo 63* and the broader avant-garde movement of those years, one cannot help feeling that his major early work *La ragazza Carla* does not sit entirely easily with the other texts in the *Novissimi* volume.

However, this text does lie at the more experimental end of what we might call the spectrum of poetic realism. It marks, according to Di Paola, an evolutionary moment in contemporary poetic language, in the transition 'dal neorealismo alla neoavanguardia'.[xviii] In this extended poetic text, Pagliarani is clearly influenced also by Pavese's experiments with narrative verse in *Lavorare stanca*: this can be seen for example in the long lines, the choice of a young working class woman as protagonist, and in certain echoes of Pavese's particular rhythmic patterns. One may also detect distant echoes of the *crepuscolari*, with their world of pathetic objects and ironic tonalities. On the other hand, Pagliarani's tendency towards linguistic experimentalism and an ethical or ideological critique of reality also clearly resonates in the 1950s with the contemporary experimentalism of Pasolini's *Officina*. Perhaps the most consistent element in Pagliarani's poetry is the element of ethical tension that underpins his various formal approaches over different periods: at the heart of his work lies what Raboni calls an 'implacabile volontà didascalica' of Brechtian derivation.[xix]

Giovanni Giudici

Another relatively isolated figure is Giovanni Giudici (1924-), whose poetry, though largely coinciding with the post-war years of neo-realism and the subsequent period of experimentalism in the 1950s and '60s, is conceived and developed following a very personal vein of autobiographical realism, as encapsulated in the title of his first major collection, *La vita in versi* (1965). Born near La Spezia, he lived as a young man in Rome (where he received the 'educazione cattolica' that he would later recall with ironic affection in his verse), eventually becoming a journalist and settling in Milan in the late 1950s, where we worked for Olivetti. It is the Milan of the early 1960s, the years of the Italian 'economic miracle', that provides the setting and material for *La vita in versi*: a collection that charts the vicissitudes of everyday life and ponders some of the practical and ethical dilemmas faced by the *io-impiegato*, a sort of caricature or double, portrayed with some ambivalence, and with an ironic and resolutely non-lyrical voice that owes something to Saba, as well as to the *crepuscolari*, not to mention Caproni and, in some respects, Montale. Giudici eschews the experimentalism of the neo-avantgarde in favour of a communicative voice, giving us a series of 'metafore intense del tran-tran giornaliero', within broadly conventional verse and strophic forms.[xx] The overall effect, in Lorenzini's words, is not so much one of straightforward lyrical realism as of defamiliarization, a 'descrivere straniato'.[xxi]

Giovanni Raboni

Raboni's native city of Milan is a constant presence in his work, especially in his first major collection *Le case della Vetra* (1966). Raboni (1932-2004) is a poet who finds his voice broadly within the strands of the modern tradition represented by Saba and Montale, and whose work resonates clearly with elements of the *linea lombarda*, notably with the work of Sereni. In the poem presented here, Raboni writes of the changing Milan of the 1960s, and, like Giudici, he uses a language and tone that often border on the prosaic or colloquial, his stylistic refinement masked by a 'tono dimesso, conversevole'.[xxii] He is a poet of 'understatement morale e stilistico', and though the world of objective reality is strongly in evidence, there are also frequent allusions to the voices of the dead, and his portrait of the city appears at times 'spettrale e spaesato'.[xxiii] Raboni was also a notable translator, for example of Baudelaire and Proust, and critic (see for example his exemplary essay 'Poeti del secondo Novecento' in the Garzanti *Storia della letteratura italiana*.[xxiv]

Endnotes

[i] Giancarlo Majorino, *Poesia e realtà: 1945-2000* (Milan: Tropea, 2000), p. 35. Majorino presents a kind of alternative anthological portrait of the decades in question, tracing a 'realist' vein through the works of many (and diverse) poets.

[ii] See Cucchi and Giovanardi, *Poeti italiani del secondo Novecento*, pp. xi-xxi.

[iii] The crudely prescriptive nature of some of these positions is noted by Giorgio Barberi Squarotti and Anna Maria Golfieri in *Dal tramonto dell'ermetismo alla neoavanguardia* (Brescia: La Scuola, 1984), pp. 5-22.

[iv] Giorgio Luti and Caterina Verbaro, *Dal Neorealismo alla Neoavanguardia* (Firenze: Le Lettere, 1995), p. 53.

[v] Ermanno Krumm, *Poesia italiana del Novecento* (Milan: Skira, 1995), p. 599.

[vi] See Cucchi and Giovanardi, *Poeti italiani del secondo Novecento*, pp. xvii-xviii.

[vii] This idea of 'lirica nuova' had been highlighted as the dominant trend for example in the important 1953 anthology, *Lirica del Novecento*, ed. by L. Anceschi and S. Antonielli (Firenze: Vallecchi, 1953).

[viii] On Pasolini and *Officina*, see Robert S.C. Gordon, *Pasolini. Forms of Subjectivity* (Oxford: Clarendon Press, 1996), pp. 40-47. See also Luti and Verbaro, pp. 23-27.

[ix] In Raboni's view, however, the significance of *antinovecentismo* has been somewhat overstated. See Giovanni Raboni, *La poesia che si fa* (Milan: Garzanti, 2005), p. 211.

[x] See Luciano Anceschi, *Linea lombarda: sei poeti* (Varese: Magenta, 1952).

[xi] Fortini, for example, brings together many of the names represented in this chapter, along with those of Montale, Sereni and Luzi, under the avowedly broad heading of 'poesia dell'esistenzialismo storico' (*I poeti del Novecento*, pp. 6-7 and 163-4), while

Mengaldo warns against over-simplistic periodizations 'a senso unico' (*Poeti italiani del Novecento*, pp. lvii-lviii).

xii   On Pavese's use of narrative mouthpieces for the *io lirico*, see Giorgio Barberi Squarotti, *La poesia del Novecento*, pp. 263-87.

xiii   See respectively, Mengaldo, *Poeti italiani del Novecento*, p. 701; and Beccaria, in Caproni, *Poesie (1932-1986)* (Milan: Garzanti, 1989), p. 809.

xiv   See Raboni, *La poesia che si fa*, p. 135.

xv   Mengaldo, *Poeti italiani del Novecento*, p. 702.

xvi   On Pasolini's work in general, see Gordon, *Pasolini. Forms of Subjectivity*.

xvii   Raboni, *La poesia che si fa*, p. 194.

xviii   Gabriella Di Paola, *La ragazza Carla: linguaggio e figure* (Roma: Bulzoni, 1984), p. 11.

xix   Raboni, *La poesia che si fa*, p. 207.

xx   Majorino, *Poesia e realtà*, p. 43.

xxi   Lorenzini, *La poesia italiana del Novecento*, p. 149.

xxii   Fausto Curi, *La poesia italiana nel Novecento*, p. 397.

xxiii   Mengaldo, *Poeti italiani del Novecento*, p. 987.

xxiv   Raboni, 'Poeti del secondo Novecento' in *Storia della letteratura italiana*, diretta da Emilio Cecchi e Natalino Sapegno, nuova ed. a cura di N. Sapegno, vol. VII, *Il Novecento* (Milan: Garzanti, 1986), pp. 209-248.

Poetic texts

Cesare Pavese
Le poesie, a cura di Mariarosa Masoero (Turin: Einaudi, 1998)

Salvatore Quasimodo
Poesie e discorsi sulla poesia, a cura di Gilberto Finzi, I Meridiani (Milan: Mondadori, 1971)

Giorgio Caproni
Complete editions are:
Poesie: 1932-1986 (Milan: Garzanti, 1989), which includes a selection of key critical writings on Caproni;
L'opera in versi, I Merdiani (Milan: Mondadori, 1998).

Pier Paolo Pasolini
Bestemmia: Tutte le poesie, a cura di Graziella Chiarcossi and Walter Siti (Milan: Garzanti, 1993)

Franco Fortini
A wide selection of his poems is in: *Versi scelti: 1939-1989* (Turin: Einaudi, 1990)

Elio Pagliarani
Tutte le poesie (1946-2005), a cura di Andrea Cortellessa (Milan: Garzanti, 2006)

Giovanni Giudici
I versi della vita, a cura di Rodolfo Zucco, I Meridiani (Milan: Mondadori, 2000)

Giovanni Raboni
L'opera poetica, a cura di Rodolfo Zucco, I Meridiani (Milan: Mondadori, 2006)

Further reading

Anceschi, Luciano, *Linea lombarda: sei poeti* (Varese: Magenta, 1952).
Barberi Squarotti, Giorgio, and Anna Maria Golfieri, *Dal tramonto dell'ermetismo alla neoavanguardia* (Brescia: La Scuola, 1984)
Bazzocchi, Marco, *Pier Paolo Pasolini* (Milan: Bruno Mondadori, 1998)
Beccaria, Gian Luigi, 'Caproni, la poesia, e oltre', in Caproni, *Poesie (1932-1986)* (Milan: Garzanti, 1989), pp. 809-12
Berardinelli, Alfonso, *Franco Fortini* (Florence: La Nuova Italia, 1974)
Brevini, Franco, *Per conoscere Pasolini* (Milan: Mondadori, 1981)
Calvino, Italo, 'Il taciturno ciarliero', in Caproni, *Poesie (1932-1986)* (Milan: Garzanti, 1989), pp. 803-806

Colombo, Gianfranco, *Guida alla lettura di Pavese* (Milano: Mondadori, 1988)

Dei, Adele, *Giorgio Caproni* (Milan: Mursia, 1992)

Di Paola, Gabriella, *La ragazza Carla: linguaggio e figure* (Roma: Bulzoni, 1984)

Gigliucci, Roberto, *Cesare Pavese* (Milano: Bruno Mondadori, 2001)

Gordon, Robert S.C., *Pasolini: Forms of Subjectivity* (Oxford: Clarendon Press, 1996)

Guglielminetti, Marziano, *Cesare Pavese: introduzione e guida allo studio dell'opera pavesiana* (Florence: Le Monnier, 1980)

Leonelli, Giuseppe, *Giorgio Caproni: Una guida alla lettura di un grande poeta del Novecento* (Milan: Garzanti, 1997)

Luti, Giorgio and Caterina Verbaro, *Dal Neorealismo alla Neoavanguardia* (Florence: Le Lettere, 1995)

Majorino, Giancarlo, *Poesia e realtà: 1945-2000* (Milan: Tropea, 2000)

Mazzoni, Guido, 'La poesia di Raboni', *Studi novecenteschi*, 19 (1992)

Mengaldo, Pier Vincenzo, 'Per la poesia di Fortini', in *La tradizione del Novecento: da D'Annunzio a Montale* (Milan: Feltrinelli, 1975), pp. 387-405

Muñiz Muñiz, M. de las Nieves, *Introduzione a Pavese* (Roma-Bari: Laterza, 1992)

O'Healy, Áine, *Cesare Pavese* (Boston: Twayne, 1988)

Raboni, Giovanni, *La poesia che si fa* (Milan: Garzanti, 2005)

Surdich, Luigi, *Giorgio Caproni: un ritratto* (Genoa: Costa & Nolan: 1990)

Thompson, Doug, *Cesare Pavese: A study of the major novels and poems* (Cambridge: Cambridge University Press, 1982)

Zanzotto, Andrea, 'Pasolini poeta', in *Aure e disincanti del Novecento letterario* (Milan: Mondadori, 1994), pp. 153-60

Contents

CESARE PAVESE

From *Lavorare stanca* (1936)

Pensieri di Deola

Deola passa il mattino seduta al caffè
e nessuno la guarda. A quest'ora in città corron tutti
sotto il sole ancor fresco dell'alba. Non cerca nessuno
neanche Deola, ma fuma pacata e respira il mattino.
Fin che è stata in pensione, ha dovuto dormire a quest'ora   5
per rifarsi le forze: la stuoia sul letto
la sporcavano con le scarpacce soldati e operai,
i clienti che fiaccan la schiena. Ma, sole, è diverso:
si può fare un lavoro piú fine, con poca fatica.
Il signore di ieri, svegliandola presto,   10
l'ha baciata e condotta (*mi fermerei, cara,*
a Torino con te, se potessi) con sé alla stazione
a augurargli buon viaggio.

                  È intontita ma fresca stavolta,
e le piace esser libera, Deola, e bere il suo latte
e mangiare brioches. Stamattina è una mezza signora   15
e, se guarda i passanti, fa solo per non annoiarsi.
A quest'ora in pensione si dorme e c'è puzzo di chiuso
— la padrona va a spasso — è da stupide stare là dentro.
Per girare la sera i locali, ci vuole presenza
e in pensione, a trent'anni, quel po' che ne resta, si è perso.   20

Deola siede mostrando il profilo a uno specchio
e si guarda nel fresco del vetro. Un po' pallida in faccia:
non è il fumo che stagni. Corruga le ciglia.
Ci vorrebbe la voglia che aveva Marí, per durare
in pensione (*perché, cara donna, gli uomini*   25
vengon qui per cavarsi capricci che non glieli toglie
né la moglie né l'innamorata) e Marí lavorava
instancabile, piena di brio e godeva salute.
I passanti davanti al caffè non distraggono Deola

che lavora soltanto la sera, con lente conquiste　　　　　　　30
nella musica del suo locale. Gettando le occhiate
a un cliente o cercandogli il piede, le piaccion le orchestre
che la fanno parere un'attrice alla scena d'amore
con un giovane ricco. Le basta un cliente
ogni sera e ha da vivere. (*Forse il signore di ieri*　　　　　35
mi portava davvero con sé). Stare sola, se vuole,
al mattino, e sedere al caffè. Non cercare nessuno.

Pensieri di Deola

Lavorare stanca was first published by the Florentine journal *Solaria* in 1936, but this poem dates to 1932. Here as elsewhere, Pavese's long lines are not just *verso libero*, but have a particular rhythmic pattern, with four or five main accents in the line, in a succession of trisyllabic feet, with the stress on the third syllable (e.g. 'per rifàrsi le fòrze: la stuòia sul lètto'): a rhythm suited to a narrative tone and measure.

1-4:   Straightforward, descriptive impressions of an urban scenario (including hints of the anonymity it provides); **'pacata'**: calm.

5-9:   Deola recalls her work **'in pensione'** (here meaning in a brothel) before starting to work alone; **'rifarsi le forze'**: get one's strength back; **'stuoia'**: (straw) mat; **'scarpacce'**: rough shoes; **'fiaccan la schiena'**: break your back (note language of concrete realism); **'sole'**: on your own (fem. plur. of 'solo', in impersonal sense).

10-16:   She recalls yesterday's client: note the inclusion of his direct speech, multiplying the voices in the text; **'intontita'**: dazed; **'una mezza signora'**: almost a lady (with clear ironic overtones).

17-20:   **'puzzo di chiuso'**: again note crude corporeal language in the description of the 'pensione'; **'da stupide'**: for stupid people; **'locali'**: bars, cafés; **'presenza'**: attractive 'presence', good looks (emphasising Deola's belief that her current work is on a superior level); **'quel po' che ne resta…'**: a hint perhaps that she is past her prime, deluding herself that her life is improving.

21-23:   The image of the mirror emphasises her introspection but also suggests a kind of doubling of the self in a constructed image. **'non è il fumo che stagni'**: 'it is not the smoke stagnating', i.e. her pale complexion is not just due to the smoky atmosphere.

24-28:   **'la voglia'**: enthusiasm, attributed to Marí, her one-time colleague; **ll.25-27**: again, another voice, that of Marì, giving her view of their clients in the colloquial tones of a spoken exchange; **'cavarsi capricci'**: to satisfy desires, whims.

29-36:   Deola gives her 'slow conquests', with their musical backdrop, an illusory, romantic veneer, her role as **'attrice'** in implicit contrast to crude reality. There is an alternation of matter-of-fact calculation (**'Le basta un cliente…'**) and dreamy fantasy (***'Forse il signore…'***)

36-37:   Her self-contained solitude conceals, perhaps, a deeper existential isolation. Barberi Squarotti calls her 'un personaggio fondamentalmente tragico' (Barberi Squarotti, *La poesia del Novecento*, p. 264).

SALVATORE QUASIMODO

From *Giorno dopo giorno* (1947)

Alle fronde dei salici

E come potevamo noi cantare
con il piede straniero sopra il cuore,
fra i morti abbandonati nelle piazze
sull'erba dura di ghiaccio, al lamento
d'agnello dei fanciulli, all'urlo nero   5
della madre che andava incontro al figlio
crocifisso sul palo del telegrafo?
Alle fronde dei salici, per voto,
anche le nostre cetre erano appese,
oscillavano lievi al triste vento.   10

Alle fronde dei salici

The opening text in Quasimodo's short 1947 collection, this poem marks decisively (in both theme and style) the poet's adoption of a new literary stance, in keeping with the broader ideological and cultural climate of the post-war years. In his 1946 essay 'Poesia contemporanea', he distances himself expressly from his own hermetic roots while stressing the ethical responsibilities of the writer: 'Per quelli che credono alla poesia come a un gioco letterario, che considerano ancora il poeta un estraneo alla vita, uno che sale di notte le scalette della sua torre per speculare il cosmo, diciamo che il tempo delle "speculazioni" è finito. Rifare l'uomo, questo è l'impegno.' (*Poesie e discorsi*, p. 272). '**Alle fronde dei salici**': on the branches of the willows.

1:     The validity of a lyrical approach is questioned, while a direct allusion to Psalm 136 establishes a tone of epic solemnity (what might be called a 'generica tonalità oratoria': see Luti and Verbaro, p. 54), underlined by the use of the hendecasyllable throughout. Note the '**noi**', in place of a lyrical *io*.

2-7:   The reality of occupation and conflict are foregrounded in the images of death and violence. And yet simultaneously there is a note of declamatory rhetoric: the particularly brutal image of l.7 for example, clearly plays also on religious overtones (along with the echo of the psalm and the '**lamento d'agnello**' of ll. 4-5).

8-10: Like the '**cetre**' (lyres) of the Psalm, the poet's lyricism is 'suspended'. And yet there remains in this image, and in the elevated stylistic modes adopted, an idea of the 'sacrality' of poetry (Lorenzini, *La poesia italiana del Novecento*, p. 123), in keeping with Quasimodo's 'impegno epico-lirico del dopoguerra' (Finzi, in Quasimodo, *Poesia e discorsi*, p. xxix).

GIORGIO CAPRONI

From *Il seme del piangere* (1959)

L'uscita mattutina

Come scendeva fina
e giovane le scale Annina!
Mordendosi la catenina
d'oro, usciva via
lasciando nel buio una scia   5
di cipria, che non finiva.

L'ora era di mattina
presto, ancora albina.
Ma come s'illuminava
la strada dove lei passava!   10

Tutto Cors'Amedeo,
sentendola, si destava.
Ne conosceva il neo
sul labbro, e sottile
la nuca e l'andatura   15
ilare — la cintura
stretta, che acre e gentile
(Annina si voltava)
all'opera stimolava.

Andava in alba e in trina   20
pari a un'operaia regina.
Andava col volto franco
(ma cauto, e vergine, il fianco)
e tutta di lei risuonava
al suo tacchettìo la contrada.   25

L'uscita mattutina

This text is part of the section *Versi livornesi*, an idiosyncratic series of love-poems centred on the figure of the poet's mother (Anna Picchi), as imagined in her youth and beauty in Livorno. Thus the 'reality' of the city is in fact a kind of dream landscape, and the everyday is evoked with a distinct note of 'elegia' (Calvino, in Caproni, *Poesie: 1932-1986*, p. 804). The poem is largely based on the traditional shorter metrical forms of *settenario* and *novenario*, giving it the air of a popular *canzonetta*, with its rhyming couplets and tercets underlining the *cantabile* element.

1-6:   The opening rhyme sequence of '**-ina**' recurs throughout, helping to create the dominant notes of lightness and delicacy. The figure of the mother is portrayed with a mix of child-like innocence ('**mordendosi la catenina**': biting her gold chain) and implied sensuality, with the 'wake' of '**cipria**' (make-up) trailing behind her. Note how the regular metre and rhyme scheme is subtly disrupted by the repeated enjambements.

7-10:   The image of a street 'illuminated' by her passing may be an ironic allusion to the *dolce stil novo* tradition; '**albina**': white.

11-12:   The dream-like vision is now located firmly in the urban setting of a specific Livorno street that 'wakes up' at her passing, as the focus widens to include a collective or social experience.

13-19:   The subject of 'conosceva' is Corso Amedeo (i.e. the inhabitants of the street). The rhyme '**Amedeo**' – '**neo**' (mole) stands out for its idiosyncratic specificity amidst the otherwise delicate and rather conventional rhyme sequence. Corporeal details (along with the coquettish glance of l. 18) reinforce the erotic aspect of the vision, which is linked implicitly (l. 19) to the busy activity of the surrounding scene; '**nuca**': nape of neck; '**andatura ilare**': cheerful gait; '**acre**': sharp, pungent.

20-21:   Her youthful elegance is given a specifically working-class dimension; '**alba**': here, worker's smock; '**trina**': lace; '**pari**': equal.

22-23:   Her figure combines innocence and allure; '**franco**': suggests an absence of any false modesty; '**fianco**': side (of body).

24-25:   The poem closes with a renewed emphasis on the '**contrada**' or district surrounding her, which becomes suffused with her presence (encapsulated in the echoing sound of her heels: '**tacchettio**'), as ordinary reality is transformed in the magic of an individual experience.

PIER PAOLO PASOLINI

From *Il pianto della scavatrice* (1956)

VI

Nella vampa abbandonata
del sole mattutino — che riarde,
ormai, radendo i cantieri, sugli infissi

riscaldati — disperate
vibrazioni raschiano il silenzio   5
che perdutamente sa di vecchio latte,

di piazzette vuote, d'innocenza.
Già almeno dalle sette, quel vibrare
cresce col sole. Povera presenza

d'una dozzina d'anziani operai,   10
con gli stracci e le canottiere arsi
dal sudore, le cui voci rare,

le cui lotte contro gli sparsi
blocchi di fango, le colate di terra,
sembrano in quel tremito disfarsi.   15

Ma tra gli scoppi testardi della
benna, che cieca sembra, cieca
sgretola, cieca afferra,

quasi non avesse meta,
un urlo improvviso, umano,   20
nasce, e a tratti si ripete,

così pazzo di dolore, che, umano
subito non sembra più, e ridiventa
morto stridore. Poi, piano,

rinasce, nella luce violenta,   25
tra i palazzi accecati, nuovo, uguale,
urlo che solo chi è morente,

nell'ultimo istante, può gettare
in questo sole che crudele ancora splende
già addolcito da un po' d'aria di mare...   30

A gridare è, straziata
da mesi e anni di mattutini
sudori — accompagnata

dal muto stuolo dei suoi scalpellini,
la vecchia scavatrice: ma, insieme, il fresco   35
sterro sconvolto, o, nel breve confine

dell'orizzonte novecentesco,
tutto il quartiere... È la città,
sprofondata in un chiarore di festa,

— è il mondo. Piange ciò che ha   40
fine e ricomincia. Ciò che era
area erbosa, aperto spiazzo, e si fa

cortile, bianco come cera,
chiuso in un decoro ch'è rancore;
ciò che era quasi una vecchia fiera   45

di freschi intonachi sghembi al sole,
e si fa nuovo isolato, brulicante
in un ordine ch'è spento dolore.

Piange ciò che muta, anche
per farsi migliore. La luce   50
del futuro non cessa un solo istante

di ferirci; è qui, che brucia
in ogni nostro atto quotidiano,
angoscia anche nella fiducia

che ci dà vita, nell'impeto gobettiano   55
verso questi operai, che muti innalzano,
nel rione dell'altro fronte umano,

il loro rosso straccio di speranza.

From *Il pianto della scavatrice* (1956)

The setting for this poem (from the 1957 volume *Le ceneri di Gramsci*) is Rome during the period of the economic boom, tangibly present in the sights and sounds of a building site, with its workers embodying both the oppression of the working class, and its potential energy. This is the final section: after wandering the streets the previous evening and exploring far-ranging personal and historical anxieties into the night, the poet's persona awakes to the sounds of construction work. For all its ideological and 'realist' thrust, the poem is in many ways a very personal exploration, with moments of unrestrained lyricism and elegy. As Fortini notes in a highly ambivalent essay on Pasolini, the style is full of contradictions and inconsistencies: the apparently 'communicative' choice of the discursive *poemetto* form expresses quite a different 'verità stilistica e sentimentale'; the 'situazioni epico-liriche di *racconto*' are twisted under the gridwork of the 'false terzine', leaving us with a 'furioso stridio' in this final section (Fortini, *Saggi italiani*, pp. 137-41).

1-5: In the morning heat of the building site, mechanical noises (**'vibrazioni'**) break the silence (literally 'scraping' or 'grating' it: **'raschiano'**). The diction is a mix of the concrete or realistic (**'cantieri'**: building sites, **'infissi'**: door frames) and the more literary (**'vampa'**: blazing heat, **'riarde'**: burns). From the outset, the sounds are given a strong emotive charge with **'disperate'**.

5-7: The silence has a sense of (**'sa di'**: lit. 'tastes of') melancholy desolation, expressed in images that recall the crepuscular repertoire of abandoned objects and places, adding a further note to the eclectic tonal mix.

8-15: Amidst the growing noise, the human figures are almost overwhelmed. The 'poverty' of the workers, their suffering and vulnerability, is underlined to an almost hyperbolic degree, as the poet indulges in a rhetorical/emotional identification with their plight: **'povera'**; **'anziani'**; **'stracci'** (rags); **'arsi'** (burned); **'sudore'**; **'lotte'**. As they struggle with **'fango'** and **'colate di terra'** (flows of earth), what is most notable is the loss of their 'voices', which, already **'rare'**, are 'undone' (**'disfarsi'**) by the noise (**'tremito'**) of the machines.

16-30: Against the background noise of the **'benna'** (mechanical grab bucket suspended from a crane), a new sound arises, initially like a 'human' cry (l. 20), then becoming a 'dead' mechanical noise (**'stridore'**), and finally sounding like the cry of a dying person (ll. 27-28). This **'urlo'** (subject of verbs **'nasce'**, **'si ripete'**, **'sembra'**, **'ridiventa'**, **'rinasce'**) is, as clarified in the subsequent tercets, the 'cry' of the ageing **'scavatrice'** or mechanical digger, of the poem's title. The connotations of the mechanical noises are contradictory and shifting: from the initial 'blind' grasping of the **'benna'**, an image of the inhuman, destructive side of progress, apparently with no clear aim (**'meta'**); to the ambiguous cry of the other machine, which seems to echo the suffering of the workers (**'pazzo di dolore'**; **'morente'**), and elicits the sympathy of the poet's persona. There is further ambivalence in the evocation of the atmosphere, with its **'luce violenta'**, **'palazzi accecati'** (windowless buildings) and 'cruel' sun, but immediately mitigated by a 'sweet' sea breeze (l. 30).

31-40: The source of the 'cry' is identified, but its metaphorical nature is immediately underlined, as it seems also to emerge from the **'sterro sconvolto'** (disturbed earth of the building site), then the whole **'quartiere'**, the city, and indeed **'il mondo'**. The 'scavatrice' emits this cry in apparent solidarity with its 'mute' gang (**'stuolo'**) of labourers, whose torments it shares (**'straziata'**: tortured). The background is again ambiguous, containing both the stifling **'orizzonte novecentesco'** of the modern urban landscape and also an allusion to the city as a vital place, with its **'chiarore di festa'**.

40-48: It is a lament for the sense of loss that is inseparable from change, in this case the transformation of the urban fabric itself: green spaces (l. 42) become enclosed courtyards, 'decorous', but also full of 'rancour'; the jumbled **'fiera'** (fair) of old houses, with their uneven plastered walls (**'intonachi sghembi'**), becomes the new **'isolato'** (city block), **'brulicante'** (crowded), its 'order' concealing hidden suffering.

49-58: The voice of the 'scavatrice' expresses the poet's own ambivalent perspective, lamenting loss even if change brings improvement (ll. 49-50). Time and change (**'la luce del futuro'**) are unceasing, 'wounding' and 'burning' us at every moment of our present, generating 'anguish' even in our faith in progress, in our urge to identify with the oppressed workers. **'impeto gobettiano'**: 'Gobettian urge', referring to Piero Gobetti, murdered by the Fascists in 1926, who sought to bring together liberal cultural ideas with socialism (an extreme example of Pasolini's heterogeneous lexical and tonal range, which can bring together such an abstract political term with the likes of 'benna', 'scavatrice'). The final lines present a poignant image of the workers themselves, **'muti'**, but raising the tattered red flag of their political hopes (all but defeated in the Italy of the economic miracle). **'rione dell'altro fronte umano'**: neighbourhood of the other half of humanity, that of the oppressed.

FRANCO FORTINI

From *Una volta per sempre* (1963)

Traducendo Brecht

Un grande temporale
per tutto il pomeriggio si è attorcigliato
sui tetti prima di rompere in lampi, acqua.
Fissavo versi di cemento e di vetro
dov'erano grida e piaghe murate e membra   5
anche di me, cui sopravvivo. Con cautela, guardando
ora i tegoli battagliati ora la pagina secca,
ascoltavo morire
la parola d'un poeta o mutarsi
in altra, non per noi più, voce. Gli oppressi   10
sono oppressi e tranquilli, gli oppressori tranquilli
parlano nei telefoni, l'odio è cortese, io stesso
credo di non sapere più di chi è la colpa.

Scrivi mi dico, odia
chi con dolcezza guida al niente   15
gli uomini e le donne che con te si accompagnano
e credono di non sapere. Fra quelli dei nemici
scrivi anche il tuo nome. Il temporale
è sparito con enfasi. La natura
per imitare le battaglie è troppo debole. La poesia   20
non muta nulla. Nulla è sicuro, ma scrivi.

Traducendo Brecht

The setting for this poem arises out of Fortini's translating, along with his wife Ruth, of work by Bertolt Brecht for an Italian edition of *Poesie e canzoni* (published 1961). The image of working on Brecht (an important intellectual and ideological model for Fortini) becomes an occasion for him to question the function of poetry (and of writing more generally) in the face of an oppressive reality.

1-3:   A gathering and breaking storm presents one image of external reality, implicitly threatening the figure of the writer, seen as enclosed and isolated in the following lines, but also offers a vision of natural energy and vitality in contrast with the 'dry' exercise of literature; '**attorcigliato**': twisted, tangled. The storm here may be an echo of Rebora's 'Dall'intensa nuvolaglia'.

4-6:   The *io* is absorbed ('**fissavo**': I stared) in literature, which is characterized in terms suggesting both concrete durability ('**cemento**') and fragility ('**vetro**'). The words on the page encapsulate the suffering of humanity ('**grida e piaghe**': cries and wounds), which also includes the poet's own suffering, portrayed as physical parts ('**membra**') of the self, whose dismemberment he survives. It is a contradictory image of self-absorption and awareness of wider reality.

6-10:   The reality outside ('**tegoli battagliati**': 'embattled' roof-tiles) is compared to the 'dry' sterility of the poetic page, leading the *io* to lose faith in the vitality of the poetic word, or see it transformed into something no longer valid for 'us' (collective present reality).

10-13:   The stanza closes on a note of dejection and disorientation in the face of injustice. Both oppressed and oppressors are '**tranquilli**' (the former resigned, the latter self-assured), hatred is 'courteous', has lost its meaning in bland niceties, the poet's own ideological certainties are undermined.

14-17:   The response is twofold: he must write and he must 'hate' those responsible for perpetuating injustice, in particular those who do so hypocritically, '**con dolcezza**'. Meanwhile, there is a certain ambivalence in the attitude to the 'oppressed' (with whom the *io* associates himself also), seen as lacking belief in their own ability to understand the world ('**credono di non sapere**').

17-18:   The ambivalence running through the poem comes to the surface here: the *io* as a writer and intellectual is part of the very system of oppression that he seeks to oppose and that 'dismembers' him (l. 6).

18-21:   The poem closes on further notes of ambivalence and paradox. The storm itself now seems impotent as it 'emphatically' disappears. Poetry is apparently futile in the face of reality. But despite the triumph of uncertainty, the poet's final injunction to himself is to write (even if, as in ll. 17-18, writing may be a self-denunciation on the part of poetry itself).

ELIO PAGLIARANI

From *La ragazza Carla* (1960)

Carla Dondi fu Ambrogio di anni
diciassette primo impiego stenodattilo
all'ombra del Duomo

      Sollecitudine e amore, amore ci vuole al lavoro
      sia svelta, sorrida e impari le lingue   5
      le lingue qui dentro le lingue oggigiorno
      capisce dove si trova? TRANSOCEAN LIMITED
      qui tutto il mondo...
                      è certo che sarà orgogliosa.

      Signorina, noi siamo abbonati   10
      alle Pulizie Generali, due volte
      la settimana, ma il signor Praték è molto
      esigente – amore al lavoro è amore all'ambiente – cosí
      nello sgabuzzino lei trova la scopa e il piumino
      sarà sua prima cura la mattina.   15

      UFFICIO A UFFICIO B UFFICIO C

Perché non mangi? Adesso che lavori ne hai bisogno
             adesso che lavori ne hai diritto
                          molto di piú.

S'è lavata nel bagno e poi nel letto   20
s'è accarezzata tutta quella sera.
      Non le mancava niente, c'era tutta
      come la sera prima – pure con le mani e la bocca
      si cerca si tocca si strofina, ha una voglia
      di piangere di compatirsi   25
                ma senza fantasia
      come può immaginare di commuoversi?

      Tira il collo all'indietro ed ecco tutto.

From *La ragazza Carla* (1960)

Written between 1954 and 1957, this is a five-part *poemetto* depicting the world as experienced by a young office-worker in Milan. This extract is from the opening of part 2, as the humdrum reality of office life is juxtaposed with the protagonist's restless anxiety and uncertain sense of self. The poem interweaves strands of narrative, dialogue and commentary involving a wide range of linguistic and tonal registers, from the conversational to the technical and commercial.

1-3:   Carla's situation on her first day at work is summed up in the language of dry administrative formulae, one of the recurring registers of the poem: '**fu Ambrogio**': 'daughter of the late Ambrogio'; '**anni diciassette**': inversion typical of bureaucratic usage; '**stenodattilo**': short-hand typist. The Duomo is that of Milan.

4-9:   As marked by the indented text, a different voice is now heard, apparently that of an office superior instructing Carla on her tasks in a patronising tone, urging high ideals of commitment ('**sollecitudine**': attentiveness). The use of '**amore**' (here, love of work) has clearly ironic overtones, as does the reference to the 'pride' she will feel; '**sia ... sorrida ... impari**': 3rd person (Lei) imperative forms. The loose punctuation in these lines reflects the spoken register as well as suggesting Carla's somewhat confused state of mind as she tries to make sense of her surroundings. '**TRANSOCEAN**': the upper case introduces another element of tonal dislocation, bringing the company name, stated in all its formal appearance (as on a name plate), into the fragmented poetic discourse.

10-16:   The voice continues, explaining the twice-weekly arrangement with an outside cleaning company ('**abbonati**': contracted) and how demanding the boss is in matters of cleanliness. The parenthesis in l. 13 apparently repeats the boss's motto: 'love of work means love of your surroundings'. But the high moralising tone is undermined by the juxtaposition with the following lines, where the practical reality is seen: she must clean the office every morning; '**sgabuzzino**': broom cupboard; '**scopa**': broom; '**piumino**': duster. '**UFFICIO A...**': the upper case again suggests signs on office doors, whose anonymity underlines the alienating character of the working environment.

17-19:   Yet another voice, this time apparently that of Carla's mother at the family dinner table. The typical motherly concern is subtly coloured by her insistence on the value of work and linking of this to Carla's 'need' and even 'right' to eat. It seems that even within the family, Carla's identity is now defined by her economic role.

20-27:   The closest we come to the protagonist's own viewpoint is through a third-person narrative voice. The tone, in contrast with the numerous other voices in the *poemetto*, is compassionate, if matter-of-fact, with the lexical emphasis on the domestic and the corporeal. The sphere of the personal and the private is reduced to the bathroom and bedroom, where we see Carla attempting to verify or reclaim her own identity in some way (with a hint of autoeroticism: '**si tocca si strofina**'). While she can account for her physical integrity ('**c'era** tutta': she was all there), she is left anxiously unsure of the psychological and emotional parameters of the self, feeling herself bereft of **'fantasia'** and thus incapable of emotion (**'commuoversi'**).

28: **'Tira il collo all'indietro'**: she pulls her neck back. The exact meaning of her physical gesture here is unclear (perhaps simply a stretching of the neck to relieve some muscular ache) but the closing **'ecco tutto'** strongly suggests a sense of resignation, as if the sphere of emotional interiority is closed off to her.

GIOVANNI GIUDICI

From *La vita in versi* (1965)

Tempo libero

Dopo cenato amare, poi dormire,
questa è la via più facile: va da sé
lo stomaco anche se il vino era un po' grosso.
Ti rigiri, al massimo straparli.

Ma – chi ti sente? – lei dorme più di te,   5
viaggia verso domani a un vecchio inganno:
la sveglia sulle sette, un rutto, un goccettino
– e tutto ricomincia – amaro di caffè.

Tempo libero

One of the shorter texts that alternate throughout this collection with longer more narrative pieces, this poem does, for all its brevity, evoke implicitly the whole routine of daily life, with its endlessly recurring cycle. It contains many typical elements of Giudici's work: the exploration of everyday experience in the consumer society, a quasi-prosaic rhythm in a predominantly hendecasyllabic framework, an observant eye for detail (including that of the distinctly unlyrical realm of corporeal reality), and a strong dose of self-deprecating irony in the presentation of the poet's persona. The ironic nature of the title is clear from the overall sense of a life constrained by routine.

1-4:   These lines describe **'la via più facile'**: suggesting a failure on the part of the poet's persona (addressed in the poem as *tu*) to engage fully in the ethical challenges of life, renounced in favour of the hollow, mechanically repeated gestures of mere physical subsistence, encapsulated in the three verbal forms of l. 1 (**'Dopo cenato'**: having had dinner). An emphasis on the baser elements of bodily reality emerges in ll. 2-3, as the focus shifts to the digestion of the strong (**'grosso'**) wine; **'va da sé'**: the stomach carries on regardless, by itself. The effects are felt in a restless night (l. 4), including an element of almost delirious or uncontrolled speech (**'straparli'**), again undermining the credibility of the lyrical voice.

5-6:   The voice of the *io* fails to communicate, even within the private realm of the couple, as 'she' seems locked in her own isolation, with her own delusional dreams of tomorrow.

7-8:   The reality of **'domani'** is the reprise of the routine, seen in its most banal aspects, including a **'rutto'** (belch), resolving the night's digestive problems on a low, comic note (underlined by alliteration on -tt-). The closing image of 'bitterness' (**'amaro'** qualifies **'goccettino'**), hints at a deeper unease behind the monotony of a disillusioned alienated existence.

GIOVANNI RABONI

From *Le case della Vetra* (1966)

Risanamento

Di tutto questo
non c'è più niente (o forse qualcosa
s'indovina, c'è ancora qualche strada
acciottolata a mezzo, un'osteria).
Qui, diceva mio padre, conveniva   5
venirci col coltello... Eh sì, il Naviglio
è a due passi, la nebbia era più forte
prima che lo coprissero... Ma quello
che hanno fatto, distruggere le case,
distruggere quartieri, qui e altrove,   10
a cosa serve? Il male non era
lì dentro, nelle scale, nei cortili,
nei ballatoi, lì semmai c'era umido
da prendersi un malanno. Se mio padre
fosse vivo, chiederei anche a lui: ti sembra   15
che serva? è il modo? A me sembra che il male
non è mai nelle cose, gli direi.

Risanamento

The title refers to the 'redevelopment' or 'regeneration' of a less salubrious area of Milan near the Naviglio, originally a canal that was then covered over (see ll. 6-8). The theme recalls that of Pasolini's 'Pianto della scavatrice', although it is treated here with a rather lighter touch.

1-4:   An understated declaration of nostalgia for what is lost, matter-of-fact rather than elegiac. The prosaic tone is reinforced by **'tutto questo'**, as if a reference to the topic of a conversation already underway, on which we are eavesdropping; **'s'indovina'**: you can guess; **'acciottolata'**: cobbled.

5-8:   The father's voice recalls the gritty reality of a poor area, whose dense fog appears a visible sign of the dangers lurking in its streets (**'conveniva…'**: 'you would have to carry a knife coming here'). The memory of the father expands the time-frame of the poet's nostalgia, opening up a dialogue with the ghosts of memory, both personal and collective (the dialogue with the dead recalls numerous poems by Sereni). The repeated breaks ('**…**'), along with the colloquial **'Eh sì'**, increase the sense of a conversational tone, although this is balanced by the use of hendecasyllabic metre here and elsewhere in the poem.

8-14:   The poet's voice questions the real significance of a merely physical regeneration, with its focus on the demolition of an albeit squalid urban fabric, which was not the source of **'il male'**; **'ballatoi'**: balconies or open walkways giving access to flats; **'umido da prendersi un malanno'**: damp that would make you catch your death of cold.

14-17:   The putative dialogue with the ghost continues in truculent terms (**'è il modo?'**: 'is this the way to do things?'). It opens up a line of ethical questioning, placing the emphasis finally on human responsibilities, notwithstanding the importance of **'le cose'** or the world of physical objects.

7
Vittorio Sereni (1913-1983)

Sereni belonged to the same generation as Luzi and other hermetic poets, but from an early stage his work follows quite different lines of inspiration and development, linked in part to his geographical roots in Lombardy, where he grew up in the town of Luino on Lake Maggiore. Thus, he comes to be regarded later as a key figure in a 'linea lombarda', focused on a more existential and objective poetics, as against the Florentine hermetic tradition with its *poetica della parola* and orphic stance. It is true that Sereni's early work has elements in common with that of his hermetic contemporaries. The poems of *Frontiera* (1941) frequently present lyrical evocations of the lakeside landscape, using a 'poetic grammar' that has many affinities with that of the hermetic poets of the 1930s.[i] But, as Memmo argues, even from his first collection, Sereni's poetic vision eschews the mystic tendencies of the hermetics: 'non ha mai incarnato il ruolo del poeta che possiede la verità, non ha mai creduto alla "sacralità" della poesia'.[ii] And while he undoubtedly owes stylistic debts to Ungaretti (as pointed out by Isella), it is difficult not to see the influence of Montale (and Saba) coming to the fore as Sereni's work progresses.[iii]

It was as a student in Milan (his degree thesis was, tellingly, on Gozzano) and then as a teacher in the late 1930s, that Sereni wrote the poems of *Frontiera*. The 'frontier' of the title referred, as Sereni would explain later, both to the geographical reality of the Swiss border near Luino and to a more profound 'sentimento della frontiera', whose meaning lay 'tra la chiusura antidillica della vita italiana di quegli anni, d'anteguerra, e la tensione verso quello che stava al di là, verso un mondo più grande'.[iv] In these poems, the lyrical vision of the poetic persona is frequently interrupted by the echoes of other presences from beyond that frontier, or from beyond the personal/existential barrier of the individual's isolation.

With the outbreak of war, Sereni served as an infantry officer. In 1942 his unit was posted to Athens (destined ultimately for North Africa), only to return to Italy some months later having seen no action. In July 1943, he was stationed in Sicily and, with the capitulation of Italian forces after the Allies invaded the island, he was taken prisoner and transferred to Algeria, where he spent the next two years in a succession of POW camps. His second collection, *Diario d'Algeria* (1947) encapsulates many of his wartime experiences and the essentially contemplative lyricism of the first collection is in part replaced by a posture of direct engagement with the surrounding world. And yet this engagement is, paradoxically, from a perspective of profound isolation, as the *io* comes to terms with his frustrating exclusion from the events of the war and the Resistance in Italy, a sense of exclusion that will, in many ways, continue to be felt in the poetry of the post-war decades. While elements of a 'lingua ermetizzante' continue in *Diario*, this is now combined with a new density of content and increasing prominence of narrative or quasi-narrative forms, with a move from 'purezza del vocabolario' to 'concretezza'.[v]

After the war. Sereni settled in Milan, initially resuming his teaching career and in 1952 taking up a post in the Pirelli press office. From 1958 he worked as a literary editor with Mondadori. During the post-war years, Sereni continues to struggle with some of the sense of alienation and disillusionment experienced during his period of enforced exile from the events of Italian history, and this difficult relationship with his times is reflected in the evolution of his poetry. There is an ever greater 'contamination' between verse and more prosaic elements (and indeed in 1962 he publishes a first volume of prose writings, *Gli immediati dintorni*) and when Sereni's third major collection, *Gli strumenti umani*, is published in 1965, it marks a decisive development in his style.[vi] Any idea of lyric 'purity' is now superseded by a complex layering of thematic and linguistic registers, as the poet intersperses fragmentary sketches of contemporary urban life, encounters and dialogues with second- and third-person voices, and 'reticent' monologues, all in a 'plurilinguistic' style.[vii] It is, as Mengaldo writes, 'una scrittura a più strati, polifonica', subsuming the voices of others into 'la propria voce, rabbiosa e tenera', a formula that neatly sums up the shifting unpredictability of tone, by turns conversational, polemical, bewildered, contemplative, but always somehow reserved, never emphatic.[viii] (Elements of this style almost certainly influenced, among others, Montale in his later work of the 1960s and 1970s.)

While there is a substantial degree of continuity between the language and themes of the 1965 volume and those of Sereni's last collection, *Stella variabile* (1982), it is also possible to discern a growing tendency in this work towards introspection, towards contemplation of the mysteries of life and death, with a recurrence of motifs of dream or vision, including encounters with the ghosts of the dead. Perhaps the most important section of this work is the long poem 'Un posto di vacanza', a complex meditation on poetry, landscape and history set on the coast at Bocca di Magra, where Sereni spent his summers (this poem is not represented in the selection below, as no individual segment of it stands alone easily). We now find emerging a visionary or metaphysical strain, which, at its most extreme, touches on a kind of 'smiling nihilism', in which 'le immagini ... si cristallizzano finalmente nell'assoluto del negativo e del nulla'.[ix] And yet, while there persists a 'linea petrarchesca', a vein of stylistically refined lyricism throughout his work, this is constantly counterbalanced by the antidote of the prosaic.[x] Sereni's poetry always remains grounded in the reality of individual experience, in the world of objects and humanity.

Endnotes

[i]   Pier Vincenzo Mengaldo, 'Il linguaggio della poesia ermetica', in *La tradizione del Novecento, terza serie* (Turin: Einaudi, 1991), pp. 131-57 (pp. 143-4).

[ii] Francesco Paolo Memmo, 'Ancora sui rapporti fra Sereni e l'ermetismo', in *La poesia di Vittorio Sereni: Se ne scrivono ancora*, a cura di Alfredo Luzi (Grottammare: Stamperia dell'Arancio, 1997), pp. 51-61 (p. 55). This essay gives an excellent overview of Sereni's relationship with the major poetic tendencies of his times.

[iii] Dante Isella places Sereni's first two collections more within the sphere of influence of Ungaretti and the early Quasimodo than that of Montale (although the critic goes on to list the widespread presence of Montalean imagery and motifs in Sereni). See Isella, 'La lingua poetica di Sereni', in *La poesia di Vittorio Sereni: Atti del Convegno* (Milan: Librex, 1985), pp. 21-32 (pp. 26-7).

[iv] From a 1965 interview in Ferdinando Camon, *Il mestiere di poeta* (Milan: Lerici, 1965), 139-46 (p. 141). On the connotations of 'frontier', see also Stefano Raimondi, *La 'Frontiera' di Vittorio Sereni: Una vicenda poetica (1935-1941)*, (Milan: Unicopli, 2000), pp. 39-44.

[v]   Pier Vincenzo Mengaldo, 'Il solido nulla', in *La tradizione del Novecento, nuova serie* (Firenze: Vallecchi, 1987), pp. 377-86 (p. 378) and Niva Lorenzini, *La poesia italiana del Novecento*, p. 129.

[vi] The title of the volume is explained by Sereni as meaning 'tutti i mezzi e anche gli espedienti con cui l'uomo, singolo o collettività, affronta l'ignoto, il mistero, il destino' (*Poesie*, 483).

[vii] On the idea of 'reticenza', see Franco Fortini, 'Di Sereni', in *Saggi italiani* (Milan: Garzanti, 1987), pp. 172-203 (p. 181). For 'plurilinguismo', see Lorenzini, *La poesia italiana del Novecento*, p. 147.

[viii] Mengaldo, *Poeti italiani del Novecento*, p. 751.

[ix] Mengaldo, 'Il solido nulla', p. 384. On 'nihilism', see also Gilberto Lonardi, 'Di certe

assenze in Sereni', in *La poesia di Vittorio Sereni: Atti del Convegno*, pp. 106-18 (p. 113).

x   See Isella, 'La lingua poetica di Sereni', p. 29.

Poetic texts

Poesie, edizione critica a cura di Dante Isella, I Meridiani (Milan: Mondadori, 1995) (This volume contains many invaluable fragments of commentary by the author in the critical apparatus, as well as a useful selection of essays by key critics.)
It brings together the individual collections:
Frontiera (1941); *Diario d'Algeria* (1947); *Gli strumenti umani* (1965); *Stella variabile* (1982).

Prose texts

Gli immediati dintorni (Milan: Il Saggiatore, 1962)
Gli immediati dintorni primi e secondi (Milan: Il Saggiatore, 1983)
The content of these two volumes is subsumed in:
La tentazione della prosa, ed. by Giulia Raboni (Milan: Mondadori, 1998)

Further reading

Particularly useful are two volumes of conference proceedings (some individual contributions in these are also cited below):
La poesia di Vittorio Sereni: Atti del Convegno (Milan: Librex, 1985)
La poesia di Vittorio Sereni: Se ne scrivono ancora, a cura di Alfredo Luzi (Grottammare [Ascoli Piceno]: Stamperia dell'Arancio, 1997)

Other sources:
Baffoni-Licata, Maria Laura, *La poesia di Vittorio Sereni: alienazione e impegno* (Ravenna: Longo, 1986)
Barile, Laura, *Sereni* (Palermo: Palumbo, 1994)
Bonalumi, Giovanni, 'In margine a un "vecchio" testo', in *La poesia di Vittorio Sereni: Atti del Convegno*, pp. 134-42
Camon, Ferdinando, ed., *Il mestiere di poeta* (Milan: Lerici, 1965), pp. 139-46 [interview with Sereni]
Caretti, Lanfranco, 'Il perpetuo presente di Sereni', *Strumenti critici*, 1 (Oct. 1966), 73-85
Fortini, Franco, 'Di Sereni', in *Saggi italiani* (Milan: Garzanti, 1987), pp. 172-203
Grignani, Maria Antonietta, '*Lavori in corso*: addetti e dintorni', in *La poesia di Vittorio Sereni: Atti del Convegno*, pp. 119-133
Grillandi, Massimo, *Vittorio Sereni* (Florence: La Nuova Italia, 1972)
Isella, Dante, 'La lingua poetica di Sereni', in *La poesia di Vittorio Sereni: Atti del Convegno*, pp. 21-32
Lonardi, Gilberto, 'Di certe assenze in Sereni', in *La poesia di Vittorio Sereni: Atti del Convegno*, pp. 106-18
Memmo, Francesco Paolo, 'Ancora sui rapporti fra Sereni e l'ermetismo', in *La poesia di Vittorio Sereni: Se ne scrivono ancora*, pp. 51-61
Mengaldo, Pier Vincenzo, 'Il linguaggio della poesia ermetica', in *La tradizione del Novecento*,

terza serie (Turin: Einaudi, 1991), pp. 131-57

Mengaldo, Pier Vincenzo, 'Il solido nulla', in *La tradizione del Novecento, nuova serie* (Firenze: Vallecchi, 1987), pp. 377-86

Mengaldo, Pier Vincenzo, 'Iterazione e specularità', in *La tradizione del Novecento: da D'Annunzio a Montale* (Milan: Feltrinelli, 1975), pp. 359-86

Raimondi, Stefano, *La 'Frontiera' di Vittorio Sereni: Una vicenda poetica* (1935-1941), (Milan: Unicopli, 2000)

Contents

From *Frontiera* (1941)

Concerto in giardino

A quest'ora
innaffiano i giardini in tutta Europa.
Tromba di spruzzi roca
raduna bambini guerrieri,
echeggia in suono d'acque   5
sino a quest'ombra di panca.

Ai bambini in guerra sulle aiole
sventaglia, si fa vortice;
suono sospeso in gocce
istante   10
ti specchi in verde ombrato;
siluri bianchi e rossi
battono gli asfalti dell'Avus,
filano treni a sud-est
tra campi di rose.   15

Da quest'ombra di panca
ascolto i ringhi della tromba d'acqua:
a ritmi di gocce
il mio tempo s'accorda.

Ma fischiano treni d'arrivi.   20

S'è strozzato nel caldo
il concerto della vita che svaria
in estreme girandole d'acqua.

Concerto in giardino

As hinted at in the title, this 1935 poem is presented as a kind of musical fantasia, suggested by the sounds of water sprinkling on a garden as 'luogo d'incanto e d'idillio' (Raimondi, p. 42). The musicality is inherent in the poem's patterns of assonance and repetition (e.g. *ora-Europa-roca*; *acque-panca-bianchi-campi-panca-acqua*). But the poem also registers an acute awareness of a wider world beyond this enclosed contemplative space. Giovanni Bonalumi notes how strikingly different this poem seemed in the 1930s when compared with those of the hermetic poets, especially in its openness to a European dimension (Bonalumi, p. 135).

1-2:   The opening sets out some parameters in time and space for what follows: the poem is set in a tangible present (**'a quest'ora'**), but reaches out to include a broad geographical/cultural setting; **'innaffiare'**: to water.

3-11:   The sound of water (the **'tromba'** here being the spout of a watering-can or hosepipe) introduces via the connotation of a bugle (albeit a 'hoarse' one) a delicate fantastical picture of children's war-games, and also brings us back from the broader European setting to the concrete reality of **'quest'ombra di panca'** (echoing the demonstrative of l.1, to give a strong sense of a personal experience). The fantasy-impressions continue in ll.7-8, where the earlier 'tromba' fans out (**'sventaglia'**) in a vortex on the **'aiole'** (flowerbeds), and a quasi-hermetic note is introduced as auditory and visual sensations merge in ll.9-11, with the sound 'mirrored' momentarily in dark green (the single-word-line **'istante'** highlights the fleeting nature of the individual insight). Meanwhile, the image of **'bambini guerrieri'** suggests perhaps echoes of distant conflicts.

12-15:   Suddenly other images intrude, fragmentary glimpses of the Europe already mentioned. **'siluri'**: racing cars (torpedo-shaped); **'Avus'**: Berlin racetrack; **'treni'**: a recurring image in Sereni, recalling the international railway line passing by Luino and evoking ideas of adventure and exotic promise beyond the frontier.

16-19:   The alternation between 'there' and 'here' continues, with a return to **'quest'ombra...'**, where the *io* finds some harmony with the rhythm of reality; **'ringhi'**: growls.

20-23:   The idealized trains of l. 14 now become a more tangible present reality, abruptly interrupting his reverie. The water-fantasia is finally evoked again with its shifting **'girandole'** (carousels), only to be 'strangled' as the outside world intrudes. (There may be an echo of Montale's 'rivo strozzato' in 'Spesso il male di vivere...'; see Baffoni-Licata, p. 37).

Inverno a Luino

Ti distendi e respiri nei colori.
Nel golfo irrequieto,
nei cumuli di carbone irti al sole
sfavilla e s'abbandona
l'estremità del borgo.   5
Colgo il tuo cuore
se nell'alto silenzio mi commuove
un bisbiglio di gente per le strade.
Morto in tramonti nebbiosi d'altri cieli
sopravvivo alle tue sere celesti,   10
ai radi battelli del tardi
di luminarie fioriti.
Quando pieghi al sonno
e dài suoni di zoccoli e canzoni
e m'attardo smarrito ai tuoi bivi   15
m'accendi nel buio d'una piazza
una luce di calma, una vetrina.

Fuggirò quando il vento
investirà le tue rive;
sa la gente del porto quant'è vana   20
la difesa dei limpidi giorni.
Di notte il paese è frugato dai fari,
lo borda un'insonnia di fuochi
vaganti nella campagna,
un fioco tumulto di lontane   25
locomotive verso la frontiera.

Inverno a Luino

Written in 1937, this is one of a number of poems in this collection evoking the landscapes of Luino and Lago Maggiore.

1:       The *tu* is Luino itself, depicted in terms that suggest an idyllic calm and beauty.

2-5:   Almost immediately, a different note is struck, with the anxiety of the 'restless' bay threatening the town, and the realistic detail of coal-heaps (an allusion to the railway) shifting the focus to an urban dimension (although this in turn seems strangely languid – **'s'abbandona'**); **'irti'**: spiky, bristling; **'sfavilla'**: sparkles.

6-12:   The focus shifts to the poet's own persona for whom the 'heart' of the town lies in the juxtaposition of the idyllic calm just outlined with the **'bisbiglio'** (whisper) of human presences. Unlike in other settings, he feels 'alive' here amidst the lakeside landscape, evoked in almost impressionistic, lyrical terms. **'fioriti'**: refers to 'battelli' – the boats are 'blossoming' with lights in the dusk.

13-17: The town itself, with its sounds and sights, is the protagonist here (and the subject of the main verbs), but also provides the firmly urban setting for a central moment of introspection by the *io*, whose sense of bewilderment (**'smarrito'**) in the empty streets is not entirely dispelled by the sudden oasis of light of a shop-window. (Sereni later described this in terms of a Montalean *occasione*, showing the important influence of Montale on the younger poet in these years – see *Poesie*, pp. 340-41).

18-21: The momentary enchantment is dispelled by the thought of winter storms and the desire to flee, underlining the precarious nature of any idyllic experience here, which provides no 'defence' in the face of a hostile nature or unknown other forces. (Again there are echoes of *Le occasioni*, with its repeated threatening storms.)

22-26: The closing lines depict the town surrounded by signs of other presences, from the 'probing' searchlights (those of the border patrol-boat on the lake – see *Poesie* p. 340) to the restless lights of long-distance trains, with their promise of potential escape beyond the frontier, an image both of the suffocating isolation of pre-war Italy and also the isolation of the individual in the face of personal/existential barriers.

From *Diario d'Algeria* (1947)

Italiano in Grecia

Prima sera d'Atene, esteso addio
dei convogli che filano ai tuoi lembi
colmi di strazio nel lungo semibuio.
Come un cordoglio
ho lasciato l'estate sulle curve   5
e mare e deserto è il domani
senza più stagioni.
Europa Europa che mi guardi
scendere inerme e assorto in un mio
esile mito tra le schiere dei bruti,   10
sono un tuo figlio in fuga che non sa
nemico se non la propria tristezza
o qualche rediviva tenerezza
di laghi di fronde dietro i passi
perduti,   15
sono vestito di polvere e sole,
vado a dannarmi a insabbiarmi per anni.

Pireo, agosto 1942

Italiano in Grecia

Like others in this collection, this poem is back-dated to the time of the events described, but was probably completed during Sereni's time in Algerian POW camps in 1943-45 (see *Poesie*, p. 417).

1-7:   Opening in appropriately diaristic mode, the poem sums up in a few lines the new landscape of Sereni's verse: occupied Greece and, in the years to come, the desert where time will stand still. The recurring motif of trains (**'convogli'**) is one of many elements of continuity with the world of *Frontiera*, but the evocative trains passing through Luino are replaced now by troop-transports, with all their **'strazio'**, torment (or perhaps the **'convogli'** may refer to trains loaded with deportees glimpsed in stations; see Baffoni-Licata, p. 84). This pain is also the **'cordoglio'** or grief for a lost idyll (l. 5). The language, for all the autobiographical realism of the piece, retains a notably elegiac element (**'esteso addio'**, **'colmi di strazio'**, **'semibuio'**).

8-15:   The poet's heartfelt address to Europe is immediately subsumed within a lyrical discourse that continues to explore the inner reality of the *io*. These lines are shot through with a tension between the external/historical reality of the **'schiere dei bruti'** (ranks of the brutes), the occupying armies of which the poet is a part, and his own self-perception as **'inerme'** (defenceless), fleeing and clinging to his **'esile mito'**: a fragile personal mythology summed up in the evocation of his lost landscape of **'laghi'** and **'fronde'** (leafy branches). Once more the diction and tones of *ermetismo* can be traced here in ll. 12-15, in the use of generic nature imagery and the emphasis on emotional abstractions (**'tristezza'**, **'tenerezza'**); **'rediviva'**: revived.

16-17:   The persona and scenario of the actual Algerian diary (the second section of the book) are introduced as the *io* (retrospectively) foresees his destiny of defeat and imprisonment; **'insabbiarmi'**: get stuck in the sand (here both literally and figuratively).

Non sa più nulla, è alto sulle ali
il primo caduto bocconi sulla spiaggia normanna.
Per questo qualcuno stanotte
mi toccava la spalla mormorando
di pregar per l'Europa   5
mentre la Nuova Armada
si presentava alla costa di Francia.

Ho risposto nel sonno: – È il vento,
il vento che fa musiche bizzarre.
Ma se tu fossi davvero   10
il primo caduto bocconi sulla spiagga normanna
prega tu se lo puoi, io sono morto
alla guerra e alla pace.
Questa è la musica ora:
delle tende che sbattono sui pali.   15
Non è musica d'angeli, è la mia
sola musica e mi basta –.

Campo Ospedale 127, giugno 1944

Non sa più nulla, è alto sulle ali...

From the central section of the book (itself sub-titled 'Diario d'Algeria'), this poem juxtaposes the frustrating isolation of the North African POW camps with distant echoes of the Allied landings in Normandy. The essentially narrative thrust of this poem, and the inclusion of different voices (including that of the *io*) in dialogue, is something that recurs repeatedly in his later verse.

1-2:   The momentous events in Normandy are introduced through the imagined, poignant figure of a single fallen soldier (**'bocconi'**: face down). There is a mixture of concrete realism (l. 2) and a hint of lyric potential, with the image of **'alto sulle ali'** suggesting perhaps the dead soldier's spirit (although Sereni elsewhere makes specific – if somewhat fanciful – reference to the aerial evacuation of the dead and wounded; see *Poesie,* pp. 442-43).

3-7:   Notwithstanding the epic sweep of the historical canvas (**'l'Europa ... la Nuova Armada ... la costa di Francia'**), the poet's dreamlike encounter with the voice or ghost of the dead soldier (**'qualcuno'** – clearly also a kind of *alter ego*) is recounted in understated, matter-of-fact language (see the almost apologetic tone of l. 4), highlighting the intimate connection between the individual and collective dramas of these years.

8-13:   The reply by the poet's persona seeks to dismiss the voice as a trick of the wind and also encapsulates his sense of impotence and frustration, cut off from historical events which are yet felt so keenly. The theme of death becomes a kind of death of the soul, an enforced renunciation of any active role in the unfolding struggle (ll. 12-13), what Sereni called a 'situazione di estraneità, di emarginazione, di miseria' (*Poesie,* p. 444).

14-17:   The poet seeks to define a new voice and timbre, already suggested by the **'musiche bizzarre'** of l. 9, now crystallized as an image of poetry itself, an impoverished music of tents flapping in the wind, distinctly non-celestial, but music nonetheless. It is a perfect image of the subdued, problematic lyricism of Sereni's mature style, both engaged with and detached from historical events. Another feature of this style will be the frequency of repetition, seen here in ll. 2 and 11, as well as in recurrence of the terms 'pregare', 'vento', 'musica'.

Non sanno d'essere morti
i morti come noi,
non hanno pace.
Ostinati ripetono la vita
si dicono parole di bontà   5
rileggono nel cielo i vecchi segni.
Corre un girone grigio in Algeria
nello scherno dei mesi
ma immoto è il perno a un caldo nome: ORAN.

Saint-Cloud, agosto 1944

Non sanno d'essere morti...

Echoing the opening of the previous text, Sereni elaborates on the idea of the prison camp as a sort of living death, an existence of stasis and frustration. Critics have seen echoes of Dante's Purgatory here: note the sense of a provisional existence between life and death, the exchange of **'parole di bontà'**, the reading of celestial signs, and especially the term **'girone'** (circle) and the image of endless circling around a fixed point (**'perno'**: pivot) in the closing lines (Segre and Ossola, *Antologia della poesia italiana*, p. 579; Baffoni-Licata, p. 107). See also *Gli immediati dintorni* (pp. 27-28) for the Purgatorial image and an account of moving from one camp to another, but always revolving around the same location.

9:     **'ORAN'**: Algerian city.

From *Gli strumenti umani* (1965)

Le ceneri

Che aspetto io qui girandomi per casa,
che s'alzi un qualche vento
di novità a muovermi la penna
e m'apra a una speranza?

Nasce invece una pena senza pianto   5
né oggetto, che una luce
per sé di verità da sé presume
– e appena è un bianco giorno e mite di fine inverno.

Che spero io più smarrito tra le cose.
Troppe ceneri sparge attorno a se la noia,   10
la gioia quando c'è basta a sé sola.

Le ceneri

The setting for this 1957 poem is the private space of the home, one of the recurring poetic locations in this very urban collection.

1-4:   Despite the different circumstances, an element of continuity with *Diario d'Algeria* is quite evident in the sense of frustration and enclosure (e.g. the image of 'girandomi' – although here the nature of the paralysis is clearly artistic/existential). Note also the recurrence of **'vento'** as an image linked to poetic inspiration – here frustratingly absent. **'alzi'**, **'apra'**: subjunctive forms, expressing the hypothetical nature of the event.

5-8:   The reality is a kind of dull inexpressive (**'senza pianto'**) suffering that presumes a 'light ... of truth', i.e. takes on, of and for itself, an appearance of truth – even if this light is merely the unremarkable reality of a winter's day.

9:        Sums up the stance of the *io* in *Gli strumenti umani*: one of resignation and bewilderment at the multiple phenomena of reality

10-11:   **'ceneri'**: an earlier title was 'Mercoledì delle ceneri', which perhaps colours the poet's **'noia'** here with a note of renunciation or self-sacrifice, overwhelming any momentary 'joy' (liberating creativity?) posited at the close, which seems to exist in some other, self-contained sphere. (We may note perhaps an echo of Ungaretti's 'allegria' in Sereni's putative 'gioia'.)

Le sei del mattino

Tutto, si sa, la morte dissigilla.
E infatti, tornavo,
malchiusa era la porta
appena accostato il battente.
E spento infatti ero da poco,   5
disfatto in poche ore.
Ma quello vidi che certo
non vedono i defunti:
la casa visitata dalla mia fresca morte,
solo un poco smarrita   10
calda ancora di me che più non ero,
spezzata la sbarra
inane il chiavistello
e grande un'aria e popolosa attorno
a me piccino nella morte,   15
i corsi l'uno dopo l'altro desti
di Milano dentro tutto quel vento.

Le sei del mattino

This 1957 poem again uses the setting of the home, presented as part of yet another dream-like fantasy, as the poet imagines the empty house after his own death, adding a further dimension of ambivalence to his treatment of this space, and to that of the lyrical *io*, depicted as split between an observing self and an absent/dead observed self.

1:      A somewhat enigmatic line, perhaps best understood as suggesting that death unlocks or 'breaks the seal' (**'dissigilla'**) on all mysteries.

2-6:   **'tornavo'**: the imperfect tense of a dream narrative. **'malchiusa ... appena accostato'**: the limits of the domestic haven are breached, an image of the 'undoing' (l. 6) of normal reality with the imagined death of the self.

7-13:   The focus of the fantasy is the house itself, presented in ambivalent terms, **'smarrita'**, unsure of its own bearings, filled only by its emptiness (the paradox of l. 11); a space whose boundaries are now no longer effective (ll. 12-13); **'sbarra'**: bar, barrier; **'chiavistello'**: bolt.

14-17: The spatial perspective is now opened up completely, with the external spaces of Milan dwarfing the self, who is portrayed (with an almost comically reductive 'piccino') as an insignificant presence (or indeed, non-presence, in death) amidst the awakening, crowded city streets (**'corsi'**). Thus the image of the home, far from being a safe haven of individual identity, is open to the flux of collective urban life seen in ever-ambivalent terms.

Nel sonno

IV

Abboccherà il demente all'esca
dei ragazzi del bar?
Certo che abboccherà
                            e per un niente
nella sua nebbia si ritroverà
dalla parte del torto.   5
Lo picchieranno, dopo, più di gusto.
C'era altro da fare delle domeniche?
I giornali attorno ai chioschi
garruli al vento primaverile:
viene un tale, canaglia in panni lindi,   10
su titoli e immagini avventa un suo cagnaccio.
– La sporca politica
e noi sempre pronti a rifondere il danno,
Pantalone che paga –
e getta soldi all'accorso edicolante.   15
Approvazioni, intorno, risa.

V

L'Italia, una sterminata domenica.
Le motorette portano l'estate
il malumore della festa finita.
Sfrecciò vano, ora è poco, l'ultimo pallone
e si perse: ma già   5
sfavilla la ruota vittoriosa.
E dopo, che fare delle domeniche?
Aizzare il cane, provocare il matto…
Non lo amo il mio tempo, non lo amo.
L'Italia dormirà con me.   10
In un giardino d'Emilia o Lombardia
sempre c'è uno come me
in sospetti e pensieri di colpa
tra il canto di un usignolo
e una spalliera di rose…   15

Nel sonno, IV (Abboccherà il demente all'esca...)

'Nel sonno' is a six-part poem whose origins lie in the years 1948-1953, from the electoral defeat of the left to the beginnings of the economic boom (a period seen in distinctly negative terms by Sereni, as one of 'involuzione della democrazia'), but largely written in 1962-63 (see *Poesie*, pp. 566-83). The poem is one of several engaging openly with the collective realities of the time, but in a highly individual way, and without offering any easy ideological answers. Opening sections recall the memory of the Resistance and register the poet's sense of deep disappointment at the 1948 election result. Here instead we find a vivid sketch of an urban scene in the new Italy, marked by cynicism and barely-contained violence.

1-6: Brutalized social relationships (set in a specifically public space) are epitomized in the bullying of a **'demente'** (mentally ill person) by a group of youths, who set a 'bait' (**'esca'**) for him (presumably some practical joke), leading to his confusion (mental 'fog') and the sadistic cruelty of a casual beating (**'lo picchieranno'**); **'abboccherà'**: 'he will take the bait'.

7: The poet annunciates with fierce irony a sense of collective futility, as if there never was any other way of living (but implying strongly the loss of genuine values).

8-9: Newspapers flapping garrulously in the wind (an implicit image of public/political discourse).

10-16: These lines typify Sereni's tendency to present snatches of narrative and multiple voices in direct speech, while the present tense gives a strong sense of immediacy (on Sereni's present tense, see Caretti); **'un tale'**: a person, a guy; **'canaglia in panni lindi'**: 'scoundrel in clean clothes'; the image suggests hypocrisy, while the character's denigration of all political ideals recalls the cynicism of political *qualunquismo* (an anti-ideological post-war political movement of the right). The **'cagnaccio'** (an ugly or brutish dog) gives another image of latent violence in the face of cultural values. **'Pantalone che paga'**: referring to the *commedia dell'arte* character, the phrase expresses the sense of grievance of the common man forced to support others through taxes, etc., epitomized also in his disdainful throwing of money; **'edicolante'**: person running the *edicola* (news-stand).

Nel sonno, V (L'Italia, una sterminata domenica...)

1: Recalls l.7 in the previous section, but now expanded to convey a sense of generalized futility embracing the new Italy, whose lazy endless (**'sterminata'**) Sunday suggests also a kind of ethical torpor (note the title of the poem, and see also l.10 here)

2-8: Archetypal images of post-war Italy with its material well-being, motor-scooters and football, are interwoven with intimations of discontent (l.3) and loss (l.5, where the image of a lost football game carries overtones of the historic defeat alluded to earlier in the poem), culminating in a reprise of the mindless brutality seen in the previous section (l. 8); **'Aizzare'**: to incite.

9:      Sereni's blunt declaration of historical alienation suggests a stance of profound detachment, but also, paradoxically, a sense of belonging (**'il *mio tempo*'**). It is an expression of aggrieved dissatisfaction, not resignation.

10-15: An ironic depiction of the lyric persona, in his putative retreat into the private sphere of the garden (cf. 'Concerto in giardino'), adorned with the clichéd trappings of poetic idyll (**'usignolo'**: nightingale), as the *io* is reduced to an almost parodic stereotype of **'uno come me'**, mocked by his own moral doubts.

Un sogno

Ero a passare il ponte
su un fiume che poteva essere il Magra
dove vado d'estate o anche il Tresa,
quello delle mie parti tra Germignaga e Luino.
Me lo impediva uno senza volto, una figura plumbea.   5
«Le carte» ingiunse. «Quali carte» risposi.
«Fuori le carte» ribadì lui ferreo
vedendomi interdetto. Feci per rabbonirlo:
«Ho speranze, un paese che mi aspetta,
certi ricordi, amici ancora vivi,   10
qualche morto sepolto con onore».
«Sono favole – disse – non si passa
senza un programma.» E soppesò ghignando
i pochi fogli che erano i miei beni.
Volli tentare ancora. «Pagherò   15
al mio ritorno se mi lasci
passare, se mi lasci lavorare.» Non ci fu
modo d'intendersi: «Hai tu fatto –
ringhiava – la tua scelta ideologica?».
Avvinghiati lottammo alla spalletta del ponte   20
in piena solitudine. La rissa
dura ancora, a mio disdoro.
Non lo so
chi finirà nel fiume.

Un sogno

This dream/fantasy poem is an allegorical narrative of the poet's encounter with a sinister figure that embodies ideological dogmatism and blinkered cultural *impegno*.

1-4:   The possible locations are his two preferred poetic landscapes: Bocca di Magra on the Tuscan coast and the area around Luino (the river Tresa). The bridge is a characteristic image of uncertain or marginal physical co-ordinates (like the earlier Frontier), an in-between space, mirroring the poet's inner tensions.

5:       The 'leaden' figure's 'faceless' form clearly indicates a lack of humanity.

6-8:   The initial exchange sets the tone of the encounter, between menace and mutual incomprehension (**'ingiunse'**: he ordered; **'ferreo'**: rigid). Here as elsewhere, any purely lyrical perspective is replaced by the interplay of contending voices in a dramatic/narrative framework. **'le carte'**: transparently, an image of writing itself, as well as of ideological credentials; **'interdetto'**: here means taken aback, stunned. **'Feci per...'**: 'I made as if to placate him'.

9-11:   In typically self-effacing terms, the *io* emphasises the authenticity of the individual experience, of personal relationships and memories. **'un paese'**: here probably 'village' rather than 'country' (in keeping with the modest, personal tone of the declaration).

12-14:   The polemical or satirical note comes to the fore here, as the interlocutor becomes more inflexible and grotesque in his sneering disdain, 'weighing' the poet's papers. **'favole'**: trivial nonsense.

15-24:   While the snarling (**'ringhiava'**) dogmatism of the ideologue is highlighted again, the *io* is also presented in problematic terms: his position seems weak, ineffectual (15-17) and, though he is forced into the bitter struggle, there is also a clear note of self-censure (**'a mio disdoro'**: to my shame), part of a wider presence of images of impotence on the part of the poet's persona (see Lonardi). Ultimately, however, the struggle seems futile, continuing **'in piena solitudine'**, in isolation from the real world of human intercourse.

Dall'Olanda

Amsterdam

A portarmi fu il caso tra le nove
e le dieci d'una domenica mattina
svoltando a un ponte, uno dei tanti, a destra
lungo il semigelo d'un canale. E non
questa è la casa, ma soltanto   5
– mille volte già vista –
sul cartello dimesso: «Casa di Anna Frank».

Disse più tardi il mio compagno: quella
di Anna Frank non dev'essere, non è
privilegiata memoria. Ce ne furono tanti   10
che crollarono per sola fame
senza il tempo di scriverlo.
Lei, è vero, lo scrisse.
Ma a ogni svolta a ogni ponte lungo ogni canale
continuavo a cercarla senza trovarla più   15
ritrovandola sempre.
Per questo è una e insondabile Amsterdam
nei suoi tre quattro variabili elementi
che fonde in tante unità ricorrenti, nei suoi
tre quattro fradici o acerbi colori   20
che quanto è grande il suo spazio perpetua,
anima che s'irraggia ferma e limpida
su migliaia d'altri volti, germe
dovunque e germoglio di Anna Frank.
Per questo è sui suoi canali vertiginosa Amsterdam.   25

Dall'Olanda

From a three-part 1961 poem, this text belongs to an extensive strand of travel poems in Sereni, but here the experience of the tourist opens up an exploration of the complex relationship between the individual and history.

1-7:   The opening recounts the experience of the *io* in terms that are both specific in time and place and also generic, ordinary and random: **'fu il caso'** (chance) **...** **'uno dei tanti'**). The tone and diction are understated; the setting, as elsewhere, unremarkable city streets. **'mille volte già vista'**: the familiarity of this sight to so many does nothing to diminish its uniqueness, captured in the arrestingly familiar proper name on a **'cartello dimesso'** (modest sign). **'Anna Frank'**: (1929-45) author of the well-known diary written in hiding from the Nazis in Amsterdam, and victim of the Holocaust.

8-13:   An interlocuter's voice poses ethical problems for the *io*, once more concerning the potentially privileged cultural status of the writer, amidst the faceless suffering of others. l.13 could be an afterthought by the 'compagno', or a riposte by the *io*. If the latter, then the tone (with **'è vero'**) seems almost *sottovoce*, uncertain of the value of writing.

14-16:   From this point, the poem shifts from the level of narrative to that of a fantastic or dream-like musing, in which different lexical and structural elements recur in shifting variations (e.g. **'svoltando ... svolta'**; **'cercarla... ritrovarla... ritrovandola'**). As demonstrated by Mengaldo, this text thus encapsulates Sereni's use of reiterative, repetitive figures and structures throughout *Gli strumenti umani* (see Mengaldo, 'Iterazione e specularità'); **'svolta'**: corner.

17-25:   The repetitive topography of Amsterdam's canals and bridges is both singular and infinitely variable (**'insondabile'**: unfathomable, immeasurable) and becomes an image of the unknowability and yet recurrent familiarity of human experience; the city is a single soul 'radiating' through countless **'altri volti'** (ll. 22-23), it is, throughout (**'dovunque'**), the 'seed' of Anne Frank, a dizzying amalgamation of individual and collective experience. Here and in similar texts, as Grignani observes, beyond the virtuoso spatial and colour impressions, Sereni gets 'under the skin' of the modern city to discover 'una persistenza dolorosa della storia' (Grignani, p. 121).

From *Stella variabile* (1982)

Autostrada della Cisa

Tempo dieci anni, nemmeno
prima che rimuoia in me mio padre
(con malagrazia fu calato giù
e un banco di nebbia ci divise per sempre).

Oggi a un chilometro dal passo   5
una capelluta scarmigliata erinni
agita un cencio dal ciglio di un dirupo,
spegne un giorno già spento, e addio.

Sappi – disse ieri lasciandomi qualcuno –
sappilo che non finisce qui,   10
di momento in momento credici a quell'altra vita,
di costa in costa aspettala e verrà
come di là dal valico un ritorno d'estate.

Parla così la recidiva speranza, morde
in un'anguria la polpa dell'estate,   15
vede laggiù quegli alberi perpetuare
ognuno in sé la sua ninfa
e dietro la raggera degli echi e dei miraggi
nella piana assetata il palpito di un lago
fare di Mantova una Tenochtitlán.   20

Di tunnel in tunnel di abbagliamento in cecità
tendo una mano. Mi ritorna vuota.
Allungo un braccio. Stringo una spalla d'aria.

Ancora non lo sai
– sibila nel frastuono delle volte   25
la sibilla, quella
che sempre più ha voglia di morire –
non lo sospetti ancora
che di tutti i colori il più forte
il più indelebile   30
è il colore del vuoto?

Autostrada della Cisa

Written around 1978-79, this poem is one of a number of meditations on death in Sereni's last collection. The title refers to the La Spezia-Parma motorway, named after the mountain pass of La Cisa through which it runs (see *Poesie*, p. 834). The journey depicted is the one from Sereni's summer retreat in Bocca di Magra back towards Milan, but the image of the mountain pass clearly connotes the passage between life and death. The motorway is an extreme example of Sereni's use of marginal spaces or non-places as settings for his poetry.

1-4: The prospect of his own inevitable death recalls that of his father. **'Tempo dieci anni'**: 'Ten years time [is all that will pass]' (colloquial); **'rimuoia...'**: his own death will 'replay' his father's; **'calato giù'**: probably the moment of burial; **'nebbia'**: the impenetrable life/death barrier.
5-8: **'a un chilometro dal passo'**: nearing the top of the pass (but strongly suggests also the approach of death). The enigmatic image of the tousled **'erinni'** (Erinys or Fury) may be suggested by a real human figure on the rocky slope (Segre and Ossola, *Antologia della poesia italiana*, p. 606), but has clear overtones of ill omen, particularly in her action of 'extinguishing' the day; **'cencio'**: rag; **'dirupo'**: crag.
9-13: **'qualcuno'**: another disembodied voice, perhaps simply an unnamed acquaintance, but the echo of 'Non sa più nulla' suggests this may also be a voice from beyond the grave, here exhorting the *io* to believe in an afterlife. **'di là dal valico'**: the image of finding better weather 'beyond the pass' is a further metaphor for the hoped-for afterlife.
14-20: The voice is defined as that of hope, which is **'recidiva'** (incorrigible), clinging to illusions, seeking the memory of summer in the water-melon's flesh, images of immortal nymphs amidst the trees, or, in a distant glimpse of Mantua on the 'thirsty' plain below, the fantastic mirage of the lake of Tenochtitlan (the ancient Aztec city).
21-23: The moment of truth, as the *io* seeks to touch whatever ghost is speaking, only to grasp emptiness. **'di abbagliamento in cecità'**: the blinding alternation of light and darkness of motorway tunnels. 22-23: There are clear literary precedents here, notably in Dante (*Purgatorio* II), but also in Montale (the encounter with the father's ghost in 'Voce giunta con le folaghe' – but there are also other Montalean echoes in this poem, e.g. l. 4 recalls the *mottetto* 'Non recidere...', while the third stanza has overtones of 'Casa sul mare').
24-31: The oracular voice of a sibyl (**'sibilla'**), hissing (**'sibila'**) incongruously through the noisy 'vaults' of motorway tunnels, concludes the poem with an unflinching look at the void, seen in paradoxical terms as a strong, positive presence. Again, Montalean notes can be heard here, this time the serenely sceptical Montale of the later years (cf. *Xenia* I, 14).

Altro compleanno

A fine luglio quando
da sotto le pergole di un bar di San Siro
tra cancellate e fornici si intravede
un qualche spicchio dello stadio assolato
quando trasecola il gran catino vuoto   5
a specchio del tempo sperperato e pare
che proprio lì venga a morire un anno
e non si sa che altro un altro anno prepari
passiamola questa soglia una volta di più
sol che regga a quei marosi di città il tuo cuore   10
e un'ardesia propaghi il colore dell'estate.

Altro compleanno

Probably written in 1980 for the poet's own birthday (27 July), this poem is placed at the close of his last collection. Here again Sereni is the poet of Milan, of the urban fabric in its topographic specificity, but he presents the empty urban space as an image of anguish and loss. (See also the earlier prose piece 'Il fantasma nerazzurro', in *La tentazione della prosa*, pp. 81-3.)

2:      '**San Siro**': The area in Milan where Sereni lived and whose stadium is home to the AC Milan football team.

3-4:   '**fornici**': archways; '**spicchio**': literally 'segment'; a partial view, glimpsed from the bar; '**assolato**': sunlit.

5-8:   The 'empty bowl' ('**catino**') of the stadium becomes an image, a 'mirror' of time passing, of lost or 'squandered' ('**sperperato**') time, and of the anguish of uncertainty about the future. '**trasecola**': literally 'to be astonished' (the verb has overtones of feeling no longer of this world).

9:      The image of passing a '**soglia**' (threshold) recalls the various other 'frontiers' etc. in Sereni (this time with the idea of the threshold of an unknown future).

10-11: '**sol che**': provided that (takes subjunctive following); thus these lines read: 'as long as your [i.e. my] heart can withstand these city sea-storms and [as long as] a slate [roof-slate] can propagate the colour of summer'. This final, enigmatic image has a lyrical quality that recalls early, quasi-hermetic expressive modes (e.g. the key images of '**cuore**', '**estate**'). Despite living on the threshold of the void, it is a quiet assertion of continuing survival in contact with the world.

8

Edoardo Sanguineti and the *neoavanguardia*

The *neoavanguardia* (or 'new avant-garde') of the late 1950s and 1960s is a movement concerned above all with forging a radically new approach to poetic language and form, backed up by a profound and attentive engagement with developments in contemporary philosophy and culture in a European and global context.[i] The movement emerged in the mid-1950s from the same atmosphere of crisis and dissatisfaction that gave rise to the 'neo-experimentalist' line headed by Pasolini and theorized in the pages of the journal *Officina* (see chapter *Engaging with Reality*, above). Like the *Officina* group, the *neoavanguardia* rejects both the stagnant legacy of hermeticism and the post-war neorealist domination of Italian culture. However, notwithstanding some early points of contact between the two groupings, there soon emerges a clear division between Pasolini's circle and that of the new avant-garde writers, who look to the example of the *avanguardia* of the 1900s (rejected by Pasolini in favour of earlier models such as Pascoli), and whose polemical focus is, from the outset, on the problematization of language itself.[ii] But it would be wrong to assume that the *neoavanguardia* represents merely a reprise or imitation of the experience of the Futurists and their travelling companions. The historical and cultural contexts have changed beyond recognition and the writers and theoreticians of the new avant-garde display an in-depth knowledge of a vast range of contemporary thought and cultural movements, ranging from phenomenology to psychoanalysis, from marxism to structuralism, which feed into their work in varying degrees, but always with a marked degree of critical acumen and with ambitions worthy of 'il grande sperimentalismo europeo'.[iii]

The writers and critics who form the core of the group were mostly in their twenties or early thirties when, in Milan in 1956, Luciano Anceschi founded the literary and cultural quarterly *Il Verri* which soon became the key forum for their work. But it was in 1961 that the profile of the poetic *neoavanguardia* was defined most effectively with the publication of a short anthology of new poets under the title of *I Novissimi: Poesie per gli anni '60*, containing verse and essays by Elio Pagliarani, Alfredo Giuliani (editor of the volume), Edoardo Sanguineti, Nanni Balestrini and Antonio Porta.[iv] These are the poets who, along with other novelists, critics and cultural operators went on to form the *Gruppo 63*, which came into being at a meeting in a hotel in Palermo in 1963, and which, through a series of annual events and publications through the 1960s, constituted the most publicly visible manifestation of the new avant-garde.

Alfredo Giuliani's Introduction to the anthology *I Novissimi* remains one of the most telling documents in defining the poetics of the movement. He stresses repeatedly the centrality of language, the importance of the signifier and of the process of writing as much as that of its 'content': 'Ciò che la poesia *fa* è precisamente il suo "contenuto" [...] E nei periodi di crisi il *modo di fare* coincide quasi interamente col *significato*.' He writes of a moment of 'rottura' in which everything has changed: vocabulary, syntax, structure, but also 'tone', the perspective implicit in the very the act of 'fare poesia'. The new, prosaic 'parlare in versi' collides both with the everyday 'commercial' exploitation of language and with the inertia of the 'codice letterario'. Giuliani writes of a 'schizomorphic' vision, characterized by 'discontinuità', 'asintattismo' (a disruption or absence of syntax) and a 'violence' against 'segni', all of which places the *Novissimi* not at the margins but at the centre of a contemporary 'precarietà'. He also underlines a desire to displace the poetic *io* (on a specifically linguistic/structural level: 'una reale "riduzione dell'io", quale produttore di significati'), and a detailed attention to innovative metrical solutions.[v] All of this, of course, should not be taken as an indication of any compact uniformity within the group, and indeed Giuliani himself points out the diversity of their poetic outcomes. Yet, there is undeniably a common concern with form and with the theory and process of literary creation, a recognition, writes Cataldi, of the primacy of 'il momento dei significanti' for this first truly 'post-Saussurian' Italian movement.[vi] These are writers fully aware of the 'artificiality' of poetic language, which is subject to the same processes of 'alienation' as the rest of reality: language becomes an 'object', to be treated with the same 'detachment and irony' as all other objects.[vii]

The *neoavanguardia* as a whole, like the smaller *Novissimi* grouping, was never a monolithic or cohesive movement. From the time of its first meeting, the *Gruppo 63* was characterized by internal divisions and polemics of an essentially ideological nature (hardly surprising given the highly ideologized and theorized visions of language, writing, culture and society that lay at the basis of its multifarious activities).[viii] Furthermore, it was a movement marked apparently by inherent contradictions: despite its iconoclastic fervour (and, in many cases, left-wing revolutionary agendas), the movement as a whole was remarkably quick to embrace what one may call the cultural industry, with all its paraphernalia. So, leading *avanguardisti* became prominent figures through their roles in mainstream publishing houses, through their academic roles or through engagement with the burgeoning mass media of post-boom Italy.[ix] Notwithstanding the conscious desire on the part of some to subvert these institutions from within, it is hard not to see the emergence, as the 1960s go on, of a new cultural 'establishment' revolving around the *enfants terribles* of the *Gruppo 63* (Sanguineti and Umberto Eco are two names that spring to mind readily in this respect). There were, inevitably, some areas of inauthenticity or mannerism surrounding the *neoavanguardia*, especially as it came to greater prominence (though it is hard to agree with Barberi Squarotti and Golfieri when they characterize the proceedings of the 1963 meeting as merely a proliferation of more or less facile 'parole in libertà', differing from their Futurist antecedents only in their greater degree of 'sbracatura' [slovenly coarseness].[x] And there were also risks of the new writing turning inwards, becoming a closed, self-reflexive game of experimentation and pastiche for the initiated.[xi] Nevertheless, the work of the *neoavanguardia*, with its rigorous attention to language and text, in the context of the profound social, historical and cultural changes underway in the 1960s, marks a real and lasting shift in the paradigms of poetic language, and one may ultimately concur with Alfredo Giuliani when, in his preface to the 1965 edition of *I Novissimi*, he sees in the group's writings 'la costituzione di un linguaggio letterario che *fa epoca* e da cui non si può tornare indietro'.[xii]

Edoardo Sanguineti

Born in Genoa, Sanguineti (1930-) spent most of his youth in Turin, where, having graduated with a dissertation on Dante, he went on teach Italian Literature at the University. He subsequently taught in Salerno before taking up a post at the University of Genoa in 1974. Part of the group that formed around *Il Verri* on its foundation in 1956 (which was also the year that Sanguineti's first poetic collection was published, the ground-breaking

Laborintus), he emerged as one of the most important voices in the *Novissimi*, both as poet and theorist. He went on to become a key figure in the *Gruppo 63* and in the *neoavanguardia* as a whole. His creative and critical activities cover a wide range: alongside his poetry he has published narrative and theatrical works, as well as a number of highly-significant critical texts (notably on Dante and Gozzano) and an important anthology, *Poesia italiana del Novecento* (Einaudi, 1969), which set out to re-draw the profile of the modern verse tradition. Sanguineti's vision of that tradition leans decidedly towards the futurist and crepuscular lines of development (with a clear intent to link these to the new avant-garde), rather than towards the *ermetici* and *lirici nuovi* who appeared at the time to dominate. He has also taken an active interest in the visual arts and in music, notably collaborating with composer Luciano Berio on the libretti of *Passaggio* and *Laborintus II*. His literary ideology has always been inseparable from his marxist politics, also given practical expression when he was elected as an independent PCI member of Parliament in 1979. His private life (marriage to Luciana in 1954 and subsequent birth of 4 children) is repeatedly brought into the forefront of his verse, with a sometimes disconcerting directness and intimacy.

It was Sanguineti who, in 1960, coined the term 'novissimi', subsequently adopted by Giuliani in the title of the 1961 anthology. The meaning of the word merits careful attention: as Fausto Curi explains, the primary, literal meaning of the Latin term *novissimus* is 'last', 'final', while it was also used by Caesar meaning the 'rearguard' of the army. Thus, its use by Sanguineti is laden with irony: the new avant-garde are the last or the rearguard of their kind, they represent a conclusion and a critique of a literary epoch rather than a fresh new beginning (although, of course, the term also carries strong etymological connotations of 'newness').[xiii] Sanguineti's first collection, *Laborintus* (1956), lives up to the apocalyptic overtones of the word: it is, in its foreshadowing of the wider *neoavanguardia* movement, a work of extraordinary originality, a 'poesia furiosamente negativa', whose energy seems primarily a destructive one, intent on dismantling the mechanisms of language and meaning.[xiv] But behind the polemical assault on language is a wider polemic against society and all of contemporary history: the 'Palus Putredinis' (swamp of decay) is that of collective reality, as well as of the individual subconscious. When Zanzotto suggested that *Laborintus* might have some value only if it were the 'sincera trascrizione di un esaurimento nervoso', Sanguineti retorted that it was in fact an 'esaurimento storico' that was transcribed here.[xv] The 27 numbered sections build into a *poemetto*, whose 'plot', in so far as there is one, lies in the laborious elaboration of a descent into the infernal 'Palus'. However, to speak of plot or content as something distinct from form or language would be ultimately to misconstrue this work, where content is inseparable from language. Equally, to limit the work's range of reference to the area of the individual psyche would be mistaken. In short, it is a collection which challenges the whole lyrical canon and mixes 'pulsioni sociali e sessuali, immagini oniriche e ideologia politica'.[xvi]

As Sanguineti's work progresses, there is a gradual shift away from the 'finimondo liquido-sintattico' of *Laborintus* towards almost a kind of narrative (albeit a fragmentary, nightmarish and surreal one).[xvii] In *Erotopaegnia* (1960) and *Purgatorio de l'Inferno* (1964), some of the furious impenetrability is mitigated as human figures emerge (along with the *io*, there are various *tu* figures, notably that of the erotic poems and those of the poems addressed to his son), in presumably autobiographical snatches of narrative, encapsulated in ironic or grotesque scenes. And with the poems of *Reisebilder* (1971), and *Postkarten* (1977), although the poet's underlying urge to challenge the syntactical, lexical and semantic strictures of language survives as part of a now-consolidated technique, the more mature style settles, notwithstanding the fractured physiognomy of the texts, into an unexpectedly communicative 'parlato prosaico, quotidiano, quasi banale' (but always sharpened with a strong streak of critical irony).[xviii] This is the manner which will dominate much of Sanguineti's poetry for the following decades, along with an ever greater presence of sarcastic humour and biting self-deprecation expressed through playful technical and linguistic bravura.

Alfredo Giuliani

Giuliani (1924-2007) was a key figure in the *neoavanguardia*, both as poet and critic. A native of Pesaro, he lived most of his life in Rome, and held academic posts in Bologna (1971-79) and Chieti (1980-95). Part of the group associated with *Il Verri* from the outset, he came to particular prominence through his role in editing the anthology *I Novissimi* in 1961 (he wrote the incisive Introduction, as well as being one of the five poets featured), and went on to play an important part in the *Gruppo 63* (editing, with Balestrini, the proceedings of the 1963 gathering). He also directed the journal *Quindici* from 1967-69 and has been a regular contributor to national newspapers, as well as writing various 'poesie per teatro' (included in *Povera Juliet*, 1965), and an experimental prose work, *Il giovane Max* (1972). Following a trajectory almost directly opposite to that of Sanguineti, his poetry develops from relatively conventional beginnings to become, during the 1960s, increasingly challenging and radical in its formal features, from neologistic excesses to extreme syntactic and semantic fragmentation as part of what he calls his 'schizomorphic' vision.[xix]

Nanni Balestrini

A native of Milan, Balestrini (1935-)was one of the *Novissimi* and part of the *Gruppo 63*, and has been given to radical forms of innovation and experimentation in his poetic and narrative/theatrical works. He was closely associated with the student movement in 1968-69 and went on to participate in extreme left-wing politics in the 1970s (he was part of *Autonomia operaia*), until he was indicted in 1979 for alleged involvement in terrorist activity. After a period of exile in France he was eventually cleared of these charges in 1984. He has also worked extensively as a visual artist, exhibiting, for example, at the Venice *Biennale* in 1993.

Manacorda writes of Balestrini's 'tecnica del nonsenso', in which divergent elements of discourse are brought together apparently 'per pura casualità', although the process is actually carefully planned to allow multiple readings.[xx] The poems of *Come si agisce* (1963) are preceded by a note in which the author states that the texts, arranged on a 'flat surface', can be read in different sequences and interrelationships (and he appends specific 'tables' of possible reading sequences at the end of the volume).[xxi] The apparent 'gratuitousness' of Balestrini's early poetic work, its 'non-significato', comes to signify, according to Giuliani, 'il ripudio della società costituita', through the metaphor of its own forms of 'structural disruption'.[xxii]

Antonio Porta

The poetry of Antonio Porta (1935-1989), especially in its earlier phase, is filled with the fragmentary objects and phenomena of a physical world that is transformed into a nightmarish hallucinatory vision, with frequent elements of grotesque, corporeal horror and violence, expressed through a 'lingua radicalmente espressionistica'.[xxiii] Indeed, there is a dual 'violenza espressiva' in Porta, involving both the formal and the thematic levels.[xxiv] No lyrical *io* here, but at times a kind of impersonal *io*-surrogate, what Porta calls a '*poeta-oggettivo*', an unidentified protagonist immersed in this uncomfortable world.[xxv] External reality is inescapably present, as the poet feels 'l'importanza dell'evento esterno, da cui sentiamo colpita la comunità e non più, soltanto, la persona del poeta isolato: e lì ci si specchia, noi, uomini.'[xxvi] But external events are filtered through a highly individual perspective and captured in images of bodily suffering and distortion, in fragmentary details, partly glimpsed and brought together in a confused and confusing accumulation, lacking clear syntactic co-ordination or semantic cohesion.

Like many other poets of the *neoavanguardia*, Porta also experimented with the narrative and theatrical genres, while in his later poetic work, from around the end of the 1970s, there is a shift towards a more directly communicative style, though his voice remains recognizable always for its 'energia lucida'.[xxvii]

Note: The texts reproduced here by Giuliani, Balestrini and Porta have all been chosen from among those included in the original *Novissimi* volume, with the intention of giving a clear flavour of that particular cultural moment. In the case of Sanguineti, a wider selection of poems is given.

Endnotes

[i] For a useful general overview, see Fabio Gambaro, *Invito a conoscere la neoavanguardia* (Milan: Mursia, 1993).

[ii] Renato Barilli, himself a member of the original *neoavanguardia* circle around the journal *Il Verri*, gives a spirited account of how Pasolini's approach differed from that of his own grouping. See Barilli, *La neoavanguardia italiana. Dalla nascita del "Verri" alla fine di "Quindici"* (Bologna: Il Mulino, 1995), pp. 16-24.

[iii] Ezio Raimondi, *Le poetiche della modernità in Italia* (Milan: Garzanti, 1990), p. 96. See also Fausto Curi, *La poesia italiana nel Novecento*, pp. 360-63. Elsewhere, Curi underlines the idea of a common thread connecting the 'historic' and 'new' avant-gardes, in a volume covering both movements: F. Curi, *La poesia italiana d'avanguardia. Modi e techniche* (Napoli: Liguori, 2001).

[iv] *I Novissimi. Poesie per gli anni '60*, a cura di Alfredo Giuliani, Biblioteca del Verri (Milan: Rusconi e Paolazzi, 1961); republished in 1965 by Einaudi, with an additional Preface (and republished again by Einaudi in 2003, with a further, characteristically incisive preface by Giuliani). The only one of the Novissimi not included in this chapter, Elio Pagliarani, is represented in the earlier chapter *Engaging with Reality*.

[v] Giuliani, 'Introduzione', in *I Novissimi*, pp. xiii-xxxii (pp. xv-xix).

[vi] Pietro Cataldi, *Le idee della letteratura: Storia delle poetiche italiane del Novecento* (Roma: La Nuova Italia Scientifica, 1994), p. 160.

[vii] Fausto Curi, *La poesia italiana nel Novecento*, p. 364

[viii] The proceedings of the Palermo meeting are in N. Balestrini and A. Giuliani (eds), *Gruppo 63. La nuova letteratura. 34 scrittori. Palermo ottobre 1963* (Milan: Feltrinelli, 1964), which contains an extensive selection of writings in prose and in verse, as well as critical essays and the transcription of key points in the theoretical debates (see especially pp. 371-406). For a summary of the main ideological lines of division, see

Manacorda, *Storia della letteratura italiana contemporanea 1940-1996*, pp. 485-497. A further collection of critical essays arising out of the Gruppo 63 and its debates can be found in Renato Barilli and Angelo Guglielmi (eds), *Gruppo 63: critica e teoria* (Milan: Feltrinelli, 1977; see also new edition published in 2003).

ix   See Cataldi, *Le idee della letteratura*, pp. 158-9 and Giorgio Barberi-Squarotti and A.M. Golfieri, *Dal tramonto dell'ermetismo alla neoavanguardia*, (Brescia: Editrice La Scuola, 1984), pp. 87-95.

x   Barberi-Squarotti and Golfieri, *Dal tramonto dell'ermetismo alla neoavanguardia*, p. 98.

xi   Niva Lorenzini, *Il presente della poesia*, p. 42.

xii   Giuliani, 'Prefazione alla presente edizione', in *I Novissimi. Poesie per gli anni '60*, Nuova edizione riveduta (Torino: Einaudi, 1965), p. 9. The publication of the second edition by Einaudi rather than by the original relatively obscure publisher under the imprint of *Il Verri* is in itself a reflection of the progress made by the *neoavanguardia* within 'official' Italian culture.

xiii   Fausto Curi, in Sanguineti, *Opere e introduzione critica* (Verona: Anterem, 1993), pp. 13-14.

xiv   Gabriella Sica, *Sanguineti* (Firenze: La Nuova Italia, 1974), p. 24. Guido Guglielmi describes *Laborintus* as 'una sapientissima a stridente partitura musicale'; see Guglielmi, 'La poesia italiana alla metà del Novecento', in *Genealogie della poesia nel secondo Novecento. Giornate di studio, Siena 23-24-25 marzo 2001*, a cura di Maria Antonietta Grignani (Pisa-Roma: Istituti editoriali e poligrafici internazionali, 2002), pp. 15-33 (p. 22).

xv   Sanguineti, 'Poesia informale?', in *I Novissimi*, 1961, p. 169.

xvi   Lorenzini, *La poesia italiana del Novecento*, p. 143. Curi identifies three major thematic areas in Sanguineti's work: the area of 'metadiscorso'; political themes; and 'l'area erotico-coniugale' (*Opere e introduzione critica*, p. 17). Baccarani writes of Sanguineti's dual assault on the 'institution' of literature, alternating between frontal attacks using 'scrittura bassa, prosastica e prosaica' and, on the other hand, 'le sofisticate tecniche della iperletterarietà'; Elisabetta Baccarani, *La poesia nel labirinto: razionalismo e istanza antiletteraria nell'opera e nella cultura di Edoardo Sanguineti* (Bologna: Il mulino, 2002), p. 13.

xvii   It is worth quoting Giuliani's penetrating description of *Laborintus* more fully: 'La sua prima opera, il Laborintus, è una faustiana discesa all'inferno che ha tutto l'aspetto di un supremo divertimento: la tecnica della confessione psicanalitica mima in verità una ricognizione nella mitologia collettiva, dove l'alchimia e le larve dei sogni, le scoperte erotiche e filologiche, il decadimento sociale, la suggestione dottrinale di una cultura tra medioevale e barocca, le figure dell'esperienza quotidiana, s'inseguono per giustapposizioni verticali, in un finimondo liquido-sintattico che dà subito l'idea della "serie" dodecafonica trasposta nel linguaggio letterario." See Introduction to *I Novissimi* (1961), p. xxvi.

xviii   Gabriella Sica, *Sanguineti* (Firenze: La Nuova Italia, 1974), p. 53.

xix   Introduction to *I Novissimi*, p. xviii. In the preface to the 2003 edition Giuliani glosses the phrase 'visione schizomorfa' as meaning 'l'intenzionalità alla forma scissa': the aim or intention of divided/fragmented form. (2003 edition, p. viii).

xx   Manacorda, *Storia della letteratura italiana contemporanea*, p. 476. Fabio Gambaro also speaks of a duality between carefully calculated structures and a chaotic disorder within them (*Invito a conoscere la neoavanguardia*, p. 184).

xxi Balestrini, *Come si agisce* (Milan: Feltrinelli, 1963); see note on page following index (unnumbered), and tables on pp. 191-4.

xxii Introduction to *I Novissimi*, p. xxviii. On Balestrini's early work, see also Sanguineti's reading 'Come agisce Balestrini', in Sanguineti, *Ideologia e linguaggio*, 3rd ed (Milan: Feltrinelli, 2001), pp. 72-6.

xxiii Niva Lorenzini, 'Postfazione', in Porta, *Poesie (1956-1988)* (Milan: Mondadori, 1998), pp. 179-195 (p. 180). On Porta, see also Lorenzini, *Il presente della poesia*, pp. 90-100; and John Picchione, *Introduzione a Porta* (Roma-Bari: Laterza, 1995), especially pp. 31-34 on 'Europa cavalca un toro nero'.

xxiv See Stefano Agosti, 'Porta e la scena della "crudeltà"', in *Poesia italiana contemporanea* (Milan: Bompiani, 1995), pp. 153-65 (p. 153).

xxv Porta, 'Poesia e poetica', in *I Novissimi*, pp. 159-62 (p. 161)

xxvi 'Poesia e poetica', p. 160.

xxvii Maurizio Cucchi, 'Introduzione' to *Poesie (1956-1988)*, p. v.

Poetic texts

Edoardo Sanguineti

There are two principal collected editions:

Segnalibro: poesie 1951-1981 (Milan: Feltrinelli, 1982)
This brings together previous individual volumes: *Laborintus* (1956); *Erotopaegnia* (1960); *Purgatorio de l'Inferno* (1964); *Wirrwarr* (1972); *Postkarten* (1978); *Stracciafoglio* (1980); *Scartabello* (1980); *Cataletto* (1981).
Il gatto lupesco: Poesie (1982-2001) (Milan: Feltrinelli, 2002)
Includes: *Novissimum Testamentum* (1986) *Bisbidis* (1987) *Senzatitolo* (1992) *Corollario* (1997) *Cose* (2001).

Alfredo Giuliani

There is no single collected edition.
Versi e nonversi (Milan: Feltrinelli, 1986), brings together the main earlier collections:
Il cuore zoppo (1955); *Povera Juliet e altre poesie* (1965); *Il tautofono* (1969).
Later works include:
Ebbrezza di placamenti (Lecce: Manni, 1994); *Poetrix Bazaar* (Napoli: Pironti, 2003).

Nanni Balestrini

There is no single collected edition.
Poesie pratiche, 1954-1969 (Turin: Einaudi,1976), brings together the main earlier poetic works: *Il sasso appeso* (1961); *Come si agisce* (1963); *Altri procedimenti* (1966); *Ma noi facciamone un'altra* (1968);
Later works include:
La ballata della signorina Richmond (1977); *Blackout* (1980); *Ipocalisse: 49 sonetti* (1986); *Il ritorno della signorina Richmond* (1987); *Il pubblico del labirinto* (1992); *Estremi rimedi* (1995); *Sfinimondo* (2003).

Antonio Porta

A very good selected edition is:
Poesie (1956-1988), a cura Niva Lorenzini, con introduzione di Maurizio Cucchi (Milan: Mondadori, 1998).
Previous partially collected works are:
I rapporti (Milan: Feltinelli, 1966) (brings together all his early collections);
Quanto ho da dirvi (Milan: Feltrinelli, 1977) (collects all poems up to 1975);
Nel fare poesia (Florence: Sansoni, 1985) (a selection of his work with useful commentary by the poet).

Further reading

Agosti, Stefano, 'Porta e la scena della "crudeltà"', in *Poesia italiana contemporanea* (Milan: Bompiani, 1995), pp. 153-65
Baccarani, Elisabetta, *La poesia nel labirinto: razionalismo e istanza antiletteraria*

nell'opera e nella cultura di Edoardo Sanguineti (Bologna: Il mulino, 2002)

Balestrini, Nanni and Alfredo Giuliani, eds, *Gruppo 63. La nuova letteratura. 34 scrittori. Palermo ottobre 1963* (Milan: Feltrinelli, 1964)

Barberi-Squarotti, Giorgio and A. M. Golfieri, *Dal tramonto dell'ermetismo alla neoavanguardia* (Brescia: Editrice La Scuola, 1984)

Barilli, Renato and Angelo Guglielmi, eds, *Gruppo 63: critica e teoria* (Milan: Feltrinelli, 1977, 2nd edn 2003).

Barilli, Renato, *La neoavanguardia italiana. Dalla nascita del "Verri" alla fine di "Quindici"* (Bologna: Il Mulino, 1995)

Cataldi, Pietro, *Le idee della letteratura: Storia delle poetiche italiane del Novecento* (Roma: La Nuova Italia Scientifica, 1994)

Curi, Fausto, Introduction in Sanguineti, *Opere e introduzione critica* (Verona: Anterem, 1993), pp. 13-21

Curi, Fausto, *La poesia italiana d'avanguardia. Modi e techniche* (Napoli: Liguori, 2001).

Gambaro, Fabio, *Invito a conoscere la neoavanguardia* (Milan: Mursia, 1993)

Giordano, Luigi, ed., *Sanguineti. Ideologia e linguaggio* (Salerno: Metafora Edizioni, 1991) (proceedings of 1989 Salerno conference on Sanguineti)

Giuliani, Alfredo, ed., *I Novissimi. Poesie per gli anni '60*, Biblioteca del Verri (Milan: Rusconi e Paolazzi, 1961) (republished in 1965 and 2003 by Einaudi)

Guglielmi, Guido, 'La poesia italiana alla metà del Novecento', in *Genealogie della poesia nel secondo Novecento. Giornate di studio, Siena 23-24-25 marzo 2001*, a cura di Maria Antonietta Grignani (Pisa-Roma: Istituti editoriali e poligrafici internazionali, 2002), pp. 15-33 [special edition of *Moderna*, 3 (2001)]

Ó Ceallacháin, Éanna, 'Sanguineti and Montale: Travelling Companions in the 1970s', *Modern Language Review*, 102 (January 2007), 89-107

Picchione, John, *Introduzione a Porta* (Roma-Bari: Laterza, 1995)

Pietropaoli, Antonio, ed., *Per Edoardo Sanguineti: 'good luck (and look)'. Atti del convegno per il settantennio* (Naples: Edizioni Scientifiche Italiane, 2002)

Pietropaoli, Antonio, *Unità e trinità di Edoardo Sanguineti. Poesia e poetica* (Napoli: Edizioni scientifiche italiane, 1991)

Raimondi, Ezio, *Le poetiche della modernità in Italia* (Milan: Garzanti, 1990)

Sanguineti, Edoardo, *Ideologia e linguaggio*, 3rd ed (Milan: Feltrinelli, 2001)

Sica, Gabriella, *Sanguineti* (Florence: La Nuova Italia, 1974)

Siti, Walter, *Il realismo dell'avanguardia* (Turin: Einaudi, 1975)

Contents

EDOARDO SANGUINETI

From *Laborintus* (1956)

Laborintus 1

composte terre in strutturali complessioni sono Palus Putredinis
riposa tenue Ellie e tu mio corpo tu infatti tenue Ellie eri il mio corpo
immaginoso quasi conclusione di una estatica dialettica spirituale
noi che riceviamo la qualità dai tempi
                                          tu e tu mio spazioso corpo
di flogisto che ti alzi e ti materializzi nell'idea del nuoto   5
sistematica costruzione in ferro filamentoso lamentoso
lacuna lievitata in compagnia di una tenace tematica
composta terra delle distensioni dialogiche insistenze intemperanti
le condizioni esterne è evidente esistono realmente queste condizioni
esistevano prima di noi ed esisteranno dopo di noi qui è il dibattimento   10
liberazioni frequenza e forza e agitazione potenziata e altro
aliquot lineae desiderantur
                            dove dormi cuore ritagliato
e incollato e illustrato con documentazioni viscerali dove soprattutto
vedete igienicamente nell'acqua antifermentativa ma fissati adesso
quelli i nani extratemporali i nani insomma o Ellie   15
nell'aria inquinata
                    in un costante cratere anatomico ellittico
perché ulteriormente diremo che non possono crescere

tu sempre la mia natura e rasserenata tu canzone metodologica
periferica introspezione dell'introversione forza centrifuga delimitata
Ellie tenue corpo di peccaminose escrescenze
                           che possiamo roteare   20
e rivolgere e odorare e adorare nel tempo
                        desiderantur (essi)
analizzatori e analizzatrici desiderantur (essi) personaggi anche
ed erotici e sofisticati
                desiderantur desiderantur

Laborintus 1

'**Laborintus**': Sanguineti provides the following epigraph, taken, according to Giuliani, from a marginal gloss in a 13th-century rhetorical tract of the same name: 'Titulus est / laborintus / quasi laborem / habens intus' ('the title is *laborintus*, as though having hard work inside'). Thus from the outset the work is marked by the tendency to learned word play as the quotation points to the title being a play on 'labyrinth' and 'labour'.

The notes in Giuliani's 1961 anthology (pp. 61-63) provide an extremely useful key to Sanguineti's texts. The *poemetto* as a whole is described there as 'una psicanalisi patita dal protagonista e condotta da personaggi … alquanto lacunosi' (the 'characters' are Ellie, discussed below, Laszo, a masculine/solar figure, and Ruben, the analyst and/or the synthesis between the other two; see Curi, *La poesia italiana*, pp. 270-72). This opening poem is 'the description of a disintegrating mental landscape', centred on the '**Palus Putredinis**' (swamp of decay) as an archetypal image of the maternal body, of chaos in the world and of 'the desire to abolish opposites'. The character '**Ellie**' is the Jungian Anima (although to speak of 'character' is perhaps an exaggeration in this labyrinth of signs); the poem is a 'descent into the underworld'.

1-3:   '**composte terre**': perhaps the world, reality, in its composite and chaotic nature; '**complessione**': character, nature, essence; **l.3**: the figure of Ellie is the 'outcome of an ecstatic dialectic'.

4-7:   '**noi che riceviamo…**': a quotation from Foscolo, stating that poets bear the mark of their times, thus anchoring this apparently abstract text in historical reality; similarly, in ll.9-10, a quotation from Stalin reminds us of the 'reality' of the 'external' world; '**flogisto**': phlogiston, a lighter-than-air substance believed by alchemists to be released in the burning process; '**costruzione…**': contradicting the previous images of lightness and incorporeality, here the imagery is of hard, constructed physicality: part of the constant oscillation between opposites in these poems (indeed, the '**corpo**' goes on to become a disembodied '**lacuna**' in the next line).

8-12:   The 'world' is characterized also by abstractions, 'distensions' and 'insistences'. These, along with many other words ending in 'ione', etc., are an example of the kind of intellectual jargon, the professional language of the academic, the 'critichese' which may have been the last semantic area to be excluded from the poetic register and which Sanguineti now so courageously incorporates (Barilli, *La neoavanguardia italiana*, p. 51). **l.11**: the succession of abstractions (presumably features of the '**dibattimento**' of history) without any syntactic coordination (except the neutral 'e') is typical of the whole *poemetto* and its flouting of any requirement for communicative clarity; '**aliquot…**': almost by way of commentary on l.11, the Latin phrase means 'some lines [lines of intepretation?] are desired (needed/required)'.

12-17: There is an increase in the level of corporeality, from the two-dimensional 'cuore' ('**ritagliato e incollato**': cut out and pasted), to its 'visceral' documentation, to the '**acqua antifermentativa**' (antiseptic fluid) in which are 'fixed' the **'nani extratemporali'** ('dwarfs outside of time'): perhaps an image of preserved, aborted foetuses? (Giuliani says they are 'the movements of the unconscious', but he also calls them 'i figli spirituali e fisiologici', who cannot grow in the 'anatomic crater' of the disintegrated landscape – an image which also, surely, suggests the womb). In these lines it is notable how the grammatical subject seems to change almost arbitrarily from *tu* (l.12) to *voi* (l.14) to *noi* (l.17), giving an instability of meaning and perspective wholly in line with the 'riduzione dell'io' noted by Giuliani as characteristic of the *Novissimi* (on the 'schizophrenic' instability of the subject, see Baccarani, pp. 54-64).

18-19:   **'canzone metodologica'**: a highly apposite image of this poetry itself, where any idea of lyricism is overwhelmed by the frenzy of abstraction, linguistic artifice, formal inventiveness. **l.19**: an accumulation of abstract terms marked by extreme tensions between opposites, between a self-centred and an outward-looking   world-view,   between   the   **'introspezione dell'introversione'** and the terms **'periferica'**, **'forza centrifuga'** (the latter constrained in turn by the further tension with **'delimitata'**).

20-23:   The piece closes with another descent into the corporeal, this time with distinctly erotic overtones in the evocation of the body of the Ellie/Palus figure; **'peccaminose escrescenze'**: sinful growths. She can be handled (**'roteare e rivolgere'**), smelled, adored (always **'nel tempo'**, within historical time), but immediately overlaid on this is the intellectual imperative of analysis, with the urgent repetition of **'desiderantur'** (they are desired/needed) referring to the **'analizzatori…'**, but also to the **'personaggi'**, elements constantly suggested but also negated in *Laborintus*.

On a formal level, this poem serves as the deliberately provocative introduction to Sanguineti's new and challenging style. Barilli notes that the very 'look' of the poems on the page with their extraordinarily long lines possessed a 'rivoluzionarietà quantitativa' (Barilli, *La neoavanguardia italiana*, p. 50). Traditional or conventional metre is completely abandoned and the long lines obey a kind of rhythm which is based on syntactic and semantic units, but always unpredictable and open to arbitrary variations. Words accumulate in associative chains bereft of context and in which logical indicators of coordination and subordination are almost completely absent, where sense appears to derive as much from the dense texture of repetition and alliteration as from semantic elements. The language used tends, on one hand, to approach lower registers of 'parlato', but, on the other, draws on a vast range of erudite sources, including foreign and 'dead' languages, in a highly intellectualized literary artifice, whose outcome is the deliberate 'morte di ogni naturalezza' (Curi, *La poesia italiana*, p. 269). Language itself becomes the protagonist and replaces the *io* as the very source of meaning.

Laborintus 14

con le quattro tonsille in fermentazione con le trombe con i cadaveri
con le sinagoghe devo sostituirti con le stazioni termali con i logaritmi
con i circhi equestri
                con dieci monosillabi che esprimano dolore
con dieci numeri brevi che esprimano perturbazioni
                               mettere la polvere
nei tuoi denti le pastiglie nei tuoi tappeti aprire le mie sorgenti   5
dentro il tuo antichissimo atlante
                    i tuoi fiori sospenderò finalmente
ai testicoli dei cimiteri ai divani del tuo ingegno
intestinale
        devo con opportunità i tuoi almanacchi dal mio argento escludere
i tuoi tamburi dalle mie vesciche
                il tuo arcipelago dai miei giornali
pitagorici
        piangere la pietra e la pietra e la pietra   10
la pietra ininterrottamente con il ghetto delle immaginazioni
in supplicazioni sognate di pietra
                 ma pietra irrimediabilmente morale

il tuo filamento patetico rifiuta le scodelle truccate
i corpi ulcerati cosí vicini al disfacimento
                   con la lima ispida
devo trattare i tuoi alberi del pane
               devo mangiare il fuoco e la teosofia   15
trattare anche l'ospedale psichiatrico dei tuoi deserti rocciosi

Laborintus 14

This poem typifies the range of referents in the collection (to speak of 'themes' is perhaps problematic) as well as a number of the formal features already seen in the opening text. As elsewhere, the identity of the grammatical subjects *tu* and *io* is far from clear, their dialogue apparently an abstract linguistic engagement with a world in physical, intellectual and psychological chaos, represented by a bewildering accumulation of fragments and signs.

1-4:   Tonsils, trumpets, corpses, synagogues, spa-resorts (**'stazioni termali'**), logarithms, circuses, monosyllables, numbers: all 'must' be 'substituted' for the *tu* (the verb **'devo'** is the one clear element of syntactical/logical cohesion in the text).

5-9:   The infinitives here still refer back to 'devo' in l. 2: *tu* and *io* must be simultaneously interwoven ('I' putting powder in 'your' teeth, pills in your carpets, opening 'my' springs in 'your' atlas) and separated (excluding 'your' almanacs from 'my' silver, 'your' drums from 'my' blisters/bladders…). There is an extraordinary range of semantic areas, from that of banal everyday objects (dust, carpets), to that of cultural artefacts such as **'atlante'**, **'giornali pitagorici'** (Pythagorean journals), to that of a vivid corporeality, culminating in the bizarre juxtapositions of ll.7-8: **'testicoli dei cimiteri'** (testicles of cemeteries), **'ingegno / intestinale'** (intestinal genius).

10-12: One of the most extreme forms of alliterative musicality found repeatedly in Sanguineti is that of obsessive repetition, as here.

13-16: Further puzzling juxtapositions of imagery and register: 'your pathetic filament' refuses **'scodelle truccate'** (made-up or falsified bowls) and 'ulcerated bodies'; **'vicini al disfacimento'**: close to disintegration. Meanwhile the *io* must eat fire and theosophy, and, using a **'lima ispida'** ('prickly file'), must engage with the psychiatric problems, the 'rocky deserts' of the *tu*.

From *Erotopaegnia* (1960)

4.

in te dormiva come un fibroma asciutto, come una magra tenia, un sogno;
ora pesta la ghiaia, ora scuote la propria ombra; ora stride,
deglutisce, orina, avendo atteso da sempre il gusto
della camomilla, la temperatura della lepre, il rumore della grandine,
la forma del tetto, il colore della paglia:
                                                                 senza rimedio il tempo   5
si è rivolto verso i suoi giorni; la terra offre immagini confuse;
saprà riconoscere la capra, il contadino, il cannone?
non queste forbici veramente sperava, non questa pera,
quando tremava in quel tuo sacco di membrane opache.

Erotopaegnia 4

Sanguineti's second collection, *Erotopaegnia* ('erotic games') marks the beginning of a move away from the intensely challenging wall of words presented to the reader in *Laborintus*. Even on first glance, the texts appear less as a compact mass and more approachable to the eye, and their content becomes undoubtedly more intelligible as human figures, especially those of the poet and his wife, are portrayed no longer as intellectual 'ciphers', but more 'figuratively' and with a disarming directness (See Barilli, pp. 56-7). The style however, remains tensely controlled, full of artifice and invention.

In this poem, addressed like others to the beloved *tu*, the 'erotic' element is displaced onto the objective and subjective realities of birth and the newborn child.

1:     The 3rd person grammatical subject is the foetus/child; **'fibroma'**: fibroma, a benign tumour; **'tenia'**: tapeworm (as ever, the field of the imagery is wide and eclectic).

2-5:   **'ghiaia'**: gravel; **'stride'**: shouts; **'deglutisce'**: swallows; **'orina'**: urinates; **'lepre'**: hare. The range of the child's first experiences of the world, both fundamental bodily functions and the simple sensory pleasures of physical experience, has a naïve arbitrariness, from shaking its own shadow to anticipating the colour of straw, bordering almost on the surreal with **'la temperatura della lepre'**.

5-9:   **'si è rivolto'**: *rivolgersi*, to turn (towards). In this second part, time, in its relentless progress towards the present (**'i suoi giorni'**: his/her days, i.e., of the child) introduces a note of clear disappointment with the reality of the world, which is confusing and problematic, with a strong hint of hostility (**'il cannone'**). **'sacco di membrane opache'**: the womb.

From *Purgatorio de l'Inferno* (1964)

10.

questo è il gatto con gli stivali, questa è la pace di Barcellona
fra Carlo V e Clemente VII, è la locomotiva, è il pesco
fiorito, è il cavalluccio marino: ma se volti il foglio, Alessandro,
ci vedi il denaro:
        questi sono i satelliti di Giove, questa è l'autostrada
del Sole, è la lavagna quadrettata, è il primo volume dei Poetae   5
Latini Aevi Carolini, sono le scarpe, sono le bugie,
        [è la Scuola d'Atene, è il burro,
è una cartolina che mi è arrivata oggi dalla Finlandia, è il muscolo massetere,
è il parto: ma se volti il foglio, Alessandro, ci vedi
il denaro:
        e questo è il denaro,
e questi sono i generali con le loro mitragliatrici, e sono i cimiteri   10
con le loro tombe, e sono le casse di risparmio con le loro cassette
di sicurezza, e sono i libri di storia con le loro storie:

ma se volti il foglio, Alessandro, non ci vedi niente:

Purgatorio de l'Inferno 10.

In *Purgatorio de l'Inferno* there is an increasingly clear emergence of historical circumstances, not through any grand epic representation but through the very particular and ironic vision of the poetic *io* in his personal experiences, 'la storia recuperata attraverso la microstoria' (Curi, in *Opere e introduzione*, p. 15). In this poem, an intimate scene of a father teaching his young son about the world becomes an ironic unmasking, from a Marxist perspective, of the capitalist system with its reduction of all human endeavour to the level of monetary exchange. Formally, the construction of the poem as a child-like list, whose only co-ordinating structures lie in the repetition of **'questo è'**, **'questi sono'** and **'e'/'ma'**, emphasises the alienating lack of differentiation in a world organized around **'il denaro'**.

1-4: **'il gatto con gli stivali'**: Puss in Boots; **'la pace di Barcellona'**: treaty signed in 1529; **'pesco'**: peach tree; **'cavalluccio marino'**: sea-horse; **'Alessandro'**: name of the poet's second son, born 1958; The ironic tone is established immediately through the incongruous inclusion of the Barcelona treaty in the list of things more plausibly to be shown to a young child, as well as through the light repetitive rhythm based on 'questo è...', echoed throughout the text (alluding to the nursery rhyme 'Questo è l'occhio bello, questo è suo fratello...'). Behind all the phenomena of the world lies money, the capitalist system: the poem's overtly left-wing ideological message.

4-8: A further catalogue of objects, reduced, through a complete absence of hierarchy, to apparent meaninglessness: **'Giove'**: Jupiter; **'Poetae Latini...'**: a collection of Carolingian Latin poets; **'Scuola d'Atene'**: Raffaello's famous fresco in the Vatican; **'il muscolo massetere'**: the masseter, a cheek muscle.

9-13: The final list, flowing from **'il denaro'** takes a distinctly darker turn, with **'mitragliatrici'** (machine guns) leading on to cemeteries, but also inseparable from **'casse di risparmio'** (savings banks) and their **'cassette...'** (safe deposit boxes – though there may be an echo here also of 'cassa da morto', coffin); **'storia... storie'**: here the repetitive variation has a distinctly satirical slant, as 'storia' (history) is reduced to 'storie' (in the sense of fictions, lies). **'niente'**: underlying the capitalist society, where all values are reduced to that of money, is an absence of meaning or value.

From *Reisebilder* (1971)

1.

che cosa potevo fare o dire, Vasko, quando quella seria Shirley
Temple in technicolor mi ha raggiunto correndo sulla Lijnbaan, agitando
la sua rossa coda, ridendo? ho subito sentito i suoi artigli – come
si dice – nel mio cuore:
                                 tiene il mio teschio tra le sue zampe, ma la sua faccia,
adesso, è pulita: e succhia la mia spina dorsale sopra questo deserto   5
di Rotterdam, dentro questo Number One, in questo literary supper:
è una cosa (lei) del genere Holbein d.J. (penso al *Portret
van een onbekende vrouw*): non è riuscita cosí bene, si capisce, ma
è piú magra: e con il pipistrello in testa, per esempio:
                                 [e senza tutto quel velo giallo:
le ho chiesto anche il nome (lo hai sentito anche tu):
                                 [una parola come Inneke,   10
credo:
      e poi, che cosa posso scrivere, ormai, se devo ancora discutere
fino alle sei del mattino, camera 348, con l'europeo Tchicaya,
con Breyten, con te?
                     (non riesco nemmeno a telefonare a mia moglie, vedi, a finire
le *Affinità elettive*): e ho anche un paio di pustole in faccia:

Reisebilder 1

The opening poem in *Reisebilder* (German: 'travel pictures', after Heine), marks the transition to an apparently discursive, quasi-diaristic style, in which self-portraiture goes hand-in-hand with an ironic and at times grotesque self-deprecation, expressed through the fragmentary experiences of the European intellectual nomad, against the backdrop of a degraded, banal social and cultural reality. Behind the almost facile appearance of autobiographical narration, however, lies a highly self-conscious literary construction, 'un parodico e tutt'altro che solipsistico soliloquio: [...] inscenato da un io grottesco e oggettivato' (Lorenzini, *Il presente della poesia*, p. 175). The poem is a good example of what Curi calls a 'cinematic technique' of 'rapidissime zumate' ('zoomings') in a 'playful narrative' built on a discontinuous syntax and written in a 'registro medio-basso' (Curi, *Opere e introduzione*, p. 15).

1-2:   **'Vasko'**: the Serbian poet Vasko Popa; **'Shirley Temple'**: the Hollywood child-star of the 1930s is brought to mind by the sight of the young woman who stops him in the street; **'Lijnbaan'**: street in Rotterdam.

3-4:   **'artigli'**: claws; the poet underlines (with **'come si dice'**) the banality of his sudden infatuation, one of many episodes of passing sexual desire on the part of the wandering cosmopolitan intellectual (which tend, usually, to ridicule the protagonist).

4-6:   The infatuation turns into a nightmarish, masochistic vision. **'Number One'**: presumably the name of the establishment where the **'literary supper'** takes place.

7-10:   The figure of the woman merges with the culturally layered image of a portrait by Holbein the Younger.

11-13:   The poet gives us, simultaneously, a picture of the life of the contemporary writer, immersed in an ongoing, frenetic series of more or less informal encounters and dialogues, surrounded by 'il "chiacchiericcio" intellettuale' (Cucchi and Giovanardi, *Poeti italiani*, p. 393), and, at the same time, a statement of the impotence of the poetic/creative *io* (**'che cosa posso scrivere...?'**); **'Tchicaya'**: Tchicaya U Tam'si, (Congolese poet); **'Breyten'**: Breyten Breytenbach (South African writer).

13-14:   **'*Affinità elettive*'**: novel by Goethe; **'pustole'**: pimples. The self-deprecation is brought down to the intimate level of personal relationships, a sense of intellectual impotence and, in grotesque/humorous contrast, the most banal corporeal phenomena.

From *Postkarten* (1978)

1.

tutto è incominciato con una stupida storia di soprabiti scambiati
al ristorante, da Rosetta: (e con quel tuo correre cieco, oltre gli uffici
dell'Alitalia, distratta, astratta):
                    eh, c'è poco da ridere, cara mia,
mi sembra, allora, lí al bar d'Amore, se perdiamo con tanta facilità
la nostra identità, i nostri vestiti, i segni caratteristici, i punti   5
di riferimento, l'orientamento, il buon senso:
                    (siamo smarriti un'altra volta
nel mondo, ognuno come può: e come merita): (e se ti scrivo dall'aeroporto
di Capodichino, in partenza per Amsterdam, con i voli AZ 424 e AZ 382,
è già per pura scaramanzia, alla fine: e non per altro, proprio, per niente):

Postkarten 1

There is a large degree of stylistic and thematic continuity in Sanguineti's work from
Reisebilder to *Postkarten*, and indeed on through to the collections of the early 1980s:
Stracciafoglio (1980), *Scartabello* (1981), and *Cataletto* (1982). These 'postcards',
often addressed, as here, to the poet's wife, record minimal events and circumstances
in a markedly prosaic manner. In this poem, the letter of the text, the story of a mix-
up involving overcoats (**'soprabiti scambiati'**), is almost entirely transparent. **l.2: 'da
Rosetta'**: presumably the name of the restaurant; **l.4: 'bar d'Amore'**: the name of a
bar, but used clearly for its ironic and banalizing effect; **l.8: 'Capodichino'**: Naples
airport; **l.9: 'scaramanzia'**: superstitious gesture.

Barilli speaks of an ironic adoption by Sanguineti of a quasi-Montalean type of
'occasione' in these years, but an 'occasione' stripped of any sublime intent or effect:
'la vita è per intero una sequenza di occasioni, un orrido impasto di scampoli, detriti,
frammenti...' (Barilli, p. 58). It is a procedure, as Barilli and others have noted, not
without parallels in Montale's own verse from *Satura* onwards, although the two
poets put the overturning of lyrical intensity to very different uses. Echoes and
parallels with Montale's *Xenia* are particularly evident in this poem, from the
mention of specific of bars and restaurants, to the 'correre *cieco*' on the part of the *tu*,
to the central motif of loss of identity (See Siti, p. 93 and Ó Ceallacháin, 'Sanguineti
and Montale', pp. 103-4).

From *Cataletto* (1981)

12.

a domanda rispondo:
                   lo ammetto, ho messo in carte, da qualche parte,
                         [con arte, questa mia
storia cosí: faccio il pagliaccio in piazza, sopra un palco: (io sono il cavadenti,
il mangia- e sputafuoco, l'equilibrista contorsionista,
                         [il domatore di tigri e pulci,
il ciarlatano con l'orvietano, l'incantatore di basilischi, il carto- e il chiro-
mante, il zingaro, la spalla di un tony nano, il marrano): (mi cinge e preme
                        [un'orda di   5
medicini stile Petrolini, à la manière de Molière, con le sperticatissime siringhe
(e scarpe lunghe con le lunghe stringhe), che mi atomizzano, a destra e a
                         [manca, in giro,
una nuvola densa di un deodorante disinfettante):
                         mi infilo in bocca una
                         [mia mano,
scendo nella mia gola piú profonda, con il mio braccio, e avanti, e sotto,
                         [sempre piú
dentro, giù, passe-passe di passe-partout, finché mi afferro infine,
                         [lì in fondo fino   10
al fondo, con il mio dito (che mi è l'indice mio),
                         [l'anello del mio elastico sfintere:
e tiro forte, è fatta, mi rovescio le viscere,
                         [e mi sembro la scuoiatura del coniglio,
forse: e grido, su dall'ano, ma piano:
                         venite qui, e vedete: è questo l'uomo nudo,
il vivo e il vero, se lo prendi nell'intimo dell'imo (servito al naturale):

Cataletto 12

Along with the thematic area surrounding the conjugal relationship, there are frequent instances during these years of self-portraits, including those which focus on the figure of the *io* specifically *as poet*, texts whose underlying concern is with the purpose and nature of poetry itself. This poem from *Cataletto* (meaning 'coffin', but perhaps with overtones of 'catalettico', cataleptic) presents the *io* in a *tour-de-force* of alliterative word-play, ironic self-deprecation and imagery of a visceral corporeality.

1-2:　　'**a domanda rispondo**': a bureaucratic formula used in police records etc. ('in response to questioning, I reply'); '**faccio il pagliaccio...**': the image of the poet as clown and public performer recalls the early work of Palazzeschi (with his clown-like display in 'Lasciatemi divertire' or his self-definition as 'saltimbanco dell'anima mia'), a reminder of Sanguineti's debt to the historic avantgarde.

2-5:　　A catalogue of street-performers and characters of dubious integrity: '**cavadenti**': tooth-puller (not a qualified dentist); '**mangia- e sputafuoco**': fire-eater and spitter; '**domatore...**': tiger- and flea-tamer; '**ciarlatano**': charlatan; '**orvietano**': spurious medical remedy; '**incantatore di basilischi**': basilisk charmer; '**il carto- e il chiro- / mante**': two types of fortune-teller, respectively readers of cards and palms; '**la spalla di un tony nano**': in a variety double-act, the 'spalla' is the straight man; '**nano**': dwarf; '**marrano**': traitor or scoundrel.

5-8:　　The protagonist is surrounded by a crowd of somewhat dubious doctors: '**medicini**': a diminutive of 'medici', suggesting 'mean little doctors'; '**stile Petrolini**': in the manner of Ettore Petrolini (1884-1936), hugely popular Roman variety performer, author of comic songs, etc.; '**à la manière de Molière**': in the manner of Molière; '**sperticatissime**': extremely long, a grotesquely comic detail, as are the '**scarpe lunghe**' with long '**stringhe**' (laces); '**mi atomizzano...**': they spray perfume and disinfect the patient with mock ceremony (in preparation for his 'performance'). The phonic texture of the piece grows particularly dense here in the proliferation of alliteration and assonance, increasingly typical of Sanguineti's later work.

8-13:　　The poet-*pagliaccio* puts his hand down his throat and pulls himself inside out; '**passe-passe**': sleight of hand; '**passe-partout**': master key; '**l'anello del mio elastico sfintere**': the ring of my elastic sphincter; '**mi rovescio...**': I turn my innards inside out; '**scuoiatura**': skinning; '**l'ano**': the anus.

13-14:　'**l'imo**': the lowest point; '**servito al naturale**': suggests a culinary context, i.e. served without condiments. The poem closes on a note of extreme self-disclosure with connotations of both honesty and self-abasement, the display of '**l'uomo nudo**' as having nothing to hide, but also stripped of any vestiges of human dignity or identity beyond the mere fact of bodily existence. (On this text, see Pietropaoli, pp. 131-4.)

From 'Alfabeto apocalittico' (in *Bisbidis*, 1987)

Z

> zinne & zanne di zanni in zanzariera,
> zìngare con zigàni in zuccheriera,
> zecche di zecca & zane di zerbini,
> zanfate di zolfare in zatterini,
> zebre alla zuava, a zimarre, a zucchetti,
> zighe zaghe di zuffe con zibetti:
> zuppo di zeta è il zozzo zibaldone,
> zampilla zuppa di zuzzurellone:

Z

The last of a sequence of octaves based on the alphabet, this piece is representative of an increasingly important strand in Sanguineti's work, that of the verbal or formal *divertissement* as the latest expression of the problematic attempt to wring meaning from the world. Here he ostensibly adopts the classic *ottava* form, made up of eight hendecasyllables. He deliberately transgresses, however, against the required rhyme scheme, using rhyming couplets instead, and subverts the expectations of rhythm and stress patterns within the hendecasyllabic metre. The text appears, on one level, as an exercise in formal elaboration emptied of semantic value, any kind of 'content' entirely undermined by the vacuous, arbitrary succession of terms linked only by what one might call 'z-ness'. But, on another level, because of the absence of a structured discourse, one is forced to have recourse to a kind of purely semantic reading, focusing on the atomized 'meaning' of each term in the sequence, but always with a heightened awareness of the visual and aural effects of the text. The search for these meanings may be carried out with minimal effort by any reader in the 'z' pages of a good dictionary! The penultimate line sums up the effect: 'saturated with z is the filthy mixture'.

ALFREDO GIULIANI

From *Povera Juliet e altre poesie* (1965)

Prosa

a Nanni Balestrini

Bisogna avvertirli Les essuie-mains ne doivent servir qu'à s'essuyer
les mains Non sputate sul pavimento Uscita, son tutti uguali, falsissimo,
se ne sentono tante, fenomeno facile da spiegare, lascia un'idea (nitrito)
di esaltata padronanza, ma sai che poi svanisce, è bene o male?, la flussione
particolarmente intensa delle regole elementari, la prescrizione è contenuta   5
nel prodotto (è un nitrito, potrebbe essere), se ne sta ai giardini a leggere
l'Ordine Pubblico o Il Cavallo. Inutile lamentarsi, avrà la pensione,
Les théories déductives sont des systèmes hypothètiques... Il pleut... Cette
proposition est vraie ou fausse suivant le temps qu'il fait. La figura siede
dolcemente astratta presso la fontana. E tu? me lo ripeto sempre.   10

Prosa

The visual impact of this text is, at least on first glance, similar to that of *Laborintus*: the long lines (although it should be said that these are not entirely typical of Giuliani's verse), the use of foreign phrases, including erudite and abstract terminology, the relative lack of conventional punctuation, all combine to place the text decisively within the avant-garde mode. However, the overall effect is quite different: instead of the sense of obsessively layered analysis of *Laborintus*, here there is more of an air of sceptical playfulness and absurd futility, as the text doggedly refuses to coalesce into coherent meaning. The poem is made up of seemingly random fragments of sense, phrases representing heterogeneous registers and semantic areas juxtaposed in a kind of arbitrary collage.

1:     **'Bisogna avvertirli'**: there is no indication of *who* should be 'warned', but the next line and a half consist of the kind of notices found in public places; **'Les essuye-mains…'**: 'hand-wipes should be used only to wipe the hands'.

2:     between **'Uscita'** and **'son tutti uguali'** there is an apparent hiatus, as the text jumps to a completely different area of reference, with the following phrases suggesting a kind of cynical nihilism (also in **'Inutile lamentarsi'** in l.7). There are similar moments of hiatus in almost every line in the text, which thus acquires a fundamental instability of sense; **'se ne sentono tante'**: you hear so many things said.

3:     **'nitrito'**: neighing (of a horse).

4:     **'padronanza'**: mastery; **'flussione'**: fluxion (mathematical term).

7:     **'avrà'**: grammatical subject is completely unclear.

8-9:   **'Cette propostion…'**: 'this proposition is true or false according to the weather' – referring to **'Il pleut'**, this is a most banal and yet precise observation; **'La figura'**: the referent is completely obscure.

10:    **'E tu?…sempre'**: unexpectedly, a first and second person dialogue is opened at the close of an almost entirely impersonal piece. The *io*, in so far as it is present at all, is denied any possibility of lyrical expansion. Giuliani's own note speaks of a 'personaggio' who abandons himself to his situation, where important and irrelevant issues, interior and exterior elements are amalgamated and inverted continually, in a moment full of 'uncertainty and failure' (*I Novissimi*, p. 50). For Curi, Giuliani's 'riduzione dell'io' tends in fact towards a radical 'estinzione dell'io lirico' (*La poesia italiana d'avanguardia*, p. 166).

NANNI BALESTRINI

From *Come si agisce* (1963)

Apologo dell'evaso

La massima della mia azione difforme,
infausto al popolo il fiume
che al cinema videro spopolare

il delta, i fertilissimi campi
e i più nocivi insetti (chiara   5
minaccia ai vizi dei governanti!).

Fra i pampini ovunque liberi
galleggiavano, gonfi – e si fa vano
l'ufficio dello storico. Ma saremo

a lungo preservati dal morso   10
del tafano azzurro, da iniezioni
di calciobromo, dall'unghie della zarina?

Lucenti strani corpi
violano il cielo; sbanda
il filo di formiche diagonale   15

nel cortile riemerso; ancora
il sole sorge dietro
la Punta Campanella incustodita

dai finanzieri corrotti e un argine
ultimo crolla. Lode   20
a un'estate di foco. S'io fossi

la piccola borghesia colata
nelle piazze fiorite e nei dì
di festa che salvi c'ignora

dalla droga e dalla noia per un po'   25
d'uva lavata in mare
presso la marcia catapulta; rifugiati

al primo tuono nelle gelaterie – chi fuggirei?
Passato il temporalaccio d'agosto
i graspi giungono a riva   30

fra i remi ai contrabbandieri salpati
nel novilunio e anzitutto conviene
(usciti dal vico cieco chiamammo

e orme erano ovunque
dell'abominevole uomo delle nevi)   35
fare l'amore intanto

che sui ponti la Via Lattea dilata.
Il Po nasce dal Monviso;
nuvole… ma di ciò, altra volta.

Apologo dell'evaso

'**Apologo dell'evaso**': Apologue (fable) of the escapee. Giuliani states that the true 'content' of this work lies in the process of its construction, bringing together fragments from different contexts, cut, mixed and pasted together in a 'proiezione di oggetti amorosi, considerazioni di poetica, preoccupazioni esistenziali e storiche', in the face of which the reader must not try to solve any 'enigma' but rather enter into the 'open order' of the contexts and 'far funzionare la macchina' (although he also notes the objective presence of certain 'themes', notably the 'cinematic' evocation of a flood and threatening images of water; *I Novissimi*, pp. 103-4). According to Curi, Balestrini's verse does not so much give us meaning as 'suggest a direction' (Curi, *La poesia italiana*, p. 375). This poem has an apparent structural regularity, being composed of a succession of *terzine* consisting of lines with three main accents, but not based on any regular syllabic metre.

1:      The opening line, with its suggestion of a first-person protagonist, is left suspended before the catalogue of disparate phenomena that follows.

2-9:   A vision of a flooded river, '**infausto**' (adverse or ominous) to the population, 'depopulating' the delta and the fields. The harmful ('**nocivi**') insects are, in an apparently random association, a threat to the governing classes; some objects (corpses?) float swollen ('**gonfi**') amidst vine leaves ('**pampini**'); '**l'ufficio dello storico**': the task of the historian (which is 'in vain').

10-12:   A series of apparently unrelated threats, from which we may perhaps be saved; '**tafano**': horsefly; '**l'unghie della zarina**': the nails of the Tsarina.

13-21:   Any attempt to create linear sense must fail here as images from the most diverse contexts pile up together: '**lucenti strani corpi**': strange luminous bodies (UFOs?); '**sbanda**': disbands; '**Punta Campanella**': promontory near Sorrento; '**finanzieri corrotti**': corrupt customs police; '**argine**': dyke; '**lode**': praise.

21-28:   '**S'io fossi**': the *io*, barely introduced in l.1, resurfaces here only to be almost submerged again in the ensuing evocation of the 'borghesia'. (The hypothesis is completed in l.28: 'If I were the bourgeoisie, ...who would I flee?'). The juxtaposition of images surrounding the bourgeoisie becomes extremely disjointed (it includes the Leopardian '**dì di festa**', drugs, grapes washed in the sea, a rotten catapult). In any case they seem threatened by an impending storm (l.28).

29-37:   The aftermath of the storm: '**graspi**': stems of grapes; '**contrabbandieri salpati...**': smugglers who have set sail under the new moon; **ll. 32-37**: '**conviene [...] fare l'amore ...**': the main proposition ('one should make love while the Milky Way spreads over the bridges') is interrupted by the rather surreal insertion of the 'abominable snowman' and his footprints.

38-39:   As if the poem is progressing backwards, from effect to cause, we see the river Po back at its source at the slopes of Monviso, and its ultimate source in the clouds, until the text breaks off, with the voice of the *io* really engaged in some other discourse, elsewhere.

ANTONIO PORTA

From *I rapporti*, 1966 (originally in *La palpebra rovesciata*, 1960)

Europa cavalca un toro nero [extracts]

1
Attento, abitante del pianeta,
guardati! dalle parole dei Grandi
frana di menzogne, lassù
balbettano, insegnano il vuoto.
La privata, unica, voce   5
metti in salvo: domani sottratta
ti sarà, come a molti, oramai,
e lamento risuona il giuoco dei bicchieri.

[...]

5
Il treno, il lago, gli annegati,
i fili arruffati. Il ponte nella notte:
di là quella donna. Il viola
nasce dall'unghia e il figlio
adolescente nell'ora prevista dice: 5
"Usa il tuo sesso, è il comando."
Dentro la ciminiera, gonfio di sonno
precipita il manovale, spezzata la catena.

[...]

7
Con le mani la sorella egli
spinge sotto il letto. Un piede
slogato dondola di fuori.
Dalla trama delle calze sale
l'azzurro dell'asfissiato. Guarda.   5
Strofina un fiammifero, incendia
i cappelli bagnati d'etere
luminoso. Le tende divampano

crepitando. Li scaglia nel fienile,
il cuscino e la bottiglia di benzina.   10
Gli occhi crepano come uova.
Afferra la doppietta e spara
nella casa della madre. Gli occhi
sono funghi presi a pedate.
Mani affumicate e testa   15
grattugiata corre alla polveriera,
inciampa, nel cielo lentamente
s'arrampica l'esplosione e i vetri
bruciano infranti d'un fuoco
giallo; abitanti immobili   20
il capo basso, contando le formiche.

[…]

8
Osserva della notte l'orizzonte,
inghiottita la finestra dal gorgo del cortile,
l'esplosione soffiò dal deserto
sui capelli, veloce spinta al terrore:
tutto male in cucina, il gas   5
si espande, l'acqua scroscia,
la lampada spalanca il vuoto.
Richiuse la porta dietro di sé,
e gli occhi punse il vento dell'incendio
corso sugli asfalti, macchiato d'olio: 10
Saltati i bottoni alla camicia estiva
la ferita si colora, legume
che una lama rapida incide.

Europa cavalca un toro nero

1. Attento, abitante del pianeta...

'Europa cavalca...': 'Europa rides a black bull', a reference to the Greek myth of Europa, the Phoenician princess carried off to Crete by Zeus, who had assumed the form of a white bull (the change in the bull's colour foreshadows the rather dark subject matter of much of the sequence). Giuliani calls this series of ten short poems an 'emblematica *suite* di episodi di cronaca', thus highlighting a significant streak of what might be called 'realism' in the texts (this is certainly true when compared to some of the work of other *Novissimi*, who are more focused on the centrality of language and form). Giuliani notes that part 1 is inspired by 'summit conferences and the prevarications of political power' (*I Novissimi*, p. 131). Years later, Porta would write of a 'passione civile e letteraria' underlying this poem, a desire to denounce 'il vuoto maligno del nuovo autoritarismo' (Porta, *Nel fare poesia*, pp. 9-10). In all the poems, however, the content is the starting point for a highly literary process of fragmentation, arbitrary juxtapositions and surreal description, leading to a heightened, defamiliarized vision of reality.

1-4:   The strong opening lines with their call to attention place the focus of the text on external reality rather than any lyrical introspection. '**guardati!**': (imperative) beware!; '**frana di menzogne**': landslide of lies (i.e. the words of 'i Grandi'); '**balbettano**': they stammer.

5-8:   The admonition to protect ('**mettere in salvo**') the private voice has a quasi-apocalyptic overtone in its vision of a future where this will be taken away and replaced with lamentation, but the advice is also steeped in irony, as Porta himself refuses to deploy any 'unique, private' voice in his verse.

5. Il treno, il lago, gli annegati...

Giuliani notes that this (and poem no.4) 'evocano incidenti tipici della nostra organizzazione; tra l'incidente ferroviario e l'infortunio sul lavoro, s'incastra un'immagine di prostituzione'. In what seems initially a depiction of a train crash by a lake, there is a disconcerting combination of directly presented reality and bizarre discontinuity in the juxtaposition of images. '**fili arruffati**': tangled wires; '**usa il tuo sesso**': an apparent incitement to prostitution; '**ciminiera**': chimney stack; '**precipita il manovale**': the worker falls.

7. Con le mani la sorella egli...

1-3:   '**egli**': 'Il protagonista della strofa 7 è un pazzo che fa saltare un paese dopo aver ucciso la sorella' (Giuliani). '**slogato**': dislocated (the first shocking indication that the sister is actually a corpse); '**dondola**': dangles.

4-8:   '**trama**': weave; the overall image suggests strangulation with a pair of stockings. In the description of violence and horror in these and the following lines, there is a bizarre co-existence of direct simplicity and grotesque expressionism; '**strofina**': rubs, i.e. strikes a match (apparently to set fire to the corpse).

8-10:   'divampano / crepitando': blaze up crackling; 'Li scaglia nel fienile': he throws them [the pillow and bottle of petrol of l.10] into the hayloft.

11-14: 'gli occhi crepano...': 'the eyes crack open like eggs'. Along with l.14 (where the eyes are 'mushrooms given a kicking'), the poem reaches a climax of grotesque corporeal horror here; 'doppietta': double-barrelled shotgun.

15-19: The episode culminates in a violent explosion. 'grattugiata': 'grated' [i.e. the head]; 'polveriera': munitions store; 's'arrampica': climbs up (subject is 'l'esplosione'); 'infranti': shattered.

20-21: An image of the inhabitants of the place, in a kind of shocked paralysis, able only to scrutinize minute details of ants on the ground.

8.   Osserva della notte l'orizzonte...

Another anonymous 3rd person protagonist, this time a person caught up in a nuclear explosion (as noted by Giuliani). Throughout the poem the apocalyptic destruction is recounted through minimal incidental details and matter-of-fact description.

1-4:   'inghiottita...': the window is 'swallowed' by the 'gorgo' (vortex) outside; 'dal deserto sui capelli': the spectrum of destruction goes from the vast landscape down to intimate physical details; 'spinta': push (noun).

5-7:   'tutto male in cucina': a most incongruously understated, domesticated summary of the catastrophic effects of the explosion; 'spalanca': opens up wide.

8-10:   The futile individual gesture of closing the door is followed by the fiery blast: 'the wind of the fire that ran over the asphalt, stained with oil, stung his eyes'.

11-13:   Further incongruous detail, as the buttons pop off his summer shirt. 'la ferita': the destruction of the body is given in an almost surreal image centred on colour, shape and texture, with a wound compared to a 'legume' (a pulse, i.e. pea or bean, etc) sliced open by a knife.

9

Andrea Zanzotto (1921–)

Zanzotto is widely regarded as one of the major poetic voices of twentieth-century Italy, with his place in the modern canon reflected for example in the publication during his lifetime (a relatively rare honour), of an edition of his work in Mondadori's 'Meridiani' series (*Le poesie e prose scelte*, 1999). However, his is also a highly individual and often isolated voice. In his early work of the 1950s, his style seems in some ways doggedly anachronistic, displaying the influence of the hermetic tradition at a time when the pursuit of any sort of 'pure' lyricism was politically and culturally suspect. In other respects however (especially in his poetry of the 1960s and beyond), Zanzotto can be seen to be keenly in tune with contemporary literary trends. Throughout, his work reflects his immense culture and erudition, ranging over the literary traditions of Italian and many other European cultures, while also echoing contemporary developments in linguistics, psychology, and philosophy.

The landscape, history and inhabitants of his birthplace of Pieve di Soligo, a small town amidst the hills near Treviso in the Veneto region, figure repeatedly in different guises throughout his work. Indeed he has resided for most of his life in the area. From a young age, his family life was marked by suffering and tragedy: the death of his two sisters (one in 1929 and the other in 1937) was deeply traumatic, and the sense of precariousness was accentuated by the frequent absence of his father, unable to work in his home town due to his intransigent anti-Fascism.[i] Zanzotto also suffered from asthma and related ailments from his youth, and psychological problems have repeatedly led him to undertake a variety of therapies. Having graduated in *Lettere* at Padua in 1942, he was conscripted into the army, until, following the armistice between Italy and the Allies in 1943, like many young men, he became involved with the Resistance against Fascism and took to the hills for a time in 1944-45. Apart from a period spent working in Switzerland in 1946-

47, he would spend most of his working life as a school teacher in and around his home town, until his early retirement in 1975. By this time he was a prominent cultural figure, and a regular contributor to literary journals and the national press.

Zanzotto's verse first came to prominence when he won the San Babila poetry prize for his unpublished work in 1950 (awarded by an impressive jury including Ungaretti, Montale, Quasimodo, Sereni and Sinisgalli) which led to the publication of his first collection, *Dietro il paesaggio*, in 1951. His early work is, in Agosti's words, 'intensamente e addirittura dichiaratamente letteraria'.[ii] It is an apparently ahistorical exploration of the landscape and of what lies 'behind' it, an 'imaginative rearrangement' of reality owing much to the modern traditions of symbolism, *ermetismo* and surrealism and to the work of Ungaretti.[iii] At a time when questions of ideological commitment and possible forms of realism were at the centre of much literary and cultural debate in Italy, Zanzotto's early work swims against the tide, with its extreme (though by no means naive or unproblematic) commitment to poetry itself as a locus of authenticity.

With the next two collections, *Elegia e altri versi* (1954) and *Vocativo* (1957), we are still in the first phase of Zanzotto's work. Nevertheless, in *Vocativo*, there is a heightened level of 'alienazione linguistica', and a new 'tensione al colloquio' (as reflected in the title), but it is a problematic dialogue, where both *io* and *tu* are are potentially absent or unidentifiable. Still, in Zanzotto's own words, 'la tentazione della poesia continua', and the thematic area of the landscape, albeit a less comforting presence than in the first book, indicates a substantial thread of continuity.[iv]

IX Ecloghe (published in 1962 and containing poems written between 1957 and 1960) marks a 'decisive turning point' according to Mengaldo, the beginning of a new phase, that of Zanzotto's full artistic maturity, in which he attacks 'l'assolutezza del linguaggio illustre e la certezza dell'io come depositario dell'autentico'.[v] Thematically and lexically, there is an opening up to a variety of fields, including science and technology, and, centrally, metalinguistic concerns. Meanwhile, in all areas, the poet's irony creates an ambivalent distance between the *io* and the multiple banalities of contemporary reality. Indeed, for Raboni one of the defining characteristics of Zanzotto's work is the strange combination of 'grande stile' (high style, with a 'tragic' voice and outlook) and 'ironia' (one of whose functions, of course, is to undermine the former element).[vi]

The 1968 collection *La Beltà* marks the culmination of Zanzotto's idiosyncratic experimentalism (or, as Agosti has it, 'il punto più basso', meaning that of his most in-depth penetration of language, a level of 'verbal

experience' that goes on to form the basis of all of his subsequent work).[vii]
The collection is written against the background of the 'trasformazione
antropologica, conoscitiva, percettiva' of 1960s Italy, the years of the
economic boom, the rise of the mass media and the consumerization of
culture. Language itself is infected with this 'inauthenticity' and Zanzotto
confronts the phenomenon head-on, through the very medium that is so
debased.[viii] There is now an irremediable break between language and the
world, signifier and signified, and such meaning as can be construed emerges
from 'segni irrelati … balbettii e silenzi'. *La Beltà* also includes instances of a
descent into pre-rational language, including the 'petèl' (a dialect term for
baby-talk) found in a number of texts, which can be seen as an attempt to
access the deep origins of language, part of a broader concern with the
exploration of the unconscious (related to the author's readings of Freud,
Lacan and others), whereby reason and *logos* are interwoven with 'le voci del
sonno (con le voci del sogno)'.[ix]

It is easy to discern parallels between Zanzotto's poetic experimentalism
and that undertaken by the Novissimi and others in these years (see Chapter
on Sanguineti and *neoavanguardia*). At the very least they share a
preoccupation with language, with linguistic form, which is foregrounded
often at the expense of any unequivocal meaning. In both cases, we find
phenomena of fragmentation and discontinuity, whether on the level of the
individual word, of syntax, of poetic metre or on the broader structural levels
of the poem or the collection as a whole. There is at times, to put it simply, a
similar degree of difficulty for the reader in approaching some of their
respective texts. But there is a broad critical consensus that crucial differences
exist between Zanzotto's work of the 1960s and that of the *neoavanguardia*.
Agosti emphasises the ideologically-driven nature of the neo-avantgarde
project, which sees conventional language and meaning as inseparable from
political power structures. And in contrast to the 'asemantic' avant-garde
texts, he sees in Zanzotto a 'strenuous construction' of sense, accessing deep,
hidden origins.[x] For Mengaldo, Zanzotto's 'libera attività del significante' is
quite distinct from the external 'aggression' towards language perpetrated
'programmatically' by the *neoavanguardia*.[xi] However, it is clear that these
different poetic experiences arise from the same background of a deep cultural
and sociological crisis. According to Cucchi and Giovanardi, Zanzotto's
accessing of his 'magma primordiale', could only have taken place outside of
the overly ideologized confines of the avantgarde, but is born of the same
'disagio culturale' given such violent expression by the latter.[xii] Indeed,
Mengaldo also notes that the 'freedom' of Zanzotto's language 'presupposes'
the 'aggression' carried out by the Novissimi. At the very least, bearing in

mind that *La Beltà* was written largely in the mid-1960s when the Novissimi had already come to prominence (and indeed that *IX Ecloghe* post-dates Sanguineti's *Laborintus*) it seems likely that Zanzotto was to some degree influenced by the formal radicalism of the *neoavanguardia*.[xiii] But the latter came to represent a kind of organized cultural iconoclasm, focused on language as just one of the institutions of an iniquitous political power structure, with an ideological dogmatism that is quite alien to Zanzotto's troubled ontological excavations in the deep strata of linguistic expression.

After *La Beltà*, Zanzotto's poetry continues to explore new thematic, structural and linguistic avenues. However, the stylistic novelty marked by the 1960s collection is not matched by any subsequent radical shift in expressive paradigms. The second major centre of gravity of his work is what he calls his 'pseudo-trilogy' of *Il Galateo in bosco* (1978), *Fosfeni* (1983) and *Idioma* (1986). Of these, *Il Galateo in bosco* is probably the best-known work, with its re-reading of the poet's landscape through the lens of the violence of the First World War. The collection also includes a rich diversity of styles and poetic forms, including accomplished pastiche and parody of texts from the Italian tradition, notably in the 'Ipersonetto'. As John Welle writes, 'Zanzotto's singular idiom magnifies the problematic nature of the Italian language while contributing to the rich literary experience that has grown out of it'.[xiv] The second and third parts of the trilogy involve, respectively, a rather more abstract contemplation of the mountain landscape of the Dolomites and an exploration of the human and linguistic world of the poet's home town itself. (There is a notable presence here of texts in dialect, also a feature of the 1976 collection *Filò*. However, dialect poetry falls outside the necessarily limited scope of the present anthology.) The entire trilogy is characterized by what Lorenzini calls 'una coscienza ossimorica', founded on polarities between 'compostezza e magma, forma ed entropia, sublime e basso-livellato'.[xv] Zanzotto has continued to write and publish through the 1990s and beyond, and throughout his work we find the awareness of 'un tessuto disgregato della civiltà'.[xvi] His work continually pushes at the boundaries of what may be called lyric poetry in a contemporary world transformed by technology and mass communication, testing 'il limite ultimo della parola lirica'.[xvii]

Endnotes

i   See 'Cronologia' in *Le poesie e prose scelte*, a cura di Stefano Dal Bianco e Gian Mario
        Villalta, I Meridiani (Milan: Mondadori, 1999), pp. xcvii-cxxxii.

ii   Stefano Agosti, Introduction in Zanzotto, *Poesie (1938-1986)*, a cura di Stefano Agosti

(Milan: Mondadori, 1993), p. 8.

iii   Vivienne Hand, *Zanzotto* (Edinburgh: Edinburgh University Press, 1994), pp. 2-3.

iv   See Dal Bianco's note in *Le poesie e prose scelte*, pp. 1435-6.

v   Mengaldo, *Poeti italiani del Novecento*, p. 872.

vi   Giovanni Raboni, 'Poeti del secondo Novecento', in *Storia della letteratura italiana*, vol. IX, 2nd edn (Milano: Garzanti, 1987), pp. 209-48 (p. 227).

vii   Agosti, Introduction to *Poesie*, p. 7.

viii   Lorenzini, *La poesia italiana del Novecento*, p. 151; see also *Le poesie e prose scelte*, p. 1483.

ix   Agosti, Introduction to *Poesie*, pp. 19 and 27-8; see also *Le poesie e prose scelte*, pp. 1483-4.

x   Agosti, Introduction to *Poesie*, p. 21. See also Romano Luperini, *Il Novecento* (Torino: Loescher, 1981), p. 779. Hand takes issue with the critical consensus, insisting that Zanzotto's subversion of language *is* both programmatic and bent on the destruction of meaning (although she also draws distinctions, notably in the area of ideological intent). See V. Hand, *Zanzotto*, pp. 130-5.

xi   Mengaldo, *Poeti italiani del Novecento*, p. 874.

xii   Cucchi and Giovanardi, *Poeti italiani del secondo Novecento 1945-1995*, p. xxxv.

xiii   In the course of a highly polemical discussion of Zanzotto's work, Fausto Curi suggests a strong influence of Sanguineti in the 'plurilinguismo' and the problematization of language found from *IX Ecloghe* onwards. But Curi is concerned above all to distinguish Zanzotto from the *neoavanguardia* (with whom the critic is closely aligned), as his essay turns into a savage *stroncatura* of Zanzotto's work (asking, for example, whether the poet's 'maliziosamente ingenui giochi infantili' have ever really caused his readers to 'lose any sleep', and suggesting that Zanzotto's work has been manipulated ideologically by critics seeking a counter-balance against the work of the *neoavanguardia*). Curi, *La poesia italiana nel Novecento*, pp. 335-53 (at pp. 339, 347, 352-3).

xiv   John P. Welle, *The Poetry of Andrea Zanzotto. A Critical Study of 'Il Galateo in Bosco'* (Roma: Bulzoni, 1987), p. 13.

xv   Lorenzini, *Il presente della poesia*, p. 203.

xvi   Luigi Tassoni, *Caosmos. La poesia di Andrea Zanzotto* (Roma: Carocci, 2002), p. 14.

xvii   Lorenzini, *La poesia italiana del Novecento*, p. 154.

Poetic texts

Le poesie e prose scelte, a cura di Stefano Dal Bianco e Gian Mario Villalta, I Meridiani (Milan: Mondadori, 1999).
This contains the individual collections:
Dietro il paesaggio (1951); *Elegia e altri versi* (1954); *Vocativo* (1957); *IX Ecloghe* (1962); *Gli sguardi i fatti e senhal* (1969); *Pasque* (1973); *Filò* (1976); *Il Galateo in bosco* (1978); *Mistieròi* (1979); *Fosfeni* (1983); *Idioma* (1986); *Meteo* (1996).
There is also a subsequent volume, *Sovrimpressioni* (Milan: Mondadori, 2001)

Critical works by Zanzotto

Aure e disincanti nel Novecento letterario (Milan: Mondadori, 1994)
Scritti sulla letteratura, a cura di Gian Mario Villalta (Milan: Mondadori, 2001)

Further Reading

Note: The apparatus of notes and other materials in the collected edition, *Le poesie e prose scelte*, constitutes a fundamental starting point for exploring Zanzotto's poetry.

Allen, Beverly, *The language of Beauty's Apprentice* (Berkley: University of California Press: 1988)
Agosti, Stefano, Introduction in Zanzotto, *Poesie (1938-1986)*, a cura di Stefano Agosti (Milan: Mondadori, 1993).
Conti-Bertini, Lucia, *Andrea Zanzotto o la sacra menzogna* (Venezia: Marsilio, 1984)
Hand, Vivienne, *Zanzotto* (Edinburgh: Edinburgh University Press, 1994)
Motta, Uberto *Ritrovamenti di senso nella poesia di Zanzotto* (Milan: Vita e pensiero, 1996)
Nuvoli, Giuliana, *Andrea Zanzotto* (Firenze: La Nuova Italia, 1979)
Raboni, Giovanni, 'Poeti del secondo Novecento', in *Storia della letteratura italiana*, vol. IX, 2nd edn (Milano: Garzanti, 1987), pp. 209-48
Tassoni, Luigi, *Caosmos. La poesia di Andrea Zanzotto* (Roma: Carocci, 2002)
Welle, John P., *The Poetry of Andrea Zanzotto. A Critical Study of 'Il Galateo in Bosco'* (Roma: Bulzoni, 1987)

Contents

From *Dietro il paesaggio* (1951)

Ormai

Ormai la primula e il calore
ai piedi e il verde acume del mondo

I tappeti scoperti
le logge vibrate dal vento ed il sole
tranquillo baco di spinosi boschi;   5
il mio male lontano, la sete distinta
come un'altra vita nel petto

Qui non resta che cingersi intorno il paesaggio
qui volgere le spalle.

Ormai

This poem is unusually short in the context of Zanzotto's first collection, but is characteristic of its thematic concerns and stylistic features. It evokes the landscape in spring through a series of refined, rather literary images that initially suggest a quasi-idyllic atmosphere. However this becomes less clear in the closing lines where the *io* can be seen to turn to the landscape almost as a last resort (**'Qui non resta che...'**) in the face of an unspecified negativity (**'male'**, **'sete'**) which, though 'distant' is none the less real. The title, **'Ormai'** ('by now') links the text firmly into the sense of an ongoing, dynamic relationship with the landscape (there is a clear seasonal progression within the collection).

1-2: **'primula'**: primrose; **'il calore / ai piedi'**: may suggest the nurturing warmth of spring emerging from the soil itself, indicating a corporeal intimacy between the lyrical persona and nature (but Dal Bianco states that this is a reference to chilblains acquired by Zanzotto during the war years, a 'realistic' element, along with the 'tappeti' and 'logge' in the following lines; *Le poesie e le prose*, p. 1404); **'acume'**: intensity or extremity.

3-5: **'logge'**: loggias (balconies); **'ed il sole...boschi'**: These lines reflect Zanzotto's proximity at this early stage to the stylistic paradigms of a now somewhat outmoded *ermetismo*, both in their semantic and conceptual tensions and in the elliptical form of the analogy (omitting any verb of being or resemblance). The **'baco'** here is the silkworm (once widely kept in this area of the Veneto), as if the sun creates the woods out of silk.

6-7: Negativity is within him, but here felt as separate and distant.

8-9: The stance of the *io* is one of a decisive (and unavoidable) immersion in and identification with the landscape (**'cingersi'**: to wrap around oneself), turning his back on something unspecified (possibly contemporary, historical reality; see Curi, *La poesia italiana*, p. 338).

From *Vocativo* (1957)

Caso vocativo

I

O miei mozzi trastulli
pensieri in cui mi credo e vedo,
ingordo vocativo
decerebrato anelito.
Come lordo e infecondo   5
avvolge un cielo
armonie di recise ariste, vene
dubitanti di rivi,
e qui deruba
già le lampade ai deschi   10
sostituisce il bene.
Come i cavi s'ingranano a crinali
i crinali a tranelli a gru ad antenne
e ottuso mostro
in un prima eterno capovolto   15
il futuro diviene.
Il suono il movimento
l'amore s'ammollisce in bava
in fisima, gettata
torcia il sole mi sfugge.   20
Io parlo in questa
lingua che passerà.

Caso vocativo I

The title of Zanzotto's third collection reflects a desire to open a channel of communication with some 'tu', whether nature or poetry itself, but it also emphasises the limitations of this communicative urge, which struggles to go beyond an abstract grammatical level and which, while calling out, does not necessarily provoke any response or true dialogue. This is particularly pointed in this poem, given the title and the closing emphasis on language itself. The poem belongs to the ironically titled first section 'Come una bucolica'. As in the earlier work, a sophisticated and literary level of style is present here in terms of syntax, vocabulary and metre (a mixture of classic metres such as *settenari, quinari, endecasillabi*), which still owe much to the hermetic/symbolist/ Petrarchan traditions, although these are challenged by other heterogeneous elements.

1-4:   In keeping with the title, the poem opens with a direct address to the poet's **'trastulli'** (playthings or delights: nature? poetry? – in any case immediately identified as interior phenomena, **'pensieri'**), which are, somehow, truncated (**'mozzi'**), cut short, mutilated. No sooner is the address pronounced than it is characterized negatively in ll.3-4 (**'ingordo'**: greedy), with a certain tension created by the mix of semantic fields and registers in each pair of terms, particularly between **'decerebrato'** (decerebrated, a medical/scientific term), and the very literary **'anelito'** (yearning).

5-11:   The poet's gaze turns to nature, but this offers no promise of refuge or idyll. Instead it too is characterized by contradictory notes: the ears of wheat (**'ariste'**) are cut, but form 'harmonies' (in an image redolent of hermetic imagery and syntax), streams (**'rivi'**) are 'doubtful', and meanwhile all is enveloped by a filthy (**'lordo'**), sterile sky (an echo of Baudelaire: see *Le poesie e le prose*, p. 1442), which collides with human culture (**'deschi'**: tables) and replaces 'goodness' (with what, is less certain).

12-16: What is certain is that here the relationship with the natural landscape, although still at the centre of Zanzotto's verse, has been deeply problematized as nature encounters contemporary human technological or scientific endeavour, even as **'crinali'** (ridges) intermesh (**'s'ingranano'**) with cables, cranes, aerials. These lead on to a future seen in highly dubious terms as an 'obtuse monster', an eternal replay of the past, but inverted (**'capovolto'**).

17-20: The negative notes now dominate entirely as the landscape is interiorized again: the unreachable sun is a 'discarded torch' and the most elevated emotion or abstraction of **'amore'** is doubly degraded, first 'softening' to a 'dribble' or 'slaver' (although **'bava'** can also mean the 'floss' created by silkworms) and then to a (rather banal and colloquial) **'fisima'** (whim).

21-22: The issue of language, implicit in the title and in the opening lines, is baldly foregrounded here, as the poet highlights the transience, and by extension, the arbitrary and problematic nature of the linguistic system with which he must try to 'address' these multi-faceted realities. The attempted dialogue is apparently a monologue (and yet one may also read in this a kind of dogged determination to maintain the poetic discourse).

Idea

E tutte le cose a me intorno
colgo precorse nell'esistere.
Tiepido verde il nitore dei giorni
occulta, molle li irrora,
d'insetti e uccelli s'agita e scintilla.   5
Tutto è pieno e sconvolto,
tutto, oscuro, trionfa e si prostra.
Anche per te, mio linguaggio, favilla
e traversia, per sconsolato sonno
per errori e deliqui   10
per pigrizie profonde inaccessibili,
che ti formasti corrotto e assoluto.
Anche tu mio brevissimo nitore
di cellule mentali, tronco alone
di gridi e di pensieri   15
imprevisti ed eterni.
Ed esanime il palpito dei frutti
e delle selve e della seta e dei
rivelati capelli di Diana,
del suo felice dolcissimo sesso,   20
e, agra e vivida, l'arsura
che all'unghie s'intromette ed alle biade
pronte a ferire,
e il mai tacente il mai convinto cuore,
tutto è ricco e perduto   25
morto e insorgente
tuttavia nella luce
nella mia vana chiarità d'idea.

Idea

This text (from the second section of *Vocativo*, 'Prima persona') considers some of the complex interactions between the exterior world of nature and the inner world of the poet's persona. The world of the 'idea' and of abstractions faces a difficult relationship with the richly varied and yet troubling phenomena of external reality; however the two are closely intertwined, not least through the medium of language. The language and imagery here still owe much to hermetic influences, including a certain difficulty or obscurity of sense, although some of this difficulty also arises out of the proliferation of oxymoronic contradictions. Metrically, the poem is dominated by *endecasillabi* and *settenari*.

1-2: The phenomena of reality are pre-empted by the poet's perception (**'colgo'**) which prefigures their existence even as it captures them; **'precorse'**: past participle of *precorrere* (to prefigure).

3-5: Description of nature: the 'greenery' [subject of the following 3rd person verbs] conceals (**'occulta'**) the clarity (**'nitore'**) of the days, irrigates them (**'irrora'**) with life, and 'sparkles' (**'scintilla'**) in agitation.

6-7: One of the central tenets of the poem: all of life is suffused with irreconcilable contradictions, at once obscure, triumphant and prostrate.

8-16: The tensions found in nature apply also to the poet's language, the addressee of these lines: it too is both a positive **'favilla'** (spark, recalling the sparkle of nature in l.5) and 'misfortune' (**'traversia'**). The recurring **'per'** in ll.9-11 should be read as 'due to' (**'deliquio'**: loss of consciousness). The pairing of **'corrotto e assoluto'** in l.12 sums up the problem of language: it is 'corrupt', unable to give an authentic representation of reality, and yet it is the ultimate tool of representation, absolute and unavoidable. The recurrence of **'nitore'** in describing language in l.13 creates a further parallel with the external world of nature.

17-24: Nature is represented again in oxymoronic terms, as the catalogue of its 'palpitating' elements is apparently lifeless (**'esamine'**), its 'burning' (**'arsura'**) is both 'bitter and vivid'. The evocation of the moon-goddess Diana leads into a depiction of the landscape as a locus of sexuality and fertility (but this is negated a priori by 'esanime' in l.17). Nature's burning pervades all, from fingernails to **'biade'** (grain crops; which are inexplicably threatening). The catalogue ends with the inclusion of the heart in l.24, an image of the inner world apparently assimilated in the landscape, but like it characterized by ambiguities.

25-28: All of the foregoing phenomena, whether of the mind or of the exterior world are brought together in perhaps the strongest oxymoron yet, where all is **'morto e insorgente'** (rising up). But the final lines make it clear that all of this takes place in the 'light' of the inner, mental world of ideas. The reconciliation/assimilation of contradictions and tensions belongs to the sphere of mental 'clarity', but this, in turn, is trapped in its own oxymoronic tension: **'vana chiarità'**.

From *IX Ecloghe* (1962)

13 settembre 1959 (variante)

Luna puella pallidula,
Luna flora eremitica,
Luna unica selenita,
distonia vita traviata,
atonia vita evitata,   5
mataia, matta morula,
vampirisma, paralisi,
glabro latte, polarizzato zucchero,
peste innocente, patrona inclemente,
protovergine, alfa privativo,   10
degravitante sughero,
pomo e potenza della polvere,
phiala e coscienza delle tenebre,
geyser, fase, cariocinesi,
Luna neve nevissima novissima,   15
Luna glacies-glaciei
Luna medulla cordis mei,
Vertigine
per secanti e tangenti fugitiva

La mole della mia fatica   20
già da me sgombri
la mia sostanza sgombri
a me cresci a me vieni a te vengo
. . . .
. . . .
(Luna puella pallidula)
. . . .

13 settembre 1959 (variante)

In this volume Zanzotto's work begins to take on some of the recognizable features that will characterize his major collections in the following decades: the literary tradition, while still very much in evidence, is subject increasingly to fierce irony (as for example in the use of the term 'eclogue' in this book), and the focus shifts notably towards exploring language itself, with an emphasis on the play of the signifier as a key factor in generating the poetic text (see Agosti, Introduction to *Poesie*, p. 18). The dialogue between self and nature tends now to give way to a more multi-faceted discourse which includes ever more diverse aspects of contemporary reality (including scientific and technological developments) and which challenges any assumption of a privileged status for the *io*. The historical occasion for this poem is the successful landing of the first (unmanned) Soviet lunar probe, leading Zanzotto to address an ironic litany, a mock prayer, to the once-untouched, now violated moon, age-old embodiment of mystery, poetry and beauty. Among others, Leopardi must surely lurk in the background of this poem.

1-3:   **'puella pallidula'** (Latin): pale young girl (a literary allusion to the Emperor Hadrian's 'Animula vagula blandula'). Already from l.1, the element of word-play is foregrounded in the striking alliteration and assonance (and the *sdrucciolo* rhythm established here is one of the unifying formal features of the whole text); **'flora eremitica'**: hermitic (i.e. solitary, contemplative) flower (or the Roman goddess Flora). l.3: A sarcastic nod to the emptiness of the real moon, so unlike its literary/mythological image (**'selenita'**: moon dweller; the moon itself is its only inhabitant).

4-14:   Having established the litany form in the repetitive structure of ll.1-3, there follows a long catalogue of the moon's attributes and associations, where repeatedly signifier and sound take precedence over logical sense. There are parallel pairs, such as **'distonia'**/ **'atonia'**, both meaning a loss or lack of muscle tone or strength, but leading in to an apparent lack of distinction between **'traviata'** (led astray) and **'evitata'**; there are alliterative sequences, such as that of l.6 where the transliterated Greek term, the colloquial **'matta'** and the medical/scientific **'morula'** (an early embryonic phase) are brought together primarily on phonic grounds; there are couplings of opposing terms, as in l.9, where the striking oxymoron suggests a quasi-mystical disregard for reason (**'peste'**: plague; **'patrona'**: patron saint); **'glabro'**: hairless. The pseudo-religious note is underlined by allusions to the cult of the madonna (**'protovergine'**, and later, in the distorted form of a cosmic 'Vertigine'), and, in l.10, by 'alfa', leading one almost to expect 'alpha and omega', an expectation thwarted with **'alfa privativo'** (the Greek prefix 'a-' used to negate meaning). Throughout these lines the tone and linguistic register shift from the medical to the technical/scientific to the magical or mystical, all subsumed in an overarching play on sound and sense: **'degravitante sughero'**: 'degravitating cork'; **'pomo'**: fruit; **'phiala'**: phial; **'cariocinesi'**: form of cellular reproduction.

15-19:   Mock solemnity is underlined by the return of the anaphoric structure and the accumulation of Latin terms: **'glacies-glaciei'**: 'ice, of ice'; **'medulla cordis mei'**: 'marrow of my heart'. In l. 19 the Latin element recurs in the mathematical terms 'secant' and 'tangent' (characterizing the 'vertiginous' movement of the moon) and in **'fugitiva'** (Latin plural, as opposed to the Italian 'fuggitivi').

20-25: The poem closes with a further mock prayer, a grateful recognition of the moon's removal (**'sgombri'**) of the burden of the poet's own 'substance' (**'mole'**), as if a (highly improbable) form of salvation or transcendence could be achieved by this event of, as it were, touching the moon, leading to the wholly ironic rapture of l.24, with the blending of *io* and *tu* (until the poem ends in aphasia, in a silence which can be broken only by a repetition of the ritual words, underlining the fruitlessness of this technological breakthrough).

From *La Beltà* (1968)

Oltranza oltraggio

Salti saltabecchi friggendo puro-pura
nel vuoto   spinto   outré
ti fai più in là
intangibile – tutto sommato –
tutto sommato   5
tutto
sei più in là
ti vedo nel fondo della mia serachiusascura
ti identifico tra i non i sic i sigh
ti disidentifico   10
solo no solo sì solo
piena di punte immite frigida
ti fai più in là
e sprofondi e strafai in te sempre più in te
fotti il campo   15
decedi verso
nel tuo sprofondi
brilli feroce inconsutile nonnulla
l'esplodente l'eclatante e non si sente
nulla non si sente   20
no   sei saltata più in là
ricca saltabeccante   là

L'oltraggio

Oltranza oltraggio

In *La Beltà*, as Zanzotto's work moves into its fully mature phase, we find the 'assolutizzazione del significante' (Cucchi and Giovanardi, p. 302): it is the interplay of forms and sounds of the signifier that itself comes to constitute meaning, rather than pointing towards extraneous rationalizations. This, the first poem in the collection, sets the scene for a work full of formal experimentation and inventive verbal exuberance (executed frequently with a good degree of humour and linguistic irony). **'Oltranza'**: excess; **'oltraggio'**: outrage; the title (bipartite in form, like many of Zanzotto's) sets out the key thematic concern of seeking to go 'beyond' (beyond the limitations of language, or of normal perception and experience?), in pursuit of some unnamed feminine *tu* (probably best identified as the eponymous 'beltà', and/or poetry itself or inspiration).

1-3:   The opening lines establish the nervous energy and unexpected lexical leaps that characterize the text; **'saltabecchi'**: you move jerkily, by jumps. There is a sense of grammatical precariousness in the non-commital **'puro-pura'** and of formal openness in the empty spaces of l.2, reflecting the specific sense of **'vuoto'**, **'spinto'** and of 'jumping beyond' ('outré', borrowed from French, means 'excessive' or 'outraged', and is related of course to the Italian *oltre* and its compounds which are so visible in this poem). All of this converges on the simple statement of l.3 (but nonetheless enigmatic in the absence of a clearly identified *tu*), which subsequently emerges (with slight variations) as the obsessive key-phrase of the text.

4-8:   Again, repetitive variation is the dominant stylistic 'tic'; **'serachiusascura'** (sera chiusa scura): typographically creates the opposite effect to that of the extra spaces used elsewhere, here giving a sense of the *io* enclosed in a dark restricted habitat.

9-11:   The logical tenor of the text is challenged by a series of direct contradictions, even as the linguistic texture becomes more unconventional and inventive, juxtaposing the Latin **'sic'** with the English **'sigh'** (used in Italian in the language of comic strips and pronounced 'sig'), and introducing the neologism **'disidentifico'** ('disidentify').

12:      The *tu* acquires distinctly hostile overtones (**'immite'**: cruel; with a note of sexual hostility in **'frigida'**).

13-19:   The poet's elusive interlocutor is associated with increasingly heterogeneous attributes. While still 'going beyond' (**'strafai'**: you overdo it), she is apparently also ever more self-absorbed (**'più in te'**, with a direct structural parallel to l.13), but this is followed by another 'departure' in the energetically-coined gallicism of **'fotti il campo'** (cf. French *foutre le camp*), only to merge into further expressions of static decay (**'decedi'**: you decease; **'sprofondi'**: you sink down), followed in turn by indications of 'brilliance', nothingness (**'nonnulla'**), explosive energy (**'eclatante'**) and silence.

20-23:   The opening verb is repeated, but now in the past tense, giving a clear sense of a break in the meaning, marked also by repeated typographic 'jumps', which lead on to the closing **'oltraggio'** (conveying a sense of 'outrage', or 'offence', but also of going 'beyond' the limit of what is reachable). The lines repeatedly ending in '**là**' may perhaps point to the identity of the *tu* being phonically evoked as the absent part of the rhyme: 'la beltà' (*Le poesie e le prose*, p. 1487).

La perfezione della neve

Quante perfezioni, quante
quante totalità. Pungendo aggiunge.
E poi astrazioni astrificazioni formulazione d'astri
assideramento, attraverso sidera e coelos
assideramenti assimilazioni –   5
nel perfezionato procederei
più in là del grande abbaglio, del pieno e del vuoto,
ricercherei procedimenti
risaltando, evitando
dubbiose tenebrose; saprei direi.   10
Ma come ci soffolce, quanta è l'ubertà nivale
come vale: a valle del mattino a valle
a monte della luce plurifonte.
Mi sono messo di mezzo a questo movimento-mancamento radiale
ahi il primo brivido del salire, del capire,   15
partono in ordine, sfidano: ecco tutto.
E la tua consolazione insolazione e la mia, frutto
di quest'inverno, allenate, alleate,
sui vertici vitrei del sempre, sui margini nevati
del mai-mai-non-lasciai-andare,   20
e la stella che brucia nel suo riccio
e la castagna tratta dal ghiaccio
e – tutto – e tutto-eros, tutto-lib. libertà nel laccio
nell'abbraccio mi sta: ci sta,
ci sta all'invito, sta nel programma, nella faccenda.   25
Un sorriso, vero? E la vi(ta) (id-vid)
quella di cui non si può nulla, non ipotizzare,
sulla soglia si fa (accarezzare?).
Evoè lungo i ghiacci e le colture dei colori
e i rassicurati lavori degli ori.   30
Pronto. A chi parlo? Riallacciare.
E sono pronto, in fase d'immortale,
per uno sketch-idea della neve, per un suo guizzo.
Pronto.
Alla, della perfetta.   35

«È tutto, potete andare.»

La perfezione della neve

Placed immediately after 'Oltranza oltraggio', this poem picks up and develops some of that poem's stylistic modes and thematic motifs ('themes' may be too strong a word). In the title, and in the repeated allusions to cold, ice and stars, there is a strong suggestion of a winter landscape (one could interpret the 'perfections', star-formations, movements, etc. as impressions of falling snowflakes). However, this is never explicitly delineated, but emerges from the repertoire of images of the absolute, of abstract perfection (images of snow, etc., with similar connotations have already occurred frequently in Zanzotto's work and will also be explored later in *Fosfeni*, the second part of the 'pseudo-trilogy'). The overall effect, however, is of a poem centred on questions of poetic (and, generally, linguistic) communication.

1-2: The visual perfection suggested in the title is immediately related to a more abstract and absolute concept of 'totality'; **'pungendo'**: stinging or prickling.

3-5: To the opening 'totalities' are 'added' (l.2) yet more elements, in a seemingly open-ended process. The phonic and formal texture becomes extraordinarily dense, with a series of overlapping and interweaving word-plays based on sound (e.g. 'astr-'), grammatical forms ('-ione') and etymology (**'astri'**, **'assideramento'**, **'sidera'**, all based on the meaning of 'star'). One term appears to generate the next spontaneously, with a kind of free-associative inventiveness: **'astrificazioni'** is a coinage (translatable as 'astrifications'); **'assideramento'** (normally meaning 'frostbite' or 'exposure') is, according to the author, used here in a pseudo-etymological sense of 'influence of a star' (*Le poesie e le prose*, p. 349); **'sidera'**, **'coelus'** are Latin terms (star, sky).

6-10: Faced with these abstractions/perfections, the *io* seems tempted to assume the role of potential visionary (but this hypothesis is framed entirely in the conditional mood). As in 'Oltranza oltraggio', the problem seems to be one of going 'beyond' ('più in là'), in this case beyond the **'abbaglio'** (a polivalent term, meaning dazzlement, but also error or deception), or beyond 'fullness and emptiness' (perhaps beyond rational distinctions). For all the sense of doubt, there is a tentative hope of certainty in **'saprei, direi'**.

11-16: Initially the **'Ma...'** might seem to block that hope, but in fact it serves more as an emphatic conjunction ('but also...'); **'soffolce'**: sustains; **'ubertà nivale'**: rich abundance of snow. This line is, in fact, a textual allusion to *Paradiso* XXIII, 130, reinforcing the idea that the poet's persona here is engaged in an arduous ascent or pursuit of some truth. Meanwhile the snow seems to multiply its 'perfections' or validity, both **'a valle / a monte'** (upstream, downstream) of the mysterious **'plurifonte'** (many-sourced) light (recalling the **'abbaglio'** in l.7); **'radiale'**: radial, radiating outwards. The *io* then explicitly posits an upward movement, but the thrill of ascent is too unequivocal not to be ironic and soon leads to the first moment of anti-climax. As 'they' (he and others like him? the 'perfections' or absolutes that he pursues?) set out, their 'challenge' leads to a dead end: **'ecco tutto'**.

17-25: The thrust towards some perfection is, however, apparently unstoppable, as the poet now turns to a relationship with a *tu* (which we may again identify with 'beltà' or poetry or meaning), and seeks to align his own *io* with it/her (note '**la tua... la mia**' in l.17); '**insolazione**': sun-stroke (combined incongruously with '**consolazione**'); '**allenate**': trained. With their 'alliance' comes a further ascent to '**vertici vitrei**' (glassy peaks, identified with '**il sempre**'), snow-topped mountains, ice and stars, all summed up in a '**tutto-eros**' which is both libido (see author's note, *Le poesie e le prose*, p. 349) and liberty, but also both '**laccio**' (snare) and '**abbraccio**', an ambiguous union with the other who is now quite willing ('**ci sta**'); '**castagna**': chestnut; '**tratta**': pulled. Again purely phonic imperatives seem to play a large part in the fabric of these lines.

26-30: The 'smile' of ecstatic union seems distinctly forced and open to question. The object of his erotic attention is now a strangely truncated '**vi(ta)**' (to be understood, the poet's note states, as 'ideare-vedere'; *Le poesie e le prose*, p. 349). Even as she seems ready, on the 'threshold', to be caressed, the consummation is frustated (by both parenthesis and question mark). Finally the irony is unconcealed as his ecstasy is expressed with the highly literary-archaic '**Evoè**' (a cry of joy), and the landscape (such as it is) becomes a pure play of colours and verbal sounds; '**colture**': cultivations.

31-36: The ecstatic-erotic-ascensional mood is unceremoniously broken by the banal ordinariness of an interrupted telephone call; '**Riallacciare**': to hang up the phone (evoking the 'rapporti banalizzati' of ordinary communication; see Lorenzini, *Il presente della poesia*, p. 114). It is a merciless deflation of the poet's fraught preoccupation with the problems inherent in linguistic and literary communication. The hypothesis of some rarefied communion with beauty or life itself is unsustainable, replaced now by his modest aspiration to provide a '**sketch-idea della neve**', a rough sketch ('**guizzo**') of perfection. The apparently blunt final leave-taking conceals a number of ironic allusions: it echoes the closing formula of the liturgy of the mass, as well as the 'congedo' of the poetic tradition, in which an author takes leave of his text (see *Le poesie e le prose*, p. 1488); but also the statement '**è tutto**' overturns the '**totalità**' of the opening, from 'all' it has turned to silence, to nothing.

Al mondo

Mondo, sii, e buono;
esisti buonamente,
fa' che, cerca di, tendi a, dimmi tutto,
ed ecco che io ribaltavo eludevo
e ogni inclusione era fattiva   5
non meno che ogni esclusione;
su bravo, esisti,
non accartocciarti in te stesso in me stesso

Io pensavo che il mondo così concepito
con questo super-cadere super-morire   10
il mondo così fatturato
fosse soltanto un io male sbozzolato
fossi io indigesto male fantasticante
male fantasticato mal pagato
e non tu, bello, non tu «santo» e «santificato»   15
un po' più in là, da lato, da lato

Fa' di (ex-de-ob etc.)-sistere
e oltre tutte le preposizioni note e ignote,
abbi qualche chance,
fa' buonamente un po';   20
il congegno abbia gioco.
Su, bello, su.

Su, münchhausen.

Al mondo

Here the poet confronts the problem of the relationship between the *io* (subjective perception) and the world (objective reality), in an ironic exhortation to the latter to exist in its own right. However he cannot overcome the problems that arise from our necessity to perceive and formulate reality through language, and the inevitable cross-contamination between self and world that results.

1-3:   Verbs in the imperative set up the direct exhortation to the world ('Be, world, and [be] good'), and the tone from the outset is of a kind of playful, mock intimacy. Zanzotto calls attention to language itself and its mechanisms, from the slightly elliptical syntax of l.1, to the coinage **'buonamente'** of l.2, to the semantically incomplete imperatives of l.3. **'fa' che, cerca di, tendi a'**: all would logically require some further verb or action to follow; as it is, they signify the *io*'s desire for action in itself on the part of the 'world', for the world to 'speak' to him, rather than the other way around.

4-6:   With the shift to the imperfect tense, the poetic voice assumes a distance from his foregoing address to the world, commenting on it from a detached perpsective. He suggests that his approach was flawed (**'ribaltavo'**: inverted), that whether 'including' or 'excluding' the world from his own reality, he was engaging in a 'constructive' or 'artificial' (**'fattiva'**) relationship with it.

7-8:   He switches back to the original direct address, again calling on the world to exist unproblematically, to be neither isolated within itself (**'accartocciarti'**: roll up in a ball) nor existing purely in the subjective mind. Again, the tone is one of *bonhomie* (**'su bravo'**: 'come on...').

9-16:   The return to the imperfect tense indicates a further distancing, but now his presumed present viewpoint must surely be read in an ironic key. In other words what he says he 'thought' is in fact what he *thinks*: that the world conceived as naively as suggested in the opening stanza *is* in fact just a distorted, manipulated (**'fatturato'**) reflection of an *io* that is undeveloped (**'male sbozzolato'**: not properly emerged from the cocoon), lacking in understanding or clarity of thought, misunderstood, and that the world is *not* in fact some 'sacred' entity, just out of reach or or in some other place (l.16 recalls the unreachable 'beltà' of 'Oltranza oltraggio'). The terms **'super-cadere super-morire'** may refer to a world in a state of entropy (*Le poesie e le prose*, p. 1501).

17-21:   The good-humoured exhortations to the world now find expression in terms that are strongly marked by references to the problematic nature of language. What is urged ironically is for the world to **'-sistere'**, to somehow 'be', regardless of the precise meanings formed by the logical mechanisms of language (the various prefixes), to exist 'beyond' all linguistic forms, to 'do' (even if what is to be done is unclear); for the **'congegno'** (mechanism) to come into play.

22-23:   The overall ironic effect of the poem depends to a large degree on the incongruous juxtaposition of different registers, tones, semantic fields and cultural references. This culminates here in the abrupt shift from the colloquial familiarity of **'Su, bello, su'** (something like: 'come on, old thing') to the unexpected literary reference to R.E. Raspe's 18th-Century character, Baron von Münchhausen. The precise allusion (following the poet's indications; *Le poesie e le prose*, p. 1500) is to the Baron escaping from a swamp by pulling himself up by the hair. Clearly the prospect of reality existing in some entirely innocent form, bringing itself into being independently of our human formulation of it, is remote. And yet, in the spirit of Münchhausen, we are left with a residual aspiration for such a heroic absurdity.

From *Pasque* (1973)

Proteine, proteine

E tu t'inoltri per entro la città e schiacci
entri col piede, così apprendi a fondo, nel vivissimo.
Così – qui t'incoccio – vollero i duci
sui culmini dei lucri, così i seguaci.
   «Proteine in quantità – per la Sua felicità,   5
   mille vasi di Loyal – e di Kik e Ciappi e Pal;
   pieno colmo vo' che sia – ogni étage giardino o via
   della kukka del mio Lassi – che a ciascun suggelli i passi,
   vo' che il cantico di Fido – nelle psichi faccia nido;
   proteine, proteine – bilanciate, sopraffine» –   10
E nell'alba   quella del chiaro
E nella sera   quella d'oscuro
tu nel denso di Lassi metti i passi
incendiato di odore abbaiante vai vai
fin oltre, dove nel sordo   désir delle nebbie   15
nell'occhio del falò
splende la bimba di paraffina,
fin dove inchimichita si sgrana l'aura dei campi
fin sul molo ultimo   sull'ultimo alt
a cerca – vano escapismo – di nettarti la zampa,   20
non trovi, t'ingiri, in asfittiche ire t'inventri:
   ecco già la mossa nascosta –
   una linea di eoni e di dèi
   la muta una muta di anubi
   enciclopedizza chiosa accusa   25
     verità e vanità
     passioni e svenimenti

   in minoranza infinitamente cadi/sei

Proteine, proteine

This poem is in some ways uncharacteristic of *Pasque*, whose major texts include lengthy explorations of themes of pedagogy and meditations on the meanings and symbolism of Easter. Also unusually, it presents an urban landscape, which in itself carries negative connotations in Zanzotto's world, rendered even more repugnant by the abundance of canine excrement (to which the title makes ironic allusion).

1-4:   The *tu* of this poem may signify an address to the self and/or directly to an imagined reader. **'t'inoltri'**: move further on; **'schiacci'**: squash (this and **'entri'** refer to a dog-turd on the street). The theme of pedagogy, explored so earnestly elsewhere, is now the subject of sarcastic mockery: here is where you learn the reality of life **'a fondo'** (in depth); **'t'incoccio'**: I bump into you. The **'duci'** and **'seguaci'** may consitute a further ironic allusion to the idea of education (and to the Latin meaning of *educare*), but now reduced to the image of owners 'leading' their dogs. Their wish, apparently fulfilled, is the accumulation of excrement, related closely to a society based on accumulation of profit (**'lucri'**).

5-10:   A block of text marked by a metrical pattern of *ottonari doppi*, an incongruous revival of an archaic verse form, in comic contrast to the content, an exaltation of commercial brands of dog food (e.g. **'Ciappi'**, Italianized form of *Chappie*) and their inevitable consequences after the digestive process, a veritable ode to excrement. **'Vo'**: 'voglio'; **'kukka'**: a variant form of 'cacca'; **'Lassi'**: Lassie (dog's name); **'suggelli i passi'**: that it should 'seal' their footsteps, i.e. stick to their shoes; **'sopraffine'**: of highest quality.

11-14:   The more 'normal' Zanzottian voice returns, although the irony is no less evident as he pictures the poem's protagonist 'barking' (**'abbaiante'**) with rage at his misfortune.

15-21:   The attempt to escape leads you on, **'oltre'** (a highly-charged word in Zanzotto, as we have seen above), looking perhaps for some other, more rarefied landscape of **'nebbie'**, or more profound perception of reality, only to find instead further nightmarish scenes in what seems to be a kind of peripheral zone, where the archaic/poetic **'aura'** (air, breeze) of the countryside disintegrates (**'si sgrana'**) in chemical pollution; **'la bimba di paraffina'** may be a reference to prostitutes standing around bonfires (**'falò'**) at the edge of the city (*Le poesie e le prose*, p. 1545). At the last halt, the foot turns into an ironic/animal **'zampa'** even as you try to clean it (**'nettarti'**) in your **'escapismo'** (another Zanzottian neologism), and you are left 'choking' with rage (**'ire'**), turning inwards on yourself (**'inventrarsi'**, to penetrate deeply, is a Dantesque term, and lends a similar flavour to the coinage **'ingirarsi'**, to turn in on oneself).

22-28:   A hidden force emerges: Anubis the Egyptian jackal-god, god of the dead (or rather a whole 'pack' of them) replaces the other gods (**'la** [object pronoun referring to 'la linea'] **muta** [verb mutare] **una muta** [subject, a 'pack of dogs']...'), and goes on to monopolize the whole spectrum of knowledge, truth, etc. (**'chiosa'**: glosses, explains) until the poet's persona is forced into an absolute minority (**'infinitamente'**). And yet there is a kind of resistance in the closing words, **'cadi/sei'**: this 'fall' is still a form of possibly authentic 'being'.

From *Il Galateo in bosco* (1978)

Rivolgersi agli ossari. Non occorre biglietto.
Rivolgersi ai cippi. Con il più disperato rispetto.
Rivolgersi alle osterie. Dove elementi paradisiaci aspettano.
Rivolgersi alle case. Dove l'infinitudine del desìo
               (vedila ad ogni chiusa finestra) sta in affitto.   5

E la radura ha accettato più d'un frondoso colloquio
ormai, dove, ahi,
si esibì la più varia mostra dei sangui
  il più mistico circo dei sangui. Oh quanti numeri, e rancio speciale. Urrah.
Vorrei bucarmi di ogni chimica rovina   10
per accogliere tutti, in anteprima,
nello specchio medicato d'infinitudini e desii
di quel circo i fermenti gli enzimi
dentro i succhi più sublimi dell'alba, dell'azione, in piena diana. E si va.
E si va per ossari. Essi attendono   15
gremiti di mortalità lievi ormai, quai gemme di primavera,
gremiti di bravura e di paura. A ruota libera, e si va.
Buoni, ossari – tante morti fuori del qualitativo divario
              onde si sale a sicurezze di cippo,
fuori del gran bidone (e la patria bidonista,   20
che promette casetta e campicello
e non li diede mai, qui santità mendica, acquista).
Hanno come un fervore di fabbrica gli ossari.
Vi si ricevono ordini, ordinazioni eterne. Vi si smista.
All'asilo, certi pazzi-di-guerra, ancora vivi   25
allevano maiali; traffici con gli ossari.
Mi avete investito, lordato tutto, eternizzato tutto, un fiotto di sangue.
Arteria aperta il Piave, né calmo né placido
ma soltanto gaiamente sollecito oltre i beni i mali e simili
          e tutto solletichio di argenti, nei suoi intenti, a dismisura. 30
Padre e madre, in quel nume forse uniti
          tra quell'incoercibile sanguinare
            ed il verde e l'argenteizzare altrettanto incoercibili,
in quel grandore dove tutti i silenzi sono possibili
voi mi combinaste, sotto quelle caterve di   35
os-ossa, ben catalogate, nemmeno geroglifici, ostie

rivomitate ma come in un più alto, in un aldilà d'erbe e d'enzimi
erbosi assunte,
in un fuori-luogo che su me s'inclina e domina
un poco creandomi, facendomi assurgere a   40
Così che   suono a parlamento
per le balbuzie e le più ardue rime,
quelle si addestrano e rincorrono a vicenda,
io mi avvicendo, vado per ossari, e cari stinchi e teschi
mi trascino dietro dolcissimamente, senza o con flauto magico   45
   Sempre più con essi, dolcissimamente, nella brughiera
io mi avvicendo a me, tra pezzi di guerra sporgenti da terra,
si avvicenda un fiore a un cielo
dentro le primavere delle ossa in sfacelo,
si avvicenda un sì a un no, ma di poco   50
differenziati, nel fioco
negli steli esili di questa pioggia, da circo, da gioco.

Rivolgersi agli ossari

With this text we are back in the poet's most deeply-experienced landscape where, in the area near his home, the wood of Montello was the scene of fierce combat in the First World War. One of the central themes of *Il Galateo in bosco* is the presence in this landscape of the '**ossari**', commemorative structures containing the bones and thus the physical, cultural and spiritual memory of the unknown war dead. This is one of several elements that are woven together in this multi-faceted and stylistically heterogeneous collection: the subjective perceptions of the *io*, as ever, are in dialogue with the landscape, but this is also deeply contaminated by the violence of history and the complexities of human culture. The title of the collection reflects the coexistence of such elements. The term *Galateo* recalls the 16th-century book of manners written in this same area by Monsignor Giovanni Della Casa, a term which Zanzotto adopts in the sense of a set of rules or norms of what constitutes civilization and human history, as it confronts the 'bosco' of nature, uncodified reality, at once innocent and chaotic. In this poem, in a thematic scenario which has had many illustrious precedents in the literary tradition, from Dante to Foscolo to Montale, Zanzotto consults the dead, whose remains are seen to have fused with the landscape.

1-5:   The repetition of '**rivolgersi**' (to turn to) establishes an atmosphere of questioning, seeking answers, while '**Non occorre biglietto**' both demystifies the pilgrimage, downgrading it to the level of a free tourist attraction, and also distinguishes it from the sordid commercial world; '**cippi**': memorial stones. But the poet does not divorce the 'ossari' from life. Indeed, in these opening lines, he tends to amalgamate the two, turning the questioning mind also to '**osterie**' and '**case**', the abodes of pleasure and desire ('**desìo**').

6-9:   The '**radura**' (clearing) has seen the rhetoric of official commemoration ('**frondoso**' meaning both 'leafy' and 'excessively rhetorical'), but the matter-of-fact '**mostra** (show) **dei sangui**' deflates the rather tendentious '**mistico circo**'. Such mysticism is cut short by the scathing irony of 'special rations' ('**rancio**') being distributed to the innumerable dead, and their hollow, poignant '**Urrah**'.

10-14:   The poetic *io* has a visceral, corporeal response, wanting to '**bucarmi**' (inject himself), to assimilate the chemistry of the dead within himself, in the 'mirror' of the landscape/circus, 'medicated' by infinities, letting their essence ferment with the very '**succhi**' of the dawn, as a (remembered or imagined) reveille ('**diana**') plays. So his true pilgrimage starts.

15-24:   The ossuaries are approached with a mixture of humble reverence and honesty. They are laden ('**gremiti**') with mortality (in contrast to the unholy 'eternalizing' rhetoric of commemoration; see l.27). They are like spring buds and are, unashamedly, places of both '**bravura**' and '**paura**', quite alien to distinctions of honour or otherwise (the 'qualitative distinctions' that lead to memorial 'certainties'), and are far removed from the '**bidone**' (fraud) that saw so many men die in hopes of social reform ('**casetta e campicello**') cynically promised by the '**Patria**' which now seeks to 'beg' some sacred glory here. In contrast, the 'ossari' conserve their own dignified 'fervour', remain alive in their eternity, their inmates 'taking orders', being assigned to groups (**'si smista'**).

25-26: The reference here is to traumatized survivors, some of whom were still living in mental asylums when Zanzotto wrote, constituting a living point of contact (**'traffici'**) with the dead.

27: The poet's central accusation against the establishment, which, by 'eternalizing' the real human loss, the 'flood' of blood, has fouled (**'lordato'**) the memory of it.

28-40: The river of blood becomes the Piave, the scene of great slaughter, and thus now **'nume'** (a kind of pagan divinity) in the eyes of national rhetoric, but actually indifferent to the horror; **'gaiamente sollecito'**: cheerfully diligent; **'solletichio'**: stimulation. Rather, for him, the Piave represents his intimate, physical, biological roots, the place of his conception (in the years immediately following the Great War), in the shadow of those piles (**'caterve'**) of bones (whose violent physical reality is again reinforced with **'ostie rivomitate'**: 'vomited hosts'), now high above and almost indeed 'assumed' into a kind of rarefied **'aldilà'** (beyond) of nature. Thus the remains of the dead are seen to be assimilated again into the landscape in a kind of osmosis, by **'enzimi'**, in the very fabric of the land that created the poetic *io*. Any possible ascent (**'assurgere'**) of his own is, however, abruptly truncated in l.40, its destination remaining void.

41-43: He turns now to his perennial theme, that of the problematic nature of poetry and language, which he deploys **'a parlamento'** (here in the sense of a 'parley' between opposing forces), with 'arduous' rhymes that strive to pursue one another; **'balbuzie'**: stammering.

44-52: We are left with the image of the poet as a kind of Pied Piper, calling the bones to follow him as opposing concepts and images blend in the 'circus' of the landscape: **'stinchi e teschi'**: shinbones and skulls; **'brughiera'**: moor; **'sporgenti'**: sticking out; **'sfacelo'**: decomposition; **'steli'**: stems. These lines revolve around the verb **'avvicendarsi'**, 'to alternate (with one another)', emphasising the interchangeability between elements in this landscape and by extension between the self and the landscape, positive and negative, the living and the dead.

10
Amelia Rosselli (1930–1996)

Rosselli belongs to the same generation as key members of the *Gruppo 63*, and indeed her poetry of the early 1960s may appear, at first sight, to fall naturally within the parameters of the neo-avantgarde. However, while the innovative language and experimental character of her work points to affinities with some of the *Gruppo 63* (and in particular with the poetry of Antonio Porta), she remains ultimately on the margins of the *neoavanguardia* as she develops her own highly personal and idiosyncratic style of writing.[i]

In considering the individuality of her poetic voice, some weight must surely be given to the peculiar and dramatic circumstances of her life and personal background: born in 1930 in Paris, she was the daughter of the exiled anti-Fascist Carlo Rosselli, who was murdered by Fascists along with his brother Nello in 1937 and would subsequently be revered as a martyr of the Italian left. Amelia Rosselli's childhood and youth were scarred by this traumatic event, but were also marked by further elements of instability in the formation of her cultural and linguistic identity. She was brought up speaking mainly French at first (although her father spoke to her in Italian), but in 1940 her English mother led the family to the relative safety of England and then on to the United States for the duration of the war. It was not until 1946 that she first came to Italy, where she eventually settled (in Rome) in 1948. She had meanwhile begun studying music in earnest, but following the death of her mother she was obliged to start working part-time as a translator and soon underwent, in her own words, 'un forte esaurimento nervoso' (marking the early stage of a long struggle with mental and physical illness).[ii] Music and ethnomusicology continued to be a major focus of her cultural activity, alongside her literary work (and indeed comparisons have been made between, for example, her use of 'variations' and contemporary experimental music).[iii] The first significant publication of her poetry was the appearance in the journal *Il menabò* in 1963 of a group of 24 poems with a note by Pasolini, followed in 1964 by her first collection, *Variazioni belliche*. Most of her poetic work dates to the 1960s and 1970s. She took her own life in Rome in 1996.[iv]

Her trilingual background almost certainly plays a role in forging the complex linguistic character of her work: her poetry is marked by a problematic relationship with language itself, but also by an acute awareness of the creative potential inherent in the music, mechanisms and rhythms of language, and in the interferences between one linguistic code and another, one word and another, one syllable and another. The poet Giovanni Giudici asserts that language itself, as 'a means of exploration, experimentation and invention', is the principle theme of Rosselli's work. He maintains that her various collections of verse essentially constitute a continuum in which a number of components interweave and interact: a 'magmatic' linguistic component, leading to a constant instability of meaning; an almost 'confessional' autobiographical element, whose referents remain, however, nameless and faceless (this component also brings in the presence of her 'malattia nervosa'); a 'visionary and literary' component with clear roots in the modern literary tradition (e.g. Campana, Montale, Rimbaud, Kafka); and a prosodic component (related to the author's musical studies) involving a sense of rhythmic control even where the verse tends towards prose, giving rise to a poetic text close in its essence to a musical score, where at times the 'cosa-vuol-dire' is less important than the 'dire-in-sé'.[v]

Pasolini, in presenting her poems in 1963 (a presentation that tends somewhat to play down the experimental character of Rosselli's work as Pasolini pursues his own polemical agendas), introduces the term 'lapsus', meaning Freudian slip or error, to describe some of her curious linguistic aberrations.[vi] It is a term that has proved perhaps more enduring than illuminating in Rosselli criticism. For Pasolini, her use of the 'lapsus' is a means of liberation from the weight of convention, but the word itself also suggests a lack of conscious control, an element of surrender to the irrational or the subconscious, which can point to an implicitly reductive reading of the work. Mengaldo, who in 1978 gave a first 'canonical' recognition to Rosselli by including her as the only female voice in his *Poeti italiani del Novecento*, also tends to emphasise an irrational element: 'la poesia è qui vissuta anzitutto come abbandono al flusso buio e labirintico della vita psichica e dell'immaginario'.[vii] Giudici, however, in his 1981 preface to *Impromptu*, cautions against any assumption of an 'unconscious' force guiding Rosselli, 'un'artista così consapevole del proprio operare', but he does suggest that she uses the 'lapsus' as a form of '"errore" creativo', releasing a creative potential that she finds within language itself.[viii] Emmanuela Tandello also emphasises the element of formal control in Rosselli, underlining in particular the poet's preoccupation with the 'laws' of form, notably as set out in the dense theoretical framework of her 1962 essay 'Spazi metrici'.[ix]

Often in Rosselli's poetry, one has the sense that the individual texts, in their fragmentary unpredictability, allude or refer implicitly to some larger narrative scheme that has somehow been displaced or frustrated.[x] The technique of 'variations', with the playful and inventive repetition (and distortion) of lexical and phonic elements from one poem to the next, adds to this quasi-narrative perspective. One recurring element in whatever fragmented narrative the reader may be invited to reconstruct is the presence of an unidentified 'tu' at the heart of many poems. There is a difficult, sometimes confrontational or polemical dialogue with this figure (or rather, these figures, as the identity of the interlocutor seems by no means stable – and more than once the reader is led to suspect that the dialogue is a wholly interior one), a dialogue which, as Lucia Re notes, is part of a broader 'dialogic structure', a perennial tension between opposing ideas, themes and images (such as love and death, mysticism and scepticism, *impegno* and disillusionment).[xi]

Although Rosselli, especially in her earlier poetry, shares with elements of the *neoavanguardia* an interest in exploring the possibilities of language and form at a time when the construction of meaning seems almost impossible amidst a chaotic reality, her poetic voice remains throughout a highly individual one, making it difficult to place her work neatly within any established critical or historiographical category (and indeed it has been repeatedly observed that influences on her work come from far beyond the contemporary Italian literary scene, reaching deep into anglophone and francophone territories, with influences such as Joyce, the English metaphysicals and the French surrealists). She remains, on the one hand, a somewhat isolated figure in the midst of the literary polemics of the 1960s and beyond, but can also be seen as opening important areas of exploration for writers of her own and subsequent generations.[xii]

Endnotes

i   In a later interview, she was dismissive of the Gruppo 63 – 'usano tecniche superatissime' – although she still expressed esteem for Porta and Pagliarani. See Elio Pecora, 'Un incontro con Amelia Rosselli', in *Amelia Rosselli*, ed. by Daniela Attanasio and Emmanuela Tandello, special issue of *Galleria*, vol. 48 (1997), 150-54 (p. 153). Fausto Curi suggests, with a note of condescension, that while the Novissimi have a clear sense of the 'innaturalezza' of poetic language, Rosselli, for all her distortions and word-play, uses language as an essentially 'natural' communicative medium for the experiences of the psyche and the emotions (Curi, *La poesia italiana*, p. 389).

ii   See interview with Spagnoletti in Amelia Rosselli, *Antologia poetica*, ed. by G. Spagnoletti (Milan: Garzanti, 1987), pp. 149-163 (pp. 153, 157).

iii   See Lucia Re, 'Amelia Rosselli and the esthetics of experimental music', in *Amelia Rosselli*, ed. by Attanasio and Tandello, pp. 35-46.

iv   On her life and works in general, see: Segre and Ossola, *Antologia della poesia italiana* (bio-bibliographical note, pp. 1155-58 and introductory essay by Laura Barile, pp. 959-63); Catherine O'Brien, *Italian Women Poets of the Twentieth Century* (Dublin: Irish Academic Press, 1996), pp. 150-61; interview with Spagnoletti in *Antologia poetica*; also various memoirs and interviews in *Amelia Rosselli*, ed. by Attanasio and Tandello; and in *Amelia Rosselli: Un'apolide alla ricerca del linguaggio universale* (Atti della giornata di studio Firenze, Gabinetto Viesseux, 29 maggio 1998), ed. by Stefano Giovannuzzi (Quaderni del Circolo Rosselli, 1999).

v   Giovanni Giudici, 'Prefazione' in Amelia Rosselli, *Poesie*, ed. by Emmanuela Tandello (Milan: Garzanti, 1997), pp. vii-xiii (pp. ix-x).

vi   On Rosselli and Pasolini, see Stefano Giovannuzzi, ' "La libellula": Amelia Rosselli nel labirinto degli anni sessanta', in *Giornale storico della letteratura italiana*, 182 (2005), fasc. 597, 69-92 (pp. 84-87).

vii   Mengaldo, *Poeti italiani del Novecento*, p. 995.

viii   This preface appeared subsequently as 'Per Amelia Rosselli', in the 1987 *Antologia poetica*, ed. by Spagnoletti, pp. 5-11 (see pp. 6-7).

ix   See Emmanuela Tandello's introduction to *Amelia Rosselli*, ed. by Attanasio and Tandello, pp. 10-11.

x   Lorenzini speaks of 'sviluppi narrativi bloccati' (*Il presente della poesia*, p. 110).

xi   See Lucia Re's introductory note on Rosselli in Picchione and Smith, *Twentieth-Century Italian Poetry: An Anthology* (Toronto: University of Toronto Press, 1993), pp. 452-3.

xii   See Monica Venturini, 'Alla luce della critica: la poesia di Amelia Rosselli', in *Trasparenze*, nn.17-19 ed. by Giorgio Devoto and Emmanuela Tandello, Supplemento non periodico a *Quaderni di Poesia* (Genova: Edizioni San Marco dei Giustiniani, 2003), pp. 107-18 (p. 117).

Poetic texts

Collected edition
Le poesie, a cura di Emmanuela Tandello, prefazione di Giovanni Giudici (Milan: Garzanti: 1997).

A good selection is in:
Amelia Rosselli, *Antologia poetica*, edited by Giacinto Spagnoletti (Milan: Garzanti, 1987).

Individual collections
Variazioni belliche (1964); *Serie ospedaliera* (1969); *Documento* (1976); *Impromptu* (1981); *Sleep: Poesie in inglese*, trans. by Emmanuela Tandello (Milan: Garzanti, 1992)

Prose texts

Amelia Rosselli, *Una scrittura plurale: saggi e interventi critici*, edited by Francesca Caputo (Novara: Interlinea, 2004).

Further reading

Attanasio, Daniela, and Emmanuela Tandello, eds, *Amelia Rosselli*, special issue of *Galleria*, vol. 48 (1997)

Devoto, Giorgio, and Emmanuela Tandello, eds, *Trasparenze*, nn.17-19, Supplemento non periodico a *Quaderni di Poesia* (Genova: Edizioni San Marco dei Giustiniani, 2003) [contains comprehensive bibliography of works by and on Rosselli]

Giovannuzzi, Stefano, '"La libellula": Amelia Rosselli nel labirinto degli anni sessanta', in *Giornale storico della letteratura italiana*, 182 (2005), fasc. 597, 69-92

Giovannuzzi, Stefano, ed., *Amelia Rosselli: Un'apolide alla ricerca del linguaggio universale (Atti della giornata di studio, Firenze, Gabinetto Viesseux, 29 maggio 1998)*, (Quaderni del Circolo Rosselli, 1999)

O'Brien, Catherine, *Italian Women Poets of the Twentieth Century* (Dublin: Irish Academic Press, 1996), pp. 150-61

Re, Lucia, Introductory note on Rosselli in *Twentieth-Century Italian Poetry: An Anthology*, edited by John Picchione and Laurence Smith (Toronto: University of Toronto Press, 1993), pp. 450-53

Tandello, Emmanuela, 'Doing the splits: Language(s) in the poetry of Amelia Rosselli', in *Journal of the Institute of Romance Studies*, 1 (1992), 363-73.

Contents

From *Variazioni Belliche* (1964)

i rapporti più armoniosi e i rapporti più dissonanti, tu povero
che corri armoniosamente tu intelligente che corri con
la dissidenza, voglia io unirvi
in un universo sì cangiante sì terribilmente dissidente
che solo la Gloria di Dio noi crediamo porti Gloria   5
sa riunire. E se veracemente con tutta la fiaccola di dio oh ordine
che cadde consumato, si rinnovò e non fu per sempre e fu solo
una balugine, io perdo! io non resto! riposato sulle erbe
tranquille dei né paradisi né terra né inferno né normale
convenienza con te ho cercato l'immenso e la totale   10
disarmonia perfetta, ma basse corde risuonano anche se tu non
le premi anche se tu non sistemi le valanghe i gridi e
le piccole sgragnatiture in quell'unico
sicuro scialle.

'i rapporti più armoniosi e i rapporti più dissonanti...'

This poem is from the volume's first section, titled *Poesie*, dating to 1959 and containing texts which are, on the whole, less marked by formal experimentation than those of the second section. Here Rosselli uses a form of *verso libero* with a preponderance of longer lines, anticipating in part the more systematic and uniform metre of her subsequent work.

1-5: The title of the collection as a whole ('War Variations') can best be interpreted as referring to the poet's inner struggles, as well as reflecting the recurring presence of deeply conflictual relationships with various *tu* figures – as found in the opening lines here, where one might perhaps discern the presence to two interlocutors, one 'harmonious', one 'dissident', but one may equally assume these to be two sides of the poet's own persona which she apparently should aspire to unite (**'voglia'**: 'that I might wish'); so that this text, like many others, becomes an examination of the make-up and the expectations of the poetic *io*. In such a chaotic world (**'cangiante'**: changing), this unification is an impossible task, except for a God, whose 'glory', however, is no sooner posited than it is undermined (**'noi crediamo...'**: to be read as a parenthesis: 'we think he bears glory').

6-8: Even with a 'divine' illumination, though this is a mere **'fiaccola'** (torch) or **'balugine'** (glimmer), there is no stable order, leading to the defeat and retreat of the *io*.

8-11: '[...] with you I have looked for [neither] gods (**'dei'**) nor paradises [...etc] nor normal conventions [but] immensity and [...] perfect disharmony'.

11-14: Despite the quest for *dis*harmony, 'low-pitched strings' sound spontaneously, even if 'you' do not neatly wrap up the chaotic phenomena of life in a single 'shawl'; **'sgragnatiture'**: a typical Rossellian coinage/distortion, in this case a kind of 'portmanteau' word, combining (according to her own 'glossarietto') *sgraffiature, sgranare, sgramaticato* [sic], *sgranocchiare, sgraziato, gragnolare* (now in Devoto and Tandello, *Trasparenze*, p.18); thus the sense hovers between 'scratches', 'ungrammaticalness', 'munching', 'gracelessness' (among other things). The poem as a whole presents a vision of the inner life in perennial tension between 'dissidence' and 'harmony', in a text full of syntactic and semantic tensions (perhaps best summed-up in **'totale / disarmonia perfetta'**).

Se nella notte sorgeva un dubbio su dell'essenza del mio
cristianesimo, esso svaniva con la lacrima della canzonetta
del bar vicino. Se dalla notte sorgeva il dubbio dello
etmisfero cangiante e sproporzionato, allora richiedevo
aiuto. Se nell'inferno delle ore notturne richiamo a me   5
gli angioli e le protettrici che salpavano per sponde
molto più dirette delle mie, se dalle lacrime che sgorgavano
diramavo missili e pedate inconscie agli amici che mal
tenevano le loro parti di soldati amorosi, se dalle finezze
del mio spirito nascevano battaglie e contraddizioni, –   10
allora moriva in me la noia, scombinava l'allegria il mio
malanno insoddisfatto; continuava l'aria fine e le canzoni
attorno attorno svolgevano attività febbrili, cantonate
disperse, ultime lacrime di cristo che non si muoveva per
sì picciol cosa, piccola parte della notte nella mia prigionia.   15

'Se nella notte sorgeva un dubbio...'

This poem, like the following ones, comes from the second part of the collection, *Variazioni* (1960-1961), a lengthy sequence in which Rosselli experiments with a more systematic metrical form, as theorized in her essay 'Spazi metrici' (published along with this collection). The line length, based on a rhythmic measure similar to that of the beats in a bar of music (rather than on the traditional syllabic system of Italian verse), is set by the opening line and remains rhythmically and typographically constant, giving rise to a symmetrical block of text, or 'forma cubo'. Yet within this formal framework, and, as it were, in counterpoint with it, language, syntax and imagery flow freely, passionately and with sometimes arresting surprises. Another prominent formal device (in keeping with the title) is the use of repetitive structures akin to those of the musical variation, along with other 'musical' effects of repetition and variation on the phonic level of alliteration and assonance. The poet herself described the theme of this collection as 'il nascere e morire di una passionalità da principio imbrigliata e contorta [...]', along with, in parts, 'una problematica religiosa' (see interview in *Antologia poetica*, p.156).

1-5:   Spiritual self-questioning is juxtaposed and fades away with the banal reality of an overheard sentimental song. l.4: **'etmisfero'**: according to Rosselli's glossary, a fusion of 'emisfero' (hemisphere) and 'atmosfera', used to 'bring space down to a human level' (see Devoto and Tandello, *Trasparenze*, p.18).

5-7:   The nocturnal meditation becomes explicitly anguished, an **'inferno'**, which in turn leads to the invocation of angelic and saintly protection; **'protettrice'**: patron saint (but the author distances herself from any idea of 'directly' accessing those 'shores'); **'salpavano'**: set sail; **'sponde'**: shores.

7-10:   With her anguish now flooding over (**'sgorgavano'**) into tears, we glimpse irascible, belligerent relationships with friends found lacking and also a difficult and divided self; **'diramavo'**: I released; **'pedate'**: kicks; **'mal tenevano le loro parti'**: 'played their roles badly'.

11-12: The outcome of all these problematic conditions is, unexpectedly, an affirmation of 'allegria', but it is framed in curiously negative terms, with **'noia'** dying, and with the **'malanno'** (affliction) left 'unsatisfied' and 'disturbed' (**'scombinava'**) by joy.

13-15: Similarly here the songs are 'feverish', leading to **'cantonate'** (blunders) and **'lacrime di cristo'** (a possible ironic allusion to the wine known as 'lacrima Christi'?). This (lower case) 'christ' does not intervene in her anguished nocturne for **'sì picciol cosa'**: such a small thing (a literary/archaic phrase, probably used with ironic intent).

Per le cantate che si svolgevano nell'aria io rimavo
ancora pienamente. Per l'avvoltoio che era la tua sinistra
figura io ero decisa a combattere. Per i poveri ed i malati
di mente che avvolgevano le loro sinistre figure di tra
le strade malate io cantavo ancora tarantella la tua camicia   5
è la più bella canzone della strada. Per le strade odoranti
di benzina cercavamo nell'occhio del vicino la canzone
preferita. Per quel tuo cuore che io largamente preferisco
ad ogni altra burrasca io vado cantando amenamente delle
canzoni che non sono per il tuo orecchio casto da cantante   10
a divieto. Per il divieto che ci impedisce di continuare
forse io perderò te ancora ed ancora – sinché le maree del
bene e del male e di tutte le fandonie di cui è ricoperto
questo vasto mondo avranno terminato il loro fischiare.

'Per le cantate che si svolgevano nell'aria...'

This text follows immediately after the one given above and provides a good illustration of Rosselli's use of variation and repetition running from one poem to another, leading to an overall sense of continuity, albeit fragmentary and intermittent, in the collection. The poem is part of an ongoing belligerent dialogue with a *tu*. The **'cantate'** of l.1 (followed throughout the text by a series of cognate terms) picks up immediately on both 'canzonetta'/'canzoni' and also, in purely phonic terms, 'cantonate' from the preceding poem ('svolgevano' and 'aria' also echo the previous text). Meanwhile, there is also a pattern of variation within this poem on a structural level with the repetition of **'Per...'**.

1-2: The opening suggests a potentially optimistic view of poetry. Rosselli frequently uses the verb *rimare* (to rhyme) in the rarely used sense of 'to write poetry'.

2-6: The darker and more 'sinister' elements in the figures of the *tu* and others (**'avvoltoio'**: vulture, is underlined by the alliteration and repetition in l. 4) are counterbalanced by the 'song' of the *io*, which blends in surreal fashion into **'tarantella'** (a frenetic folk-dance) and **'la tua camicia'**.

6-10: 'We' sought 'song' in another individual amidst streets reeking of petrol. She now finds the reason to sing in 'your' heart, compared to a **'burrasca'** (storm), but one that is 'preferred'; **'casto'**: chaste. It is an image, perhaps, of poetry springing out of suffering (see La Penna on the 'metafora ventosa', in *Trasparenze*, pp. 309-32).

11-14: Progress is blocked and the poem closes with a premonition of loss and separation in a quasi-apocalyptic vision of a world overwhelmed by the 'tides' of good and evil and **'fandonie'** (lies, tall tales). The fact that these are all 'whistling' recalls again the image of wind, out of which the poet's 'canzone' may emerge. As the text proceeds there is at times a sense that musical imperatives of repetition and variation take precedence over semantic cohesion.

Se per il caso che mi guidava io facevo capriole: se per
la perdita che continuava la sua girandola io sapevo: se
per l'agonia che mi prendeva io perdevo: se per l'incanto
che non seguivo io non cadevo: se nelle stelle dell'universo
io cascavo a terra con un tonfo come nell'acqua: se per   5
l'improvvisa pena io salvavo i miei ma rimanevo a terra
ad aspettare il battello se per la pena tu sentivi per
me (forse) ed io per te non cadevamo sempre incerti nell'avvenire
se tutto questo non era che fandonia allora dove rimaneva
la terra? Allora chi chiamava – e chi rinnegava?   10

Sempre docile e scontenta la ragazza appellava al buio.
Sempre infelice ma sorridente mostrava i denti. Se non
v'era aiuto nel mondo era impossibile morire. Ma la morte
è la più dolce delle compagnie. La dolce sorella era
la sorellastra. Il dolce fratello il campione delle follie.   15

'Se per il caso che mi guidava...'

Again we find a structure of repetition and variation, with an accumulation of enigmatic hypotheses, where any unequivocal sense is constantly challenged by the presence of oppositions and semantic tensions.

1-3:   The hypotheses are predominantly centred on negativity, chance, loss, **'agonia'** (dying), with initially 'positive' outcomes (turning somersaults, knowing), only to turn to the negative of **'perdevo'** in l.3 (but one suspects that this may be invoked at least in part simply by the phonic echo of **'perdita'** and **'prendeva'**).; **'capriole'**: somersaults; **'girandola'**: turning motion.

3-7:   The hypotheses become even more abstruse and contradictory: an enchantment (**'incanto'**) *not* followed leads to *not* falling, stars lead to a fall to earth (**'tonfo'**: thud), **'pena'** leads to salvation (but only for others – an echo perhaps of Montale, one of Rosselli's favourite authors, or possibly also of Dante, where the souls are conveyed to purgatorial salvation by boat).

7-10:   **'se per la pena tu sentivi...'**: an example of Rosselli's idiosyncratic Italian syntax, with the omission of the relative pronoun probably based on English ('la pena [che] tu sentivi'). Again, suffering is seen as a potential path to a kind of salvation (but characterized in strangely negative terms), until finally all of these hypotheses are swept aside as spurious **'fandonie'** (nonsense), leaving only uncertainty (probably another Montalean allusion, echoing the closing line of 'La casa dei doganieri').

11-15:   A further series of oppositions, focused initially on **'la ragazza'** (the poet's own persona?), then finally on death and madness (**'follie'**). These, however, are surrounded and counterbalanced by the repetition of **'dolce'**; **'appellava'**: to call, rare in Italian, probably influenced here by French *appeller*; **'sorellastra'**: stepsister.

Ma se nell'amore io intravvedevo un barlume di gioia; se nella
notte improvvisamente levandomi vedevo che il cielo era
tutta una rissa di angioli: se dalla tua felicità risucchiavo
la mia; se dai nostri occhi incontrandosi prevedevo il
disastro se nella melanconia combattevo il forte drago del   5
desiderio; se per l'amore facevo salti mortali se per le
tue canzoni rimanevo illusa: era per meglio nascondere il
premio di bontà tu non desti. Non a tutte le bontà si può
rispondere.

'Ma se nell'amore io intravvedevo un barlume di gioia...'

In the course of the inner battle transcribed in these 'bellicose' variations, there are
flashes of ecstatic joy amidst the anguish (**'intravvedevo'**: I glimpsed; **'barlume'**:
glimmer). Even the elation of love, however, is portrayed in problematic and quasi-
combattive imagery: the angels are engaged in a **'rissa'** (brawl); the *io* 'sucks'
(**'risucchiavo'**) her happiness out of the *tu*; there is a premonition of disaster; desire
is a 'dragon' to be fought; l.7: Her being left **'illusa'** (under an illusion) is another rare
moment of positivity, indulging in the illusion of joy/love, whereas so many of the
poems centre on disillusionment, as indeed, ultimately, does the collection as a whole.
However, even this 'prize' must, it seems, remain hidden and unacknowledged. l.8:
Relative pronoun is again omitted '... bontà [che] tu non desti' (**'desti'**: 2nd pers. pass.
remoto of dare). Note again in this 'variation' the recurrence of familiar elements
such as **'notte'**, **'angioli'**, **'occhi'**, **'canzoni'**.

Tutto il mondo è vedovo se è vero che tu cammini ancora
tutto il mondo è vedovo se è vero! Tutto il mondo
è vero se è vero che tu cammini ancora, tutto il
mondo è vedovo se tu non muori! Tutto il mondo
è mio se è vero che tu non sei vivo ma solo   5
una lanterna per i miei occhi obliqui. Cieca rimasi
dalla tua nascita e l'importanza del nuovo giorno
non è che notte per la tua distanza. Cieca sono
chè tu cammini ancora! cieca sono che tu cammini
e il mondo è vedovo e il mondo è cieco se tu cammini   10
ancora aggrappato ai miei occhi celestiali.

'Tutto il mondo è vedovo se è vero che tu cammini ancora...'

The last poem in *Variazioni belliche*, this is a disenchanted leave-taking, not without notes of bitterness. The image of the world being **'vedovo'** (widowed) due to the *tu* remaining alive constitutes the central paradox, implying his definitive separation from the *io*. Around this central conceit, the poem unfolds as a series of musical variations (in which meaning appears subordinated to sound) arising from the words **'mondo'**, **'vedovo'**, **'vero'**. The poem has an almost abstract quality and indeed, in 'Spazi metrici', Rosselli calls it her only attempt at 'astratto ordinamento' (*Le poesie*, p.341). The other principal metaphor, that of eyes, sight and blindness, picks up on a motif recurring throughout the collection. As elsewhere, contradiction and oppositions are in evidence: he is a 'light' for her eyes, but she is blinded; his absence turns new day into night. l.9: **'chè'** (normally with an acute accent): because, since; **'aggrappato'**: holding tight.

From *Serie ospedaliera* (1963-1965)

la vita è un largo esperimento per alcuni, troppo
vuota la terra il buco nelle sue ginocchia,
trafiggere lance e persuasi aneddoti, ti semino
mondo che cingi le braccia per l'alloro. Sebbene
troppo largo il mistero dei tuoi occhi lugubri   5
sebbene troppo falso il chiedere in ginocchio
vorrei con un'ansia più viva ridirti: semina
le piante nella mia anima (un tranello), che
non posso più muovere le ginocchia pieghe. Troppo
nel sole la vita che si spegne, troppo nell'ombra   10
il gomitolo che portava alla capanna, un mare
gonfio delle tue palpebre.

'la vita è un largo esperimento per alcuni...'

This collection, published in 1969, contains two sections, firstly *La libellula*, a *poemetto* (long poem) which the author dates to 1958 (but this date probably refers only to an early draft, as suggested by Giovannuzzi); secondly, the section titled 'Serie ospadeliera', a sequence of 80 short texts from which the following poems are taken. In the original edition, these were printed as facsimiles of a type-written text. The poems are characterized by a certain sense of withdrawal from the tense confrontations of the previous work, displaying 'un'emotività ferita e dispersa' (Cucchi and Giovanardi, *Poeti italiani*, p. 458). Rosselli herself describes them as reflecting 'una melanconica privazione di vita', but with a greater 'rigore linguistico', adding: 'La "serie" è "ospedaliera" in quanto anche rassegnata a un ritornare criticamente sui propri passi, in quanto non più bellicosa nei confronti di sentimenti e intuizioni anche più rari o rarefatti' (*Antologia poetica*, pp.157-8). The metrical and rhythmic scheme used in *Variazioni* is essentially maintained here (in this case, a line based on 5 main stresses).

1-2:   This poem is permeated with a sense of excess, of the world in disproportion to the individual: **'largo'**, **'troppo vuota'**, **'buco'**, etc. The sense of frighteningly open possibilities in the first few lines is supported by an uncertainty of the grammatical person: the relationship between the 3rd person of **'sue'** and the subsequent *tu* and *io* is far from clear (the latter two seem, in fact, almost interchangeable).

3-4:   The meaning is extremely problematic, with a rather surreal juxtaposition of images; **'trafiggere lance'**: to transfix lances; **'persuasi aneddoti'**: convinced anecdotes; **'ti semino mondo...'**: it is unclear whether the sense is 'I sow the world for/to you' or 'I sow you, world' (similarly, the relationship of this to the following clause is as unclear as the sense of the clause itself); **'cingere'**: to encircle; **'alloro'**: laurel.

5-9:   Despite the sense of intolerable excess (**'troppo largo... troppo falso'**), the *io* wants to engage in a dialogue, is compelled to assume a begging/praying posture to have her own soul 'sown' with seeds, though this may be a **'tranello'** (trap); **'pieghe'**: neologism for 'piegate'.

10-12:   As usual, opposing forces (sunlight and shadow) leave little respite; **'il gomitolo...'**: the ball of wool or thread leading to some refuge suggests perhaps the myth of Ariadne; **'mare...'**: the image may suggest tear-laden eyes.

Tènere crescite mentre l'alba s'appressa tènere crescite
di questa ansia o angoscia che non può amare né sé né
coloro che facendomi esistere mi distruggono. Tenerissima
la castrata notte quando dai singulti dell'incrociarsi
della piazza con strada sento stridori ineccepibili,   5
le strafottenti risa di giovinotti che ancora vivere
sanno se temere è morire. Nulla può distrarre il giovane
occhio da tanta disturbanza, tante strade a vuoto, le
case sono risacche per le risate. Mi ridono ora che le
imposte con solenne gesto rimpalmano altre angosce   10
di uomini ancor più piccoli e se consolandomi d'esser
ancora tra i vivi un credere, rivedo la tua gialla faccia
tesa, quella del quasi genio – è per sentire in tutto
il peso della noia il disturbarsi per così poco.

'Tènere crescite mentre l'alba s'appressa...'

This dense and difficult poem evokes another night-time scene, with the (sleepless) poetic *io* enclosed in an interior setting, disturbed by the strident sounds of an unreflecting life outside. Given the title of the collection, and the biographical background, one may perhaps imagine that the poem involves a hospital setting.

1-3: A typically contradictory series of images: her 'anguish' undergoes 'tender' growth (**'crescite'**), it loves neither self nor others, those others who simultaneously give life and destroy; **'s'appressa'**: approaches.

3-7: The repetition of **'tenerissima'** and the portrayal of the night as 'castrated' or helpless suggests initially a broader world in affinity with the *io*, but this is then contradicted by the arrogant (**'strafottente'**) laughter of the youths outside for whom life is unproblematic, untouched by fear or mortality; **'singulti'**: sobs; **'stridori'**: strident noises; **'ineccepibili'**: faultless.

7-9: Despite the self-assuredness of youth, nothing can hide the emptiness of the world that is so disturbing; **'disturbanza'**: an anglicizing coinage; **'risacche per le risate'**: the image is that of laughter echoing back from the walls ('risacca' is the backwash of waves from the shore: the lexical choice seems determined largely by phonic aspects).

9-14: The laughter seems directed specifically at the *io*, as her view turns inwards once more. Literal meaning is problematic, not least due to the use of the verb **'rimpalmare'**, probably here meaning 'to close [the shutters] together [again] (like a pair of hands)', as well as the uncertain subject of this verb (**'altre angosce di uomini'**: possibly some other individuals present with the poet?); **'se consolandomi ... credere'**: 'if, taking consolation that there is belief/faith among the living...'. The identity of *tu* remains unclear. The poem closes on the weight of her anguish, but also an ironic suggestion that all of this was not worth getting upset about (**'il disturbarsi'**). Much of the force of the poem derives from the relentless rhythm of its long lines and the dense internal network of alliterative and assonant echoes (for example in the many permutations of st-/ str-/-a-).

E accomodandosi tutto lei piangeva, disperatina
nella sua cella, biochimica la sua reazione. Son
un tantino rincretinita, rispose al padrone di
casa – ma che fai con la pistola?

La spingo nel suo buco.   5

E ne partì un colpo che traversalmente prese la
rete retinica, poi si lasciò cadere morbido sul
divano, ma era per terra i mattoni quadri rossi
e grigi.

'E accomodandosi tutto lei piangeva, disperatina...'

A nightmarish vision of violence and death, with a heightened awareness of corporeal reality. The main event is clearly a violent death, but far less clear is the detail, which is subject to a number of grammatical and syntactic ambiguities: the masculine **'tutto'** of l.1 appears incongruous, cannot be applied to **'lei'**, but equally cannot be applied with certainty to any 'lui'; both the identity of the *io* in l.5 and the referent for 'suo' are unclear (the latter perhaps referring to 'its', i.e. of the gun); meanwhile the present tense verb in this line is out of keeping with the overall sequence (it may be direct speech quoted within the overall narrative); finally, both the perpetrator and victim of the shooting are unclear, but are probably 'him' (see **'morbido'**). What is clear, however, is that the events portrayed are brutally traumatic, not least for 'lei', in her 'cell' (prison? hospital? or metaphorical mental space?), conditioned strongly by bodily reactions. In the description of the shooting, there is a kind of detached precision, both clinical and hallucinatory, reminiscent perhaps of the grotesque physicality of some Porta texts in its morbid lingering on details of bodily trauma, texture and colour (**'rete retinica'**: retina). There is an interesting tonal incongruity between this and the conversational register of the earlier **'disperatina'** and **'un tantino rincretinita'** ('a bit stupefied'). As Mengaldo observes, Rosselli's poetry gives us 'la percezione della normalità dell'orrore, della quotidianità come dominio privilegiato del terribile' (Mengaldo, *Poeti italiani del Novecento*, p. 996).

Poter riposare nel tuo cuore, nel tuo fuoco
a bracie spente, liberamente rinnegando
la mia libertà. O commuoverti in perdono
perdendo l'ora, che trionfante vuole
un cuore duro, selciato, minaccioso   5
finché ne perdi la causa, l'origine
dell'ardore.

Poter danzare con le ore, gaiamente
intravedendo scienze, e non stampare
la tua faccia sul sasso. Poter rinsaldare   10
con te le mille pietre, che congiunte
in anello, sono edera leggiera
avvinta ai nostri occhi. Poter castrare
i desideri, slacciarli puri nel fiume
dove orgiastiche passano le ballerine   15
suicide di notte. Poter annunciare
che i desii non sono assurdi, ma
canto vero, una pulce nell'orecchio
atto d'amore, oppure vero verbo
che sale nel tuo cuore.   20

'Poter riposare nel tuo cuore, nel tuo fuoco...'

Here we find a rare moment of affirmation, of a positive aspiration to authentic human intimacy and the liberation that this might bring. The fact that this remains strictly hypothetical (indicated through the repeated **'Poter...'**: 'Oh to be able...') does not detract from the power of this vision, but does add pathos to it.

1-3:   The desire of the *io* to 'rest' in the other's heart is not daunted by the fact of its **'bracie spente'** (spent embers): rather, hers is an unconditional, quasi-religious desire, summed up in the oxymoron of ll.2-3, with its echoes of the Christian paradox of free-will subject to divine will.

3-7:   She may perhaps move to pity (**'commuoverti in perdono'**) the heart of the other, triumphant in its hardness, until the origin of passion is lost; **'selciato'**: paved with stone.

8-13:   Further striking contrasts, between the lightness of dance to which she aspires and the image of 'your' face imprinted in stone, lead in to an image of delicate beauty, in which the hardness of **'sasso'** turns to that of gemstones, set in a ring (**'rinsaldare'**: to reinforce), that metamorphoses into a climbing plant (**'edera'**: ivy), entwining (**'avvinta'**) with the lovers' eyes.

13-16: There is an increasing violence and irrationality in the aspiration to both 'castrate' desires and also to untie or unleash them (**'slacciarli'**), culminating in the surreal image of **'orgiastiche ... ballerine / suicide'**, a vision of desire unleashed as a self-destructive force.

16-20: Almost as if in response to the preceding image, the poem closes on a moving affirmation of the authenticity of desire (**'desio'**: archaic literary form for 'desire') and love (even though this may consitute **'una pulce nell'orecchio'**, an inconvenient or unwelcome truth), love which is both **'atto'** and **'canto'**/**'verbo'** penetrating the other's heart.

From *Documento* (1966-1973)

Quale azione scegliere, prevedere, ereditare?
Un pezzo di pane a cane senza museruola
è meglio che questo scrivere in bianchi
versi di getti lacrimogeni, a branchi
di gente tutta senza importanza o museruola   5

che scrive vincendo e perdendo tutte
le cause: mentre fuori il tempo gode
e esplode, senza la tua intima perplessità
intimità di cose andate e perdute mentre
tutt'occupata a scrivere versi bianchi   10
andavi leggendo quel che non si poté

fare.

'Quale azione scegliere, prevedere, ereditare?...'

Documento is Rosselli's last extensive collection (with the exception of *Impromptu*, a *poemetto* published in 1981) and, while the major thematic elements show a substantial continuity with her earlier work, there is, perhaps, a sense of heightened tension and uncertainty in the exercise of the poetic act, as the author clings to structure and form as a defence against bland anonimity of expression in the 1970s: 'diventa per lei urgente, drammatico, il bisogno di non arrendersi a un linguaggio che si fa "rasoterra", "decifrabile"...'; rather, hers is 'una lingua-corpo percorsa da tensioni telluriche e da una carica psichica conflittuale...' (Lorenzini, *La poesia italiana del Novecento*, p. 165). In Rosselli's own words, 'i contenuti sono dei veri e propri gridi' (*Antologia poetica*, p.158).

1-2: This poem illustrates a tendency towards an intermittent opening-up of thematic range towards what might be called 'external' reality, in this case through a consideration of the question of 'action' or *impegno* (although the ultimate focus in this text is on the apparent impotence of poetry in this respect). The image in l.2 suggests some concrete action, feeding hungry mouths (**'museruola'**: muzzle).

3-7: In comparison, **'bianchi versi'** seem to serve no purpose (**'lacrimogeni'**: tear-provoking, lends them a particularly negative connotation), other than to satisfy the **'branchi'** (herds) of the cultured middle classes, characterized as lacking any commitment or clarity of purpose (l.6).

7-12: External reality or history (**'il tempo'**) carries an explosive energy, in opposition to the **'intima perplessità'** of the poet (here addressed as 'tu'), occupied with the futile pursuit of studying her own impotency, her inability to **'fare'** (ll.11-12).

È una soneria costante; un micidiale compromettersi
una didascalia infruttuosa, e un vento di traverso
mentre battendo le ciglia sentenziavo una
saggezza imbrogliata.

Conto di farla finita con le forme, i loro   5
bisbigliamenti, i loro contenuti contenenti
tutta la urgente scatola della mia anima la
quale indifferente al problema farebbe meglio
a contenersi. Giocattoli sono le strade e
infermiere sono le abitudini distrutte da   10
un malessere generale.

La gola nella montagna si offrì pulita al
mio desiderio di continuare la menzogna indecifrabile
come le sigarette che fumo.

'È una soneria costante; un micidiale compromettersi...'

1-4: This poem of artistic disenchantment opens with a merciless critique of the poetic voice itself, dismissed as a mere **'soneria'** (chiming or jingling noise), a 'deadly' compromise, fruitless **'didascalia'** (explanatory discourse), a pompous **'sentenziare'** (solemnly declaring) – but while 'fluttering the eyelashes – of a confused (fraudulent?) 'wisdom'.

5-9: Even in bidding farewell to 'form', the poet engages in characteristic formal or linguistic play, in variations on 'contenuti' and a series of internal rhymes and assonances based on '-enti', '-ente' (**'bisbigliamenti'**: whisperings). There is a strong element of self-deprecatory irony in these lines, with the soul described as a 'box' that should try to 'contain itself'.

9-11: In contrast with the preceding word-play, a numbing vision of everyday life (with 'habits' seen as 'nurses' suggesting the constant presence of illness in the daily routine); 'distrutte / da un malessere generale': destroyed by a general malaise.

12-14: An enigmatic combination of images, suggesting perhaps the throat, cleansed by mountain air provoking the desire to smoke, a habit as incorrigible (as unhealthy/unclean?) as that of the 'menzogna' of poetry.

Propongo un incontro col teschio,
una sfida al teschio
mantengo ferma e costante
chiusa nella fede impossibile
l'amor proprio   5
delle bestie.

Ogni giorno della sua inesplicabile esistenza
parole mute in fila.

'Propongo un incontro col teschio...'

The 'bellicose' vein running throughout Rosselli's verse comes to the fore again in this challenge to death ('**sfida al teschio**': challenge to the skull) The poet's persona holds to an 'impossible' faith in life, in a physical, biological sense ('**l'amor proprio / delle bestie**'). In the penultimate line, '**sua**' is ambiguous, but is perhaps best understood as referring to the skull, to death, whose presence is constant but incomprehensible, provoking the poet's only response of '**parole mute**'.